Midpoints

Unleashing the Power
of the Planets

MIDPOINTS
Unleashing the POWER of the Planets

Michael Munkasey

ACS PUBLICATIONS
Astro Communications Services, Inc.
San Diego, California

International Standard Book Number 0-935127-11-9

Cover Design by Maria Kay Simms

Printed in the United States

Published by ACS Publications, an imprint of
Astro Communications Services, Inc.
PO Box 34487
San Diego, CA 92163-4487

Publisher's Note

This book contains delineations of the correspondences between
planetary pairs and health issues. A note of caution is in order,
for as the author, himself, says on page 16 "further development
needs to be done in the area of medical astrology." Medical
astrology is extremely theoretical and provisional, so great
caution is required in the application of its "rules." The correspondences given under the paragraphs entitled "With Body or
Mind" should be used, at best, as only an adjunct to the
information available through other, more proven sources,
such as laboratory tests and diagnosis by medical professionals.
The astrological correspondences given herein are in no way
intended to replace competent medical advice.

Dedication

I wish to thank my family and friends,
but in particular the members of the
Board of Directors of
The National Council for Geocosmic Research
NCGR
who over the years have provided me
with stimulation, ideas, direction,
advice—and a lot of fun.
I dedicate this book to these wonderful people.

Acknowledgements

I explicitly wish to acknowledge my appreciation and gratitude for the pioneering work of the Ebertin family and in particular Dr. Reinhold Ebertin, whose book, "The Combination of Stellar Influences" and the Ebertin family's subsequent work in Cosmobiology, was instrumental in giving me important inspiration for this present work. I also wish to thank Dr. Baldur Ebertin for his permission to emulate the format so successfully used in that book.

I also wish to thank Sarah Fleming, who made this book possible, and the many people who have given me advice and insight into astrology. In particular I wish to acknowledge the help, advice, teachings, ideas, and criticism of Charles Emerson over the years we have known each other, and the specific advice given by Kathleen Hanna, Margie Herskovitz, Delphine Gloria Jay, Grace Lents, Marilyn Muir, and unnamed but not forgotten others who read through and commented on early versions of this work or contributed ideas about the page layouts. For her assistance in the final editing, and for her work on the format and the cover of the book, I wish to thank Maria Kay Simms

Table of Contents

The 78 Midpoints

A Four-Page Guideline to the Delineation of
Each Midpoint Combination **60**

Appendix A **373**

Appendix B **382**

Appendix C **390**

Appendix D **392**

An extensive and detailed index to this work is to be found in its
companion book, *The Concept Dictionary.*

Introduction

An Eastern teaching precept asks the question, "If I divide in half with every step I take the distance to my goal, when shall I arrive?" The answer is **never**, but, clearly, the teaching is revealed that, during the neverending journey, I will constantly be refining my knowledge of the distance I travel. I will know with continuously more detailed awareness the nature of my quest. I will see how where I was relates to where I am going.

Midpoints in astrology represent this kind of synthesis of two symbolisms. Introducing a third symbolism at the midpoint position or in aspect to it adds still another component to the synthesis, and we are able to know even more. Synthesis expands as we harness the nuances of astrological symbolisms. Meanings in astrology gain mass.

Anyone who has known Michael Munkasey over the past fifteen years knows that "key words" have been a daily focus of research and studied application in his life. Now, all that work has come together in this book: Michael has established imposing verbal substance for the theoretical considerations of planetary synthesis. We now have a richness of considerations to help us bring gulps of planetary synthesis to personal significance.

This book is not a revelation of any new technique: Michael is quick to point out the legacy of the extraordinary work accomplished with midpoints by the Ebertins and, before that, by Witte in the Hamburg school. Rather, this book is a copious sharing of rich conceptualization. It is a reference work for rumination. It establishes a sense, a feel, an embrace of thought to bring us closer to our goal in astrology: to understand the planets working together in the lives of human beings and the events of history. In short, this book takes us beyond traditional astrological aspects.

In my opinion, the most important mission of any textbook is to make the reader think afresh or further. Michael does both here, with concepts galore, and with meticulously organized and graded key words that press us into the challenges and rewards of synthesis. We are forced to come to grips with the antithetical concept of Mars relating to Saturn; the alarming concept of Saturn relating to Pluto; the elusive concept of Venus relating to Neptune, for particularly apt examples. We are then led further to embrace these sensitively articulated concepts in relation to yet another planetary symbol . . . **all** the others, in fact . . . and we are well on our way indeed to more complete knowledge of the distances we travel in every horoscope.

Michael Munkasey's book helps us to think more completely analytically. It helps us perform closer to our best in the realm of synthesis. And for this, we astrologers should be markedly grateful.

Noel Tyl
McLean, VA

Preface

What is this book? Who should own it and why?

This book translates important astrological images into modern American ideas. In its simplest definition astrology is a language. It is the language of the universe and it has its own alphabet and rules of grammar. The planets and the personal sensitive points (collectively called "points") are symbols which are important letters in astrology's alphabet. This work provides insight into understanding and appreciating the role of astrological symbols. Buy this book if you are interested in learning about the astrological meanings of the planets and points in familiar settings. Just as you use language or words to convey your ideas and thoughts to others, astrology uses the symbols and patterns formed by the points to bring insight and meaning to personality, love, relationships, medical concerns, events, etc. This book can help you understand the power represented by these combinations and how to recognize their symbolism in your daily experiences with life.

Midpoints express the astrological role of the points in subtle yet powerful ways. A midpoint is the middle or centered location of any pair of point influences. Powerful new images of these point combinations are unleashed through the definitions on these pages. This book was not written to teach you the basic rules of astrology or how to interpret a horoscope. But if you want to learn ideas beyond routine fundamentals this book is essential. It explains basic concepts in a new way; provides insight on how to view life; and brings additional understanding about your feelings, activities, situations, reactions, relationships, or behavior.

This book is not a guide on how to live your life or a quick "cookbook" giving astrological interpretations or meanings. It contains ideas, and can be compared to a dictionary or thesaurus. Just as a dictionary tells you the meanings of words and gives examples of how to use them properly in different acceptable ways, this book does the same for the role of the points in astrology. A dictionary or a thesaurus does not teach you to speak, write, or communicate effectively. But a skilled dictionary or thesaurus user is better able to convey his or her ideas in more effective ways. A dictionary or a thesaurus helps bring order to chaos. Understanding the powerful role which the planets and points can have in your everyday experiences may bring illumination to unfamiliar areas.

My companion book *The Concept Dictionary* provides a complete and thorough alphabetical index for all of the concepts and ideas contained in this work.

If you want to learn more about yourself and life — please read on!

Michael Munkasey
Northern Virginia, USA
October, 1989

Chapter 1
Planetary Combinations

General Introduction and Background to Astrology

Astrology has five major, significant parts: planets, personal sensitive points, harmonics, houses, and signs. This is a book about the meanings of the planets and certain of the personal sensitive points when taken together as a pair. The planets and the personal sensitive points when considered together are called "points." Midpoints are the middle position in space between any two of the planets or the personal sensitive points. The planets are the most important part of astrology, although the personal sensitive points and the harmonics (also called aspects) are also very important. Houses and signs have their role too as they lend needed shades of meaning to the basic ideas supplied by the planets, personal sensitive points, and the aspects or point separations in space.

Astrologers popularly use ten planets. Listed in their traditional astrological order, their names are: Sun, Moon, Mercury, Venus, Mars, Jupiter, Saturn, Uranus, Neptune, and Pluto. Astrologers refer to the Sun and the Moon as planets although astronomers do not refer to them this way. The planets which have been known since antiquity and which a person with normal vision can see in the night's sky are: Mercury, Venus, Mars, Jupiter, and Saturn. Uranus, Neptune, and Pluto are not visible directly by eye and were discovered by scientists using telescopes in more modern times. Astrologers define a planet as a heavenly body which rules a certain part of the heavens, or our activities or situations in life. Many planetary-type bodies exist in space but only the major planets listed above are given an astrological rulership. The planets are the mythological major "gods" or "goddesses" of our ancestors and their rulership and characters are expressed in stories passed from ancient civilizations.

A planet, for the purposes of this book, is one of the ten bodies named above. The planets as used in this book are ordered according to the hierarchy given in the table below. The planets each have unique two, three, or four letter and symbolic abbreviations and these are (reading down the left hand column and then down the right hand column for the correct planetary ordering):

Sun	SUN, or SU	☉	Jupiter	JUP, JU	♃
Moon	MOON, MO	☽	Saturn	SAT, SA	♄
Mercury	MER, ME	☿	Uranus	URA, UR	♅
Venus	VEN, VE	♀	Neptune	NEP, NE	♆
Mars	MARS, MA	♂	Pluto	PLU, PL	♇

Seven personal sensitive points are recognized, and the Node of the Moon can be considered as an eighth personal sensitive point. The personal sensitive points are called by the name shown in the left column in the table which follows, and their opposing paired point in the right hand column is always understood to be opposite in the heavens from the named point. The personal sensitive points exist as two opposite but identical placements. They represent real locations of intersections in space and serve to mark the qualities of time. Their locations are defined by combining the Earth's position in our Solar System, a place on Earth, the day of a month and year, and the time of that day in an astronomical way. Their names, their abbreviations, and their equivalent paired point are:

Ascendant	(ASC, AS, A)	Descendant	(DSC)
Midheaven	(MC, M)	Lower Heaven	(IC)
Equatorial Ascendant	(EQA, EQ)	Equatorial Descendant	(EQD)
Vertex	(VTX, VT)	Anti-Vertex	(AVX)
Co-Ascendant	(CAS, CA)	Co-Descendant	(CDS)
Polar Ascendant	(PAS, PA)	Polar Descendant	(PDS)
The Aries Point	(ARI, AR, ♈)	The Libra Point	(LIB, ♎)

The Node of the Moon can be logically included with these personal sensitive points and its name, symbolic abbreviation, and its opposing point is:

North Node	(NN, ☊)	South Node	(SN, ☋)

Although the personal sensitive points always exist in pairs lying across the chart, only one side is popularly referred to and that convention is kept here. The side most commonly referred to is in the left-most column above. Because only the ASC and MC enjoy the most common astrological use, they and the Moon's Node are the only points included in this book. A more complete definition and derivation of the other personal sensitive points may be done in another book. The words "planet" or "point" are both used to refer to any of the ten astrological planets mentioned earlier, the Moon's Node, the Ascendant, or the Midheaven.

By combining the five parts of astrology according to astronomical, astrological, and mathematical rules, a picture which astrologers call a **horoscope** or chart is formed and can be shown. A horoscope reveals information about its subject. An astrologer is a person who is trained to read the patterns and symbols within the horoscope and to translate these into words, ideas, and phrases which have meaning for people. While practiced astrologers have been trained to read horoscope patterns as information from astrology's chart forms, it is not as easy to 'read' the midpoint significance from the same stylized chart formats. Different procedures are required for seeing a midpoint's emphasis, and these are non-visual. While a trained astrologer can look at the patterns in a horoscope diagram and "see" the strength or weakness of planetary pattern, it is not possible to do this with midpoint patterns. Midpoint patterns are more subtle and few graphic techniques exist to help you visually interpret their patterns. Ways to evaluate midpoint strength or weakness in a chart are discussed more fully in Chapter 2.

Astrology is not fatalistic. Astrology does not say that you must do this or you must do that. Astrology is simply a guide which can give you a powerful means for interpreting and understanding things about yourself and life in general. Astrology is a language which conveys information in the same way a road map describes a locality. A person traveling through an unfamiliar region may not choose to use any road map, but doing so could save much time and trouble. A person living through the rigors of life can choose to ignore the knowledge shown within a natal horoscope, but knowing something about that information can save much time and energy when choosing among the various options to which life exposes us. Astrology does not judge that character traits are good or bad as astrology only conveys information about choices or options available. It is people who label these choices to be either good or bad. Astrology is very impersonal and does not care whether it is proven in a scientific sense. It is a language and it conveys information. As with any language or information it simply exists. You can not scientifically prove that Spanish or German or Japanese are technically valid. To quote an old saying, it may be easier to teach a pig to whistle — and even if you attempt this you should carefully look at what you may gain for your efforts for you shall certainly annoy the pig.

The schools of astrology are: Natal, Synastry, Medical, Mundane (or Judicial), Horary, Electional, Business, Rectification, Esoteric, Event, and Weather Forecasting. Each school uses the horoscope as its primary source of information and starting point, but the schools place different astrological emphasis on this information.

Natal astrology deals with the birth of a person and the planetary patterns surrounding that birth. Natal astrology shows patterns of life which are important to the person being studied. Synastry is concerned with relationships in general (person to person, person to company, etc.) but human relationships in particular (parent–child, male–female, etc.). Medical astrology is concerned with medical and health situations. Mundane concerns the astrological study of countries, their leaders, businesses, events, etc., often in a historical way. Horary concerns itself with the answering of questions asked, e.g., should I accept this job, should I marry person X, where did I lose my article Y. Astrologers use the rules of Electional astrology to choose a favorable time to start a business, perform a marriage, etc. Business astrologers study the different economic cycles encountered. Rectification is a practice to find the correct time of an event or person's birth from the circumstances which follow in life. This practice is useful for people who do not know their time of birth. Esoteric is concerned with the spiritual parts of life and the choices we have as creatures with souls. Event astrology studies episodes, like earthquakes, plane crashes, etc., to see what can be learned from them and what information lies behind these events. Weather forecasting uses the planetary positions to forecast the weather (farmer's almanacs have been doing that for years!).

Midpoints and Combinations

Midpoint is a specific term referring to the middle space between two points. **Combination** is a more general term which encompasses midpoints, planetary pictures, triads, etc. **Halfsum** is also a term used as a general word for midpoints. Halfsum is more commonly used in Europe. These terms will be explained more fully later in this chapter. The terms "combination," "halfsum," and "midpoint" may be used interchangeably, especially if you recognize that midpoint is a more specific application of a concept and combination is a more general term embracing not only midpoints but other related terms as well as midpoints. Midpoints are not a new concept and probably were in active use before the 16th century.

A midpoint lies in the middle of the space between two points and is one form of a combination. Points have movement in four directions (forward and backward, up and down, in and out, and in time). The middle point can be found between any two points in any of these directions. Normally, a midpoint refers to the middle place between two points in the forward and backward direction, which is more formally called **zodiacal longitude**. Midpoints have been popularized in the western world by the Cosmobiology school of the Ebertin family in Germany, whose pioneering works and writings have done much to popularize this concept among astrologers. Cosmobiologists also use the word "half-sum" to refer to midpoints.

This book explains the astrological meanings of any two of the points named before taken together as a pair. This is also called a combination. Thus the names: midpoint, combination, half-sum, or planetary pairing have all been used to refer to this same combining. Any astrologically significant grouping involving more than one point (or sign, house, etc.) forms a combination. This book is about combinations involving points. These combinations can give you much insight into events in your life or people with whom you become involved.

Points can combine in many ways to convey information. Some ways are very subtle and new forms of expression are constantly being uncovered. Just as there are many different ways to express the idea "I love you," there are many different forms of valid planetary combinations which give messages similar to each other. This book can help you understand the planetary combinations by explaining them in modern terms. This book offers suggestions on the meanings of the planets when they form combinations.

In astrology, point positions are measured along a circle in the sky called the "ecliptic." The **ecliptic** is the apparent path of the Sun in the sky, measured against the background of the fixed stars as seen from the Earth. The ecliptic is a circle and we must define a starting point for it. Normally this is taken to be that point in space defined by the Sun and the Earth working together, when they combine in a certain special way around March 21st of each calendar year. The Sun appears to pass across an extension of the Earth's equator into space with the Sun traveling from South to North. This marks the first instance of Spring in the Earth's Northern hemisphere and Fall in the Earth's Southern hemisphere. The point in the sky where this occurs is called the "**Aries Point.**" Yes, this is the same Aries Point listed as a personal sensitive point. Opposite to this is the "Libra Point" which serves to mark the start of Fall in the Northern hemisphere and Spring in the Earth's Southern hemisphere.

Starting from the Aries Point at equal thirty degree intervals in the zodiac where all the planets travel, the signs of the zodiac begin. The sign Aries starts at zero degrees of zodiacal longitude, Taurus at thirty degrees, Gemini at sixty degrees, Pisces at three-hundred thirty degrees, etc. The signs, their zodiacal order, and their abbreviations are listed in Chapter 2. Planetary positions are defined in astrology along the circle of the ecliptic, and in degrees and minutes of the zodiacal sign they occupy. An example of a planetary location stated in an astrological way is: the Sun at 13 CAN 46. This means that the Sun is in the zodiacal sign of Cancer, about half way through the zodiacal sign of Cancer, or more specifically thirteen degrees and forty-six minutes from zero degrees of Cancer. Since Cancer is ninety degrees from the Aries Point, then the Sun is ninety plus thirteen degrees, or one hundred three degrees and forty-six minutes from the Aries Point, or the Sun has one hundred three degrees and forty-six minutes of zodiacal longitude.

Similarly you may find the planet Mars at 24 GEM 40. This is stated as twenty-four degrees of Gemini, forty minutes. Reasoning as before with the Sun, then Mars is eighty-four degrees and forty minutes from the Aries Point. The midpoint of the Sun and Mars is written as: SU/MA, and this is pronounced as "the Sun–Mars midpoint," or "Sun–Mars." SU/MA in this example occurs in the zodiacal space halfway between 24 GEM 40 and 13 CAN 46. This midpoint location can be calculated many ways. One easy way is to take the planetary distances from the Aries Point, add them, and divide by two to find the midpoint position. In this example, doing that we find that adding (103° 46' + 84° 40') is equal to 188° 26'. Dividing 188° 26' by two we get 94° 13'. This is the midpoint of the Sun and Mars and written in zodiacal form it becomes 4 CAN 13 as zero Cancer is ninety degrees from the Aries Point. Using the standard astrological shorthand, the midpoint location is written as: SU/MA = 4 CAN 13, or with traditional astrological symbols: ☉/♂ = 4 ♋ 13.

Midpoints are always formed in pairs and the pairs are opposite in zodiacal longitude to each other. The same midpoint equally exists at 4 CAP 13, or 4 CAN 13, as Capricorn is opposite to Cancer in its zodiacal position. Only one side of this pair is popularly cited as the other side is understood to co-exist with the side used. Traditionally the near midpoint (the one closest to the actual position of the planets) is used. In the example above 4 CAN 13 would be used in preference to 4 CAP 13 as the midpoint location. However, both locations are valid and it is important to understand that **midpoints exist as point pairs which lie across a horoscope axis, even if only one side is popularly and consistently mentioned when writing or speaking of them.**

Planetary Pictures, Triads, and Arabic Parts

A **triad**, also called a **planetary combination** or a **hit**, is formed when a planet is at or near a midpoint, or makes an important astrological angle to a midpoint. Thus, if at the same time the SU/MA = 4 CAN 13, the planet Uranus is also near to 4 CAN 13, then you write: UR = SU/MA, or in symbolic form: ♅ = ☉/♂. When any planet is also at an appropriate aspect or angle to 4 CAN 13, then that planet also sets off, hits, or activates the midpoint. A more complete discussion of angles, aspects, or harmonics which can cause hits is given in Chapter 2.

A **planetary picture** is any combination of points which satisfies the mathematical relationship: A + B - C = D, where A, B, C, and D are points and are measured in zodiacal longitude. The name "planetary picture" was introduced by the Uranian school of astrology. This school originated from research done in Hamburg, Germany in the early part of the 20th century. Much of their work on planetary pictures relied on concepts and information from earlier and more ancient astrological theories. **Midpoints are a special case of a planetary picture**, and this can be proven using common algebra. If you care to understand the mathematical logic which relates midpoints and planetary pictures, please follow an example through:

Assume that the following planetary picture occurs:

SU + NO - UR = MA, or, symbolically
☉ + ☊ - ♅ = ♂

This is read and spoken as: the Sun plus Node minus Uranus is equal to Mars. If we treat this as an ordinary algebraic equation, which we can do since it is one, then we can add and subtract according to the rules of simple algebra and get the following results. Starting with the astrological equation above:

☉ + ☊ - ♅ = ♂

Adding Uranus (♅) to both sides, we maintain a balanced equation and get:

☉ + ☊ - ♅ + ♅ = ♂ + ♅,   or
☉ + ☊ = ♂ + ♅

Adding and subtracting Uranus to itself in the first line above yields a mathematical zero and this zero resultant means that Uranus disappears from the left side of the equation. The last line, which is mathematically equal to the preceding line, presents this. Dividing both sides of this result above by two allows us to maintain mathematical equality. Doing this we get:

$$(\odot + \Omega) \div 2 = (\mathcal{O}^{\!\!\!\!\prime} + \text{♅}) \div 2$$

But, $(\odot + \Omega) \div 2$ is the mathematical definition of a midpoint in general and the SU/NO midpoint in particular, or $\odot/\Omega$ symbolically, and $(\mathcal{O}^{\!\!\!\!\prime} + \text{♅}) \div 2$ is also the midpoint of MA/UR, or $\mathcal{O}^{\!\!\!\!\prime}/\text{♅}$, because a midpoint is defined as the sum of the zodiacal longitude of any two planets divided by two. The planetary picture we started with has been algebraically reduced to two equated midpoints. Therefore, a planetary picture is a special case where two midpoint combinations meet in space at the same location by astrological aspect. **Any time one midpoint aspects another midpoint a planetary picture is formed. This is an important concept, and it reinforces ideas on how points combine to convey messages and meanings.**

Arabic Parts are a form of planetary picture which Arabic astrologers used and defined about 900 A.D., or perhaps even earlier. Arabic Parts are similar to planetary pictures, but usually an Arabic Part includes the use of one of the personal sensitive points in its formula. Arabic Parts have special and fancy names, like the Part of Fortune, the Part of Marriage, the Part of Travel, etc. Arabic parts are just midpoint combinations. To prove this let us take an example and algebraically expand it as before. **The Part of Fortune** (PFOR) is calculated by the formula:

PFOR = $\mathbb{D}$ - $\odot$ + ASC, or, PFOR = $\mathbb{D}$ + ASC - $\odot$

But reasoning as before with algebraic combinations of points:

PFOR + $\odot$ = $\mathbb{D}$ - $\odot$ + ASC + $\odot$, or
PFOR + $\odot$ = $\mathbb{D}$ + ASC

Dividing by 2 on each side:

(PFOR + $\odot$) $\div$ 2 = ($\mathbb{D}$ + ASC) $\div$ 2

By the earlier definition for the Part of Fortune, PFOR = $\mathbb{D}$ - $\odot$ + ASC, you can substitute and replace PFOR with its equal:

($\mathbb{D}$ + ASC - $\odot$ + $\odot$) $\div$ 2 = ($\mathbb{D}$ + ASC) $\div$ 2, or,
($\mathbb{D}$ + ASC) $\div$ 2 = ($\mathbb{D}$ + ASC) $\div$ 2.

Since both sides of the equal sign are identical, this simply shows that any Arabic Part is a midpoint, equal to itself. Thus, **midpoints, planetary pictures, and Arabic Parts are simply combinations of the points** in their simplest form. Other forms of planetary combinations are discussed in Chapter 2.

This should remove some of the mystery of what midpoints and planetary combinations are and can be. They have been called by many different names and shown in many different ways throughout the years. Whatever their name and however they are used, they are simply combinations of the planets taken as pairs or triads. This book helps you interpret the combinations and triads formed by the planets and points listed earlier.

Wheels and Dials

Astrologers have invented clever graphic and visual displays called 'wheels' or 'dials' for easily spotting midpoints, triads, hits, and combinations. A dial is a round paper or plastic circular device from five to eight inches in diameter with precisely marked ruling lines which are used to visually separate horoscope information. Dials normally come in 360° or 90° formats, but other formats have also been used. See Figures 1 and 2 for pictures of a 360° and a 90° dial.

A 90° dial appears as a circle just like a 360° dial. The 90° dial looks like a 360° dial, except that its information is folded four times over on top of itself. Yet the dial appears as a circular graphic. Although the 90° dial looks like a 360° dial its degree areas are four times larger and when

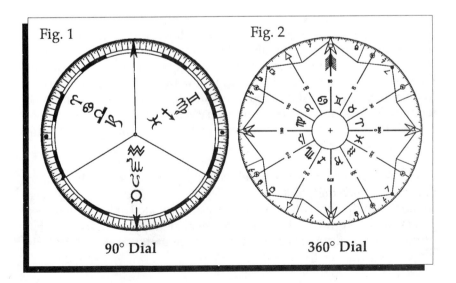

Fig. 1   Fig. 2

90° Dial   360° Dial

working manually with a 90° dial your visual accuracy is increased. The information in each 90° sector of the 360° horoscope is overlaid onto the original 90° sector of the dial. The 90° dial effectively reduces the picture of a horoscope to be Cardinal, Fixed, and Mutable transparent. Cardinal, fixed, and mutable are astrological terms which describe certain basic characteristics attributed to the signs of the zodiac. Their definition is not relevant here and can be found in standard astrological references or basic astrology books.

When working manually the 90° dial highlights certain combinations separated in space by angles based on the harmonic numbers 1, 2, 4, 8, and 16. A dial makes these angles easy to notice. The use of dials greatly simplifies the selection of midpoints and combinations when you are working manually with horoscope information. Explaining how to use dials is beyond the scope of this book. Please refer to Appendix C to find other works which explain dials.

Computing Midpoints and Finding the Important Ones

It is difficult to visualize each midpoint from a standard horoscope form. Midpoints are seen more easily if they are computed and listed in a zodiacal or other order. Several popular computer programs written for personal computers are available for purchase which will compute midpoints or similar forms of planetary combinations. Midpoints listings can be obtained this way. Astrological service bureaus also exist which will perform this service for a nominal fee. Please refer to Appendix C for a listing of these programs and services.

The easiest way to compute the location of midpoints for your purposes is to use one of these programs or services. However, you may also wish to compute midpoints manually. When doing this a calculator can be a good help. To compute each of the seventy-eight midpoints used in this book for any particular chart, please follow the example given earlier. Manually computing midpoints is not difficult, but it can quickly become tedious. It is also easy to make simple mathematical errors if you are not careful. For these reasons I recommend that you use a computer program or chart service for this task.

Once the locations of the midpoints are computed you still have to determine which midpoints are most significant in the chart. The most significant midpoints will be those which are activated or hit by the other points most forcefully. Locating the most significant midpoints is a tiresome task, and almost beyond manual computational means. Wheels and dials are somewhat helpful when doing this chore, but a computer program or computer service for astrologers which incorporates some form of "Midpoint Weighting Analysis" (MWA) is needed. Chapter 2 will give additional information on the subject of MWA's and their importance in finding the strongest or weakest midpoints.

Chapter 2
Other Combinations

House and Sign Astrology

Other astrological parts called signs, houses, and aspects can also create combinations and give the planets forms of astrological expression. The **signs of the zodiac**, or signs, are equal divisions of space along the ecliptic in a narrow band of sky referred to as the zodiac. The signs of the zodiac are different from the constellations in the sky, although unfortunately some constellations and signs share identical names. It is in this band of the zodiac that the planets travel for most of their time. The order of the signs of the zodiac, their letter and symbol abbreviations, and their offset in degrees from zero Aries are (read down the left columns first and then into the right columns for the correct order):

Aries	ARI, or AR ♈ 000	Libra	LIB, LI ♎ 180
Taurus	TAU, TA ♉ 030	Scorpio	SCO, SC ♏ 210
Gemini	GEM, GE ♊ 060	Sagittarius	SAG, SG ♐ 240
Cancer	CAN, CA ♋ 090	Capricorn	CAP, CP ♑ 270
Leo	LEO, LE ♌ 120	Aquarius	AQU, AQ ♒ 300
Virgo	VIR, VI ♍ 150	Pisces	PSC, PS ♓ 330

Popularly the signs each have one or two planetary rulers, or one ancient and one modern planet. The planetary rulers of a sign have a strong affinity for that sign, and astrological characteristics between the planet and sign are passed back and forth between the rulers and the signs. The traditional planetary rulers are:

Aries	♂	Libra		♀
Taurus	♀	Scorpio	♀	♂
Gemini	☿	Sagittarius		♃
Cancer	☽	Capricorn		♄
Leo	☉	Aquarius	♄	♅
Virgo	☿	Pisces	♃	♆

From this list notice that Mars has an affinity with both Aries and Scorpio, and that Venus has an affinity with both Taurus and Libra, etc. This association allows astrologers to draw planet and sign analogies. For example, if the Sun is in the sign of Cancer, then the combination of Sun and Moon is activated, as Cancer and the Moon are matched above. Similarly, if the Moon is in the sign of Leo then the Sun and Moon as a planetary combination are activated again, and the descriptions under the ☉/☽ combination apply. The double-columns arrangement above is intentional: it refers to a theory that will be described in a future book.

Houses are divisions of space and symbolically represent the qualities of space in the horoscope. Astrology has many different ways to divide space and show these divisions in a horoscope. A very popular method of house division is called "Placidus" and is named after a monk who lived in Europe in the middle ages. The Placidian house system was printed by a British publishing house in the early 1700's or so and for over one hundred years was the only such table of houses available to astrologers. Thus it gained in popularity and usage and is by far the most requested house system today, according to people who run computer based astrological services which print charts or horoscopes for the public. Houses lend important shades of meaning to astrological interpretations and their use is recommended.

In the astrological literature some twenty-three house systems have been described. This is not a place to elaborate on these. While the Placidian system is the most popular, all systems have a unique role in astrology depending on the circumstances of their use. Houses are formed in one of three ways using the ecliptic, equatorial, and horizon astronomical planes in space. Regardless of the house system chosen the individual houses are referred to by their numbers and are called houses one through twelve. The first house relates to the zodiacal sign of Aries, the second house to the sign of Taurus, and so forth through the twelfth house which relates to Pisces.

Through the affinity of the signs for planets, the houses also have planetary affiliations. As with the signs a planet in a house yields a combination which this book can help you understand. For instance, Saturn in the seventh house (♄ in 7th) is analogous to the ♀/♄ descriptions, due to the seventh house affiliation with the sign of Libra and Libra's rulership by Venus. Similarly, Neptune in the eleventh house (♆ in 11th) can be associated with either ♄/♆ or ♅/♆ due to the Saturn and Uranus affiliations with the sign of Aquarius. As another example for using the combinations in this book, Venus in Leo can be described by the ☉/♀ combination, and Mercury in Aquarius is described by both ☿/♄ and ☿/♅. **The 78 combinations in this book can be used to find ideas for planets in signs, planet in houses, signs on house cusps, or planets in aspect.** Please refer to Appendices A and B which cross reference this information for you.

Aspect or Harmonic Astrology

Aspects or harmonics can provide a rich and varied insight into situations. **Aspects** or **harmonics** are the angles in space between points. The difference between the term aspect and the term harmonic is that aspects are called by names (e.g., conjunction, opposition, trine, quintile, sesquiquadrate) while harmonics refer to the same separation but call them by their equivalent numbers (one, two, three, five, eight). The numbers are easier to pronounce, but the aspects are more traditional to use. In this book the word harmonics is used, but each term–aspect, harmonic, or angle–refers to the same angular separation of points in space.

The following relationship equates the planets with the harmonics. The following table is read down the left columns first for harmonic numbers one through six and then down the right columns for harmonics seven through twelve.

Aspect Name	Angle	Harmonic	Planet	Aspect Name	Angle	Harmonic	Planet
Conjunction	0°	1	☉	Septile	51° 26'	7	–
Opposition	180°	2	☽	Semi-Square	45°	8	♂
Trine	120°	3	♃	Novile	40°	9	♆
Square	90°	4	♄	Decile	36°	10	☿
Quintile	72°	5	☿	Undecile	32° 44'	11	♅
Sextile	60°	6	♀	Semi-Sextile	30°	12	♇

The angles shown above are found by dividing the 360° of a circle by the number of the harmonic, where conjunction is one, opposition is two, trine is three, etc., as shown. The seventh and eleventh harmonics have a fractional or non-integer angle. People familiar with music theory will recognize much harmony (harmonics!) within this table. Multiplying these basic angles repeats the harmonic. That is, three times the decile, or 3 times 36°, gives 108°. Thus, two planets separated by 108° of zodiacal longitude will exchange energy at a decile or Mercury vibration. Such integer multiplication gives many important angles beyond those just listed in the table above. Such repeats or multiples of the basic harmonic are called **nodes**.

Other special combinations of angles, like the sesqui-quadrate (at 135°), and the quincunx or inconjunct (at 150°) also exist. The sesqui-quadrate is a special case of the 45° aspect or the eighth harmonic, which relates to Mars. The quincunx is a unique aspect which is formed by the division of a fractional (non-integer or real) number into 360°. The harmonics listed above are formed by whole or integer numbers. Harmonics with real numbers are also valid. Harmonic theories are exciting and show very powerful ways of finding astrological significances. Other harmonics beyond those mentioned or discussed so far may also determine planetary or point activation.

You can use the information in this book to help you decipher harmonic combinations. For instance, Saturn sextile or 60° to some other point will correlate to the ♀/♄ (VE/SA) description in this book. The table above shows Venus associated with the sextile aspect, and thus 'Saturn sextile' would be equal to a ♀/♄ pairing. Similarly, a Jupiter and Saturn conjunction will incorporate ideas from all of the following combinations described in this book: ♃/♄; ☉/♃; and ☉/♄ — as well as ☉ = ♃/♄, and similar variations on this theme. See Appendices A and B for a cross reference of the harmonic equivalents.

Harmonics are significant within a narrow band of space called an **orb**. It is difficult to say, for many technical astrological reasons, what the width of this orb should be for a combination. In general for natal, synastry, medical, and mundane astrological work an orb of two degrees for a midpoint is acceptable and orbs of three degrees and more have been found to be valid in certain instances. Generally, smaller or tighter orbs are held to be more powerful. In rectification work people use an orb of only ten percent of one degree, or six minutes of arc. In business and weather forecasting astrology orbs wider than two degrees are commonly used. When wider orbs are proposed they may be used to cover astrological sins. Depending on your preference, an orb of between one and two degrees is certainly acceptable for midpoint work and orbs of up to three degrees may be used with discretion. Use your own judgment and if you are bothered by orb width, using tighter rather than looser orbs in your work is better. As an example of the use of an orb, consider the following midpoint combination occurring in a chart: AS = ♀/♄ (this is read as: the Venus/Saturn midpoint occurs in a significant aspect to the degree of the Ascendant; but is spoken as: Ascendant equals Venus/Saturn). That is, the ♀/♄ combination exists in aspect, within plus or minus the orb width, at the position where the Ascendant occurs. When this happens the combination is in orb and is said to be **activated** or **hit**.

The Cosmobiology school uses midpoints and the Uranian school uses both midpoints and planetary pictures. They each teach that any of the following harmonics can yield hits: 1, 2, 4, 8, and 16. That is, AS = ♀/♄ can occur if the midpoint combination of ♀/♄ is conjunct (0°) at the Ascendant, in opposition to (180° from) the Ascendant, square to (90° from) the Ascendant, semi-square to (45° from) the Ascendant, or semi-octile to (22 1/2° from) the Ascendant. For a working explanation of their methods please refer to a book on these schools of astrology or a book on how to use wheels or dials.

Progressions, Directions, and Solar Arc

A powerful feature of astrology is its ability to project events into the future and "see" something about the patterns which accompany these events. The different ways of doing this are: progressions, directions, and solar arc. Planets are progressed in time, but directed by solar arc. Progressions, directions, and solar arc are powerful astrological methods which bring astrological insight into how changing patterns and events can affect human consciousness. There are at least eighteen or more different forms of progressions, and at least three different ways to use solar arc. Experienced midpoint users prefer to use solar arc directions.

Solar arc is the angle between your natal Sun and your secondary progressed Sun. The secondary progressed Sun is found by taking each day of life after birth as symbolically equal to one year of life. Thus, if you are twenty-four years old and you were born on May 17, then you were twenty-four days old on June 10 of your birth year. The angular difference between your birth Sun and the Sun on June 10 in your birth year is your solar arc Sun for your 24th year of life. In astrological practice these solar arc angles are measured using more precise mathematics than described here. This solar arc Sun angle, or simply Solar Arc or SA, is then applied to all other planets and points in the chart. (Be careful not to confuse the solar arc "SA" abbreviation with the two letter abbreviation for the planet Saturn, also SA.) Half solar arc and double solar arc angles have also been proposed to be astrologically informative. The generic term 'solar arc' refers to any form of these solar arc values.

Some teachers propose that solar arc is to be used in a forward zodiacal direction only. Other teachers use solar arc in both a backward and a forward direction. Strong arguments have been raised for using both directions. The use of forward and backward for solar arc carries strong astrological implications, discussions of which are beyond the scope of this book. Additional research is recommended in this important area.

Interesting theories concerning combinations provided by progressed Sun, transiting Sun, and natal or progressed midheaven combinations exist. These are referred to as "The Meridian of the Day" and are said to show important daily focuses of activity in a natal chart. Since these parameters change daily they can provide interesting insight into activities. More study of these theories is needed.

When a planet is directed by solar arc and it hits a midpoint or a planetary picture then that midpoint or planetary picture is activated. To compute these midpoint or planetary picture hits by hand is tedious and it is easy to make simple math errors. The visual methods of using dials, wheels and other available aids are helpful with hit identification. These also require some practice to gain proficiency of usage. Professional chart calculation services exist which will compute and clearly print your solar arc and progression hits for a very reasonable fee. Inexpensive computer programs for personal computers are also available for this task. Please refer to the list of such services and programs in Appendix C.

Other Bodies

Other bodies or factors occur in space besides the astrological planets. Asteroids (the lesser gods), Chiron, fixed stars, planetary nodes (other than the Moon's Node which is included herein), hypothetical or undiscovered planets, the Solar Apex, and the Galactic Center are just a few examples. The generic term "bodies" is used to refer to these sources. The principles described in this book work equally well when such bodies activate midpoints. This book describes basic ideas about the combinations, and these ideas persist despite their being used with known or unknown examples, such as asteroids, fixed stars, etc. Some of these bodies have been shown to be powerfully significant, and investigation and research into the application of their principles is encouraged.

However, first study and understand the planets and the personal sensitive points mentioned earlier.

An example of a body activating a midpoint occurs when the midpoint falls in the same degree of zodiacal longitude as an asteroid or a prominent fixed star. For instance: ☽/♅ falling on the degree of the fixed star Sirius. Sirius is a prominent star in the heavens and has a definite astrological lore associated with it derived from the accumulation of ideas from many cultures in the world. The information in this book can be used to work with these bodies, but for specific information on the use and meanings of planetary combinations with other bodies you will have to refer to sources which explicitly address these other celestial sources.

Evaluating the Importance of Specific Midpoints

It is difficult, almost impossible, to look at a traditional horoscope format and determine what is or is not an important or emphasized midpoint. An empty or unaspected midpoint may also carry powerful astrological implications. Special new techniques are needed to evaluate the strength or weakness of individual midpoints in a horoscope. These techniques involve calculating the midpoint locations, testing the midpoints for any hits, evaluating hits to see if they are in orb, determining the closeness of hit if in orb, and then assigning a weighting factor to the hit based on the harmonic and closeness values.

Aspect or harmonic theory allows you to use number equivalents when evaluating the importance of midpoints in a horoscope. Extending harmonic theories to midpoints has already been done for years through the use of dials and wheels which highlight harmonics 1, 2, 4, etc. For this book all harmonic numbers up to twenty-five were considered for use. Harmonic usage with midpoints is an exciting tool. Astrologers have long known that various harmonics produce different effects in life. However a lengthy study of this application area has not been conducted. But now a personal computer can be used to carry these harmonic and midpoint ideas further than was previously possible using manual techniques.

In this book the same 247 persons and events were chosen for inclusion as examples for each of the 78 midpoints. See Appendix D for a listing of the people and the events chosen as examples. The evaluations of the midpoints in those 247 charts selected proved to be formidable. A totally new procedure had to be formulated and created for this task because no one before had evaluated so many charts for one purpose just on their midpoint strengths alone. To judge which people or events to rank as strongest or weakest on the midpoint explanation pages a new evaluation procedure was devised and thoroughly tested.

The procedure devised to rank and evaluate individual midpoints for strength or weakness is called a "**Midpoint Weighting Analysis**" or MWA. Computer programs were specially written to execute the MWA for the examples in this book. The MWA computed each midpoint (78 per chart), looked to see if the midpoint was hit by a point at a significant harmonic, determined if the hit was in orb for that harmonic, evaluated the closeness of hit, and then calculated a weight for the hit. Planetary hits formed by a conjunction or opposition were mathematically weighted as highest in importance, then hits formed by square or trine aspects, etc. The MWA used for this book allowed a 1.5° orb for conjunctions or oppositions, 1.2° for squares or trines, etc., in a five-tiered process with ever smaller orbs and changing weights for other harmonics. This multi-tiered orb and weighting effect helped distribute the impact of aspects which occur more frequently than, for example, a conjunction. A bell-shaped curve was further used to assign a stronger weight to activated midpoints with closer hits. Despite considerable automation through the use of a personal computer, this procedure required several months of effort. The computer determined, sorted, and ranked an average of about 700 hits for each of the 247 charts used. Only the most significant were then chosen to be listed on the midpoint pages as the book's examples.

The weighting plan devised for this book evaluated certain combination sequences in charts as being more potent than other combinations in the same charts. The MWA procedure used broke with the tradition of using only the family of conjunction, opposition, square, and semi-square aspects with midpoints. All of the harmonics described before and others too were used in the book's MWA evaluations. In retrospect the consideration and use of points in trine, sextile, quincunx, etc., to midpoints in the MWA technique gave enlightening results. New horizons were opened with this technique and the results obtained can be found on the example page for each midpoint.

Until this effort no such multi-tiered consideration of hits to midpoints had been used on such a significant and large sample of charts. Traditionally, any hit was considered to be equal in weight to another hit, and orbs for all hits were kept as a constant factor. In general practice the orb used was one to two degrees, but for research purposes narrower orbs of ±1/2° were recommended and used. This traditional method presented some problems for the purposes of evaluating example strengths and weaknesses for this book's charts. Using such methods the conjunction of two points just over one degree apart in a chart would have been ignored in analysis if a ±1/2° orb had been blindly followed, since the midpoint created would be over 1/2° apart from either of the points. A significant pattern in the chart would have been missed. The MWA however allowed a ranking of hits and all significant combinations were noted and given their appropriate input and respective weight.

For the 247 charts used as examples in this book only those persons or events having the highest and strongest hits after this MWA evaluation were chosen for inclusion as examples on the combination pages. Typically people or events in the top two percent of their category are listed. This is an extreme selection process but it ensures that only the most significant results are included. As a contrast those people from the test group with the weakest two percent of midpoint hits are also listed. These correlations are a fascinating study in the inverse use of cosmic power.

The MWA selected used about twenty harmonics in its evaluation. There was no distinction made between one harmonic and another. That is, the twelfth harmonic was treated just like the eighth harmonic for the purposes of this study. A hit by the twelfth harmonic produced a numbered evaluation like a hit from an eighth harmonic. This may be a fault because astrological theory says that the interpretation of the individual harmonics is important. However, the study to obtain the most significant examples for this book was not formulated to pursue any interpretation of the harmonics, but only to see whether or not the hits for any harmonic existed. The study sought significance, not interpretation. Further study and investigation of the meanings of the individual harmonics should be done elsewhere. Also, no differentiation was made between hits made forward in the zodiac and hits made backward in the zodiac. This too is a potential failing in the area of interpretation which must eventually be corrected by more thorough study.

No consideration was given to evaluating midpoints for this book's examples other than those formed in zodiacal longitude. Experiments done on a small scale have shown that midpoints formed in declination or latitude also have significance. Studies with midpoints along the time or distance axes probably have never been systematically done. Although these midpoint evaluations were not investigated for this book they do remain a viable area of study for interested persons.

Some commercial astrological services will print out the midpoint locations and harmonics for a horoscope. Using such services and tools it is much easier to find combinations in a horoscope today than it was a few years ago. You will have to judge whether a particular service or computer program just lists midpoint locations, lists midpoint hits, or does a complete MWA form of analysis. These are three different operations and employ different levels of complexity and sophistication. Obviously, a complete MWA is preferable to a midpoint listing or a hit listing which blindly allows a simple constant orb. Be aware of these differences when choosing your evaluation and listing methods. Please see Appendix C for listings of such specific services.

Chapter 3
How to Read and Use
the Combination Pages

Overview

Each of the seventy-eight planetary combinations contained in this book occupies four pages. These four pages explain the descriptions of the combinations and are referred to as pages one through four for each midpoint. The planets are arranged in a specific and definite order in the book and you can use this planetary ordering as an index for locating any specific combination. The planetary order used is (reading down each column of planetary name and symbol, starting on the left):

Sun	☉	Jupiter	♃	Node	☊
Moon	☽	Saturn	♄	Ascendant	A
Mercury	☿	Uranus	♅	Midheaven	M
Venus	♀	Neptune	♆		
Mars	♂	Pluto	♇		

The combination explanations start in astrologic order with ☉/☽, then ☉/☿, to ☉/MC, and then ☽/☿ to ☽/M, ☿/♀ to ☿/M, etc., to the last combination in this order which is A/M. Language purists forgive me, but the variant word "thru" is used on the pages as a substitute for "through" to save space within the three line paragraphs and allow the inclusion of more ideas.

The descriptions provided are not intended to be delineations or explanations of any person's life. The descriptions are meant to provoke visual associations or images of some of the many possibilities which exist within each combination. This is important to understand. Delineations of midpoints should include both house and sign pair interpretations as well as the midpoint interpretations provided by this book. It is not practical to try to include every possible human or material circumstance within each combination. Please do not read the planetary description in this book and say something like: "I have ☉/♂ activated and what you have written in this sentence didn't fit my client, self, or friend." It was never intended to present material which is so person specific that it could be repeated back to a person as truth or an interpretation of their circumstances. Instead the writing should provoke images and potentials of what is available through the power of the planetary combinations. You are invited to create your own personal meanings from these images, and if you want to write your ideas on the pages you may do so. If you read the material and come back and say "I can relate to what is there and the ideas behind what you have written describe my circumstances or nature in ways I can immediately relate to," then a prime purpose for this book has been achieved.

Delineations of the midpoints need to include their sign and house pair associations as well as the midpoint descriptions. Since midpoints lie across a chart they are associated with sign pairs and also with house pairs — not a specific sign or a specific house. People having their ☉/☽ across the 6th–12th house pair in the signs of ♍–♓ will have a very different delineation of the ☉/☽ midpoint from people having their ☉/☽ across the 4th–10th house pair and also in ♍–♓. Similarly sign changes for a midpoint will also affect its delineation. Thus, people with ☉/☽ in ♍–♓ will have a quite different delineation of their ☉/☽ midpoint meaning from a person with their ☉/☽ across the sign pair of ♈–♎. The explanations given in this book are "pure" in a planetary sense and are not intended to perform as a personal delineation within a particular chart for any specific person.

The power of the planets is in their symbols and the patterns they form. It is an astrologer's job to interpret their symbolism and patterning in words and ideas in a language you can understand. What are these symbols? What do they mean? As their aspects change how does this alter their shades of meaning? How do these symbols function in various and quite different areas of our daily lives? These are some of the questions addressed by this book and the information provided in it.

The layout on each of the individual four pages will be discussed in greater detail in the following paragraphs. But, as a summary, the first page of the four page layout presents an overall view of the planetary combination being described. The first page contains five separate sections relating to the combination: basic ideas, personal circumstances, relationships, medical, and political or business considerations. The second page represents the planetary synthesis as it evolves when a third planet combines with the primary two. The third page is an amalgam of miscellaneous ideas which were too important to omit from the description of the combination, but which somehow just did not fit into the overall scheme of any of the other formats. The fourth page shows the combination with itself at the top of the page. These explanations become important when you work with the combinations using progressions, directions, or transits. Following on the fourth page are examples of famous people and notable events when the combination was found to be especially strong (or weak) in their natal or event charts. The listing of the people or events shown was taken from the MWA output written to evaluate the 247 charts used as examples. The first page presents an analytical, left-brained approach to interpreting midpoints, while the third page presents ideas and sounds which stimulate the right-brain's imaging and associative activities.

The First Page

The first page contains five distinct and independent areas, called: "Basic Ideas," "In Your Personal Life," "In Your Relationships," "With Body or Mind," and "In Politics or Business." The "Basic Ideas" section presents an introduction into some of the more important thoughts associated with the combination. You should read the "Basic Ideas" section first before reading other parts of the combination, as the "Basic Ideas" section contains clues and verbal hints which will help you relate to the other areas better when you read and study them. This section is basic to the combination, but not all inclusive.

Many different concepts can be associated with any combination and the purpose of the "Basic Ideas" section is to quickly and generally introduce these ideas to you. The "Basic Ideas" section is not a description intended to be used as a definition of a person's character, but an explanation of the different ways the planetary combination can express itself in life. Although the words "you" and "your" are used in the writing, the ideas in this section apply equally well to relationships, business considerations, etc. The purpose of the "Basic Ideas" section is simply to show you some fundamental ways the combination expresses itself.

A planetary combination expresses itself in life and in the world in general in many different ways. All descriptions of a combination can not be included in the "Basic Ideas" section. Some of the ideas in there may appear trivial and some may appear important to you, but all are part of the overall concepts contained within the planetary combination. Start your study of the combination by reading the "Basic Ideas" section first before going to other specific areas. Doing this will help you better use the information in this book.

The "In Your Personal Life," "In Your Relationships," and "In Politics or Business" sections are shown in three line thesis and antithesis pairs. The pairing was intended to show a contrast of extremes in a space saving way. Each set of three lines is called a **set**. These sets represent a contrast of extremes. Nothing more and nothing less was ever intended. The sets are definitely not "good" vs. "bad" contrasts. To save space on the printed pages only the "anti" portion of the word "antithesis" is written in the areas where these pairings are used. However, "anti" does not and was not intended to mean opposite — just contrasting. The use of words like "plus or minus," or "male and female," or "good and bad" to denote opposing concepts, have their drawbacks; and the words thesis and antithesis were chosen because they do not carry a "good and bad" or any sexist connotation.

Certain planetary combinations convey ideas which many people find very difficult to accept. Some people will go out of their way to ignore ideas like: burdens, responsibility, death, devastation, maiming, etc. Some people prefer words like: peace, tranquility, relaxation, etc. However, there are different sides to life and some of the combinations just do not generate such pleasant words. It is very difficult to say positive uplifting things about some of the combinations and in an opposite way it is very difficult to write more practical and direct explanations of combinations which provide ease, light, and luxury. Everyone wants love, money, pleasure, and fulfillment, but few are willing to undertake the discipline, hard work, drive, and consistency which bring these attributes.

Some of the combinations are heavy and difficult to read. If you have trouble reading them, think about the effort it took to amass, study, and write about this material. It is easy to write about ♀/♃ and difficult to write about ♄/♇. But, both ♀/♃ and ♄/♇ exist in this world and each combination must be addressed. Do not look upon the contrasting paragraphs as being either good or bad. Especially with these two pairs, good and bad as concepts do not exist. ♀/♃ is "happiness and love" and ♄/♇ is"hard dirty work, greed, using others, etc. " In these combinations the contrasting concepts are not contrasts of good and bad. For ♀/♃ the contrasts represent two different sides of luck and love, and in the case of ♄/♇ the contrast represents two different sides of hard work, greed, and using and discarding people.

All combinations exist in every horoscope. Everyone has both a ♀/♃ and a ♄/☿ in their chart. But individuals will use them differently too, regardless of how they are accented or highlighted in their life. One person's trash is another person's treasure is an old saying. The combinations certainly enhance that idea. One person will thrive on drive and hard work and not be able to relax and enjoy life, while another person will relax too well and not work hard nor use and abuse others. In the end the sum of all of the energies available to us is zero. All of the good balances all of the bad, and vice versa. Individually however, certain people will emphasize more of one end of the pairing than the other and it is for this reason that the contrasted pairings were included. They offer alternative views of the energies of the planets and not views of their good or bad sides or shades of meanings.

You function best as an individual when you incorporate both sides of the thesis and antithesis concepts into your personality functions. You also perform best as a person when you know and realize those circumstances and situations in life where it is appropriate to express either extreme. You should not be all thesis or all antithesis, but a proper balance of these two extremes capable of either expression. You should be able to appropriately demonstrate either the thesis or antithesis side in various life's situations. Doing this shows a good balance of natural expression. Other expressions may be repressive. You may be able to relate and freely express either thesis or antithesis; but when you consistently take those forms of expression which are socially appropriate, then you show personal growth.

As an example of thesis and antithesis extremes consider this. Any person can be destructive, show destructive tendencies, speak about intentions to destroy, order destruction, etc. At times this form of activity may be necessary. There are also times when it is inappropriate. Such activity is more often inappropriate than appropriate. A person who demolishes old buildings for a living may use these characteristics in a positive way. A person who has little aim in life, suffers alienation toward people or society, and chooses to exhibit destruction in any of several ways is not using these energies effectively. Astrology does not judge good or bad attitudes. People make those judgments. Astrology simply presents you with your options — the contrasts. It is up to you as an individual to take control of your life, balance out your expressions, and repress neither side of these energies.

The "In Your Personal Life" section is intended to help you directly understand self or others. It addresses the concepts in the "Basic Ideas" section in a personhood sense. The information given here is intended to orient your thoughts toward the inner qualities of people, like your friends, parents, bosses — whomever. This section should help you view people as individuals rather than as partners or associates. Use this information to help see yourself and your relationships. Look at the sets provided and see how you balance the two contrasting views. You are best balanced for the combination when you have some traits from both sides of the pairing and feel free to move either to the thesis or antithesis sides as you choose.

The "In Your Relationships" pairings are intended to help you understand your role in interpersonal relationships. Relationships is a general term and may be taken as male-female, male-male, female-female, friend to friend, lover to lover, parent to child, employee to boss, person to pet, child to child, neighbor to neighbor, animal to animal, etc. Many such possible interactions exist. The orientation in the writing is often male to female, or from you to a partner or lover, but please do not exclude other forms of relationships. The writing slant was chosen because you are reading the ideas, and it is easier to relate to words like you, even though you may want to apply the ideas from your child to his or her playmates. When you have a combination highlighted in certain ways, this section should help you understand the interpersonal roles that will be accentuated during this period of life. If a combination is strong natally, then these pairings will help you gain insight into strengths or weaknesses you may have when working with others.

The symbology of the "With Body or Mind" combinations presents such a rich sea of ideas to choose from that it is difficult to omit the medical concepts on a general introduction page like this first page. The medical symbology is only casually defined in astrological literature for some of the planets, and not so clearly defined for the personal sensitive points. The personal sensitive points indicate your mental state more than your body's physical state, and the writing reflects this orientation. The "With Body or Mind" section was included because medicine and health considerations are an important part of your daily life. Further development needs to be done in the area of medical astrology, and interested persons are invited to use the knowledge presented here as a beginning basis for additional work.

The "In Politics or Business" section is provided for the strong interest shown for mundane ideas. Great astrological interest in mundane and business matters exists because people find that astrology gives them insight into social and business trends which are otherwise difficult to perceive. Mundane, political, governmental, event, business, and social ideas provide a rich testing ground for the concepts of astrology and the ideas presented in this "In Politics or Business" section should help people orient themselves to the information conveyed by the planets. The word "enterprise" is often used in these descriptions in an overall sense to refer to a nation, business, government, etc.

The Second Page

This page is the heart of the book, especially for astrological practitioners already familiar with and using midpoints. The second page presents ideas about the primary combination when a third point combines with the primary pair. When a third point meets a midpoint by an astrologically significant harmonic, then the midpoint is said to be hit or activated. Use this page when midpoint combinations or planetary pictures are activated or hit in the charts you are studying. People are always eager for new interpretations and ideas about point sets, and for them this page of ideas, hints, concepts, and thoughts is presented.

Examine your MWA and find the hits which occur to the midpoint you are using. Or, find a significant hit in your MWA and look up the triad activated by this hit. Use the information on this page to help you understand the meaning and impact of this hit in your life. The information should give you insight into your present circumstances. The material should help you understand the meaning associated with the three points taken together as a whole. Some of the information given is oriented to personal life and some to mundane circumstances. This mixture should help you understand the point definitions more fully. The expressions of the point symbols can take many forms and the ideas given may not always fit your immediate situation. You may wish to use the supplemental keyword information in Chapter 5 to round out the material presented on this page if the write-up does not fully explain your current circumstances.

The information given is not meant as a delineation of personal circum-stances. You need house and sign information to properly understand current contexts, and the information on this page deals only with the points involved. Use this information to gain insight and understanding into your conditions, but also view your situation through the house and sign context in which they occur.

The Third Page

Page three pulls together different ideas about the combination listed in a short phrase-like way. Use this page as a further idea generator for the midpoint, and also to help you better understand the information on page one of the combination. You will notice three columns at the top of the page with shorter images, and two columns on the lower part of the page containing longer images. The column placements carry no implications. This dual columnar arrangement allowed about one hundred images to fit onto each of these third pages.

Consider each set of words as a mental image generator. The page consists of a series of short phrases or statements each of which tells you something about how the themes of the two points manifest in life. This page is intended to be a fun page, yet also to have a serious side to it. It can bring you ideas and concepts about the combination which are not easy to describe or use in a more formal or paragraph oriented framework. The page is intended to give you a short, quick look at sides of the energy combination in small, rapid bursts of ideas. Scan the lists provided and notice the rich variety of expressions the points represent. Use this page to let your creativity flow and give yourself ideas about the portrayal of the pairing. Write in your own ideas and concepts about the pair on this page if you prefer. Have some fun and open your own avenues of creation with these concepts. They are designed to help stimulate your creative right-brain functions.

Sometimes the concepts are simply two word astrological phrase combinations. Other times more words are used to express an idea. An invented and coined word, **frases**, is applied to these individual groups. An example of a two word frase is 'effective haste' which may be found in the ☉/♂ concept page list. A more wordy example is "thinks concurrently on different ideas" which is associated with the ☿/A concept list. Both frases convey their planetary motifs well. These lists started from ideas on the combinations which were used to present images before thinking or writing about the individual midpoints. They proved to be so important and powerful that they ultimately grew into a separate page for the book. So, from a mnemonic jog to a fun concept page, a transition was made. This page adds a lot to the overall information and usage you can derive from the planetary combination.

These frases are not interpretations or delineations of the combination. They are meant to be mental images and hopefully bring you other ideas about this combination. A combination can express itself in an unlimited number of ways, but only a certain number can be included on these pages. It was difficult to cut the original material down to what was included on these pages and often a frase which was deemed important and retained in one reading was sacrificed at another reading for another frase which somehow just seemed more appropriate to include. Do not dwell too long on a specific frase if that frase has no meaning for you. Sometimes a specific frase has no exterior meaning. Think of the frases as images, like word pictures, which together with the other images and your own experience are there to give you deeper insight into the midpoint meaning.

Use this page to help you understand the material on pages one and two. Often you may just need to gain some expanded insight into the point images themselves. Scanning this page can help you achieve a better grasp. At times when you need an overview of the information, as opposed to an interpretation, this page can prove to be most useful. Make whatever notes you desire on this page and you may find, with time, that the same images keep re-appearing to you about a particular combination. When that happens note this occurrence. It is through such practices that you will gain personal insight into the meaning of the combination.

The Fourth Page

This page contains two distinct areas: the combination with itself, and examples of people and events who have their midpoint combinations activated by the planet shown. The combination with itself is useful when you are working with transits, progressions, or directions. Often you will find a transiting, progressed, or directed point activating itself, and when that happens you can use this information to help you understand the circumstances of the activity indicated. The combination with itself may also be helpful when you combine two or more charts into a composite chart. You will find that the combined positions activate themselves.

Two hundred and twenty famous people from fifteen different categories of life were chosen for use in the book's examples. Besides people, twenty-seven timed events of note, primarily oriented to the history or politics of the United States, are also included. These examples present a broad range of personalities and events rather than a concentration in any one area. Some of the categories of people you will find here are: authors, artists, politicians, actors, military people, scientists, etc. No more than fifteen people from each category were chosen to ensure that no job category predominated. The people and events selected all had known, recorded, or individually verified birth times. This is essential if they are to be used as examples — especially because the time-sensitive personal sensitive points change rapidly moment to moment for any particular location on earth. The people's names and areas of notoriety are listed alphabetically in Appendix D along with the events. Biographies of the people included in the examples can be found in the "Astro-Data" books by Lois Rodden. The history of the people or events chosen can be further checked through sources in your local libraries.

The midpoint hits from the people chosen are divided into two categories: strongest and weakest. The example listings on this page were not derived from 'eyeballed' approximations. The MWA listing generated was used to select those people from the 220 examples showing the strongest or weakest midpoint hits. The listing of the names given was copied in order by strength (or weakness) as determined by the MWA. See Chapter 2 for an explanation of the MWA selection technique used. The "strong" listings give the names of those persons who were the strongest in the combination according to the MWA. These were the people who most needed to learn and use this combination in their life. The "weak" listings are also quite informative because they show those people from the 220 examples who least needed the energies of this combination in their life.

The events listed show the strongest weighted events for this combination first. The last event is listed in parenthesis and is the weakest of the twenty-seven events analyzed for the midpoint described. The strong and weak events are another indication which can help you understand the significance of the combination in life, circumstances, and society.

The rest of the page is filled with the names of the people or events ranked most highly by the MWA in each individual category. The MWA first determined if a person or an event had this category (e.g. ♂ = ☿/♀; ♅ = ♀/♇) active, and then ranked, from strongest to weakest, the names of the people and events. It was this MWA list that was used to list the strongest examples found. In listing these names, sometimes abbreviations are used so that at least four names or descriptions could fit on each line. If the use of abbreviations confuses you then you may wish to refer to Appendix D for the full name of the person or event cited. Notice that the component points themselves are listed together in the examples (e.g., ♀ and ♄ are listed together at the ♀/♄ midpoint). A harmonic activates both planets involved in the midpoint. A person or event having any point hitting ♀/♄ will have that point, by definition, equidistant from both ♀ and ♄. Therefore, only either ♀ or ♄ need be listed for ♀/♄, or, as done, both can be listed together on the same line.

In each case the listing begins with the strongest event or person, then the next strongest, etc. As an example, of the 247 people and events selected, it was Jack Nicklaus, the professional golfer, who had the strongest ☉ = ♂/♅. This was next followed by the event which was the secession of the State of South Carolina from the Union just prior to the Civil War in the U.S. The thoughts from the second page of ☉ = ♂/♅ give considerable insight into the need of a person having ☉ = ♂/♅ activated to "correct past mistakes effectively" (which a professional golfer must do to succeed) or to "prevent the transgressions of fundamental rules" (which the legislature of South Carolina was trying to show concerning the issues involved with the slavery and states' rights questions in the 1850s and 1860s in the Southern U.S.).

The Index to this Book

The index to this book is available in a separate book called *The Concept Dictionary*, which will be referred to as the *CD*, for short. The index was too long to include in this book. This companion index is 271 pages long with two columns of entries per page. The *CD* is a comprehensive cross reference of all of the ideas presented in this book. It began as a listing and reference of the concepts from page three of each combination, but additional information was also added to the frases initially listed. *The Concept Dictionary* contains a KWIC (Key Word In Context; pronounced "quick") sort for each entry from the concept pages of each midpoint, and more. *The Concept Dictionary* is recommended as a companion for this book. The *CD* acts like a rulership book for midpoints.

A **KWIC index** references all key words within a phrase or a title. In a KWIC listing an entry, such as "Receptive to Destruction," listed under ☽/♀, would be indexed under both the word "receptive" and the word "destruction," but not the word "to" which is not considered a key word. Thus the KWIC index would have two entries for "Receptive to Destruction" and a user of the indexed list could find this reference listed alphabetically under both key words. The KWIC idea is to present an index in its simplest yet most complete and cross referenced way.

The *CD* can be a valuable companion tool when working with the material in this book. There are many different ways it can be used. You may wish to refer to the *CD* first and then work with this book, or do the reverse. In either case, do not overlook the important other information which the *CD* can furnish you.

Chapter 4
Working with this Book

With a Horoscope

An easy way to learn to use the information in this book is to test it against your personal horoscope or the horoscope of someone you know well. The midpoints from a horoscope are the most common starting point for using this book because this book is oriented to midpoint usage and then to other planetary combinations. Assume that you are working with a natal horoscope, that it was cast either by a chart service or a micro-computer program, and that you have a sorted list of the midpoints for that horoscope before you. You should have read and become familiar with the information in the preceding chapters.

If you are working without an MWA you should notice which planets or points have the most hits. Notice which midpoints are hit by more than one point. Look for recognizable and repeating patterns formed by the hits. The most active planets and midpoints will emphasize the more important areas of a horoscope. The MWA will give you a list of sorted and ranked midpoints and hits. Look up the definitions of the activated midpoints in this book, starting with the ones with the strongest hits and read their descriptions. When referencing the combination pages, always start by reading the "Basic Ideas" section of the combination first. This will introduce you to the most central parts of the themes represented and will better prepare you for the shorter descriptions in the four theme areas on page one of the midpoint report.

Repeat this procedure for all of the midpoints you care to reference. You may also wish to reference the supplemental meanings of the points given in Chapter 5. The information in Chapter 5 can be used to give you additional ideas about the meaning of a combination. There is a wealth of information in this book and there are many ways you can reference this information. Certain ideas or themes may repeat in a horoscope and it is these repeated themes or ideas which will predominate during the life of the subject. All people and all events have all combinations as their potential in life, but not all combinations will be activated or emphasized. It is the combinations which are repeatedly stressed which should prove to be the most important in a person's life or the analysis of an event.

As you become familiar with the information contained in a horoscope, you may wish to try equivalent combinations to the midpoints which are activated. Notice which midpoint themes are repeated by combination themes, for these repeats will also be important. For instance, a ♃/♄ midpoint may be very active in the chart you are examining. You may also note that this chart has either ♃ in the tenth, or ♄ in the ninth house. Either of these placements would reinforce the power behind the ♃/♄ midpoint, and vice-versa. You have to develop your own sense of how these themes repeat in a chart, because experience has shown that important themes will repeat in a horoscope in different ways. Appendices A and B help show you these alternative ways.

Dials and Templates

If you are familiar with dial techniques then you can use dials to manually find midpoints and their hits directly. The 90° dial allows all cardinal zodiacal sign placements (Aries, Cancer, Libra, and Capricorn) to overlap in the same portion of the dial or wheel. Saturn at 2 ♎ 44 and Mars at 3 ♑ 15, if drawn on a 360° dial, would appear as a square. The same positions drawn on 90° dial would appear to be a planetary conjunction. This is because a 90° dial overlaps every 90°. All cardinal sign placements overlap or share the same space, as do all fixed sign placements (Taurus, Leo, Scorpio, and Aquarius) and all mutable sign placements (Gemini, Virgo, Sagittarius, and Pisces). A clear illustrated introduction to the use of the 90° dial is available in *Dial Detective* by Maria Kay Simms.

The 360° dial (illustrated on page 9, available from Astro Communications Services) makes a good aspectarian, to help you spot major and minor aspects. Plastic overlay tools such as "AstroTemplate" and "AstroRuler" from Smart Art are also useful to determine aspects or harmonics to midpoints, planets, parts, or pictures directly. The advantage of these tools is that they highlight the minor harmonics, such as the important trine, quintile, sextile, septile, and novile (3rd, 5th, 6th, 7th, and 9th harmonics). These harmonics are difficult to see on a 90° dial which emphasizes the 2nd, 4th, 8th, and 16th harmonics.

It is up to each individual user to determine which technique, manual or machine, or combinations of both, suits him or her best. There is no right or correct way. Try a little of each and you will eventually find the method which feels most comfortable to you personally. Refer to and use the resources listed in Appendix C.

Midpoint Weighting Analysis

The MWA technique used to evaluate the examples used in this book should be available from several sources. You may also be able to purchase computer programs for your personal home computers from astrological software companies to calculate midpoint weightings for you. The advantage to using the computer services or programs is that they perform millions and millions of calculations for each chart evaluation, and the computer will do such evaluations quickly and correctly. Working at the constant pace of one arithmetic calculation per second a human being would take over forty-six days to compute and evaluate the midpoint weighting in just one chart. The MWA technique offers you the most complete analysis of a chart available and is the technique recommended for use with this book.

Other Combinations

Appendices A and B offer alternatives to seeing traditional planetary placements. Through Appendix A you can see that ♀/☊ is equal to the Node in the 2nd House, the Node in the 7th House, the Node in Taurus, the Node in Libra, or the Node sextile (anything). If you want to obtain suggestions about such placements then both Appendix B and Appendix A offer fascinating possibilities for further exploration. Use Appendices A and B as cross references to look up equivalent combinations in this book for ♄ in ♉, ♃ in ♎, ☿ in the tenth house, etc.

You may wish to perform a traditional horoscope analysis with a chart form, and note which combinations are emphasized by sign, rulership, aspect, or house placement. Having done this you can extract the equivalent midpoint information of these emphasized points and see how the equivalent midpoint combinations are hit. Several important hits should be confirmed for each midpoint. Astrologers are very good at using different techniques or schools of thought which convey the same basic information, but repeated in different ways.

Idea Searching

Another useful feature of this book helps you with idea searching. Often in astrological work you will simply want some hints and directions about an astrological combination. This is where the concepts page of each combination can be helpful. Read this page over to get general ideas and hints about the combination you wish to understand. Often these concepts will provide insight and direction for your thinking and work and point you to directions which you may not have thought of otherwise.

If you notice an event and you think that event may remind you of a certain midpoint combination, then you may wish to check the material on page three of that combination to see if similar ideas are noted. Sometimes you may just wish to get a quick overall review of the meanings associated with a midpoint without having to read or think about text. Again, page three can be helpful in this way.

The Examples

Noting the famous people or events listed as examples on page four may also help you associate with the meanings of the combinations. Knowing something about the lives of the people noted can be helpful. You are encouraged to study the personalities and lives of the people selected in the examples. If you are familiar with these people's lives or the mundane circumstances noted, then your insight into the meaning of the combination may be enhanced. If you are not familiar then you may wish to check reference books at a convenient library about these people or events. You may wish to include your own events or people on these pages by writing them in where possible. Do not overlook this valuable tool included on page four of the combination pages.

Keeping track of your own strengths and weaknesses as well as those of your friends is also a valuable tool for learning more about working with the midpoints and midpoint combinations. You may wish to start a diary about each chart you work with to note how themes repeat or unfold in an event or a person's life. This can be a very informative way of learning new ideas.

Expounding and Speculations

The MWA technique is a new astrological tool and astrologers are just beginning to recognize its potential. One advantage it has over other techniques is that it is more comprehensive than similar earlier tools which were primarily manual and visual. The MWA is more objective and when properly done will not fail to point out something that a person may miss due to hurry or worry when using manual techniques. The MWA gives new and important insight, and its use with charts is highly recommended. The MWA provided information and rankings about the people and events used as examples, but it did not provide any analysis of the implications of these rankings. Since the technique is relatively new no time for perspective on the implications of the MWA as an advanced tool has been exercised. Therefore, some cursory speculation is needed on the analysis produced from the examples selected for this book.

Examination of Certain Results

The material in the book was written first before the MWA was developed for a ranking of the examples. The MWA results were not used to alter or influence the already written book material, as the research which produced the book material had been done earlier over a fifteen or so year period. A cursory examination of the MWA results used to rank the 247 charts examples shows that people seem to be born with talents already within them, and then express these talents through the whole category of the energy spectrum available in the horoscope. For example, a musician may have world-noticed talent and express it through ☉/♅, or through ♀/♆, etc., but neither ☉/♅ or ♀/♆ necessarily indicate the presence of such musical talent or the fact that one will or will not be famous. This lack of vocational specificity in any particular midpoint or combination was perhaps the most striking outcome from the MWA. The MWA reinforced the idea that it is the overall pattern formed in a natal chart, and not a specific combination of one or two things, which shows how a talent may be utilized in a lifetime. This finding reinforces the concept of 'free will' or the ability to choose and direct your own paths in life. Thus the influence of location, family, environment, personal motivation, etc., has a great influence in how the combination patterns highlighted may be used.

Every person or event will be strong in certain midpoints and weak in others. Strong and weak are comparative terms and in general refer to the top or bottom 3% (i.e., seven occurrences) of the people or events in a category. The strong midpoints seem to indicate the areas of life which will present challenges or learning opportunities for the person in this lifetime, while the weak midpoints seem to represent talents already learned in prior lifetimes (and thus need not be emphasized now), or opportunities or talents which may be denied in this lifetime. For example, Albert Einstein had a comparatively weak ☉/☿ which showed that he did not tolerate wit or practical thinking to interfere with his conceptual thinking. A weak ☉/☿ does not always mean the absence of intelligence.   The job category which seemed to predominate in the stronger weighted ☉/☿ people was that of the TV talk show hosts, who of course have to live by a rapid analysis of people or situations, their sharp observations, and a ready wit.

The bank robber John Dillinger had a strong ☉/♀ which can show an ego involvement with the acquisition of money. John Dillinger was also noted for being a model and courteous prisoner. Certainly the ego and money aspect of ☉/♀ is an important trait likely to be cultivated by a bank robber. It is also interesting to note that artists and musicians did not dominate the ☉/♀ category as some traditional astrologers may have suggested. Traditionally ☉/♀ is a midpoint which denotes a central involvement with money, art, music, softness, appreciation, gratitude, etc. — these all being central themes of Venus. Thus, conventional wisdom holds that a person with a strong ☉/♀ is likely to concentrate on developing traits involving Sun and Venus themes in their life.

A musician or an artist does not necessarily have to have any ☉/♀ traits strong in life. They may be helpful, but they are not necessary. Audrey Hepburn, Paul Cezanne, Georges Seurat, Burl Ives, Neil Diamond, and Jimi Hendrix are all artists who have a weak ☉/♀. Audrey Hepburn, noted for her natural physcial beauty, studied hard to be a ballerina, but abandoned this career. It was not to be through ballet (which requires grace in form and movement), but acting, that she found fame. Paul Cezanne failed to gain entry to art school as he exhibited little artistic talent in his life at the time of the art school admission judgment. Georges Seurat founded a school of painting which used dots, but died with most of his works unsold. Folk singer Burl Ives was more noted for his robustness and enjoyment of life than his melodious singing voice or his desire to treat others with respect. It is difficult to say that the artistic musical style of Jimi Hendrix shows courtesy and appeasement. These people all had a weak ☉/♀ and the actions, events, and activities in their lives reflected this. However having a weak ☉/♀ did not prevent them from becoming famous in artistic fields. On the other hand the poetry of Percy Bysshe Shelley is noted for its grace and gentleness and of the 247 people or events analyzed, he had one of the strongest ☉ = ☉/♀.

Arnold Schwarzenegger has a weak ☉/♂, but a strong ♂ = ☉/☽. Thus, you should expect the unusual from the MWA but not the unthinkable. ☉/♂ represents your expenditure and regulation of energy, but not your inner strength or even your muscular strength. On the other hand a strong ♂ = ☉/☽ represents an astrological influence which could be used to develop physical body beauty, as any good body builder seeks. Arnold Schwarzenegger won the Mr. Universe title five times, and has used that fame to go on and perform in movies where he is usually cast in a macho role. Is it his acting ability or his body building results that are being represented in the movies? He has a weak ☉/♀ which can indicate a lowered appreciation for the gentle. From his MWA a strong midpoint is ♅/♇, which by its definition reflects the image he portrays in his movie roles. From the concept page of ♅/♇ the frase "Rebels with Intensity" is found in column two near the top. This could be altered slightly to read "A Rebel with Intensity" and this is the image his movie maker directors have wanted him to portray in most of his movie roles. He has done so quite successfully. He was not necessarily meant to be a movie actor, but in portraying roles which require a strong ♅/♇ as well as a weak ☉/♀ he has been financially and artistically successful. This is an indication of how the midpoints can work in life. You should work with and use your astrological strengths or weaknesses to the best of your ability.

A person may not have to work to find his or her accentuated midpoints. Perhaps, as Charles Atlas advertisements from earlier days suggested, events we encounter through other people propel us to take action to strengthen our weak points, or act on our potential strengths. In the Charles Atlas advertisements a skinny boy on a beach talking with a pretty girl has sand kicked in his face by a stronger, more muscular boy. The weaker boy is humiliated and vows to become stronger by taking the Charles Atlas body building course. He applies himself—eventually going back to the same beach and kicking sand in his adversary's face in front of the same girl who had seen his earlier disgrace. It was an inner determination (which is shown astrologically by ☉, M, and also ♄) which produced the desired results in this example. Cosmic laws indicate that we should work hard to capitalize on the talents we have chosen to emphasize through our stronger midpoints. This inference recalls the parable of the talents given to us in the New Testament of the Bible. Similarly the MWA examples in the book seem to show that in life you should use or develop what talents (e.g., midpoint strengths) you have to advantage and not grieve over what you have chosen to de-emphasize.

Perhaps a lesson from the cosmos is that the contrast between strengths and weaknesses can be turned into assets if we choose roles where others appreciate the downplaying of our de-emphasized traits — like areas where we are innately weak. Steve Wozniak has one of the weakest ♃/♅. At first consideration this would seem improbable for one of the founders of the Apple Computer company. Traditionally the ♃/♅ is a trait which computer people should want to cultivate because Uranus rules computers and Jupiter brings luck. Also ♃/♅ may be viewed as an "expansion of ideas in the computer field." But, look at some of the frases for ♃/♅ as listed on the concepts page, such as: "excessive leniency," "forgives infractions," and "happy with discontent." These portray a picture of a person who will tolerate errors or slackness in work. Any MWA weakness in ♃/♅ shouts of a drive to be without flaws. Thus the drive to become a perfectionist is, in this instance, noted by the weak ♃/♅ and it is Steve Wozniak's drive for this intolerance of error which substantially contributed to his successful corporate achievements. You should not downplay the importance of weakly aspected midpoints.

The following MWA result was initially quite puzzling. Adolf Hitler had a weak ♃/♇ (♃/♇ being equated with "large destruction"). It is difficult to reconcile this considering the incredible destruction he wrought before and during WW II to achieve his goals. However, he had two passions during the progress of the war concerning technology of a ♃/♇ sort. They were to obtain an intercontinental rocket which had a capability of delivering a payload over 2000 miles away, and a bomb of atomic destructive capabilities. He came close to succeeding in both of these categories. But, both of these ♃/♇ weapons were denied to him, possibly reflecting his weak ♃/♇ emphasis. Had he been born at a time when a stronger ♃/♇ would have been natally available the outcome of historical events on our planet may have been quite different from what we read in the history books today.

The 27 events chosen seemed to conform to traditional meanings of astrology more than the people chosen for the examples did. This seems to indicate that people are more clever in their expression of talents and impulses than events. Thus it is more likely for a Uranus event to be strong in Uranus traits than a person exhibiting Mars is to be strong in a Mars trait. There are so many different and equal ways of expressing Mars, or Uranus, or whatever, that people are usually more clever in expressing and exercising their options than events, which tend to exhibit the more traditional manifestations of the energies and symbols.

The event MWA of ♀/♂ provides an interesting example. The first statement from the mundane section states: "courtesy shown to adversaries by a combatant" and a strong event was General Robert E. Lee's surrender at Appomattox, VA for the end of hostilities of the U.S. Civil War in 1865. General Lee was known for his military precision and correctness. The ceremony is often historically portrayed with General Lee in clean and proper military dress formally handing his sword over to General Ulysses S. Grant. General Grant was recognized to be personally much sloppier in his dress and mannerisms than General Lee. However, he observed all correct decorum on this day, and that correctness is reflected suitably by the MWA for the strong ♀/♂ during that event.

Another strong ♀/♂ event was the enrollment of James Meredith at the University of Mississippi. U.S. Marshals were assigned to escort Mr.

Meredith onto the campus and enroll him. They had to endure strong opposition from people who resented this show of governmental force. The statement "a ruler with martial skills, charm, and diplomatic tendencies," and in the antithesis section "making a spectacle of prowess... " do show much of the activity surrounding this event. There were bricks and bottles thrown at Mr. Meredith and his protectors, Marshals were spit upon, and they all had to run for cover when the gunfire began from people hiding behind barricades nearby. Whatever the people's reaction or intentions, the government ultimately prevailed and the University was racially integrated. Without the strong ♀/♂ occurring at that time there may have been considerable bloodshed surrounding this important social event.

The strongest event from the ♀/♂ MWA listing was the East Coast Power Blackout which occurred suddenly and caused all electricity to be turned off for most of the East Coast of the United States for many hours. The statement : "places where the natural beauty and scenery are evident for all to see and enjoy" brings to mind a startling news photograph taken on the day of event which showed the skyline of New York City, all dark and unlighted, outlined in the beauty of the fading twilight. There was also an increased incidence of births on the East Coast some nine-and- a-half months after that event.

The events noted under the ☿/A midpoint also provide for an interesting study in midpoint application. In the ☿/A writeup the ideas about the "importance placed on clearly communicating intentions to others," and "rapidly disseminating news" are noted. The events which scored high in this regard are: the Bolsheviks seizing power in Russia in 1917, the great Alaskan earthquake of 1964, the Mt. St. Helens explosion in 1980, and the secession of South Carolina from the Union in 1860 (which effectively started actions resulting in the armed conflict of the U. S. Civil war). These are all events which caused a great stir in the news of their day. They were intended as messages of statement and emphasis. Ideas about this can be found on the concept page under this midpoint, like: "describes current conditions" and "appears restless."

The earth was showing its cycle of restlessness for two of these important ☿/A events, and an emphasis on making a statement to the world was quite evident in the other two events. The Bolsheviks wanted to impose their form of government on Russia. Although it took them some years to accomplish this the impetus for this action began with their winning their battle against the then existing government. The legislature of South Carolina wanted to put their intentions forward, and did so with their definitive statement. In both of these instances a desire to make a statement or communication of intentions was very strong.

A Final Comment

Planets may be either retrograde or direct in motion, and the MWA technique used did not differentiate between these modes of motion. The research for the written material also ignored this factor, although known differences exist in the delineation between these two modes of motion. The exploration of this important difference is left for future research. The MWA showed a strong affinity for both people and events with the nodes of the planets. This important area was left untouched, although it begs for further research and investigation. Also left for future research are the combinations of the planets with the other personal sensitive points beyond the Ascendant and the MC, as well as the importance of the fixed stars and the midpoints.

Retrograde planets, the planetary nodes, and the fixed stars: I strongly urge those people interested in future studies with midpoints to be aware of these important factors. The role of the planetary nodes and the role of the fixed stars, in particular, kept coming up in the results of the MWA studies as being important. Eventually I intend to address these factors, but I also urge you, the reader, to do your own investigation of these important topics. I also can not over emphasize the importance of the personal sensitive points beyond just the Ascendant and the MC. There is much fertile work waiting to be perfomed in areas such as these.

A midpoint, like $D/♀$, represents a general energy pattern which carries information. As such it is available to every person or event which occurs. Whether the person or event chooses to emphasize that particular energy pattern is a different story. An MWA will assess the strength or weakness of that midpoint at the time of the person's birth or the event's initiation. However, when an event or a person has a specific midpoint hit pattern, such as $☉ = D/♀$, or, $⛢ = ♂/♆$, then that specific pattern becomes more explicit in its manifestation of action for that person or event. We all have each of the 78 midpoint combinations in our chart. However, we do not all have each specific hit pattern emphasized or even present. Thus, for specific traits, look to the strong hit patterns listed in the MWA, but for general trends look for the stronger midpoints listed in the MWA.

Also, the fact that a (i.e., one) particular midpoint is listed as strongest in an MWA is not as important as the combination of the top six or seven midpoints which are strong. Do not isolate the very strongest midpoint in your MWA and say "that is me." Rather look to the set of midpoints which are strong and take them as a collective set representing the challenges and energies you have chosen as one of your life's goals to learn.

Chapter 5
Planets and Their Keywords

Meanings

The individual descriptions of the planets are the heart of this book, and this chapter summarizes the expressions and ideas of the planets included here. The layout of each of these pages is similar to the first page of the combination descriptions in this book.

What follows are a series of ideas, broken down into the four categories which mirror the divisions on page one of the planetary formats. The keyword ideas included in these divisions are not complete, because a complete word breakdown and definition keyword listing would be too lengthy. However, enough representative ideas and suggestions are given so that you may begin to understand the basic nature of each individual planet and how it works in any of the topic areas which this book addresses. The keyword categories are: "Basic Ideas," "In Your Relationships," "With Body or Mind," and "In Politics or Business." The word ideas listed on each page may apply to more than just the category in which they are listed.

Some of the words given are listed and used in more than one category. This is because their connotation and usage changes depending on whether their usage is intended in a relationship, with your body, etc. Thus, a word like "security," which is related to the Midheaven, can have many shades of meaning as a basic idea, in relationships, in politics, in business, etc. You will find such words listed in more than one category in the following pages. The idea of "security" may also be related to the Moon in another sense and Saturn, too. Much of the specific relationship of a word to a planet comes from the context in which it is used.

The words are intended not for delineation use but to present ideas about the qualities of each planet or personal sensitive point. Please understand that any of these words can be taken out of the context in which they were intended. Examine the overall context the words appear in to provide one meaning before trying to isolate any one word and stretch its meaning from one planet to another. For example, one part of understanding the concept behind something as complex as the Ascendant is to realize that each of us has a forefront to our mind, which is that part of our consciousness which doesn't think, but which does react to the stimuli that we perceive in our immediate environment. Thus a set of words like "mental focus" applies to the Ascendant, but the mental processing of ideas associated with thought or thinking is a concept that belongs to the planet Mercury. You must also be careful when using word synonyms because such synonyms can quickly change context and meaning to another planet. The ideas and concepts presented in this book closely mirror traditional western astrological thought, ideas, and teachings.

SUN ☉

Basic Ideas:

Acceptability
Achievement
Ambition
Autonomy
Capability
Certainty
Confidence
Decisiveness
Determination
Discrimination

Distinction
Domination
Encouragement
Effectiveness
Enthusiasm
Exuberance
Fortitude
Inspiration
Leadership
Mastery

Motivation
Originality
Resilience
Resourcefulness
Self-Expression
Supremacy
Trustworthiness
Uniformity
Vigor
Willpower

In Your Relationships:

Bliss
Fidelity
Faithfulness
Furnishings, Style of

Games
Individuality
Living Space
Love, Capacity for

Motivation for
Playfulness
Relationship, The
Support of

With Body or Mind:

Body
Heart
Infection, Resistance to

Infections
Iodine
Magnesium

Mind
Stress
Well-Being

In Politics or Business:

Authority
Character of Business
Character of Nation
Executives
Existence
Expression
Famous, The
Heads of State
Heat

Images
Individuality
Influence
Kings, Queens
Leaders
Leadership
Light
Men, In General
Necessities

Ornate Things
Political Leaders
Power
Presidents
Prime Ministers
Remarkable Showings
Reputation
Sovereigns
Symbolic Leaders

MOON ☽

Basic Ideas:

Attitudes	Fickleness	Obedience
Behavior	Harmony	Premonitions
Caring	Hesitation	Receptivity
Collections	Home	Responses
Compliance	Imagination	Rhythm
Concern	Instinct	Sentiments
Domesticity	Instinctive Behavior	Suspicions
Emotions	Intuition	Sympathy
Fecundity	Maternity	Uncertainty
Feelings	Melancholy	Vulnerability
Females	Nurturing	Waywardness

In Your Relationships:

Comfort, Needs for	Emotions	Partner, Intuition to
Emotional State	Mothering, Attitudes of	Romance

With Body or Mind:

Acid/Alkaline Balance	Fertility	Operations, Medical
Body Fluids, Pressure	Fungus Infections	Stomach
Emotions	Glandular System	Subconscious
Eyesight	Health, Condition of	Ulcers
Female Organs	Lymphatic System	Water Levels

In Politics or Business:

Agriculture, Food	Ideas, Popularity of	Production
Concerns, Causes for	Ideologies	Real Estate
Crowds	Land	Styles
Daily Routine	Masses, The	Symbols
Desires	Oceans, Lakes, etc.	Tradition
Family	Opinions	Water, Bodies of
Females	People	Women, In General
Home, Housing	Population	Women, Attitude To

MERCURY ☿

Basic Ideas:

Accuracy
Adaptability
Agility
Alertness
Articulation
Cleverness
Comments
Communication
Comprehension
Craftiness
Curiosity

Discernment
Discussions
Dishonesty
Eloquence
Expression
Fabrication
Flexibility
Gestures
Information
Inquisitiveness
Interpretation

Mobility
Responses
Rumors
Speeches
Suitability
Swiftness
Thoughts
Trickery
Versatility
Wit
Writings

In Your Relationships:

Adaptability toward
Assessment of, One's

Communications
Discussions

Restlessness with
Thoughts about

With Body or Mind:

Brain
Bronchi
Eyes
Fats, Breakdown of
Fingers
Food, Assimilation of
Gas, Internal

Hands
Hormones
Intelligence
Lungs
Mental Attitudes
Nervous System
Pancreas

Ribs
Shoulders
Smell, Sense of
Sternum
Sugar Balance
Tension
Tongue

In Politics or Business:

Airlines
Bridges
Business
Commerce
Communication

Information, Data
Manufacturing
News
News Broadcasts
Newspapers

Press, The
Railroads
Roads
Trade
Transportation

VENUS ♀

Basic Ideas:

Admiration	Compliments	Grace
Adornment	Composure	Gratification
Affection	Contentment	Jealousy
Affinity	Cooperation	Joy
Allure	Courtesy	Loveliness
Appeasement	Dance	Luxury
Attachment	Delight	Persuasion
Attraction	Elegance	Sensations
Beauty	Flavors	Sensuality
Charisma	Flirtation	Smiles
Charm	Gain	Values

In Your Relationships:

Appreciation	Flirtation	Pleasure
Attraction	Gratification	Sensuality
Enjoyment	Love	Touching

With Body or Mind:

Blood Supply	Larynx	Throat
Blood, Diseases of	Muscle Toning	Thyroid
Copper	Relax, Ability to	Tonsils
Kidneys	Taste, Sense of	Veins

In Politics or Business:

Art	Economy	Plants
Beauty	Fashion	Scenery
Biology	Metals	Social Trends
Culture	Music	Society
Diplomacy	Peace	Values
Economics	Plant Kingdom, The	Wealth

MARS ♂

Basic Ideas:

Acceleration
Action, Activity
Adventures
Aggressiveness
Agitation
Anger
Attempts
Beginnings
Boisterousness
Boldness
Clamor

Commotion
Competition
Defiance
Discord
Endeavors
Forcefulness
Friction
Hatred
Immediacy
Initiative
Malice

Pursuit
Pushing
Rashness
Sexuality
Speed
Strength
Threats
Treachery
Unruliness
Uproar
Virility

In Your Relationships:

Anger
Conflicts

Energy
Fights

Noise
Sexual Activity

With Body or Mind:

Accidents
Acute Ailments
Adrenal Glands
Aggression
Anemia
Breaks, Rips, Tears

Energy Levels
Exhaustion
Fevers
Hatred
Hyper-anything
Inflammation

Madness
Male Sex Organs
Muscles
Rashes
Surgery
Wounds

In Politics or Business:

Acids
Animal Kingdom
Armed Forces
Assertion
Bombs
Business Leaders
Energy

Explosions
Fires
Guns
Heat
Metals
Military Rule
Military, The

Rebellions
Strife
Threats
Violence
Warlike Conditions
Wars
Weaponry

JUPITER ♃

Basic Ideas:

Abundance
Additions
Advice
Amplification
Assumptions
Attainment
Beliefs
Benefit
Candor
Cheerfulness
Compliance
Confidence

Counsel
Doctrine
Ease
Elaboration
Encouragement
Enhancement
Ethics
Expectations
Extensions
Generosity
Judgment
Luck

Opinion
Optimism
Persuasion
Philosophy
Propositions
Rewards
Sincerity
Success
Supplements
Theory
Understanding
Wisdom

In Your Relationships:

Activities Together
Benefits

Dancing
Good Feelings

Socializing
Sports

With Body or Mind:

Acid Accumulations
Buttocks
Carbohydrate Processes
Cholesterol

Expansion
Glandular Systems
Hips
Jaundice

Lecithin
Liver
Overeating
Sciatica

In Politics or Business:

Churches
Clergy
Democrats
Expansion
Foreign, Anything
Foreigners

Increase
Integration
Justice
Laws
Lawyers
Legal Systems

Overviews
Publishing
Religion
Religious Leaders
Sky, The
Well Being, Sense of

SATURN ♄

Basic Ideas:

Abstinence	Dedication	Interference
Affliction	Defense	Lack
Ambition	Delays	Limitations
Annoyance	Desire	Old, Anything
Austerity	Detours	Patience
Berating	Duty	Permanence
Brevity	Efficiency	Reserve
Burdens	Facts	Respect
Caution	Failure	Restrictions
Cessation	Fault	Severity
Conclusions	Foundations	Silence
Constancy	Impediments	Simplicity
Curtailment	Inadequacy	Stability
Decisions	Inflexibility	Worries

In Your Relationships:

Break-ups	Honor	Stability
Dedication	Reliability	Trust

With Body or Mind:

Bones	Fingernails	Retardation
Breaks	Fungus Infections	Rheumatism
Cartilage	Hair	Skin
Colds	Hearing	Teeth
Dryness	Hypo-anything	Tuberculosis
Dull Aches	Knees	Warts

In Politics or Business:

Authority	FBI	Restraining Forces
Change	Government, The	Restrictions
Discipline, National	Limitations	Rocks
Earth, The	Police	State, The
Elderly People	Republicans	Warnings

URANUS ⛢

Basic Ideas:

Abstinence
Agitation
Aloofness
Altruism
Breaches
Change
Contrariness
Detachment
Disarray
Discontent
Discovery
Disregard

Disrespect
Disruption
Disturbances
Eccentricity
Erratic Actions
Extremes
Freedom
Impoliteness
Independence
Insolence
Invention
Liberation

Manipulation
Modernization
Modification
Novelty
Opposition
Peculiarity
Progress
Rebelliousness
Restyling
Science
Surprises
Unexpected, The

In Your Relationships:

Behavior
Discontent

Freedom
Friendship

Living Together
Uniqueness

With Body or Mind:

Ankles
Body Cramps
Deafness
Muscle Cramps

Nervousness
Onset, Sudden
Remission
Ruptures

Shins
Shock
Spasms
Stress Reactions

In Politics or Business:

Associations
Astrology
Civil Actions
Computers
Divisiveness
Freedom
Friends

Industrial Revolutions
Innovation
Legislatures
Machinery
National Ideas
Neutrality
Politics

Radicals
Reform
Revolutions
Science
Shock
Traitors
Troublemakers

NEPTUNE ♆

Basic Ideas:

Absence
Abstraction
Alcohol
Ambiguity
Artificiality
Atonement
Avoidance
Camouflage
Capitulation
Carelessness
Compassion
Confinement
Confusion
Contrivance

Costumes
Counterfeits
Craziness
Daydreams
Deceit
Deception
Devotion
Dilapidation
Drugs
Escapes
Fantasy
Flimsiness
Folly
Garbles

Holiness
Illusions
Imperfections
Indiscretion
Inspiration
Make Believe
Myths
Redemption
Release
Shabbiness
Subtlety
Temptations
Weakness
Whimsy

In Your Relationships:

Abstract Ideas of
Avoidance

Dreams of
Drugs, Use of

Emotions, Heightened
True Love

With Body or Mind:

Atony
Atrophy
Conditioning, Lack of
Drugs, Reaction to

Fungus Infections
Insect Bites
Spleen
Symptoms, Vague

Thymus Gland
Tiredness
Unease, General
Weakness, In General

In Politics or Business:

Chemicals
Delusion
Dreams, National
Drug Policies
Drug Trafficking
Drugs
Glamor

Hospital Care
Ideals, Business
Ideals, National
Illicit Undertakings
Inflation
Occult Practices
Oil

Perfection
Resignations
Scandals
Spies
Subversion
Unplanned Ventures
Visions

PLUTO ♀

Basic Ideas:

Abnormalities
Accusation
Admonishment
Adulteration
Breakdowns
Catastrophe
Censure
Cessation
Cleansing
Completion
Compulsion
Concealment
Conclusion
Condemnation

Constraints
Contamination
Control
Conversion
Corruption
Crime
Death
Debasing
Decadence
Decay
Defamation
Denunciation
Destruction
Dishonesty

Extremes
Fanaticism
Morbidity
Perversion
Pursuit
Rancor
Rebirth
Rediscovery
Restitution
Ruthlessness
Suspicions
Termination
Transition
Wilfullness

In Your Relationships:

Divorce
Dominance

Love Extremes
Power Struggles

Retribution
Sexual Extremes

With Body or Mind:

Cell Formation
Cell Regeneration
Colon
Degenerative Diseases

Endocrine Glands
Hemorrhoids
Infection
Piles

Pituitary Gland
Pus
Rectum
Toxemia

In Politics or Business:

Agencies, Secretive
Catastrophe
Chaos
Contamination
Corruption
Destruction
Dismissal

Force, Use of
Funerals
Overthrows
Poisoning
Prosecution
Punishment
Renovation

Restitution
Rubble
Subversion
Tyranny
Vengeance
Violence
Waste Products

NODE ☊

Basic Ideas:

Acquaintances
Acquisitions
Affiliations
Alliances
Annulment
Appointments
Apportionment
Assemblies
Associations
Cooperation

Criticism
Discovery
Divisions
Events
Evolution
Exchanges
Familiarity
Fate
Group Connections
Habit Patterns

Interchanges
Kinship
Life's Aim
Meetings
Obligations
Opportunities
Relinquishing
Sequences
Shows
Sources

In Your Relationships:

Attachment
Attraction
Bonding
Connections
Divorce

Familiarity
Finding Others
Groupings
Karmic Links
Marriage

Meeting Others
Partnerships
Relationships
Seeking Others
Ties to Another

With Body or Mind:

Air Passages
Arterial Walls
Attachments, Any
Conduits

Diseases, Karmic
Ducts, Saliva
Ducts, Tear
Habit Patterns

Intestinal Walls
Tubes, Attached
Tubes, Internal
Vein Walls

In Politics or Business:

Allies
Backers
Bureaucracy
Conferences
Conventions
Demonstrations
Episodes

Federations
Interviews
Joint Ventures
Kinship
Layoffs
Meetings
Mergers

Passageways
Pathways
Publicity
Relatives
Supporters
Treaties
Walls

ASCENDANT A

Basic Ideas:

Assessment	Environment, Your	Reality
Atmosphere	Experiences	Rejoinders
Attention, Focus of	Notions	Repression, Mental
Attitudes	Observations	Responses
Awareness	Observances	Self
Blocking	Peculiarities	Settings
Characteristics	Perceptions	Style, Personal
Circumstances	Personal Space	Tone (Attitude)
Cognizance	Points of View	Traits
Consciousness	Privacy	Views

In Your Relationships:

Attention to	Impressions of	Personal Responses
Attitudes toward	Inhibitions to	Pretenses toward
Communication	Introspection of	Treatment of Others
Focus Upon	Motivations for	Understanding Others

With Body or Mind:

Appearance	Demeanor	Mannerisms
Attitudes toward Life	Introspection	Sensations

In Politics or Business:

Atmosphere, The	Experiences	Responses, Formal
Attitudes	Masquerades	Settings
Conditions	Personal Style	Views of Others
Effects on the World	Portrayals	Views, An Individual's
Environment, The	Relations with Others	Views, Foreign

MIDHEAVEN M

Basic Ideas:

Accomplishment
Aims
Ambition
Aptitude
Assurances
Attainment
Authentication
Authorization
Beginnings
Behavior
Capacity, One's
Career

Competence
Conclusions
Conduct
Confirmation
Constancy
Corroboration
Credentials
Experience
Fulfillment
Goals
Guiding Principles
Mastery

Meanings
Methods
Purposes
Qualifications
Rank
Rewards
Security, Needs for
Security Seeking
Sense of Fairness
Start in Life
Trust, Personal
Word, Keeping One's

In Your Relationships:

Fulfillment
Learning and Growing

Objectives
Outcomes

Rewards from
Security Needs from

With Body or Mind:

Behavior, One's
Conscience
Coping

Defenses, Personal
Integrity
Maturity

Principles, Personal
Security, Needs for
Self-Restraint

In Politics or Business:

Assurances
Beginnings
Certification
Degrees, Scholarly
Guarantees
Integration
Objective

Origins
Outcomes
Planning
Public Projection
Reputation
Roots
Rules of Conduct

Safe Passage
Safety
Schooling
Security
Standards
Trust
Workmanship

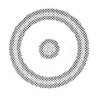

The 78 Midpoints

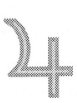

SUN/MOON   ☉/☽

Basic Ideas:

The Sun and Moon show the direction and focus of your personal awareness. Here is where you show your understanding for others, or life. Your desire to increase your authority, popularity, or sensitivity starts here. These energies show how you develop your vitality for the central themes of your life, your enthusiasm when adapting your daily routines to the needs of others, and the ups and downs you have in your creative flow. Your enjoyment for seeking and gaining public popularity or in being noticed by other people, the sensitivity you bring to your decision making processes, and the impressions you have of your spiritual origins can also start here. These points also emphasize any weakness or awkwardness you feel when you receive honors or recognition, your delight with romantic episodes, and the commitment or importance you give to your soul or spiritual life.

In Your Personal Life:

Thesis   The attention you place on whatever is important to you in life; your family and/or home situation; your desire to extend protection to yourself or your family; efforts to make yourself more acceptable.

Anti   Your lack of will or enthusiasm shown when caring about others; any personal inadequacy or lack of concern as shown through the way you live; your unfulfilled demands for public acceptance or popularity.

In Your Relationships:

Thesis   The approval you give or receive to or with another; variations in your confidence or self-image which affect relationships; the influence you exert over your partner, or vice-versa; your desire for companionship.

Anti   A lack of will to fulfill the social rituals needed to maintain your relationships; not caring about the quality of your life with others; feelings that your friends do not seriously take you into their confidence.

With Body or Mind:

Chemical, Ph, and mineral balances within the body; sensitivity to drugs; pressure near the heart; overall health and stamina; colds; flu symptoms.

In Politics or Business:

Thesis   How the will of the people is applied to taking the country into new or important directions; the international reputation of the country; reading the attitude of the people when making national policy.

Anti   National will forcefully imposed by the leadership; a loss of face in international politics; smears on the national reputation; pessimism flows through the population or lawmakers.

SUN/MOON with Planets and Points

☿ Using your education and reasoning to progress through life; absorbing the various lessons of life; increasing your search for opportunities; applying your knowledge to the different situations you meet in life.

♀ Developing skills in or appreciation for the fine arts or music; increasing gratitude for the efforts of others; admiration from others for your talents; helps you become more calm and relaxed in your personal life.

♂ Becoming more self-reliant; strengthens personal drive and initiative; a need to impose your will on others; situations where you may force or push others for quicker progress; anger; a focus on strength.

♃ Taking too many directions at once; developing a philosophy for living and coping with life's situations; seeing opportunities which you use to advantage; developing a better philosophy for experiencing life.

♄ Increased personal discipline and work habits; determination to work consistently and steadily to achieve results; helps you mold your fate; increased restrictions on your ability to progress in life.

♅ Setting yourself aside from the ordinary or mundane; applying ingenuity to complete goals or create new ways of revealing old ideas; unusual twists of fate; the use of astrological ideas or methods.

♆ Realizing the importance of thinking through your plans and ideas; dreaming about the options open to you for redirecting your plans; delusions about what you can do or how hard you will work to do it.

♇ Focusing attention on your own goals; secrecy about the care or concern you are willing to show to family; making startling new plans for enhancing the quality of your life; drastic measures to protect self.

☊ Creating the methods or procedures others need for their personal fulfillment; making sexual appraisals of others; gathering cooperation from people or groups to help yourself with your aims and purposes.

A Focusing on the immediate needs of your home or family; noticing the roles people play in your life; an ability to know the thoughts of those close to you; your awareness of how you meet and accept others.

M Choosing deliberate paths for personal development; developing through associations with your family or the general public; gaining perspective on your life's direction; stressing personal attainments.

SUN/MOON CONCEPTS

Arrogant Approval
Celebrated Caring
Emotions Dominate
Outrageous Bargains
Inadequate Importance
A Famous Maternity
Celebrated Intuition
Outstanding Melodrama
Effective Show of Sympathy
Important Compliance
Insolent and Fickle
Arbitrary Overconfidence

Emotional Pretension
Special Sensitivities
Of Doubtful Influence
Bold but Uncertain
Effective Intuition
Renowned Feelings
Special Compliance
Convincing Imagination
Common Melodrama
Healthy Distrust
Official Mistrust
Real Inconsistency

Flowery Imagination
Displays Hesitation
Genuine Feelings
Grand Mothering
Overdone Doubts
Outlandish Distress
Splendid Harmony
Decent Wariness
Lavish Mothering
Displays Maternity
Enough Orneriness
Grandiose Tradition

Respected Moodiness
Influences Motivations
Emotionally Based Concerns
Fears which Predominate
Convincing Doubts
Remarkable Craziness
The Importance of Nurturing
Determined Waywardness
Purposeful Vulnerability
Lavish Deference
Concerned with Sentimentality
Adequate Nurturing (Caring)
The Importance of Sensitivities
A Famous Imagination
Concerned with Fickleness
Important Warnings
Convincing Hesitation
Eminent Alterations
Elaborate Femininity
Dominating Behavior
Remarkable Intuition
Overdone (Flowery) Mothering
Unavoidable Acquiescence
Fundamental Uncertainties
Influences Sensitivities
Powerful Emotions
Authentic Nurturing (Caring)
Despair by Important People
The Importance of Cadence
Concerned with Fears
Unbending Sympathy (Concern)

Purposeful Fluctuations
Concerns which Go Astray
Flamboyant Imagination
Decisive Influence
Intentional Submission
Committed to Protection
Cherishes Importance
Dedicated Imagination
Distinguished Conduct
Authentic Hesitation
Sensitive to Concerns
An Official Domicile
Acclaimed Experiences
Adequate Emotionality
Old Fashioned Theatrics
Concerned with Compliance
The Significance of Mothering
Arrogant Compliance
Lavish Waywardness
Deliberate Indecision
Indisputable Subordination
Outstanding Fence-sitting
Determined Intuition
Adequate Fickleness
Sustained Emotions
Characteristic Melancholy
Grandiose Empathy
Arrogant Waywardness
Overdone (Flowery) Intuition
Dedication to Mothering
Intentional Wavering

SUN/MOON With Itself

☉ Helps you focus on the efforts you put into daily events; emphasizes the popularity and fame you achieve through basic interests; the concern you devote to the quality of your soul growth, as opposed to self or ego.

☽ Increased needs to express care or bring relief to important people in your life; women who help you determine your life's purpose; the watchfulness or protection you extend to your home, family, or values.

Significant Examples of People and Events Using Sun/Moon

General: **STRONG:** Kareem Abdul-Jabbar; Marc Edmund Jones; Carl Sagan; Guglielmo Marconi; Norman Mailer; Ernest Pyle; John Paul I; George Patton; Audrey Hepburn; Jean Francoise Millet; Johann Von Goethe
WEAK: Ralph Nader; John Dillinger; William K. Douglas; Bertrand Russell; Steve Wozniak; Earl Warren; Drew Pearson; Percy Bysshe Shelley
EVENTS: George Washington's Inauguration; Titanic Hits Iceberg; Apollo 11 Moon Landing; Lindburgh Lands in Paris (Lee's Surrender at Appomattox).

☉,☽ Enrico Caruso; Jackie Robinson; Maurice Ravel; Olivia Newton-John

☿ Shirley Jones; Lord Byron; Israel Regardie; A. Lincoln; J. Meredith enrolls at Univ. of Miss.

♀ Jack Paar; Olivia Newton-John; Marlon Brando; Georges Seurat

♂ Jimmy Carter; A. Schwarzenegger; Jean Millet; Apollo 11 Moon Landing

♃ Peter Max; Herman Melville; Mario Andretti; Sean Connery; Challenger

♄ Audie Murphy; Olga Worrall; John F. Kennedy; Carroll Righter

♅ Audrey Hepburn; Ernest Hemingway; Stephen Crane; Guglielmo Marconi

♆ Rosanno Brazzi; Jimi Hendrix; Harry Belafonte; Dane Rudhyar; J. Millet

♇ Muhammad Ali; Teilhard de Chardin; Robin Williams; Charles Addams

☊ Jack Paar; Ed. Manet; Laurence Olivier; Stonewall Jackson; USS Maine

A Jerry Rubin; Thomas Huxley; Lord Byron; Ida Rolf; Ramstein Crash

M Bob Fosse; H. G. Wells; Claude Debussy; David Frost; Challenger Explosion

SUN/MERCURY ☉/☿

Basic Ideas:
This combination helps enhance your confidence when communicating, whether by speaking or writing. It suggests a special adaptability for coping with all facets of life, and implies a mental cleverness which can respond sharply and clearly with wit to all situations. It brings a capability to think rapidly on your feet in any condition which arises, aids in giving you effective concentration and control over your thinking processes, encourages you to pursue sources of information, and helps you express your thoughts in a more authoritative manner. Information that you receive is likely to be from an authority, and your primary method of thinking and reasoning is effectively and distinctively shown. Wit and intelligence are added to your discussions, you reason more effectively and confidently in affairs of life which involve any sort of complex analysis or calculations.

In Your Personal Life:
Thesis Your primary mental and reasoning powers and the shape and orientation they take; increased determination to emphasize education and clear thinking; helps you realize the importance of information.

Anti Defects in your thinking and/or reasoning processes; a mind which is not able to keep up with the body, or vice versa; faulty or lazy thinking due to inadequate study or analysis; education which is left incomplete.

In Your Relationships:
Thesis Effective communications with your partner; an ability to communicate with your friends; how people appreciate your sense of humor; the trust you receive from others concerning their personal information.

Anti Miscommunication; the inability to tell others your basic thoughts or ideas clearly; meeting people who do not understand your thinking or point of view; jokes or wit which is not appreciated or understood.

With Body or Mind:
The vitality of your nervous system; the overall efficiency of your lungs; your ability to assimilate nutrients well; status of oxygen in your blood.

In Politics or Business:
Thesis The ability to state the character and intention of an enterprise clearly and effectively; definition of a subject's character in the media; effective press coverage about business; leaders who can communicate well.

Anti An inability to be convincing within more formal communications; an ineffective press briefing; an inability to meld the needs of the nation with the nation's businesses; a multiplicity of language barriers.

SUN/MERCURY with Planets and Points

☽ Sensitivity to the thoughts and needs of others; understanding of the everyday impact of your ability to communicate; effective communications to the masses; determined thinking about family or home.

♀ Softens the way that you put your ideas across to others; an effective understanding of the process and value of money especially as it relates to markets or market conditions; efforts to succeed at loving another.

♂ Forceful, direct ways of getting your ideas across; an irritating or loud way of communicating; hastily conceived ideas; heated conversations; rapid dissemination of ideas; an urgent need to confirm information.

♃ A line of thinking which starts with religious or philosophical terms; an increased need to communicate; overdone or flowery lines of reasoning; a love of pompous oratory; quick, clever, and funny humor.

♄ Goes directly to the heart of any matter; encourages effective lines of reasoning, clearly and simply stated; stifles conversation and thinking; a stuffed shirt; frustrating or dejecting discussions with other people.

♅ Thoughts about informal or novel ways of communicating to others; electro-mechanical devices which enhance communications or store or transmit ideas well; upsetting discussions; contrary thoughts.

♆ Artificial means of getting ideas across; deceptive communications; weakened lines of communications; finding hidden meanings in information received; idealistic thinking that you convey to others.

♇ Important information that is transmitted world-wide, perhaps through the use of satellites; concealing information that is important to others; theft or neglect of important communications devices or information.

☊ Getting your messages to the right people; telling people what they want to hear; efforts to convince others of your sincerity; finding information which helps you identify your life's destiny or path.

A A strong mental focus when communicating to others; keeping your attention on a subject; concentration; a mind which does not easily wander; a disciplined mind; improving attitudes toward effectively reaching others.

M Communicating effectively and clearly to enhance your standing among others; studying the principles of effective communications, languages, or speech; clarifying your ideas and plans for achieving your goals.

SUN/MERCURY CONCEPTS

A Significant Theft
Satisfying Shrewdness
Restless Leadership
Basic Conversation
Elaborate Interpretation
Convincing Expressions
Leading Objections
Certain about Accuracy
Special Comprehension
Determined Versatility
Special Reasoning
Facetious Communication

Acclaimed Articulation
Elevates Comprehension
Distinguished Intellect
Assures Cleverness
Influences Swiftness
Primary Reasoning
Essential Gestures
Deliberate Slyness
Special Versatility
Creates Conversation
Lavish Trickery
Illuminating Responses

A Basic Curiosity
Displays Agility
Adequate Versatility
Stately Delivery
Initial Shrewdness
Convincing Wit
Deliberate Dishonesty
Influential Ideas
Arrogant Comments
Two-way Mastery
Arrogant Inquiry
Doubly Effective

Important Information
Celebrated Thievery
A Basic Mental Restlessness
Believable Thoughts
An Important Conversation
An Exclusive Education
Reliable Information
Strengthens Observations
Clever Articulation
A Potential for Restlessness
Concerned with Languages
A Potential for Deception
Overdone (Flowery) Conversation
Responsible for Information
Boundless Curiosity
Influences Expression
Promotes Agility
Elaborate Reasoning
Education which is Influential
Distinguished in Many Ways
Influential Reasoning
Flamboyant Conversation
A Determined Speaker
Effective Fact Gathering
Concerned with Information
Adequate Language Capability
A Commitment to Versatility
Enhances Comprehension
The Importance of Flexibility
Notable Comments
Playful Trickery

Outlandish Gestures
Well Known Agility
Special Swiftness
Famous Articulation
The Importance of Swiftness
Playful Inquisitiveness
Masters Comprehension
Persuasive Wit
Uneasy Enthusiasm
A Variety of Influences
Responses Dominate
Sufficient Adjustments
Influential Thoughts
Basic Intelligence
Robust Speech
Effective Conversation
Determined Thievery
Distinguished Calculations
A Primary Observation
A Certainty with Communications
Overbearing Interchanges
Esteemed Talents
Decisive Pronunciation
Strengthens an Analogy
The Importance of Inquiry
Essential Information
A Competent Observer
Concerned with Media
Effective Thinking
Flamboyant Underhandedness
Convincing Craftiness

SUN/MERCURY With Itself

☉   Your competence in finding and then relating to others what you feel is newsworthy or important as information ; the effectiveness of your ability to present news, and adapt mentally to situations while speaking.

☿   Various clever ways you place emphasis in your speech or writing; flamboyance in speaking gestures or delivery; nuances of writing or speaking which add effective meaning in communication abilities.

Significant Examples of People and Events Using Sun/Mercury

General: **STRONG:** Bob Fosse; Amadeo Modigliani; Benito Mussolini; Steve Allen; Van Cliburn; Liberace; Rollo May; Stephen Crane; John Denver; Burl Ives; John Glenn; Charles Gordon; Albert Schweitzer
WEAK: Bob Hope; Tom Jones; Scott Carpenter; Abraham Lincoln; Jean Houston; Al Unser; Paul Newman; Pierre Teilhard de Chardin
EVENTS: Lindburgh Lands in Paris; George Washington's Inauguration; Nixon's Resignation; Mount St. Helens Explosion; (South Carolina Secession).

☉, ☿   Albert Schweitzer; Benito Mussolini; Stephen Crane; RMS Titanic

☽   Anne Murray; Edouard Manet; Lord Byron; David Frost; Mark Spitz

♀   George Washington's Inauguration; Auguste Modigliani; Richard Strauss; Bob Dylan; Olga Worrall

♂   Gen Charles Gordon; Sam Sheppard; Jonathan Winters; Vida Blue

♃   Arthur Godfrey; Gianni Agnelli; Charles Steinmetz; Mt. St. Helens

♄   Gen Charles Gordon; Israel Regardie; Ralph Waldo Emerson

♅   Hugh Downs; Audie Murphy; Sydney Omarr; Ritchie Valens

♆   Gen. Charles Gordon; Dick Gregory; Robert McNamara; John Denver; Jack Paar; Arthur Ford

♇   Mick Jagger; John Dillinger; F. Scott Fitzgerald; Steve Rosenbloom; Challenger Explosion

☊   Bjorn Borg; Ernest Pyle; Paul Gauguin; Audrey Hepburn; Lee's Surrender at Appomattox

A   Amadeo Modigliani; Jack Paar; Richard Strauss; Charles Steinmetz

M   Stephen Foster; Shirley Jones; Sally Ride; Enrico Caruso; Merv Griffin; John Glenn

SUN/VENUS ☉/♀

Basic Ideas:

This combination symbolizes developing and enhancing your appreciation and gratitude toward things, people, and opportunities which come into your life. These points also include the sincerity behind your love and affection, developing your capacity for devotion and fondness, and further developing your social grace, manners, charm, and culture. Cooperation, calmness, gratitude, and refinement are integrated into your fundamental forms of expression, and you spend much effort in focusing your will on showing charm, affection, regard, and love toward others. The pleasure you get from playful activity, the delight you feel returned when others appreciate what you do for them, and the satisfaction in seeing yourself develop grace and culture begin here. These themes also enhance your regard for beauty and peace, but can stimulate jealousy against others.

In Your Personal Life:

Thesis — Concentrating on developing grace, charm, appreciation and consideration for the needs of others; appreciation of the role of beauty and love in life; feeling pleasure when others value what you do for them.

Anti — Developing a flawed charisma because you lack honesty and sincerity in your appreciation of others; your purpose in giving affection to others is faulty as you seek material things in return for your qualified love.

In Your Relationships:

Thesis — Putting additional effort into being sincere and direct about your feelings; valuing honesty and openness in your relationships, and expecting the love you give to be returned equally.

Anti — Sensing some superficiality and a lack of sincerity in the way you or your partner care for each other; developing a relationship based on value and material goals rather than on love, affection, or pleasure.

With Body or Mind:

Your attitude toward health and your body, in general; your thyroid's ability to function; infections which affect taste, smell, etc.; the condition of your kidneys.

In Politics or Business:

Thesis — Using the wealth available to a nation or business to sustain its image or authority; how a society shapes the direction of its growth; the nature of reserves, resources, and the role they play in development.

Anti — A leadership which doesn't appreciate the role that art or culture plays in developing the character or identity; a society which is estranged from its leadership; little development of artistic or musical heritage.

SUN/VENUS with Planets and Points

☽   Enhancing the care and sensitivity you bring to the affection and love you give to others; pleasures you derive from mothering; hesitations or inconsistencies you show in appreciation or gratitude.

☿   Mental concentration or study on developing social graces; thinking about how to effectively both give and receive affection; ideas on how to be better attuned to the peace and harmony you desire in life.

♂   Urgency and passion tied to your needs for affection, and the ways you give comfort or pleasure to others; arguments which arise over how you love or are loved; stimulation of possible jealous passions.

♃   An enhanced need to show diplomacy and tact; successful ways of charming others with your basic personality; an emphasis on promises made when in love, expectations of affection, or material gifts.

♄   Lends formality to your demonstration of affection and love; adds sincerity in your desire to give and receive pure love; focuses need on loving only one person; simplifies your needs for receiving love.

♅   An enhanced need to be enterprising in showing affection; surprises at how others show their love toward you; desires to upset another through jealousy or the loss of your love; original ways of loving.

♆   Bringing elements of fantasy when showing your affection or charm toward others; temptations you experience through love; the intangible or material things you associate with showing appreciation.

♀   Increases the depth of feeling and emotion you put into your expressions of appreciation and gratitude; adds to expectations about the return of pleasure or favors given to others; a sudden ending to love or hostility.

☊   Meeting others who teach you how to develop your basic ways of showing devotion and lovingness; meeting groups which teach you the meaning of how to express your inner felt affections for another person.

A   Concentrating on your need to express kindness or courtesy; learning how to be courteous or polite without having to think about it; a basic set of habits and characteristics which convey lovingness.

M   Building your reputation for being competent in artistic fields; adding to the respect others give you in return for your appreciation of their efforts; the maturity you bring when expressing love, caring, or affection to others.

SUN/VENUS CONCEPTS

Envy which Dominates
Celebrated Influence
Lavish Embellishment
Enjoys Having Influence
Primary Sensuality
Governs Infatuation
Insolent and Envious
Melodramatic Jealousy
Supplies Temptations
Genuine Satisfaction
Lavish Parties
Potential Favors
Special Compliments

Effective Compliments
Elaborate Pleasures
Adequate Respect
Influences Choices
Charming Effectiveness
Special Delight
Impressive Politeness
Basic Sentiments
Expensive Gifts
Effective Composure
Aristocratic Serenity
Committed to Comfort
Important Respect

Expensive Pleasures
Snobbish Politeness
Promotes Favoritism
Special Feelings
Effective Jealousy
Exclusive Choices
Persuasive Charm
Lavish Gratification
Immense Value
Intentional Jealousy
Dignified Charm
Genuine Flattery
Supports Politeness

Enhances Selfishness
Capable of Compliments
A Fondness for Authority
Celebrated Flirtation
Encourages the Arts
Tempted toward Power
Motivates Infatuation
Strengthens Selfishness
Concerned with Contentment
Compelling Grace
Famous Pampering
Spontaneous Courtesy
Commanding Charisma
Essential Beauty (Loveliness)
Overdone (Flowery) Kindness
Permits Quiet Persuasion
Adequate Charm
Committed to Attachment
Concerned with Pleasure
An Exclusive Agreement
Fundamental Indulgence
Distinguished Loveliness
Overdone (Elaborate) Makeup
Characteristic Composure
Intentional Fussiness
Self-Assured Beauty
Essential Embellishments
Extravagant Compensation
The Importance of Vanity
Concerned with Charisma

Respect Dominates
Influences Favors
Genuine Refinement
Enjoys Authority
The Importance of Courtesy
Enhances Affinity
Concerned with Gain
Desires Influence
Compliments from the Famous
Delights in Jealousy
Elegant Relaxation
Important Temptations (Lures)
Supreme Enjoyment
First Consideration
Self-Assured Charm
Encourages Gratification
Haughty Indulgence
Genuine Respect
Pleases Influential People
Elaborate Satisfaction
Expensive Tranquility
Polite Famous People
A Preference for Elegance
Compliments the Influential
The Importance of Pampering
Determined Appeasement
Values Praise
Concerned with Politeness
Dignifies Pleasure
Promotes the Use of Favors

SUN/VENUS With Itself

☉ Sincerity in showing appreciation for the efforts of others; focusing and directing your feelings toward those you love or give your attention to; the emphasis you place on culture, values, or artistic ability.

♀ An increased need to be surrounded by fine things and ornaments; the needs you have to maintain better and more elaborate possessions than others; the role that music and art have in giving you personal enrichment.

Significant Examples of People and Events Using Sun/Venus

General: **STRONG:** Hank Williams; Amadeo Modigliani; Ida Rolf; Joachim Von Ribbentrop; Stephen Crane; Rollo May; Fidel Castro; Albert Speer; Helen Reddy; William Butler Yeats; Richard Byrd; Scott Carpenter; Bobby Fischer

WEAK: Manley Palmer Hall; Merv Griffin; Steve Wozniak; Alexander Graham Bell; Wayne Gretzky; Georges Seurat; Moshe Dayan

EVENTS: Lewis & Clark Expedition begins; Pearl Harbor Attack; USS Maine Explosion; Transcontinental Railroad completed; (Kent State Shootings).

☉,♀ Amadeo Modigliani; Percy Bys. Shelley; Von Ribbentrop; USS Maine

☽ Bob Fosse; Earl Warren; Sean Connery; John McEnroe; FDR Wins

☿ Edouard Manet; Steven Spielberg; Charles Addams; Rollo May

♂ Emperor Hirohito; Richard Byrd; Jerry Reed; Dick Gregory; F. D. Roosevelt Wins His First Election

♃ R. D. Laing; Arthur Rimbaud; Burt Reynolds; Norman Mailer

♄ Dick Gregory; Steven Spielberg; Bob Newhart; John F. Kennedy

♅ Ida Rolf; Sandy Koufax; Winston Churchill; Ritchie Valens; Sydney Omarr; Fidel Castro; Paul Gauguin

♆ Stonewall Jackson; Louis Pasteur; Sandy Koufax; Edward R. Murrow

♀ Robin Williams; Edgar Degas; Scott Carpenter; Harry Shoaf; Bertrand Russell; Richard Strauss

☊ Alan Leo; Erich Maria Remarque; Art Linkletter; Richard Chamberlain

A Steve Allen; Enrico Caruso; Ritchie Valens; Friedrich Nietzsche

M Nikola Tesla; Herman Melville; Paul Joseph Goebbels; Helen Reddy

SUN/MARS   ☉/♂

Basic Ideas:

These planets symbolize your regulation and expenditure of physical energy, and also encourage you to compete wholeheartedly in all details of life. They can denote a reckless and impulsive nature, and help depict you as a person who is famous for impatience. Your anger and fighting ability can be remarkable, as can your stamina and endurance. These planets show confidence in using strength and aggressiveness, but aggravation from authority figures. This is a good pair for indicating determination to perfect your movements, and mastery of your ability to appear convincing to important people. Your capacity to bring theatrics and drama to situations where energy is being expended can become legendary. You are not afraid to defy influential people, or to take risks where experts advise against being rash. You may show a marked ability to purposely aggravate others.

In Your Personal Life:

Thesis   You place great emphasis on your physical development, and your use of stamina building techniques; your dedication to body building is enhanced; becoming a noted enduring and determined competitor.

Anti   Your ego is too big for yourself and others; your concerns with personal welfare and development leaves little room for other people's interests in your life; you are noted for standing up to and irritating authority.

In Your Relationships:

Thesis   You enjoy physical and sexual contact with your partner; your concerns for a successful relationship spur you to try to meet your partner's physical needs and demands; helps you enjoy stimulation through others.

Anti   Your need for being number one in all things can affect the quality of a partner's response and intimacy; you put so much emphasis on physical training and fitness that you neglect sharing and intimacy.

With Body or Mind:

Muscular development of the body; the inner strength to overcome infection; fevers; tears in the heart muscles; wounds which tear muscle or body.

In Politics or Business:

Thesis   The development of the military as an extension of internal policy; challenges to authority or hostile actions which are subdued by guards or armed forces; a leader associated with or from a military background.

Anti   The extension of aggression as a will of the people; developing military might to be used against others; the authority of a nation or business linked to the armed forces; violence against the chosen leaders.

SUN/MARS with Planets and Points

☽   Your family's role in helping you develop a competitive drive ; timid mannerisms which you reverse by adding to your physical development and personal courage; confrontation you avoid thru indecision.

☿   Mental preparation you need for excelling at physical activity; your ability to repeat demanding physical tasks until perfected; knowledge gained through physical training; flexibility meeting competitors.

♀   Sensual flavor in your basic appeal to others; grace of movement you exhibit while in motion; pleasure you derive from physical activity; energy you put into being successful in any artistic fields of endeavor.

♃   The determination to develop physically; an awareness of the political strengths of others; inflating an already big ego; success during competitive activities; publicity about feats of courage or daring.

♄   Strengthened determination to excel at physical activities; an economy of motion to your physical movements; disappointing news from important people about progress, preference, or acceptability.

♅   Tough resolution to be a bruising and nonstop competitor; indifference about the pain and struggle you endure during rigorous activities; unexpected problems or snags in your activities or conditioning.

♆   A basic fundamental flaw in your physical development; alcohol or drugs which both weaken and strengthen your body; deception about your ability as a competitor; an idealized concept of your body.

♇   Intensified desire to vigorously compete and excel; the need to control others through physical intimidation; relentless practice to improve your physical abilities; lasting damage from intense competition.

☊   Your need to work with others as a team during activities; meeting and working with others who encourage you to be more competitive; working to be part of a team which gains renown for its physical feats.

A   Concentrating on your need to develop and practice until you meet and then exceed your goals; focusing on your competition and their activities or moves; adding to your ability to concentrate during activities or competitions.

M   The encouragement you receive due to physical or sports performances; the reputation you create as a fierce and unyielding competitor; rules of conduct you follow concerning your physical regimen when competing in life.

SUN/MARS CONCEPTS

Boundless Energy
Purposeful Anger
Authentic Panic
Intentional Protests
Authentic Attempts
Overdone Progress
Impressive Strength
Influences Initiative
Determination and Courage
Powerful Arguments
Characteristic Complaints
Spontaneous Heroes

Immense Animosity
Convincing Complaints
Purposeful Rushing
Immense Power
Outlandish Commotion
Fundamental Haste
Conceited Drive
Permits Movement
Spontaneous Masculinity
Overdone Virility
Arrogant Defiance
Supports Complaints

Powerful Urges
Exclusive Demands
Official Hysteria
Conceited Insistence
Great Hatred
Immense Courage
Ornate Stimulation
Celebrated Panic
Special Coercion
Effective Exertion
Prefers Violence
Prefers Initiatives

Deliberate Clamor
Noteworthy Irritations
Overdone Activity
Concerned with Animosity
Dominates Competitors
Annoyance with Authorities
Promotes Boldness
Splendid Efforts
Adequate Endeavors
The Importance of Coercion
Distinguished Defiance
Intentional Courage
Effective Haste
Influential Pressuring
Turmoil among the Famous
Boundless Arguments
Celebrated Excitement
Motivates Complaints
Concerned with Brutality
Notable Complaints
Successful Action/Activity
Squanders Vitality
Strengthens Boldness
Grand Masculinity
The Importance of Courage
Aggressive in Theatrical Ways
Pushes for Success
Elaborate Stimulation
A Successful Start
Irritation with Arrogance
Insists on Dedication

Impressive Energy
Concerned with Initiative
Remarkable Emphasis
Special Complaints
Defiance Predominates
Determined Pushing
Basic Sexuality
Influential Animosity
Special Panic
Flamboyant Anger
Elaborate Aggravation
Effective Aggressiveness
Influential Arm-Twisting
Basic Arguments
Deliberate Disharmony
Special Initiatives
Playful Indignation
Direct Arguments
Dramatic Courage
Enhances Recklessness
Genuine Courage
A Potential for Panic
Outlandish Noise
Characteristic Indignation
Sustains Defiance
Dedicated to Commotion
Determined Hastiness
Effective Anger
Important Competitors
Stimulates Determination
Flamboyant Arguments

SUN/MARS With Itself

☉   Being determined and forceful in competitive roles; developing an inner power to press on with activity and actions even when your overall odds for success or completion are low or diminished.

♂   Turning a rush for haste and competition into argument; an urge to fight against whatever you are now focusing upon; increased threats and danger through activities; becoming more assertive and forceful.

Significant Examples of People and Events Using Sun/Mars

General: **STRONG:** Henry Winkler; Stephen Foster; Henry Mancini; Arthur Ford; Ulysses S. Grant; Bertrand Russell; Ellen Burstyn; Claude Debussy; Paramhansa Yogananda; Mark Spitz; Moshe Dayan; Alexander Graham Bell
WEAK: Jimi Hendrix; Paul Newman; Johann Von Goethe; Jacques Cousteau; Neil Diamond; Grant Lewi; Ira Progoff; Arthur Godfrey
EVENTS: Apollo 11 Moon Landing; Bolsheviks Seize Power; Kent State Shootings; South Carolina Secession; (Pres. Nixon's Resignation).

☉, ♂   Bertrand Russell; Sally Ride; Mick Jagger; Audrey Hepburn

☽   Paramhansa Yogananda; Steve Allen; Henry Mancini; Komar; David Frost; Edmund Halley

☿   Hugh Downs; E. Fermi; Sam Sheppard; Gus Grissom; Billy Rose; John Kennedy Shot in Dallas

♀   Carl Sandburg; Scott Carpenter; Dr. Tom Dooley; Sean Connery; Albert Camus; Bob Fosse; Ivar Kreugar

♃   Stephen Foster; Robert McNamara; Toulouse-Lautrec; Arturo Toscanini; Bolshevik's Seize Power

♄   Mick Jagger; Jimmy Carter; Georges Seurat; Alexis Carrel; Carroll Righter; Jack Schwartz; Gustav Dore

♅   Sir Wm Crookes; Joseph Joffre; Henry Winkler; Gustav Dore;

♆   Moshe Dayan; Richard Byrd; William K. Douglas; Scott Carpenter

♇   Ulysses S. Grant; Stephen Sondheim; Henry Mancini; Albert Camus

☊   Bobby Fischer; Vida Blue; Helen Reddy; Claude Debussy; John Glenn

A   Elvis Presley; Ellen Burstyn; Willie Brandt; Burt Reynolds; S. Sondheim

M   Mt. St. Helens Expl.; Mario Andretti; Carl Sandburg; Henri Matisse

SUN/JUPITER ☉/♃

Basic Ideas:

This combination focuses on developing the competence and enthusiasm required to win even greater approval for your activities. Through these themes you begin to build and develop the vitality, influence, and effectiveness you need to succeed in life. The way you encourage others, the support you win from people because of the dominance and competence you build through your efforts, your confidence while doing your work, and your ability to gather acclaim for your judgment and insight all begin here. Your aspiration to motivate self and others, your personal enthusiasm for life, your need to delve into the philosophy of life and answer its mysteries, and your personal sense that success breeds success, begin here. These planets may also indicate an inner arrogant optimism that you cannot fail, lucky breaks, and beliefs that you are superior to others.

In Your Personal Life:

Thesis   Developing self-leadership; gaining increased recognition and respect; increasing your competency so others will come to you for advice and counsel; adds to the prestige and political acumen of your efforts.

Anti   You spend more time with opinions than fact, and are not always ready to back up your words with action; you give great promises, and exude self-confidence, but become arrogant and may overlook crucial things.

In Your Relationships:

Thesis   Very good feelings between partners; helps each over the more difficult parts of a relationship; feelings of excitement or joy when meeting or being with each other; good feelings about your close friends.

Anti   Spending so much effort telling your partner about your needs that you neglect theirs; your ego is great and does not allow you to comprehend how others can smooth the bumps of life; a smothering relationship.

With Body or Mind:

Your personal vitality and vigor; excessive cholesterol deposits in the heart area; a liver not able to deal with blood purification or infections adequately.

In Politics or Business:

Thesis   The reputation of the nation in the eyes of the rest of the world and the personal renown and acceptance of its leaders; the growth of the national character and reputation; the country's ability to lead others.

Anti   A religious or philosophical system which ties the effective leadership of the country to a predetermined course of action; the executive of the nation battling with the legal and justice parts of government.

SUN/JUPITER with Planets and Points

☽   An interest in people; a strong need to address the motives of others; added needs for approval from women or mother figures; trying different approaches rather than relying on one proven method.

☿   Cleverness, wit, and humor enhance abilities; a fast mind able to react quickly to rapidly changing situations; getting ideas across in discussions or by their publication; religious or philosophical thinking.

♀   Others may notice your physical beauty and sensuality, or a softness to your approach in handling others; satisfaction and pleasure from the joys and comforts in life; charm and politeness in your manners.

♂   Leadership qualities; rebuilding self confidence when facing life's problems and trials; pushing and striving for excellence in all efforts; confidence and haste in the need to progress in all areas of life.

♄   Situations which force you to learn about life the hard way; lower goals and standards, but an increased ability to gain success through persistence; frustration when you fail to properly follow through with efforts.

♅   Unexpected luck with your efforts; insight and practical ability to succeed with difficult tasks; seeing the nuts and bolts of what makes life work; disruptions from unexpected sources; an interest in astrological ideas.

♆   A sense of the unreal; purposeful deceit about the nature of another's intentions; grandiose plans for projects thought by others to be impractical; elements of doubt cloud your enthusiasm for life; an interest in illusions.

♇   Achieving the greatest of success with your efforts, or total and complete failure and despair; ideas that you can proceed in life despite the legality of your efforts; compulsive elements of destruction in your basic thinking.

☊   Meeting and influencing other people who can be central to assisting with your successes in life; more political awareness in pursuing your efforts; encountering others who provide the talent and resources you need now.

A   Focusing more closely the actions and intentions of others to see how they may contribute or detract from your aims and goals in life; becoming more introspective about your own efforts; concentration on your awareness.

M   Persevering against all odds and despite the obstacles; using your good luck and leadership skills to bring goals and projects to perfection in life; renown and rewards for efforts which you have already pursued and finished.

SUN/JUPITER CONCEPTS

Important Optimism	Intentional Assumptions	Arrogant Opinions
Effective Supplements	Influences Promises	Powerful Luck
Splendid Opportunity	Essential Premises	Famous Mistakes
Confidence in Promises	Influential Optimism	Powerful Beliefs
Acceptable Beliefs	Special Principles	Basic Theory
Positive Satisfaction	Elaborate Opinions	Lucky Decisions
Supports Premises	Fundamental Excess	Purposeful Sincerity
Gains Real Experience	Governs Happiness	Exclusive Triumphs
Special Expectations	A Remarkable Philosophy	Celebrated Idealism
Winning Propositions	Sincere Motivation	Superior Potential
Characteristic Optimism	Renowned for Beliefs	Ornate Promises
Overdone (Flowery) Theory	Lavish Optimism	Lavish Expansion

Respectable Wisdom	Positive Vindication
Inclined to Assume Importance	Improves on Competence
Spontaneous Conjectures	Committed to Extravagance
Theoretical Superiority	Conceited Presumptions
Influences Believability	Original Assumptions
Assumptions of Adequacy	Enhances Expectations
The Importance of Understanding	Arrogant Promises
Distinguished Attainment	Concerned with Honesty
Concerned with Principles	Expounds on Prestige
Impressive Sincerity	Committed to Insight
Promises from the Famous	Capable of Errors
Excellent Guesses	Basic Principles
Remarkable Promises	Your Real Inclinations
Boundless Exaggeration	Important Promises
Influences Satisfaction	Expensive Beliefs
Authorizes Promotions	Approves of Understanding
Influences Understanding	A Very Large Ego
Remarkable Boasting	Exclusive Candor
Characteristic Happiness	Special Theories
Effective Counsel	Spontaneous Insight
Genuine Expansion	Committed to Believability
Concerned with Propositions	Effective Theorizing
Influential Opinion	Adequate Expansion
Arrogant Sincerity	Determined Guidance
Concerned with Errors	Exclusive Promises
Important Beliefs	Inclined to Lavishness
Potential Faith	Influences Morals
Respectable Doctrine	Adequate Inclination
Supports Speculation	Special Understanding
Grand Summation	Outstanding Understanding
Outstanding Satisfaction	Inclined to Arrogance

SUN/JUPITER With Itself

☉   An essential directness and forcefulness when facing your challenges in life; important and influential people in your life; your sense of purpose and new potentials which you can create for yourself.

♃   An element of luck with your pursuits and endeavors; seeing the need for expansion of your goals; the understanding of the doctrine and philosophy behind all of your efforts and endeavors to succeed in life.

Significant Examples of People and Events Using Sun/Jupiter

General: **STRONG:** Dr. Sam Sheppard; Adolf Hitler; Ralph Nader; Joachim Von Ribbentrop; Audie Murphy; Johann Von Goethe; Stonewall Jackson; Carl Sandburg; Anne Murray; Henri Matisse; Muhammad Ali
WEAK: Ivar Kreugar; Lawrence Welk; Rossano Brazzi; Audrey Hepburn; Henry Mancini; Walt Whitman; Bob Dylan; Paul Joseph Goebbels
EVENTS: Wright Brothers First Flight; Chernobyl Nuclear Explosion; Pearl Harbor; RMS Titanic Hits Iceberg; Lee's Surrender at Appomattox; (South Carolina Secession).

☉, ♃ Harry Belafonte; Carl Sandburg; Erich Maria Remarque; Edward R. Murrow; Bob Fosse; Grant Lewi

☽   Shirley Jones; Jacques Cousteau; Ferdinand Foch; Erwin Rommel

☿   Jean Houston; Francisco Franco; Steven Spielberg; Mary Martin

♀   Joachim Von Ribbentrop; Bob Fosse; Ervin Nyiregyhazi; Edward R. Murrow; Ramstein Airshow Disaster

♂   Erwin Rommel; Art Linkletter; Scott Carpenter; Mary Martin; Steve Wozniak; Johnny Carson; R. D. Laing

♄   Jean Houston; Hank Williams; Carl Sandburg; Mario Andretti

♅   Audie Murphy; Earl Warren; Adolf Hitler; J. Von Ribbentrop

♆   Giacomo Puccini; Mario Andretti; Drew Pearson; Dustin Hoffman

♇   Kareem Abdul-Jabbar; Stephen Crane; Adolf Hitler; Muhammad Ali

☊   Alan Alda; John McEnroe; Peter Max; Hermann Goering; Helen Reddy; Tommy Smothers; Drew Pearson

A   Rudolph Bing; Willie Brandt; Muhammad Ali; Manly Palmer Hall

M   Carl Sandburg; Auguste Rodin; Glen Campbell; Sam Sheppard

SUN/SATURN   ☉/♄

Basic Ideas:

The Sun and Saturn themes combine your ideas on discipline and determination to lend purpose to your goals for completing your activities. These motifs impart an air of authority to your generally respectable nature, send signals of rejection from or to prominent persons, influence your inflexibility, and then give you resolve and persistence to see your way through any obstacle or over any barrier. Your dedication when aroused is usually seriously and cautiously shown, you reduce or restrict any personal embellishments or lavishness, and this seriousness helps you gain respect for your accomplishments. There is a sense of purpose in y you discipline yourself for your work assignments. You realize early that others do not always appreciate your efforts and you must work very hard to overcome their criticisms; you dedicate yourself to patience and completing work thoroughly.

In Your Personal Life:

Thesis   Great determination and the rigid appearance of control and discipline about your activities; an appearance of reserve and caution that is built upon personal power; you seem to have a sense of propriety about you.

Anti   Much pessimism about accomplishing the details of the work assigned to you; blocking or resisting others when you do not want to be moved or changed in your position or attitudes; diminishes confidence.

In Your Relationships:

Thesis   Brings seriousness and reality to relationships; motivates partners to find more practical ways to share themselves; adds a respectability to joint efforts; as the relationship matures this helps to bring stability.

Anti   Gloom and dejection may be so strong that you are afraid to make commitments in relationships; powerful forces seem to bring bars or constraints to meetings or affiliations; conceit increases with age.

With Body or Mind:

Mineral deposits in the arteries near the heart; blood and lymph circulation conditions in general; your posture; infections in general; arthritis; gout.

In Politics or Business:

Thesis   Form and definition in an enterprise; the will of the people as defined in the principal founding documents; the checks and balances within enterprises as implemented by various administrations.

Anti   Pessimism and gloom as a center focus of policy; unreasonable centralization of authority in one location; a leadership preoccupied with the various forms of law enforcement; older and more distanced leaders.

SUN/SATURN with Planets and Points

☽ Added instincts for showing caution or self-control; self-discipline comes very naturally; sensitivity to otherwise rigid frameworks; desires for romance; attention to the discipline of daily activities.

☿ Adapting to circumstances despite continuing rigidity or resistance; deft thinking added to an already highly disciplined persona; actively pursuing a need to obtain the best education or work credentials.

♀ Delight in the quiet of the moment; silence and relaxation become synonymous ideas; enhancement of desires; charm and smiles added to an otherwise stern demeanor; lessening the call for luxury or vanity.

♂ Abrupt and abrasive mannerisms with an already stern demeanor; fights through rigidity and structure; enhanced ability to stay with and endure in any competitive activities; a desire to be in charge.

♃ An increased need for an already abundant supply of self-discipline; expanded capability to maintain silence, especially in religious or formal settings; generosity added to an otherwise tightfisted person; strong sense of morals.

♅ An abrupt and unusual bent in a stern nature; computers or astrologers play important roles in life; the unexpected becomes the commonplace; the need for people who bring excitement; unexpected barriers or turns of events.

♆ Elements of uncertainty in an otherwise orderly demeanor; neglect of personal discipline and training is more commonplace than you might think; a relaxation of plans that were already too tight or rigid.

♇ A sense of overwhelming rigidity and inflexibility within self; a very disciplined person who wants and attracts power; an increased will to retaliate against others for slights; elimination of pessimism or despair.

☊ Association with people who are very controlled and disciplined; familiarity with methods of self discipline and control from past endeavors; cooperation with others who need your seriousness and organization.

A A strong focus on your need to be more serious; paying more attention or being more cautious with whatever you concentrate on; realistic and genuine reactions to others; mental pictures of your goals.

M Developing your mannerisms to appear as a more mature or serious person; no accomplishment becomes unattainable for you, and you set realistic goals for yourself in life; strong needs for increasing security and protection.

SUN/SATURN CONCEPTS

Enhances Pessimism
Simple Domination
Achieves Self-Discipline
Distinguished Reserve
Conspicuous Delays
Basic Responsibility
Genuine Simplicity
Conceited Rigidity
Primary Commitment
Committed to Being Effective
Primary Reserve
Special Postponements

Frustration is Primary
Brief Notoriety
Special Significance
Committed to Reserve
Expenses which Last
Insolent Pessimism
Simple Frustrations
Permits Prohibitions
Reliable for Silence
Authentic Objections
Elaborate Caution
Continual Domination

Exclusive Rebuffs
Lavish Restrictions
Adequate Caution
Fortifies Formality
Specific Restraints
Presumes Caution
Elaborate Restraint
Displays Patience
Expensive Penalties
Special Precautions
Lavish Frustration
Primary Seriousness

Meaningful Anxieties
Characteristic Simplicity
Influential Duties
Determined Restraint
Spontaneous Rigidity
Concerned with Restrictions
The Importance of Silence
Adequate Disappointments
Powerful Dejection
Encourages Durability
Reasonable Delays
Elaborate Postponements
Concerned with Using Time
Outstanding Objections
Influences Postponements
Esteemed Reprieves
Genuine Impediments
Authentic Admiration
Well-known Dissatisfaction
Influences Frustration
Dissatisfied with Recognition
Boundless Caution
Authentic Dissatisfaction
Avoids Conceit
Of Lasting Importance
Overpowering Responsibility
Successful Persistence
Authentic Frustration
Effective Restrictions
Influential Restraint
Essential Objections

Expensive Commitments
Special Restrictions
Inevitable Postponements
Conceited Simplicity
Fundamental Skepticism
Empowers Discipline
Effective Management
Impressive Stability
Determined Commitment
Silence is Primary
Notable Consistency
Immense Precaution
Sufficient Restrictions
Distinguished Failure
Deliberate Formality
A Certain Permanence
Successful Avoidance
Practical Motivation
Stately Silence
Caution by the Influential
Concerned about Delays
Fundamental Conclusions
Adequate Frustration
Primary Restrictions
Effective Discipline
Respectable Work Performance
Discomfort for Important People
Effective Commitment
Determined Silence
Distinguished Patience
Winning Humility

SUN/SATURN With Itself

☉   The influence and determination you bring to improving situations where pessimism has prevailed; your effectiveness in solving problems and removing anxieties which keep others from progressing.

♄   Feelings that progress is made only through slow endurance and persistance; your commitment to inflexible ways of achieving results; your ability to suspend important processes or stop influential people.

Significant Examples of People and Events Using Sun/Saturn

General: **STRONG:** Carl Sandburg; Marc Edmund Jones; Earl Warren; Steve Wozniak; Dr. Sam Sheppard; Peter Max; David Frost; F. Scott Fitzgerald; H. G. Wells; Sally Ride; Robert Redford; Gustav Dore; Mark Spitz

WEAK: James Earl Carter; William K. Douglas; Jean Houston; Evel Knievel; Bob Hope; Gen. George Patton

EVENTS: Pearl Harbor Attack; Kent State Shootings; Transcontinental Railroad completed; Nixon's Resignation; (East Coast Power Blackout).

☉, ♄ Rudolph Bing; Scott Carpenter; Gianni Agnelli; Gustav Dore; Fidel Castro; Enrico Caruso; Dr. Tom Dooley

☽   Carl Sandburg; Audrey Hepburn; Ida Rolf; Stephen Foster; Arthur Rimbaud; Lord Byron; Liberace

☿   Herman Melville; Edmund Halley; Sam Peckinpah; F. Scott Fitzgerald

♀   Edgar Degas; Benjamin Disraeli; Sam Sheppard; Mark Spitz; Jean Francoise Millet; H. G. Wells

♂   Peter Max; Liberace; Mick Jagger; Laurence Olivier

♃   Alex. Graham Bell; John Paul I; Jacques Cousteau; Gianni Agnelli

♅   Bob Dylan; Peter Max; Ida Rolf; Vittorio DeSica; Johnny Carson; Jack Nicklaus; Sigmund Freud; Johann Von Goethe

♆   Stephen Crane; Arthur Godfrey; Dick Gregory; Henry Mancini; Sigmund Freud; Dane Rudhyar; Art Linkletter

♀   Lord Byron; Robert McNamara; Percy Bysshe Shelley; Drew Pearson

☊   Sam Sheppard; F. Scott Fitzgerald; Benito Mussolini; Marc Edmund Jones; Carl Sagan; Burt Reynolds

A   Franklin Roosevelt; Param. Yogananda; Paul Cezanne

M   Walt Whitman; Komar; Francisco Franco; Burt Reynolds

SUN/URANUS ☉/♅

Basic Ideas:

This shows your determination to make a mark or to impose reforms. You set personal initiative loose in a purely individual way to force changes in the way others react to you and also to bring new types of personal excitement to your lifestyle. These planets help you develop ideas of creativity and inventiveness to raise your talents to their peak. Humanitarian concerns and friendliness toward others mark you and your lifestyle. You become known for not going along with the crowd. The significance of what you want to do is tied to your independence and the marks that you will leave in life show you to be a unique person. Also shown here are the importance you place on being known as original and distinctive, the effectiveness you have in exciting others about your ideas, your influence as being politically wise, and your personal interest in using astrology.

In Your Personal Life:

Thesis   Grabbing the attention of others and swinging it to yourself; the independent person who does not want to fit into another's mold; a strong drive to defend the individuality and freedom of self or others.

Anti   Rebelliousness as a means of getting your way in life; peculiarity as a form of attention getting; coolness toward those who do not show enough respect to you; the resolve you have to remain impersonal.

In Your Relationships:

Thesis   Your ability to balance your needs for independence and freedom against the need for a partner; your ability to allow another person to display his or her independence and authority without feeling threatened.

Anti   Trouble absorbing the independence and freedom of another into your lifestyle; aligning yourself with people who are cool and unemotional, or otherwise unable to express or demonstrate their affections for you.

With Body or Mind:

Blood pressure abnormalities; bodily reactions to stress; shock or trauma; deafness from occupational causes; stress breaks to bones in the lower leg.

In Politics or Business:

Thesis   Political changes that shape the quality of all efforts; reforms which initiate changes to authority or power; legislation mandating major reforms in policies; revolutions which bring fundamental changes.

Anti   Rebellions designed solely for the removal of an existing leader; the changes which accompany upheavals; rule makers or interpreters battling decision makers; a contrary head of state with unusual habits.

SUN/URANUS with Planets and Points

☽   Unusual rhythms; sudden allergic reactions; individual displays of tenderness ; arbitrary emotional outbursts; sensitivity to the freedoms that others demand; protecting others who want or need freedom.

☿   Talks with others about how to achieve freedom; nervousness when acting alone; clever ways to show unique individuality; observing how others are able to project their unique sense of personality.

♀   Unique forms of expressing affection or loves; variety in the ways that you approach art or music; encouragement of a peculiar sort for those interested in financial or artistic pursuits; flattery when you are you.

♂   Gathering courage to create new forms of self-expression; energy and enthusiasm in expressing individuality; abrupt or crude expressions about who you are; unusual ways of competing with others.

♃   A lot of personal ambition; an optimistic view of what you are as a person and how you are unique; opinions formed about your personal ambitions; gains in your pursuit of personal expressions of freedom.

♄   Unusual forms of business activity which displays your sense of individuality; working slowly but with determination toward making self unique as an individual; caution in the pursuit of personal freedom.

♆   Inspiration regarding your sense of self; dreams to help you leave unique marks in the world; visions of new trends which you can use in business or in life; neglect of self and/or your sense of individuality.

♇   Provoking others with constant rebelliousness and distractions; disruptions of others or events to gain recognition; direct attacks on the individuality of others to help you gain more notoriety for your interests or self.

☊   Encountering others who are able to help you with your shows of uniqueness; ties to friends who give you friendly encouragement for your activities; attracting others who are uniquely peculiar or unusual persons.

A   Development of a personal style for which you are identified; mannerisms which set you apart as an individual; repression of your uniqueness and acceptance of that part of self as normal; attitudes toward unique people.

M   Growth of character and self through learning what it is that you want and how to achieve that as a person; taking the means to protect self or family from others who want to curtail your freedoms; happiness by being unique.

SUN/URANUS CONCEPTS

Abrupt Authorization
Determined Disobedience
Overdone Rudeness
Defiance is Primary
Potential Insight
Varying Influence
Flamboyant Discontent
Acceptable Contrariness
Purposeful Restyling
Restless with Responsibility
Expensive Deviations
Grandiose Opposition

Famed Uniqueness
Independence is First
An Effective Astrologer
Adequate Regulation
Influences Revisions
Striking Misfits
Arrogant Regulation
Jocular Individuality
Approves of Disruptions
Adequate Revisions
Determined Deviation
Influential Insight

Novel Influences
Boundless Impudence
Bold Peculiarities
Authentic Surprises
Primary Deviation
Special Regulation
Elaborate Obstinacy
Special Peculiarity
Exclusive Variations
Lavish Version
Arrogant Innovation
Haughty Discontent

Outstanding Discontent
Important Innovation
Essential Indifference
Facetious Eccentricity
Flamboyant Opposition
Adequate Disruption
Imperious Impartiality
Prefers Independence
Capable of Detachment
Intentional Disobedience
Concerned with Reform
Superior Originality
Approves of Abstinence
Distinguished Revisions
Concerned with Astrology
Immense Indifference
Influences Reforms
Flamboyant Disruption
Fundamental Disinterest
Modern Influences
Progressive Acceptance
Prefers Waywardness
Remarkable Indifference
Astrological Influences
Important Innovations
A Neutral Commander
Concerned with Regulation
Uniquely Remarkable
The Importance of Liberation
Influences Innovation
Overdone (Flowery) Disruption

Audacious Peculiarity
Imperious Detachment
Concerned with Peculiarity
Distinguished Astrologer
Friendly Persistence
Special Uniqueness
Determined Contrariness
Supports a Revolution
Impressive Interference
Spontaneous Surprises
Distinguished Innovation
Bold Surprises
Peculiar Approval
Determined Regulation
Arrogant Indifference
Primary Uniqueness
Authentic Variations
Remarkable Discontent
Adequate Astonishment
Special Novelty
Original Decisions
Overdone Rebelliousness
Basic Defiance
Authentic Insight
Effective Obstinacy
Competent Insight
Fundamental Revisions
Surprising Prestige
Expensive Innovation
Important Deviations
Successful Infraction

SUN/URANUS With Itself

☉   A need to be known as an independent person and one who is your own self; concern shown for personal freedoms and individuality; determination to to proceed with distinct and original objectives in life.

♅   The novelty and inventiveness you show as an individual; the detachment you exhibit when exciting others about your ideas or interests; enhanced personal resolution to go your own way in life despite all opposition.

Significant Examples of People and Events Using Sun/Uranus

General: <u>STRONG</u>: Melvin Belli; Vittorio DeSica; William K. Douglas; Gugliel. Marconi; Liberace; Albert Camus; Enrico Caruso; Arnold Schwarzenegger; Dr. Tom Dooley; Pierre Teilhard de Chardin; Steve Wozniak
<u>WEAK</u>: Claude Debussy; Paul Joseph Goebbels; Joseph Joffre; Henry Winkler; Sir William Crookes; Tom Smothers; Dave Garroway
<u>EVENTS</u>: South Carolina Secession; Watergate Burglary; Wright Brothers First Flight; Woman's Suffrage Amendment Adopted (First Medicare Patient Applies).

☉,♅   Richard Alpert; William K. Douglas; Arturo Toscanini

☽   Elton John; Steve Rosenbloom; Jimmy Carter; Arthur Rimbaud

☿   Sandy Koufax; Elvis Presley; Marlon Brando; Herman Melville

♀   Bjorn Borg; J. Von Ribbentrop; Melvin Belli; Chernobyl; Louis Pasteur

♂   Edouard Manet; S. Carolina Secession; Sigmund Freud; Anne Murray

♃   Bob Dylan; Liberace; Giacomo Puccini; Audie Murphy; H. Matisse

♄   Moshe Dayan; Hank Williams; Steven Spielberg; P. Yogananda

♆   Dr. Tom Dooley; Charles Addams; Hank Williams; Van Cliburn

♇   Sam Peckinpah; Grant Lewi; Elton John; Auguste Rodin; Ira Progoff

☊   Harry Shoaf; Bolshevik Gov't; Bobby Fischer; Van Cliburn; Bob Dylan

A   Jonathan Winters; Edgar Degas; Billy Rose; Evel Knievel; Van Cliburn

M   Albert Camus; Richard Byrd; Jerry Reed; Melvin Belli; Scott Carpenter

SUN/NEPTUNE ☉/Ψ

Basic Ideas:

This combination highlights the dreams you have about your ability and determination to present yourself as a competent and effective person. Your idealism molds your motives and purposes. You dream of competence and self-effectiveness. You become deceived by your own concepts of self-importance, and lavishly shower devotion on trivial matters. Your motivations are driven by nebulous goals, and you pull your authority from personal feelings of divinity. You mold your basic power and influence through your dreams and illusions. You encourage idealism and discourage looking at the reality of life, you deceive others with your motives, bring authenticity to mystical adventures, and confuse your will and reasoning abilities with dreams about your ability to build an ideal. Responsibility becomes a relatively meaningless concept, a topic you like to avoid.

In Your Personal Life:

Thesis   Good powers of visualizaion; building a reality from your dreams; influencing others with your dreams and visions; a deep grasp of occult or magic themes; an ability to create rituals.

Anti   Successfully deluding yourself about your abilities; adding to your own self-importance and worth; playing roles of savior or victim; escaping from reality through daydreams; expansion of your ego beyond reality.

In Your Relationships:

Thesis   Sending powerful subconscious messages to attract people to you; high ideals about people and their motivations; seeking the ideal in your relationships to fulfill your dreams of a more perfect life with another.

Anti   Becoming so enthralled with your own self-importance that you cannot adequately meet partner's needs; exploiting and then discarding people without realizing how you use them; plays the role of a victim.

With Body or Mind:

Weakened bodily constitution; decrease of willpower; potential drug addictions; visualizing and projecting yourself as healthy; lack of will to continue.

In Politics or Business:

Thesis   A leader with the ability to thrill the masses through visions of a great future; projection of the "good times;" an ability to respond to the needs of the consumers by offering products based on popular concepts.

Anti   A leadership which goes to excess and exhausts itself on impractical schemes; inflation which drains resources; budget deficits; drug problems; promises made but not backed with substance or intention.

SUN/NEPTUNE with Planets and Points

☽   Instinct which leads you into a dream world and away from reality; modesty as an illusive goal in life; receptivity to ideas and dreams of others ; ability to interpret the thoughts and intentions of others.

☿   Discussions about the occult or magical sides of life; bringing dreams into reality; a need for self-education and practice in the areas of mysticism, magical practices, ritual ceremonies, and occult ideas.

♀   Desires for and attachments to material objects; dreaming of living in beauty, wealth, comfort, and luxury; a value system based upon dreams and fancies of an easy life; delights in mental escape from life.

♂   Attempts to work out anger through dreaming; schemes to activate your dreams; ability to control more of your circumstances by visualizing changes; inner anger aroused by the actions of others.

♃   Increased desire to slip away and live in a world of illusions; expanded power to mentally visualize and create; development of a philosophy built around escape; basic and large fundamental errors.

♄   The discipline to shape reality through your dreams; persistance in working toward your ideals and dreams; frustrations in attaining goals without long practice and work; actualization of inner potential.

♅   Visualization and dreaming about astrology; adjustment of old dreams to fit newly developing situations; upsets caused by ignoring reality while you are dreaming; indifference toward life or others while you inwardly escape.

♇   Using creative visualization techniques to bring damage or harm to others; troubles you create through seeing only the ideal in people or situations; reverses in life due to a lack of clarity; increasing self-centeredness or greed.

☊   Meeting and associating with people who have dreams and desires similar to your own; links to people or groups which have ties to the occult; feeling an attachment to those you meet or associate with; ridding self of bad ideas.

A   Increased concentration on fulfilling dreams through visualizations; ability to block out unwanted influences while concentrating; personal mannerism which includes daydreaming; creativity and spontaneity.

M   Individual learning and growing about what the world is like and how your purposes can become better realized; maturing in your ability to visualize end goals; coping with reality through idealistic escapes.

SUN/NEPTUNE CONCEPTS

Subtle Displays of Power	Fundamental Devotion	Effective Escape
Ambiguous Commitment	A Creative Imagination	Special Guilt
Flamboyant Disguises	A Basic Oversight	Adequate Puzzles
Delusions of Importance	A Deceptive Lifestyle	Subtle Influences
Concerned with Subtlety	A Preference for Escape	A Bold Delusion
Inspires Influential People	An Expensive Fantasy	Stately Suppositions
Concerned with Drugs	Convincing Mysteries	Effective Disguises
Circumvents Authority	The Confidence Game	Lavish Fraud
An Inspired Achievement	Acceptable Ambiguities	Genuine Illusion
Special Disregard	A Notable Omission	Expensive Neglect
Concerned with Weakness	Effective Fantasies	Disguised Influence
Determines Pretenses	Specific Weakness	Approves of Fraud

Frivolous Attitudes	Inspired Creativity
Great Subservience	The Illusion of Influence
The Importance of Submission	Determined Inspiration
Omitting a Famous Person	Characteristic Weakness
A Genuine Miracle	Mysterious Influences
Concerned about Shoddiness	Genuine Neglect
An Illusive Famous Person	A Lack of Effectiveness
The Importance of Subtlety	Authorizes Mysticism
Dilapidation of the Once Great	The Importance of Mysteries
Fundamental Weakness	Original Dreams
Authentic Inspiration	Arrogant Pretenses
Committed to Submission	Influences Visions
Approves of Shoddiness	Lavish Inspiration
The Importance of Disguises	Positive Sanctity
Influences Omission	Arrogant Counterfeits
Official Muddles	An Inefficient Principal
Deliberate Imperfections	Authentic Confusion
Magnificent Daydreams	Effective Vagueness
Fantasy Predominates	Determined Fantasies
Deceives Influential People	An Effective Counterfeit
Competent with Concealment	Special Imagination
Special Subtlety	Reliable for Compliance
A Concealed Defect	Primary Defection
Influential Submission	Arrogant Mysteries
Overdone (Flowery) Fraud	Committed to Confusion
Essential Mysteries	Primary Carelessness
Supreme Confusion	Lavish Mysteries
Fundamental Flimsiness	Weakens Influence
A Famous Illusion	Splendid Images
Flamboyant Indiscretion	Genuine Perplexities
Subtle Effectiveness	Authorized Omissions

SUN/NEPTUNE With Itself

⊙   Personal determination to not avoid methods, procedures, or ideas which are important; the faith you bring to your dreams and visions of the future; your ability to plan and visualize future paths of action.

♆   Increased need to use artificial means or drugs to escape from pressures or demands; the work you put into not confusing or garbling important deeds or information; additional inspiration for artistic insight or achievements.

Significant Examples of People and Events Using Sun/Neptune

General: **STRONG:** Vittorio DeSica; Stephen Crane; Shirley Jones; Paul Newman; Sir Alexander Fleming; Sir William Crookes; Stephen Foster; Mick Jagger; Jean Paul Sartre; Ellen Burstyn; Jacques Cousteau; Ralph Nader
WEAK: Marlon Brando; Willie Brandt; William K. Douglas; Carl Sandburg; Hank Williams; Robert Redford; Burl Ives; Dave Garroway
EVENTS: Lewis & Clark Expedition; James Meredith's Enrollment; East Coast Power Blackout; Lee's Surrender at Appomattox; (Apollo 11 Moon Landing).

⊙, ♆   Louis Pasteur; Art Linkletter; Stephen Foster; Harry Shoaf; President Nixon's Resignation; Stephen Crane

☽   Rupert Murdoch; Sandy Koufax; Henri Toulouse-Lautrec; Charles Kettering; Scott Carpenter

☿   Ferdin. Foch; R. D. Laing; Mario Andretti; O. J. Simpson; Lindburgh Lands in Paris; Bjorn Borg; Emperor Hirohito

♀   Richard Chamberlain; Sir Alex. Fleming; Shirley Jones; Claude Debussy; Ira Progoff; Stephen Foster

♂   Cheiro; Vincent Van Gogh; Edna Ferber; Rollo May

♃   Fidel Castro; Vittorio DeSica; Moshe Dayan; Audrey Hepburn; Tom Jones; Bob Hope; Van Cliburn

♄   Paul Newman; Rex Harrison; Giacomo Puccini; Jeddu Krishnamurti; Dave Garroway

♅ ♇   Washington's Inaug.; Dr. Tom Dooley; Lawrence Welk
Sir William Crookes; Henry Kissinger; Enrico Fermi; Franklin Roosevelt; Sigmund Freud

☊   Bobby Fischer; Paul Newman; Carroll Righter; Stonewall Jackson

A   Jacques Cousteau; Ellen Burstyn; Enrico Caruso; Jimi Hendrix; Edouard Manet; Jean Paul Sartre

M   Stephen Crane; Bob Fosse; Henry Mancini; Robert McNamara; Paramhansa Yogananda

SUN/PLUTO ☉/♇

Basic Ideas:

Your fundamental urge to exert control over all situations, your capacity or determination to defeat or ally with corrupt forces as they rise around you, and the mastery you show against self-corruption are prominent with this combination. Your commitment to concentrating yourself into the essence of what you are as a person, the secret motivations you rally your inner strength around, and the obsession you have with increasing your self-confidence are also here. You appear as a person who has a deep and formidable willpower, and one who is not easily swayed from important decisions about where your life is going. You may appear to have an easygoing outer facade, but inwardly you are a tower of strength and determination. The strength and resolution you bring through these motifs to effect what you want in life is immense. You do not give up easily against anything.

In Your Personal Life:

Thesis   Force of will and determination you bring toward achieving objectives;unswerving reliability you offer to others; keeping secrets under all situations; success you achieve using threats.

Anti   Ruthless pursuit of your goals; focusing on activities which enable the accumulation of power; punishment for those who cannot perform their tasks; squandering your will by giving up on your principles.

In Your Relationships:

Thesis   You need to express your deeply felt emotions to a partner who also responds in kind; a deep need for truth between people; expressions of loyalty or respect and how these are reciprocated by your partner.

Anti   Deep feelings of hurt when another has betrayed your love or trust; an inability to find another who can respond with intense emotions; your need to dominate another person through the use of love or sex.

With Body or Mind:

The role of the colon in maintaining your overall health; susceptibility to any infections caused by toxic conditions in the body or environment.

In Politics or Business:

Thesis   Changes of policy or direction from the leadership; new leadership and the changing of policy and direction; the governing authority used to control threatened dissent or subversion despite its cause or sources.

Anti   Accumulation of an excessive amount of armed strength; the use of secret police to exert authority and control over others; the influence of criminal organizations; extremes of corruption which waste resources.

SUN/PLUTO with Planets and Points

☽   Determination to effect basic changes to the flow of life's events; efforts to bring help to those in need; fluctuations in your attempts to appear strong willed; your basic ideas about death or destruction.

☿   A mental set where you do not easily reveal anything about your self or your life; great flexibility in adapting to others impositions on you; your ability to articulate your inner motivations for control or power.

♀   Recognition of how to present beauty or adornment in intentional or basic ways; determination to show depths of feelings of love and affection ; extremes in attracting harmony or artistry to your life.

♂   Energetic sexual urges or other deep and basic needs; deep inner needs to succeed at any cost; a combative nature which will go to any lengths to conquer and solve problems; the drive to turn things around.

♃   An idealistic desire to become number one; cheer or laughter lightens your perspective on life; a need for creating a more complete set of ethics or morals; desires to study life's mysteries; a debasing of personal standards.

♄   Diminished desire to achieve power and fame; waiting patiently for results you achieve; restraint when showing your destructive tendencies or potential for fanatical ventures; a blockage of wild tendencies.

♅   Sudden obsession to acquire additional control or power; imagination for creative and powerful ideas; the use of scientific methods to achieve progress or gain power; a surprising suspicion of basic powers.

♆   Weak resolve to conquer the world alone; a lessened intensity of purpose in life's situations; receiving inspiration when you seek answers; increasing devotion; recognizing a spiritual impact on life.

☊   Attracting others into your life who can allow you to develop a stronger will and purpose; directing your dedication of purpose to that which companions feel is important; friends who help you channel your inner potential.

A   Concentrating on making changes through applying your will; noticing the weakness of others and using this knowledge for personal advantage; efforts to rid your environment of corruption, or degrading or immoral practices.

M   Working to increase your influence in your community or among your peers; pouring an excessive amount of your personal time or resources into achieving recognition and respectability; working through past mistakes.

SUN/PLUTO CONCEPTS

Achieves Purification
Expensive Cleansing
Extreme Fame
Ceases to Predominate
Influences Suspicion
Intense Resolution
Powerful Creativity
Flamboyant Excesses
Determined Contamination
Fundamental Intensity
Concerned with Depletion
Real Grieving
To Very Great Extremes
A Magnetic Presence

Prominent Destruction
Successful Corruption
Approves of Dishonesty
Respectable Funeral
Obsessed with Arrogance
Extreme Purification
Playful Wilfullness
Notable Ownership
Reliable Restitution
Expensive Corruption
Genuine Punishment
Masterful Dismissal
Special Troubles
An Intense Melodrama

Influential Control
Real Suspicion
Convincing Pursuit
Reduces Fame
Capable of Rancor
Adequate Intensity
Official Power
Lavish Curses
Drives for Power
Elaborate Failures
Influences Evolution
Capable of Mistrust
Adequate Obsessions
Certain Retribution

Potential Denunciation
Believable Suspicions
Purposeful Compulsion
Acclaimed Catastrophe
Concern over Destruction
Intentional Hiding Places
Conclusive Regeneration
The Importance of Evolution
Corruption of Famous Persons
Influences Fanatics
Punishment of the Famous
Specific Willfulness
Suspicion by Important People
Adequate Corruption
Sustained Obsessions
Remarkable Destruction
Eliminates Important People
Elaborate Endings
Fundamental Power
Leading Debasement
An Overdone Use of Force
Concerned with Purification
Characteristic Retaliation
The Decay of Influence
Great Seething
The Importance of Purification
Remarkable Corruption
Powerful Condemnation
Impressive Waste Products

Dominant Self-Assurance
Successful Transition
The End of Importance
Hiding Important Persons
Elaborate Condemnation
Sufficient Cleansing
Special Perversions
Determined Concealment
Successful Defamation
Intentional Condemnation
Depression Dominates
Influences the Prosecution
Corruption of the Influential
Well-Known Poisons
Effective Intensity
Immense Monopoly
Your Control of Resources
Effective Hiding Places
Your Role with Contaminants
Special Dishonor
Impressive Oppression
Effective Punishment
Discipline Dominates
Respectable Oppression
Melodramatic Intensity
Authentic Reduction
Important Punishment
A Compulsion to Win
Adequate Concealment

SUN/PLUTO With Itself

☉   Increasing intensity and obsession with controlling all facets of your life and the lives of others; determination to use destructive means to achieve control (whatever your justification or means for such action).

♀   Ridding yourself of unwanted forces from life and concentrating on those things which are central and important to your destiny; eliminating vengeance and ruthlessness as a means for achieving your goals.

Significant Examples of People and Events Using Sun/Pluto

General: **STRONG:** Steve Wozniak; Stephen King; William Butler Yeats; Robert DeNiro; Arthur Ford; Burl Ives; Hugh Downs; Jack Paar; Louis Pasteur; Albert Einstein; Alan Alda; Sydney Omarr; Merv Griffin; Liberace
WEAK: Gregory Peck; Sally Ride; Willi Brandt; Art Linkletter; Ellen Burstyn; Van Cliburn; Alexander Graham Bell; Audie Murphy
EVENTS: Bolsheviks Seize Power; Watergate Burglary; Lewis & Clark Expedition starts; Kent State Shootings; (First Medicare Patient Accepted).

☉, ♀   Steve Wozniak; Merv Griffin; Rupert Murdoch; Chernobyl Nuclear Disaster; Friedrich Nietzsche

☽   Winston Churchill; Jean Paul Satre; Ralph Nader; Ernest Pyle; Komar

☿   Ulysses S. Grant; Jean Cocteau; Harry Belafonte; Stephen Foster

♀   Dick Gregory; Albert Speer; Gus Grissom; Stephen Crane; Paul Joseph Goebbels; David Frost

♂   Gen Ferdinand Foch; Jimmy Carter; Paul Newman; Peter Max; A. Rodin

♃   John McEnroe; Grant Lewi; Al Unser; Carl Sagan; Hugh Downs; Pierre Renoir; Israel Regardie

♄   Richard Byrd; Dane Rudhyar; Edgar Degas; Steve Allen; Abraham Lincoln; Paul Cezanne; Tommy Smothers

♅   Alan Alda; Kareem Abdul-Jabbar; Tommy Smothers; Dick Gregory

♆   Steve Rosenbloom; Erich Maria Remarque; Ramstein Airshow Crash

☋   Jerry Rubin; Robert DeNiro; Arthur Ford; Charles Gordon; Jacques Cousteau; Stephen Crane; Elvis Presley

A   Scott Carpenter; Alan Leo; Alexis Carrel; Ernest Hemingway; Robert DeNiro; Stephen King; Steve Rosenbloom

M   Apollo 11 Moon Landing; Arnold Schwarzenegger; Bob Hope; Burl Ives; R. D. Laing; Steve Wozniak; Arthur Godfrey

SUN/NODE   ☉/☊

Basic Ideas:

This combination shows a capacity to establish relationships with people who have qualities or resources you need. Through these motifs you are able to meet new and important friends with whom you form new and close bonds or sexual ties, and remove people or circumstances from your life which you have grown beyond. They indicate circumstances where you spend more than you plan, bring opportunities which prove to be important, and increase your ties to groups or clubs which can help you. You find yourself mingling with distinguished or successful people, encounter situations where you have to face decisions about your personal destiny, and recognize ways to rid yourself of unwanted people or things. You attend meetings where speakers are arrogant, find inspiration to follow your personal destiny, are invited to meetings with important purposes.

In Your Personal Life:

Thesis | Finding individuals or groups who can help you determine or sort out your life's destiny or path; establishing ties to people or groups who are able to help you; an effective presentation of your purposes or ideas.

Anti | Meeting those who use your time or resources; an influential person who uses you and your resources; presentations from arrogant or aristocratic persons; an inability to recognize the value of new people.

In Your Relationships:

Thesis | A strong need to constantly be with another person in a meaningful relationship; the influence you exert on your partner and vice versa; finding those people who are necessary for you to achieve your destiny.

Anti | Alliances with those who are less than honest about their intentions; finding people who use your time and resources in unproductive ways; using others for sexual liaisons; bad habits repeated with a new partner.

With Body or Mind:

The blood channels or passages around the heart; clogging of these channels with deposits; connections or pathways in the spine or back; bodily stress.

In Politics or Business:

Thesis | Developing the sociology of an enterprise; the will of the leadership as explained in state of the union addresses; creating the structure for a bureaucracy; allies or associates who send added help or inspiration.

Anti | Political associations which eventually do more harm than good; formation of ties to allies which drain your vitality; a loss of respect due to unfortunate treaties, mergers, or alliances; eliminating helpful people.

SUN/NODE with Planets and Points

☽   Beneficial ties with females or with womens' groups; habits which help you to find people who can be helpful; traditional networks which bring you links to influential people; normal meetings with others.

☿   Generating ideas which influence others and simultaneously open previously closed doors for you; gathering rumors during meetings with allies; groups which impose reporting obligations on you.

♀   Affectionate feelings toward those you have recently met; a love for meeting with friends; friends bring calming influences; association with artistic individuals; meetings on issues of beautification.

♂   Impatience to meet new friends and allies; the efforts to locate the kinds of people you need; expending energy to convey your importance to others; meeting effective competitors who can become allies.

♃   Promises from influential people; ambition when arranging alliances to important organizations; genuine interest in people and their needs; publicity given to you involving important or newsworthy persons.

♄   Development of lasting ties to organizations which can exert influence on your behalf; prohibitions on developing your ties to such groups; brief encounters with famous people; weak influence within groups.

♅   Sudden breaking of ties to those who have previously helped you; friends who provide the right connections; progressive influence and bonding to those who give you help; reform or upheaval in groups.

♆   Inability to decide which destiny in life to choose; a mystical leaning to measuring your progress in life; deception from allies; finding important secret societies; fantasies about public sexual activities.

♇   The power you acquire from associating with the right people; concealing your ties to dominant and important associations or groups; secret meetings where power and influence are allocated or divided.

A   An effective concentration on maintaining or establishing ties to helpful groups; seeking attention and recognition from groups you belong to and support; rituals which occur at meetings; your evolving importance.

M   Using connections to others as a means of increasing your personal prestige or stature; the security or peace of mind you receive from your friends; meetings where you receive recognition for past work.

SUN/NODE CONCEPTS

Continuing Bureaucracy
Important Connections
Remarkable Cooperation
Effective Affiliations
Fundamental Barriers
Immense Gatherings
Successful Acquaintances
Purposeful Sexual Ties
Immense Fate
Influential Groups
Remarkable Supporters
Elaborate Hallways

Master of Your Destiny
Basic Displays
Impressive Evolution
Effective Delaying Actions
Genuine Sexual Liaisons
First at Attracting Others
Significant Meetings
Primary Runaround
Successful Relatives
Notable New Habits
Ornate Demonstrations
Joint Influences

Costly Allegiances
Special Sexual Ties
Acclaimed Removal
Competent Displays
Sincere Associates
Lavish Pathways
Important Purges
Costly Sexual Ties
Expensive Destiny
Effective Divisions
Sustains Kinship
Overpaid Colleagues

Magnificent Discourses
Overdone Sense of Destiny
Resolves New Habits
Sexual Ties to the Important
Special Presentations
Distinguished Acquaintances
Concerned with Finding Others
Official Partitions
Distinguished Gatherings
Influences Group Directions
Prefers Attracting Others
Basic Ties to the Familiar
Concerned with Presentations
Squanders Opportunities
Concerned with Karma
A Celebrated Divorce
Successful at Meeting Others
Distinguished Assemblies
The Importance of Affiliations
Cooperation Predominates
Famous for Self-Motivation
Illuminates Interchanges
Influential Attracting Others
Committed to Partnerships
An Official Annulment
Successful Meetings
Determined Cooperation
Special Meetings with Others
Adequate Relationships
Promotes Obligations
Sustains Life's Aim

Bureaucracy Predominates
Prestigious Acquaintances
Primary Ties to Others
Influences Separations
Celebrated Appointments
Flamboyant Backers
Grand Partnerships
Effective Ties to Others
Potential Pathways
Lavish Ties to Others
Achieves Acquisitions
Influential Acquaintances
Genuinely Desires Others
Wastes Close Ties to Others
Authentic Separations
Arrogant Presentations
Fundamental Kinship
Adequate Presentations
Flamboyant Sexual Ties
Determined Runaround
Motivates Alliances
Exclusive Opportunities
Confident of Ties to Others
Primary Alliances
Flamboyant Life's Aim
Deliberate Attachment
Influences Presentations
Determined Alliances
Characteristic Assemblies
Special Acquaintances
Reliable Supporters

SUN/NODE With Itself

☉   Adds importance to the personal recognition you give to others, and the help you receive in return through your ties; a memorable time with friends with whom you have special bonds; personal convictions.

☊   Relying on the work and help of friends; the realization that teamwork and cooperation will do more for achieving goals than individual and separate work; reminders of your personal fate; addressing your personal destiny.

Significant Examples of People and Events Using Sun/Node

General: **STRONG:** Benjamin Disraeli; Paramhansa Yogananda; Walt Whitman; Burt Reynolds; Guglielmo Marconi; John Glenn; Giacomo Puccini; Benito Mussolini; Lawrence Welk; Richard Alpert; Jean Cocteau
WEAK: Joachim Von Ribbentrop; Paul Joseph Goebbels; Audrey Hepburn; Ira Progoff; Grant Lewi; Auguste Rodin; Merv Griffin
EVENTS: Alaskan Earthquake; First A-Bomb Explosion; Mount St. Helens Explosion; Pearl Harbor Attack; (USS Maine Explosion).

☉, ☊   Guglielmo Marconi; Jean Cocteau; Ida Rolf; Johnny Carson; Charles E. O. Carter; Erich Maria Remarque

☽   Arnold Schwarzenegger; Charles Gordon; Jack Nicklaus; Johann Von Goethe; David O. Selznik

☿   Burt Reynolds; Lance Reventlow; Tommy Smothers; Sam Peckinpah

♀   Yehudi Menuhin; Pearl Harbor; Alex. Graham Bell; Charles Steinmetz

♂   Sean Connery; Scott Carpenter; Wins. Churchill; Nikola Tesla; R. D. Laing; Edna Ferber; Jack Nicklaus

♃   Bolshevik's Seize Power; Alan Leo; Marc Edmund Jones; Carl Sagan; Jerry Reed; Gus Grissom

♄   Bobby Fischer; Gregory Peck; O. J. Simpson; Rex Harrison; Helen Reddy; Johnny Carson; Jean Cocteau

♅   John Glenn; Richard Alpert; Burt Reynolds; Challenger Explosion; Jean Francoise Millet; Paramhansa Yogananda

♆   Emperor Hirohito; Tommy Smothers; Vida Blue; Toulouse-Lautrec

♇   Vittorio DeSica; Ada Lovelace Byron; Stephen Sondheim; Arturo Toscanini; Johnny Carson

A   A-Bomb Explosion; Alexis Carrel; Rupert Murdoch; Jack Schwartz

M   Lance Reventlow; Richard Chamberlain; John Dillinger; Apollo 11 Moon Landing

SUN/ASCENDANT   ⊙/A

Basic Ideas:

The quality of self-confidence you show through your mannerisms and temperament, the importance you place on experiencing and interpreting life's circumstances, and your use of arrogant pretenses as a mask for your feelings can all begin with this motif. The personal satisfaction you have with the way you present yourself, your dedication to learning more about the different roles you have in life, and your effectiveness at reading the motives of others can also start here. Also indicated are the role of life's experiences as conveyed through your bearing and attitudes, your enthusiasm for living, your ability to impress others with your spirit, and the importance you place on your normal daily activities. Taking an impartial look at the effect you have on others, and the immediate influence or power you exert on the people you meet are also represented here.

In Your Personal Life:

Thesis   Conveying the impression that you are in control of your life; the confidence you display in your mannerisms; the spirit and enthusiasm which you show; the personal habits which help make you unique.

Anti   Excessive attempts to seek attention from others; a personal style that shows overconfidence or arrogance; mannerisms that repel rather than attract others; your perceptions of another person's enthusiasm.

In Your Relationships:

Thesis   Bringing others into your circle of confidence and inner feelings; how you are able to harmoniously allow another to mingle with your own sense of self; the emphasis you place on learning about your partner.

Anti   Trying to overwhelm others with your own sense of importance; lacking self-confidence when relating to others; overly enthusiastic or flowery greetings; lavishness of appearance gone too far; arrogance.

With Body or Mind:

Understanding your effect on the world and feeling mentally satisfied with that; awareness of your presence and how people judge you within that.

In Politics or Business:

Thesis   How others notice expressions of the current policy; the nature of the enterprise or its people expressed directly and effectively; a leader who can show personal style and be popularly identified with an enterprise.

Anti   Imposing your demands upon neighbors; an arrogance shown by the leadership or ruling bodies; authority demonstrated in extravagant or even forceful ways; a willful or self-centered leader with ambitions.

SUN/ASCENDANT with Planets and Points

☽   Fostering feelings of closeness to others; uncertainty over how others feel about you as a person; reading the feelings that others have for you even when these are not verbalized; receptivity to cosmic information.

☿   Discussions of the interpersonal roles you have with others; a clever way of showing others that you are the person you are; information on personal needs and motivations for understanding others.

♀   Appreciation of the role others play in helping you define who you are; satisfaction with the perceptions you receive about you from others; artistically inclined people who help you identify with yourself.

♂   Enhanced levels of enthusiasm and energy; strong personality with energy and power; indignation over how others accept you as a person; noisy clamor or welcoming shouts; an active daily lifestyle.

♃   The generosity you show when relating to others; a need to give wisdom and advice to others; realizing the authority of others in ways that make them aware that you appreciate them for who they are.

♄   Self-imposed restrictions on being yourself when meeting others; simple expressions which show the nature of your personality; direct but effective ways of demonstrating your personal sense of personhood.

♅   Sudden or unexpected ways of demonstrating who you are; a strong desire to have an unconventional appearance; adapting a new sense of what you are as a person; gaining insight and ideas just by being near other people.

♆   An inability to relate clearly or effectively to another person; the feeling that you are not projecting clearly to those around you; illusions about the feelings of people you meet or encounter; shades of mystical togetherness.

♇   Obsession with how others see you as a person; desire to create a more powerful personality; drastic measures to make others notice who you are; people feel the power of your personality and your force of will.

☊   Ability to use meetings with others to build your ego and sense of self; friends who are able to help you increase your personal stature and recognition; ties to people who help you to identify with self and others more easily.

MC   Defining a personal sense of style and self; becoming more at ease with who you are as a person and how you are able to grow and develop with your personality; personal expertise recognized and appreciated by others.

SUN/ASCENDANT CONCEPTS

Influences Awareness
Audacious Disposition
Imperious Sense of Reality
Determined Motivations
Effective Sense of Reality
Lavish Relating to Others
Special Sense of Style
Effective Concentration
Winning Mannerisms
Famous Surroundings
Impacts Relating to Others
Grand Interpersonal Roles

Encouraging Conditions
Successful Observations
Influences Mannerisms
Conscious of Will Power
Prominent Demeanor
Special Surroundings
Famous Experiences
Flamboyant Reactions
Certain about Reactions
Vital Experiences
Encourages Inhibitions
Effective Personal Style

Lavish Receptions
Special Settings
Genuine Attitudes
Notes Perceptions
Effective Attitudes
Basic Conditions
Lavish Mannerisms
Special Attitudes
Genuine Responses
Positive Reactions
Primary Responses
Prefers Observance

Capable of Relating to Others
Receives Impressions from Leaders
The Importance of Personal Style
Overdone (Flowery) Attitudes
Capable of Seeking Attention
Overdone Personal Style
Relates to Enthusiasm
Concerned with Seeing Life as It Is
Remarkable Surroundings
Encourages Experiences
Influences Important People
Concerned with Relating to Others
Respectable Sense of Style
Influences Reality
Effective Ways of Motivating Self
Genuine Reactions
An Important Sense of Style
Needs a Defined Personal Space
Influences Impressions Received
Unyielding Personal Style
The Importance of Reality
Involved in Recognizing People
The Importance of Mental Focus
Encourages Repressing Events
An Important Point of View
Determined to Relate to Others
A Magnificent Sense of Style
Capable of Understanding Others
Distinguished Personal Style
Celebrated Circumstances
A Display of Attitudes

Influences Surroundings
Believable Reactions
Knows Distinguished People
Flamboyant Sense of Style
Influences Perceptions
Encouraging Attitudes
Realizes Authority
Important Personal Motivations
Authentic Reactions
Arrogant Attention Seeking
Surroundings Predominate
Overdone (Flowery) Mannerisms
First Impressions Received
Intentional Blocking of Perceptions
Purposeful Ways of Relating
Effective Sense of Style
Authentic Attention Seeking
Lavish Surroundings
The Importance of Attitudes
Arrogant Personal Style
A Cosmic Experience
Concerned with Mannerisms
Essential Interpersonal Roles
Influences Tone (Attitudes)
Special Ways of Relating to Others
Famous for Personal Attitudes
Ornate Personal Style
The Importance of Perceptions
Playful Sensations
A Focus on the Core Issues
Influences How to Relate to Others

SUN/ASCENDANT With Itself

⊙   Having more faith in the person you are; projecting the image of yourself more consciously into your environment; strengthening of character and personality; a playful disposition and demeanor.

A   Awareness of your effect on other people and what their needs and reactions are; an interest in the reactions and needs of others; motivating or using the people resources which are available to you.

Significant Examples of People and Events Using Sun/Ascendant

General: **STRONG:** Evel Knievel; Al Unser; Erwin Rommel; Abraham Lincoln; Sir Alexander Fleming; Bjorn Borg; Carl Sagan; Edmund Halley; Yehudi Menuhin; Franklin Roosevelt; Stephen Sondheim; Sir William Crookes; John Lennon
WEAK: Charles Kettering; Winston Churchill; Giacomo Puccini; Paul Newman; Liberace; Jean Francoise Millet; Alexander Graham Bell; Claude Debussy
EVENTS: Woman's Suffrage Passes; Bolsheviks Seize Power; Kent State Shootings; Watergate Burglary Discovered; (James Meredith Enrolls at U. Miss.).

⊙, A   Kareem Abdul-Jabbar; Wayne Gretzky; Edmund Halley; Ida Rolf

☽   Rex Harrison; Robert McNamara; Henry Winkler; Jean Cocteau

☿   George Patton; Israel Regardie; Ralph Waldo Emerson; Sir William Crookes; Gen. Joseph Joffre

♀   Hermann Goering; Woman's Suffrage; Arturo Toscanini; Bjorn Borg

♂   Melvin Belli; Richard Alpert; Sir Alex. Fleming; Komar; Jimmy Carter

♃   Jack Schwartz; Kareem Abdul-Jabbar; Watergate Burglary Discovered; Audrey Hepburn; Ellen Burstyn

♄   Sir William Crookes; Mt. St. Helens; Edmund Halley; Arthur Ford

♅   Billy Rose; J.F. Kennedy Shot; Arthur Ford; Walt Whitman; Anne Murray; Jean Cocteau; Hermann Goering

♆   Stephen Sondheim; Nikola Tesla; Thomas H. Huxley; Pearl Harbor Attack begins; Rudolph Bing

♀   Gus Grissom; Percy Bysshe Shelley; Jean Paul Satre; Jackie Robinson

☋   Ralph Nader; Thomas H. Huxley; Bjorn Borg; Sir Alex. Fleming

M   RMS Titanic Hits Iceberg; Willie Mays; Manly Palmer Hall; Ritchie Valens; Albert Schweitzer

SUN/MIDHEAVEN   ☉/M

Basic Ideas:

This combination represents your responsibility to both self and society to grow and mature as an individual and to realize that your contributions to life are only one person's contribution to civilization. These themes show motivation about your personal abilities, your potential to society, and the world at large. They indicate a potential for becoming a more effective manager of your personality, your time, and the natural resources inherent within your overall character. They encourage you to apply your native and natural talents to life and expand on basic social skills through learning lessons taught from schooling, practical experience, and personal efforts toward self-improvement. Other people will recognize your contributions and give you the honors and recognition you deserve, and in the amount you have earned, when you activate and use these themes.

In Your Personal Life:

Thesis   Determination to properly prepare yourself for the battles of life; a will to excel at your goals and tasks; motivation to be recognized for your efforts; gaining maturity through coping with the various lessons of life.

Anti   Overlooking humility while concentrating on your self-importance; expecting that you can succeed in life without hard work and sufficient effort on your part; using influence to gain position or power.

In Your Relationships:

Thesis   Adapting to living with another person, and allowing others room for expressing their personality within the relationship; the influence you give to another to help you modify your life's outlook and goals.

Anti   Concentrating too hard on your needs while forcing others to subordinate themselves to your ego; increasing needs for personal and family security which encourage you to retreat and become more isolated.

With Body or Mind:

Psychologically coping with life's problems; social growth and maturity; becoming a functioning member of society; adapting to parental or family bonds.

In Politics or Business:

Thesis   The ability of the leadership to place civil priorities above their own; recognition by others of a role and place in the world for business or national ideas; molding and shaping global politics or programs.

Anti   A leadership which places its personal desires above popular needs; ineffective leaders; leaders who have lost popularity; a lessening of the authority because the leadership has lost contact with the people.

SUN/MIDHEAVEN with Planets and Points

☽   Fears about what to do or how to become recognized for your contributions; understanding the primary equality of the sexes in all business, social, and family areas of life; your family's role in shaping your basic thrust in life.

☿   Communicating your intentions about your life's direction; added needs for educational credentials to achieve recognition from others; your ingenuity in making a path for yourself; accolades for scholarship.

♀   Charm and grace in your ideas of how to mature as an individual; respect from others for well-earned achievements; satisfaction and recognition for past efforts; artistic endeavors given due reward.

♂   Energy, activity, and impetus to gain recognition in life; pushing ahead with your plans for beating competitors; showing initiative in situations where progress is too slow; organizing sports activity.

♃   Success and recognition for work done; publicizing past achievements; opportunities for advancement and recognition of your self-worth due to prior contributions to life; consolidating political powers.

♄   Working hard to ensure that your efforts are better planned and implemented; indicates less public recognition but more internal satisfaction about your capabilities; a retraction of praise or honors.

♅   Attention for work with electrical, mechanical, or computing devices; recognition for work in astrology or psychology; sudden efforts to improve your standing in life through additional education or on-the-job-training.

♆   Credit for your work with disadvantaged people, or those who have substance or material dependencies; personal uncertainty or doubts about career, or your standing among your peers or within society.

♇   Increased opportunities for personal and social contributions to be recognized more universally; important secrets which help you achieve fame; reduced personal honor even if you are exceptionally honest.

☊   Ability to work with the right people or groups and have your efforts recognized; locating others to help you along in life becomes easier; recognizing your present or future potential to society or individuals.

A   Increased concentration on the need to be forthright and honest in your assessment of self, in what your accomplishments and contributions are and how they can help the lives of others or the world in general.

SUN/MIDHEAVEN CONCEPTS

Encourages Coordination	Noted Expertise	Pompous Childhood
Positive Conclusions	Overpriced Expertise	The Family is Central
Remarkable Constancy	Basic Coping	An Effective Expert
Impressive Conclusions	Imperious Philosophy	Copes with Renown
Consistent Principles	Profound Repercussions	Arrogant Experts
Effective Self-Restraint	Masterful Effects	Special Purposes
Intends to Motivate	Bona Fide Qualifications	Elaborate Aims
Flowery Assurances	Immense Rewards	Sincere Objectives
Grandiose Standards	Adequate Proficiency	Special Training
Self-Concepts Come First	Influences Results	Famous Degrees
Protects the Famous	Reliable Conclusions	Grand Outcomes
Recognizes the Famous	Personal Objectives	Central Goals

Fundamental Integrity	Personal Security is Important
Motivated to Act Maturely	Encourages Personal Reserve
Seeks Approval from the Famous	Elaborate and Expensive Planning
Expensive Methods of Protection	Sincere Self-Restraint
Bold Self-Integration	Eminent Accomplishments
Concerned with Qualifications	Remarkable Self-Concepts
The Importance of Outcomes	Flamboyant Protection
Effective Personal Development	Influences Sense of Fairness
Remarkable Attainment	Special Protection
Security for Important People	Able to Integrate Personality
Committed to Personal Needs	Successful Guarantees
Convincing Uprightness	Overpriced Training
Committed to Self-Concepts	Exclusive Confirmation
Becomes Mature Gracefully	Encourages Persevering
The Importance of Security	Confident Assurances
Splendid Results	The Importance of Protection
Prefers Validation	Heartfelt Self-Concepts
Displays Maturity	Concerned with Proficiency
Powerful Rank	Well-Deserved Recognition
Elevates Conduct	Protects the Arrogant
Essential Inner Coping	Special Trustworthiness
Expensive Lifestyle	Concerned with Credentials
A Sincere and Mature Person	Superior Personal Guarantees
Effective Learning and Growing	Inner Growth Predominates
Flamboyant Personal Conduct	Family is Origin of Influence
Expensive Schooling	Wins Proficiency
Eminent Stature (Standing)	Displays Rank
Dedicated to Personal Standards	Powerful Confirmation
Influences Perseverance	The Intentions of the Famous
Concerned with Reputation	Determined To Make Do
Special Self-Discipline	Influences Outcomes

SUN/MIDHEAVEN With Itself

☉   Gaining perspective on life direction ; examining your inner self for untapped soul growth or potential; additional notoriety and fame for efforts; recognition that you are better able now to solve your troubles.

M   Maturity in assessing your role or contributions to life; recognizing and confirming your accomplishments whether or not others give you the honors or positions you feel are due; projection of self into public notice.

Significant Examples of People and Events Using Sun/Midheaven

General: **STRONG:** Benito Mussolini; Edgar Degas; Tom Jones; Steve Wozniak; Dick Gregory; Marc Edmund Jones; Steve Allen; Gregory Peck; Bob Newhart; Gustav Dore; Jacques Cousteau; Bobby Fischer; Pierre Renoir
WEAK: Henry Mancini; Ida Rolf; Henry Winkler; Stephen Sondheim; Van Cliburn; Jonathan Winters; Winston Churchill; Neil Diamond
EVENTS: Lee's Surrender; Apollo 11 Moon Landing; Lindburgh Lands in Paris; East Coast Power Blackout; (First Atomic Bomb Explosion).

☉,M   Johann Von Goethe; Charles Steinmetz; Erwin Rommel; Carl Sandburg

☽   Dick Gregory; Burl Ives; Steve Wozniak; Olga Worrall; Komar

☿   Audrey Hepburn; H. G. Wells; Paul J. Goebbels; Louis Pasteur

♀   Steve Wozniak; Wm. K. Douglas; Wm. Butler Yeats; Woman's Suffrage

♂   East Coast Power Blackout; Ervin Nyiregyhazi; Jimmy Carter; Helen Reddy

♃   Alan Alda; Merv Griffin; Paul Joseph Goebbels; Ernest Hemingway; Bob Newhart

♄   Steven Spielberg; Audrey Hepburn; Vincent Van Gogh; Gregory Peck

♅   Transcontinental RR completed; Sam Sheppard; Erich Maria Remarque

♆   Bob Hope; Rosanno Brazzi; Charles Addams; Paul Gauguin; Yehudi Menuhin

♇   William Butler Yeats; Robert Redford; Muhammad Ali; Bob Fosse

☊   Shirley Jones; Paul Jos. Goebbels; A. Schwarzenegger; Albert Schweitzer

A   Ivar Kreugar; Rex Harrison; Enrico Caruso; Benito Mussolini; Bob Newhart

MOON/MERCURY   ☽/☿

Basic Ideas:

These planets represent your ability to communicate your emotions effectively in ways that help others understand your feelings. You are encouraged to become more aware of the separation between your intellectual or rational reasoning and intuitive or emotional sides. Feelings which originate deep within you, such as fear of the dark, phobias, etc., how calculation and logic vie against your habitual responses and impulses, and the emotions which you add to your speech are also emphasized here. The feelings you show as you speak, your use of intuition as well as logic, reasoning that is swayed by emotional speech, and intelligence which has its roots in emotions also denoted. The speech of the common people, expressions which are popular or trendy, information on the rhythms or patterns of speech, and the history of your language is also mirrored by these planets.

In Your Personal Life:

Thesis   Thinking in rhythm or rhyme; variations in the way you express concern for how others think; any romantic thoughts you have; your concepts and ideas of motherhood; rapid mood swings.

Anti   Lines of thought which lead you into insular isolation; reasoning based on sentimental concepts; the use of intuition to help you achieve a theft or swindle; a restless imagination with fluctuating mood swings.

In Your Relationships:

Thesis   Accurately reading the emotional state of others; the varieties of ways you and your partner can communicate; communicating feelings and attitudes to another; ideas about parenting within the relationship.

Anti   Fickleness with the ideas others present; relations with another where reason overpowers emotion or vice-versa; verbal arguments based on emotional states within your relationship; communal speech patterns.

With Body or Mind:

Glandular conditions which begin with nervous dysfunctioning; deeply rooted fear or phobias; allergic reactions from glandular conditions; fluid in the lungs.

In Politics or Business:

Thesis   Enhanced communications between leaders and the common people; speeches geared to the masses; propaganda efforts; helps generate excitement for popular causes through rapport with the people or workers.

Anti   Restlessness among the common people or workers over business or commerce; compiling and analyzing the attitudes of the people; talk about the need for greater personal productivity; agricultural statistics.

MOON/MERCURY with Planets and Points

☉   Ability to sincerely relate to ordinary people through communications; determination to bring analysis to the emotional needs of self or others; remarkable writing about emotions you feel for ancestral homes.

♀   Gratitude for the care others place into making your communications more effective or well received; beauty in creating symbols which represent family, heritage, or home; appreciation for family gestures.

♂   Struggles to have your concepts of communications adopted by others; movement or agitation to add emphasis to your communications; debates involving family, historical, or provincial matters.

♃   Advice received on how to display emotional appeal in discussions; theory of language or communication; an abundance of verbiage about family or home life; judgments from others on the emotional quality in your speech.

♄   Restraints on restless emotions; pessimism creeps into imagination or thinking; observations of basic changes in rhythms or cycles; caution within discussions of family matters; humdrum talk on mothering.

♅   Unpredictable reactions to speeches given without emotional appeal; indifference to responses from polls; rumors of political changes; modernizing fads which are discussed in the news and/or media.

♆   The romantic and emotional appeal books or stories have for you; neglecting to communicate your emotions to others; subtle changes in the context of information as you experience variations in emotions.

♇   Communicating emotionally powerful feelings; the transition from analytical reasoning to emotional insight; investigative research; situations which allow you to feel or make powerful moving responses.

☊   Associations with others who teach you how to control and use your feelings when communicating; attracting people who have an emotional way of defining their needs; acquaintances who discuss nurturing.

A   Concentrating on conveying emotions when speaking or talking; perceptions of the emotional level of others through their speech, discourse patterns, or information; a need to identify through personal contact.

M   Self-development through studying or identifying with the feelings of others; learning and growing through verbalizing your emotional states; gaining expertise through analyzing the feelings of others.

MOON/MERCURY CONCEPTS

Cherishes Quickness
Versatile Imagination
Caring Comments
An Uncertain Memory
Intuitive Reasoning
Sensitive to Restlessness
Maternal Thoughts
Ineffective Pronunciation
Inconsistent Reasoning
A Talk with Mother
Romantic Conversation
Secretive Observations

Protects Information
Receptive to Questions
Feelings of Agility
Common Suppleness
Rapid Caring
Traditional Nervousness
Unsteady Guile
Emotional Reasoning
Foolish Thoughts
Instinctive Gestures
Sensitive Thinking
Maternal Reasoning

Safeguards News
Impulsive Thefts
Embraces Craftiness
Innate Versatility
Basic Gestures
Erratic Maneuvers
Moody Reasoning
Hides a Thief
Vague Rumors
Arbitrary Ideas
Common Language
Private Surveillance

Concentrates on Changes
Receptive to Analysis
Discreet Larceny
Acquires Language Accents
Uncertain Adjustments
Changing Information
Concentrates on Motherhood
Illogical Disclosure
Compassionate Reasoning
A Consoling Duality
Acquires Flexibility
Uncertain Analogies
Adopts Craftiness
Modest Trickery
Commonplace Discussions
Secretive Correspondence
Maternal Doubts
Sensitive to Meaning
Intermittent Confirmation
Imaginative Pronunciation
Concentrates on Intuition
Vacillating Restlessness
Emotional Observations
Muddled Thinking
Temporary Cleverness
Clever Behavior
Conceals Information
Data on Mood Swings
Compassionate Thoughts
Everyday Sensitivities
Imaginative Reasoning

Wavering Comprehension
Fears Versatility
Imaginative in Different Ways
Nervous before Audiences
On and Off Dexterity
Periodic Correspondence
Informed on Experiences
Receptive to Inquiry
A Traditional Language
Cares about Shrewdness
Receptive to Signals
Emotional Restlessness
On and Off Insight
Examines Motherhood
Occasional Information
Rhythmic Sounds
Sensitive Conversations
Fosters Reasoning
Conflicting Data
Remembers Comments
Feels Meaning
Intuits Observation
Maintains Agility
Unconvincing Dexterity
Common Information
Ungraceful Versatility
Uneasy Conversations
Common Reasoning
Unspoken Inquiry
Alters Expressions
Thinking Behavior

MOON/MERCURY With Itself

☽ Instinctively examining and thinking about your emotional states; uncertainty about your feelings and how to verbalize or examine them; family discussions on history, with facts, data, or information.

☿ Discussing your feelings for family members in a rational and logical way; going through some self-teaching and education to allow greater emotional expression and clarity thru your speeches or writing.

Significant Examples of People and Events Using Moon/Mercury

General: **STRONG:** Alexander Graham Bell; Jack Schwartz; James Earl Carter; Steve Wozniak; Moshe Dayan; Pierre Auguste Renoir; Rupert Murdoch; Albert Speer; Lance Reventlow; Billy Rose; Richard Byrd; Charles Steinmetz
WEAK: Jack Paar; Sir Laurence Olivier; John Paul I; Paramhansa Yogananda; Bob Dylan; Gustav Dore; Johnny Carson; Willie Mays
EVENTS: Challenger Explosion; Wright Brothers First Flight; Woman's Suffrage Amendment Passed; James Meredith Enrolls; (Lee's Surrender at Appomattox).

☉ Wright Brothers Flight; Charles Steinmetz; Liberace; Gus Grissom

☽, ☿ Ira Progoff; Alex. Graham Bell; Dr. Tom Dooley; Robert Redford

♀ Paul Gauguin; Friedrich Nietzsche; Mark Spitz; Harry Shoaf

♂ Rupert Murdoch; Bob Newhart; William Butler Yeats; Bob Hope; Jeddu Krishnamurti; Edna Ferber

♃ Gen Joseph Joffre; First Medicare Patient; Marlon Brando; Bjorn Borg

♄ Olivia Newton-John; Alan Alda; Ernest Hemingway; Yehudi Menuhin

♅ Rosanno Brazzi; Henry Winkler; Dave Garroway; Jean Houston; Moshe Dayan; Norman Mailer

♆ Henry Kissinger; Hermann Goering; Adolf Hitler; Paul Cezanne

♀ Van Cliburn; Sir William Crookes; Claude Debussy; Billy Rose; Albert Speer; Charles Addams; Edward R. Murrow

☊ Richard Strauss; Benito Mussolini; Robert DeNiro; Charles Gordon

A Ivar Kreugar; Glen Campbell; John McEnroe; Hugh Downs; Marc Edmund Jones; Richard Alpert

M Pierre Renoir; F. D. Roosevelt Wins His First Election; Enrico Caruso; Percy Bysshe Shelley; Ada Lovelace Byron

MOON/VENUS   ☽/♀

Basic Ideas:

This combination mirrors the pleasure and satisfaction you derive from being a sensitive and caring person, and heightens your need for a loving environment. The enjoyment you derive from your imagination, your fluctuating and changing attitudes about being appreciated and loved, and the emotional enjoyment you receive either from people close to you or your daily activities, are represented here. Your ability to arouse people's emotion through music or art, the pleasure you derive from caring for or mothering others, and the efforts you put into getting satisfaction and enjoyment from life's simple acts, also emerge here. These two primary female indicators symbolize all aspects of your feminine nature and expressions, regardless of your physical sex. Your uncertainty about giving or receiving affection, as well as your sensitivity to jealousy, may also appear here.

In Your Personal Life:

Thesis Deriving pleasure from helping and caring for others; brings perception about the needs and moods of other people, and pleasure when they notice and appreciate your sensitive and nurturing acts.

Anti Vacillating about how you should approach and care for others; increased insecurity in social situations; enjoyment from protecting others; sensitivity by others to the care and concern shown them.

In Your Relationships:

Thesis Adds to the care, love, and tenderness you like to give or show to your partners; more enjoyment from the kindness of your partners, like gifts, caresses, and love; seeing your partner as from a higher plane.

Anti Seeking partners who bring out a more sordid side to your emotions; increases your irritation and moodiness when around others; vacillation from your partner about their receptivity to your caring.

With Body or Mind:

Female organs; your sensitivity to taste, smell, touch, etc.; glandular balances; anorexia nervosa; ability to maintain body tone; condition of the kidneys.

In Politics or Business:

Thesis Manufacturing or agricultural productivity and how it affects the overall wealth and well-being of an enterprise or the people; an ability to produce food or manufactured products; opinions of artistic attempts.

Anti The attraction visitors find to the customs and costumes of a native people; the esteem accorded to minority groups and how a country helps to preserve their heritage, customs, life-style, and culture.

MOON/VENUS with Planets and Points

☉   The importance you place on considering others and their needs; the confidence with which you are able to show caring and nurturing to others; the respect you gain when you show care and concern.

☿   Your need to talk about how you want to care and nurture others; additional ideas and thinking on how you can best support people you care about; the care and concern you show for your neighborhood.

♂   A touch of impatience and abruptness to the quality of care shown to others; wanting to nurture, but also wanting to rush into other things; heightened sexual enjoyment with those for whom you sincerely care.

♃   Luck and prosperity through refined or artistic women; encouragement from women for your ideas; meeting women who demonstrate generosity; promises of help from women; caring religious women .

♄   Desire to support those who are less fortunate; inner barriers to showing your feelings of care or backing for others; lessened pleasure from trying to be supportive; fewer caring or supportive women.

♅   Care and concern shown in unusual ways; demonstrations of impersonal or detached affections; showing creativity in ways you care for others; unexpected or sudden reversals between friends or neighbors.

♆   Increased sensitivity to the artistic side of life, and your ability to read the artistic moods of others; a temporary quality to all that you do in life; misuse of good intentions and help of others; disappearing love.

♀   Intensified needs to show concern and to help those who are less fortunate; depleting your personal resources because you care for others; reciprocation against those who take from the disadvantaged; drastic turns of fate in love.

☊   Connections to people who are receptive to your form of charm and care; you find partners who are compatible with you and who appreciate your talents; a familiarity with politeness and courtesy; love with new friends.

A   Focusing more clearly on the needs of people you meet in your daily encounters; a personal flavor to the way you care for others; your interest in people in general, and their welfare and progress; being around women.

M   Appreciating people more as you mature; further understanding of how helping and working with people affects all and brings rewards to your life in ways you may not have expected or foreseen; recognition from women.

MOON/VENUS CONCEPTS

Senses Kindness
Fosters Envy (Coveting)
Caring and Considerate
Satisfying Compassion
Conceals Charm
Ineffective Appreciation
Alters and Embellishes
Enjoys Compassion
Isolated Compliments
Apprehensive Flattery
Imagines Enjoyment
Receptive to the Arts

Hidden Jealousies
Receptive to Flattery
Everyday Compliments
Everyday Enjoyments
On and Off Politeness
Polite Changes
Discovers Enjoyment
Maintains Tenderness
Fosters Infatuation
Unsteady Serenity
Loves Inconsistencies
Feels Composure

Basic Behavior
Inconsistent Peace
Illogical Loving
Vague Satisfaction
Senses Enjoyment
Fosters Gracefulness
Protective Charms
Intuitive Pleasure
Unspoken Intimacy
Rustic Politeness
On and Off Charm
Modest Smiles

Primitive Convenience
Sympathetic Style
Intuitive Attractiveness
Pleased with Impressions
Uncertain of Preferences
Changing Attraction
Sensitive to Flattery
Conflicting Preferences
A Popular Attractiveness
Considers Psychology
Beauty (Loveliness) Aids
Pleasurable Feelings
Impressions of Calmness
Average Beauty (Loveliness)
Fluctuating Pleasures
Sympathetic to Femininity
Fundamental Sensations
Sensitive to Values
Accumulates Admiration
Pleased with Family Heritage
Provincial Favoritism
Daily Temptations (Lures)
Emotional Respect
Gentle Compliments
Inconsistent Fascination
Uncomplicated Femininity
Cares about Attraction
Enjoys Changes
Appeases Sensitivities
Inbred with Cooperation
Common Politeness

Praise for Mothering
Cares about Vanity and Styles
Feelings for Compliments
Everyday Pleasures (Delights)
Nurtures Gratification
Attracted by Rhythms
Hesitant Appreciation
Irregular Gains
Rhythmic Sensuality
Adheres to Assurances
Uneasy Composure
Feelings of Kindness
Envies other Mothers
Satisfied with the Ordinary
Uncertain Composure
Emotional Pleasure (Delight)
Enjoys Motherhood
Fluctuating Considerations
Cherishes Compliments
Instincts for Beauty Lures
Unspoken Delights
Moody Tantrums
Sentimental Preferences
Temporary Enjoyment
Incomplete Satisfaction
Maternal Composure
The Attraction of your Family
Nurtures Intimacy
Composed through Changes
Emotional Softness
Infatuated with Patriotism

MOON/VENUS With Itself

☽ Experiences which help you develop kindness and consolation about another's circumstances; illogical emotions which cause you to alter the decorative scheme in your home; sensitivity to the energy of love.

♀ Enhanced charm and beauty which may have a strong appeal to all people; attraction to people with emotional appeal; beautifying self by using makeup; a mother who preserves her femininity, charm, and grace with age.

Significant Examples of People and Events Using Moon/Venus

General: **STRONG:** Pierre Auguste Renoir; Jimi Hendrix; Hugh Downs; Edouard Manet; Elvis Presley; Ada Lovelace Byron; Steve Wozniak; Edgar Degas; Dr. Tom Dooley; Friedrich Nietzsche; Rossano Brazzi; Olga Worrall
WEAK: Giacomo Puccini; Abraham Lincoln; Vida Blue; Edm. Halley; Scott Carpenter; Rupert Murdoch; A. Modigliani; Evel Knievel; Cheiro
EVENTS: Woman's Suffrage; S. Carolina Secedes; First Medicare Patient Accepted; USS Maine Explosion; Ramstein Airshow Disaster; (Mount St. Helens Explosion).

☉ Henry Mancini; Enrico Fermi; Olga Worrall; Dick Gregory

☽, ♀ Steve Wozniak; S. Peckinpah; Richard Alpert; Alexis Carrel; John F. Kennedy; Glen Campbell; Robert McNamara

☿ Stephen Foster; Tommy Smothers; Sam Sheppard; Jimi Hendrix; Hugh Downs; Albert Schweitzer

♂ Henri Matisse; Lindburgh Lands; Rollo May; Richard Strauss; Edouard Manet; Erwin Rommel

♃ Robert Redford; Vincent Van Gogh; Walt Whitman; Dr. Tom Dooley

♄ R. D. Laing; Sean Connery; Charles Steinmetz; USS Maine Explodes in Havana Harbor; Richard Chamberlain

♅ Sigmund Freud; Glen Campbell; John Denver; Jimi Hendrix; Ira Progoff; Steve Wozniak

♆ John Dillinger; Gen Joseph Joffre; Louis Pasteur; Edward R. Murrow

♇ Ira Progoff; Friedrich Nietzsche; Steven Spielberg

☊ Winston Churchill; USS Maine Expl.; Carl Sandburg; Hugh Downs

A Albert Camus; Billy Rose; Ellen Burstyn; Enrico Caruso; Adolf Hitler

M Cheiro; FDR Wins; F. Scott Fitzgerald; Pierre Renoir; Carl Sagan

MOON/MARS   ☽/♂

Basic Ideas:

These themes combine uncertainty and hesitation with aggression and haste, or alternately, bring impulsiveness and the need for activity to soothing and caring desires. Your ability to arouse the emotions of others through movement (as in sports), and stimulation of your intuitive side is shown here. These planets symbolize a need to behave in a more caring way, sensitivity to events which turns to anger, or activities where energy ebbs and flows. The aggravation of your emotional nature and struggles for protection start here. These planets symbolize unwanted noise or clamor, represent uneven progress, and convey courage and strength to protect those who require it. They denote intuition for performing aggressively as a competitor, along with uncertainty about how far you can push or force others to stretch. You may act indecisively when trying to motivate others.

In Your Personal Life:

Thesis   Devoting more of your energy and strength to nurturing and caring for others; enjoying movement and exercise as part of your daily activities; noticing the anger which others carry; nurturing a warrior's instinct.

Anti   Showing a latent anger at having to care for those unable to care for themselves; your desire to protect or care for others sometimes exceeds your patience; irritation against those who show any weakness.

In Your Relationships:

Thesis   Seeking a partner who is more aggressive and forceful about showing or handling their emotional nature; hastily brushing another's feelings aside without added concern; sexual rhythms and receptivity.

Anti   Arguments over emotional states or feelings; differences over how to handle the anger of another person or your inner anger at others; reading wrong intentions from others; intuitive feelings of anger.

With Body or Mind:

Glandular secretions which come too quickly; heat buildup in or on the body; energy which ebbs and flows; acid stomach conditions; stomach ulcers.

In Politics or Business:

Thesis   Leaders who show concern about the welfare of others, but who don't necessarily follow through with relief; using or developing metal or mineral resources; energy usage for agriculture or land development.

Anti   Farming activities which do not receive sufficient support from the leadership; a military hierarchy which fluctuates in its effectiveness; commercial uses of land resources for military or business activities.

MOON/MARS with Planets and Points

☉   Violent influences may lead to rioting; importance of placing energy into imaginative enterprises; determination to end conflicts about initiatives or intentions; intentions to control nagging uncertainties.

☿   Discussions concerning uncertainties about the use of force; thinking or writing along these lines; information received on emotional anger; reading and studying about control of impulsive emotional reactions.

♀   Softening the angry emotional feelings you sometimes feel; increased stimulation of your imaginative side for producing art or musical works; appreciating or consoling the emotional nature or ups and downs of others.

♃   An increasing need to foster care and protection on those you feel are disadvantaged; a temporary expansion of aggression toward the common people; courageous promises from sympathetic persons.

♄   Maternal panic felt and exhibited in isolation; the responsibility you undertake for correcting uncertainties about products or activities; obligations you incur in activities involving care or concern for others.

♅   Appearing dispassionate during angry emotional outbursts; detachment of self from suspected animosity or irritation; the emotional energy to practice astrology; irregular attempts at home repairs.

♆   Disguising the causes of common complaints; becoming adept at soothing the animosity family members exhibit; enlightening others who may panic or become angry in unfamiliar situations; anger at deceitful psychics.

♇   Eliminating the anger or irritation which accompanies complaints; intensified defiance during periods of uncertainty; troubles which arise when your imagination is over stimulated; wasting common sources of energy.

☊   You may encounter people who express emotional anger; you tend to shy away from emotionally assertive people; encountering kind words hastily given; meeting people who come with complaints.

A   Concentrating on the need for alleviating the anger or irritation received by those with complaints; brings attention to arguments about women; finding a personal way of acting or behaving which stimulates your imagination.

M   The adjustments and maturing you go through to learn emotional control; adjustment of an innate need for haste when judging the actions or activities of others; efforts to gain control of a nasty temper.

MOON/MARS CONCEPTS

Ineffective Bravery	Instinctive Anger	Supports Fighting
Courageous Protection	Intermittent Refusals	Senses Anger
Energetic Imagination	Imaginative Panic	Erratic Complaints
Sympathetic to Courage	Psychological Anxiety	Aware of Heroism
Uncertain about Forcing	Asserts Feelings	Ineffective Haste
Fosters Aggressiveness	Sensitive Defiance	Senses Unrest
General Animosity	Intuits Stimulation	Feels Defiance
Warns about Speed	Moody Arguments	Avoids Resentment
Erratic Heroism	Innate Sexuality	Sensitive to Anger
Stimulates Protection	Introduces Fluctuations	Arouses Submission
Illogical Impulsiveness	Nurtures Energy	Imagines Hatred
Everyday Anger	Defies Mother	Off and On Courage

Assists Commotion	Occasional Struggles
Defensive Activity	Fosters Animosity
Stimulates Changes	Supports Defiance
Uncertain Pressures	Clamors for Romance
Sympathizes with Complaints	Fosters Arguments
Common Aggressiveness	Complains about Protection
Imagines Annoyances	Instantaneous Fears
Receptive to Complaints	An Instinctive Protector
Conflicting Initiative	Sympathetic Anger
Argues over Changes	Traditional Courage
Family Aggressiveness	Emotional Panic
Temporary Belligerence	Changes with Initiative
Home Repairs	Participates in Tradition
Emotional Energy	Ferocious Inner Conflicts
Stimulates the Imagination	Well Versed in Argument
Receptive to Movement	Commonplace Panic
Temperamental Ferocity	Off and On Complaints
Nurtures Annoyances	Noisy Sympathy
Fears Animosity	Incomplete Indignation
Imagined Slights	Feels Initiative
Changes through Coercion	Ambiguous Complaints
Aids Disturbances	Nagging Uncertainties
Defies Uncertainties	Receptive to Stimulation
Conceals Defiance	Provisional Arguments
Psychological Friction	Argues with Women
Imagines Brutality	Embraces Initiative
Protects those who Complain	Inconstant Stimulation
Uncertain and Impatient	Struggles with Feelings
Active Mothering	Feels Turbulence
Emotional Courage	Maternal Rushing
Common Defiance	Sensitive to Hostility

MOON/MARS With Itself

☽   Stimulates your intuition for romances or battles where the hero saves a heroine (or, vice versa); sympathy and caring when mothering; basic feelings about caring for those who are engaged in competitions.

♂   Generating noise or activity, in general; an instinctive reaction to defend yourself when you need protection; greater persistence even when your emotional involvement fluctuates; quick responses at an emotional level.

Significant Examples of People and Events Using Moon/Mars

General: **STRONG:** Gianni Agnelli; John Fremont; Ritchie Valens; Drew Pearson; Liberace; Arturo Toscanini; Carl Sandburg; Paul Cezanne; Georges Seurat; Bob Newhart; Lawrence Welk; Lord Byron; Ralph Nader; Hermann Goering
WEAK: Jack Paar; Vittorio DeSica; Helen Reddy; Jean Houston; Ellen Burstyn; Olivia Newton-John; Alexis Carrel; Bertrand Russell
EVENTS: East Coast Power Blackout; South Carolina Secession; Kent State Shootings; Lee's Surrender at Appomattox; (Challenger Explosion).

☉   Gustav Dore; A-Bomb Expl.; John Fremont; Henri Matisse; Bjorn Borg

☽, ♂   Bob Newhart; FDR Wins His First Election; Arturo Toscanini; Jean Cocteau; Ritchie Valens

☿   Lord Byron; Wayne Gretzky; John Denver; Kent State Shootings occur; Francisco Franco; F. Scott Fitzgerald

♀   John Lennon; Earl Warren; Bolshevik Gov't; Robin Williams; D. Selznik

♃   Rudolph Bing; Jim Thorpe; Henri Matisse; Carl Sandburg; Enrico Caruso; Louis Pasteur

♄   Carl Sandburg; Jean Cocteau; Teilhard de Chardin; Gustav Dore

♅   Jean Paul Satre; Kareem Abdul-Jabbar; Jack Schwartz; Hank Williams

♆   Jim Thorpe; Henry Mancini; Ritchie Valens; Arthur Ford; JFK Shot

♇   Gregory Peck; Komar; Johnny Carson; Olga Worrall; Jean Cocteau

☊   Johnny Carson; Vincent Van Gogh; Robin Williams; Sam Peckinpah

A   First Medicare Patient accepted; Hermann Goering; Glen Campbell; Willie Brandt; Adolf Hitler

M   Gus Grissom; Carl Sandburg; Komar; Nikola Tesla; Steve Rosenbloom

MOON/JUPITER ☽/♃

Basic Ideas:

Uncertainty, doubt, and vacillation team with expansion, advice, and opinions to show your need to understand care and sympathy for others and the personal adjustments you make to become more aware of people. These planets denote uncertainty about your personal philosophy of living, and increased desire for protecting self and family in all possible physical, financial, or emotional ways. The Moon symbolizes defensiveness and Jupiter increases and expands that tendency, so needs for personal security are activated. This pair suggests expanding your emotional perceptions, brings on internal debates over your indecisiveness, and helps you discover enjoyment by being with your family. You may also be drawn to study ancient religious or philosophical teachings. These planets may highlight intuition, but you must examine your ideas for erroneous assumptions.

In Your Personal Life:

Thesis — Increased concerns about how to protect and care for your family or self; an idealistic imagination; expansion of future schemes; luck in all areas of family life and business; belief in support and protection.

Anti — Dreaming and planing about what the future holds; possible errors in judgment; a lessened ability to act decisively or to plan clearly; greatly expanded emotional reactions to situations or people encountered.

In Your Relationships:

Thesis — Finding that your partner is pleasant to be with and has much enthusiasm for life; enjoyment of sports and outdoor activities together, and having fun due to a similar sense of humor; a pleasant contact.

Anti — Difficulty in pinning your partner down about future life together; vacillation about making a commitment to this or any relationship; meeting someone who is very sensitive about their opinions.

With Body or Mind:

Fluid retention; increased sensitivity to drugs or allergens; raises fertility conditions; a tendency to overeat; an inefficient liver; vision problems highlighted.

In Politics or Business:

Thesis — Increased agricultural production; growth in the agricultural or commercial sectors; women who make important contributions to legal or religious practices; legal situations concerning farm or land policies.

Anti — Floods; a large number of natural disasters; women's opinion is taken far beyond its significance; the legal system acts as a barrier to agricultural or commercial production; ineffective clerics or lawyers.

MOON/JUPITER with Planets and Points

☉   Increased potential for strongly influencing others through your opinions or writings; added conviction and respect for your work; need for approval from others about the basic way you approach life.

☿   Need for further study and education; publishing opinions increases your influence among people; lots of verbiage in writing and speeches, especially when expounding; ventings of great emotional impact.

♀   Charm and politeness in an already caring and sensitive person; increased comfort and pleasure in a home setting; a preference for relaxation and good music; developing artistic talent; increasing value or monetary resources.

♂   An added element of rashness and temper; increased dimensions for your opinions; harshness to your religious or philosophical ideas; energy and activity for projects done together as or for the family.

♄   Thinking deeply about religious and philosophical ideas of people; added concern about the needs and security of your family ; luck in short spurts; lasting emotional misconceptions; a large older woman.

♅   Sudden and startling bursts of luck; disruptions of large family gatherings by unusual events; detachment from family to tend to your own interests; awakening a latent talent or interest in the astro-sciences.

♆   Need for drugs to escape reality and the pressures of life; confusion about your plans for your future; your plans for the family may be unclear; you may deceive or delude yourself about emotional states.

♇   Increased ability to think about family and social implications on a very large scale; purging and cleaning out unwanted items from home or work; rejection or denunciation of your ideas or opinions about life in general.

☊   Fortunate results from activities with friends and associates; enhanced attraction to the "right" people and influences; increased ability to judge people and their needs; selecting the right friends or associates.

A   Inconsistent ideas about the role that others play in helping you in life; old memories of experiences during travels which you find pleasant; an added need to study the ideas of others and how these can be further developed.

M   Family or family activities move into a more central focus as you grow and mature in life; recognition from others for your ideas and work in expanding knowledge in areas such as philosophy, foreign affairs, etc.

MOON/JUPITER CONCEPTS

Adheres to Promises	Emotional Misjudgments	Accumulates Wisdom
Conflicting Estimates	Inconsistent Outlooks	Protects Beliefs
Propagates Romances	Common Doctrines	Embraces Theory
Maternal Success	Indecisive Counsel	Common Luck
Expands Compassion	Ordinary Expectations	Intuits Opinion
Nurtures Principles	Sentimental Ideals	Emotional Promises
Fosters Increases	Ancestral Tales	General Ease
Imaginative Ideas	Everyday Principles	Nurtures Luck
Indecisive Tendencies	Regulates Opinion	Discovers Faith
Off and On Inclinations	Receptive to Expansion	Fluctuating Beliefs
Maternal Opinion	Ambivalent Expectations	Defends Errors
Sympathetic to Theory	Sensitive to Sincerity	Ineffective Law

Compassionate Understanding	Nourishes Assumptions
Uncertain Estimates	Inconsistent Expectations
Believes in Compassion	Uncomplicated Philosophy
Receptive to Expectations	Prefers Protection
Private Generosity	Sentimental Satisfaction
Sincerely Receptive	Sympathetic Understanding
Assumes Sensitivity	Provincial Triumphs
Understands Emotions	Instinctive Confidence
Uncertain about Outcome	Common Expansion
Promises Sympathy	Inclined to the Ordinary
Provides Satisfaction	Unspoken Assumptions
Maternal Possibility	A Generous Woman
Theoretical Changes	Satisfying Nurturing
Expects the Imaginative	Ordinary Generosity
Uncertain Expansion	Unconvincing Frankness
Family Philosophy	Fickle Optimism
Irregular Principles	Large Bodies of Water
Encourages Seclusion	Ineffective Doctrines
Satisfactory Changes	Alters Theory
Sensitive to Biases	Inclined to Mother
Sincere Compassion	Judges Sentiments
Incomplete Charity	Unspoken Optimism
Unfulfilled Promises	Fosters Spontaneity
Irregular Optimism	Sensitive to Errors
Unspoken Understanding	Inconstant Assumptions
Nurtures Overstatement	Alters Promises
Consoled by Faith	Inconstant Theory
Additional Indecisions	Emotional Beliefs
Understands Uncertainty	Goes along with Opinion
Temporary Emphasis	Changing Inclinations
Psychological Propositions	Transient Speculation

MOON/JUPITER With Itself

☽   Increased needs for contacts with people as well as for understanding their motivations and inspirations; a feeling for the psychological side of life, and a need to study and understand the role of people.

♃   Added needs to expound upon a personal philosophy and goals, and a need to have others hear your opinions about life, deity, morals, and ethics; additional needs for educational recognition and extra scholarly degrees.

Significant Examples of People and Events Using Moon/Jupiter

General: **STRONG:** Helen Reddy; Johnny Carson; William K. Douglas; Adolf Hitler; Merv Griffin; Hugh Downs; Cheiro; Sam Peckinpah; Vincent Van Gogh; Steve Wozniak; Johann Von Goethe; John Paul I; H. G. Wells
WEAK: Jack Schwartz; Richard Chamberlain; Yehudi Menuhin; Tom Smothers; Nikola Tesla; Manly Palmer Hall; R. DeNiro; Arturo Toscanini
EVENTS: John F. Kennedy Shot; First A-Bomb Explosion; Pearl Harbor Attack; F. D. Roosevelt Wins First Election; (Woman's Suffrage Amendment Passed).

☉   Elton John; F. Scott Fitzgerald; First Medicare Patient; Bob Newhart

☽, ♃   Merv Griffin; Art Linkletter; Neil Diamond; Kareem Abdul-Jabbar

☿   Steve Wozniak; John Lennon; Auguste Rodin; Francisco Franco

♀   Jacques Cousteau; Dr. Tom Dooley; Lawrence Welk; Charles Addams

♂   John Denver; William K. Douglas; Stephen Foster; Jerry Reed

♄   Mario Andretti; Carl Sandburg; Mark Spitz; Stephen Foster; Art Linkletter; Guglielmo Marconi

♅   John Denver; Willie Mays; Alan Leo; Henry Kissinger; Helen Reddy

♆   George Patton; First A-Bomb Explosion; A. Modigliani; Harry Belafonte

♇   Johnny Carson; John Paul I; Sandy Koufax; Steve Allen; Henry Winkler

☊   Evel Knievel; Grant Lewi; Harry Shoaf; Henry Kissinger; Ferdinand Foch; Robert Redford; Paul Gauguin

A   John F. Kennedy; Arthur Godfrey; Sigmund Freud; Audrey Hepburn

M   Elton John; Steve Rosenbloom; Tom Jones; Bob Fosse; Transcontinental Railroad completed; Steve Wozniak

MOON/SATURN ☽/♄

Basic Ideas:

The feelings and attitudes you have about your parents, and how they influenced your potential and leanings. Your ability to acquire humility and simplicity, the restraint you show during appearances before the public, and psychological changes which help you use your time resources more effectively, all start here. These planets also concern the restrictions you place on showing your emotions, disappointments you encounter with various forms of protection (personal or material), and your attitudes toward self-discipline. The caution with which you express your emotional feelings, your willingness to follow or use the guidance your parents gave you, the silence you show when your vulnerabilities are exposed, and uncertainties you feel when you meet any restrictions or impediments to making progress in life, are also a basic part of the meaning of these bodies.

In Your Personal Life:

Thesis   The role your parents played in forming your personal habits and attitudes; the fears and concerns you experience when you encounter audiences or the public; silence which you use to go inward.

Anti   Inhibitions on being able to express the way that you feel about self or others; blocks about the role your parents had; defensive feelings about being able to discipline yourself for work you have promised to do.

In Your Relationships:

Thesis   Working with your partner as an effective team in raising children or in guiding those who are less mature; the inner strength you develop about being a parent or your need to act in a parental role.

Anti   A poor relationship model from your parents; the need to find dejection or despair when relating to others; off and on feelings about those who express care and concern to you; unneeded restrictions on relating.

With Body or Mind:

Hypo-acidity conditions in the stomach; fluids collecting in joints; water on the knee; fertility problems; calcium stones in organs; congestion.

In Politics or Business:

Thesis   An exercise of authority by the common people; institutions formed for overseeing and coordinating commerce, agriculture, or business conditions; production efficiency statistics; established agriculture.

Anti   The inability of an enterprise to grasp the intentions of the people and their needs; a lack of output or production from manufacturing or agricultural sectors of the economy; practical vs. theoretical economics.

MOON/SATURN with Planets and Points

☉   How you let your concern for others dominate your life; elaborate inner rituals to calm your emotions; how you allow small disappointments or changes affect you psychologically; effective parenting.

☿   Promoting ideas on how to offer better financial or material protection to your family; education to help you learn practical business matters or routines; studies on how to uncomplicate your emotional life.

♀   Pleasant feelings about parenting learned from various role models in your life; satisfaction from attuning to inner feelings of caring, parenting, or concern; internal musical rhythms or beats you create or use.

♂   The energy and enthusiasm with which you approach and perform your parenting roles; impulses to rush into activities geared to protect your home or family; any initiative taken to break the bonds of a restrictive home life.

♃   Expanded feelings of care and concern about your family or home matters; increased personal frustration about how family life restricts your progress at work (or vice versa); the sincerity with which you accept parenting roles.

♅   Abrupt feelings of gloom or dismay about your family obligations; unusual memories of your parents; indifference to those who need nurturing; odd or unusual ways of showing your care or concern.

♆   Envisioning yourself as an ideal parent role model; a weakened ability to show the type of inner discipline needed to pull yourself through life's daily frustrations; escape to drugs or alcohol due to this weakness.

♇   Feelings of frustration due to delays and barriers which you encounter on your road to progress; the elimination of support for family or others; strong urges and desires to control or channel your emotions.

☊   Increased chances of meeting others who need your support; separation from people requesting help; meeting people who are able to return to you the help you have given others; moody people who enter into your life.

A   Observing on how you affect others through your emotions; memories of how you overcome despair and obstacles through discipline; a personal style which has a strong need for emotional control; noticing the role of a parent.

M   Personal determination to handle your emotional side in a more mature manner; a greater understanding of motives as you mature; meeting greater needs for personal security as you mature; recognition from parents.

MOON/SATURN CONCEPTS

Feelings of Frustration	Moderate Hesitations	Instinctive Loyalty
Pessimism about Parenting	Cautious Protection	Common Simplicity
Hidden Modesty	Regulates Tyranny	Everyday Objections
Maternal Failures	Delayed Defensiveness	A Modest Creation
Instincts for Organization	On and Off Promises	Provincial Reserve
Elementary Imagination	Temporary Discipline	Aware of Objections
Drawn to Anxiety	Incomplete Dedication	Restrains Romances
Protective Custody	Nurtures Objections	Maintains Restraint
Frustrated by Feelings	Limitations on Parenting	General Pessimism
Changes Cautiously	Receptive to Limitations	Predicts Delays
Frustrating Changes	Everyday Reserve	Joyless Deliberation
Nurtures Interruptions	Maternal Precaution	Irregular Caution

Uncertainty Over Restrictions	Emotional Stability
Everyday Disappointments	Compassionate Restraint
Uncertain during Silences	Concealed Commitment
Remembers Formality	Long Term Nurturing
Uncertain Over Rigidity	Compassion in Reserve
Vacillates before Interruptions	Emotions in Reserve
Blocks Assistance	A Disciplined Mother
Avoids Annoyances	Uneven Frustrations
Restrains Protection	Compassionate Simplicity
An Abnormal Let Down	Depressing Restrictions
Imaginative Restrictions	Warns of Obligations
A Nurturing Father	Frustrating Protection
Receptive to Commitment	Conditional Delays
Sensitive about Restrictions	Receptive to Silence
Imagines Disappointments	Fosters Pessimism
Changes with Restrictions	A Moderate Intuition
Fosters Discipline	Experiences Reserve
Disillusioned with Compassion	Cautious Uncertainty
Uncomplicates Feelings	Emotional Restraint
Incomplete Conclusions	Cold Support
Lasting Emotions	Everyday Unyielding
Sensitive to Objections	Imagines Frustrations
Erratic Discipline	Lasting Protection
Receptive to Postponements	Acquires Pessimism
Father and Mother	Parental Silence
Temporary Frustrations	Cherishes Caution
A Family Commitment	Fosters Simplicity
Common Discipline	Stifles Feelings
Patient Consoling	Maternal Rigidity
Shortened Sensitivities	A Restrictive Home Life
Enduring Compassion	Postpones Parenting

MOON/SATURN With Itself

☽   Added desires for a more active parenting role or family life; maintaining a lower emotional involvement during business activities; inner conflicts about the need for protecting family; fluctuating attitudes about parenting.

♄   Sternness shown toward family members; needs to apply discipline or restrictions when managing others; envisioning a more successful business approach for commercial enterprises through planning.

Significant Examples of People and Events Using Moon/Saturn

General: **STRONG:** Harry Shoaf; William K. Douglas; Amadeo Modigliani; John Dillinger; Ada Lovelace Byron; Marc Edmund Jones; Sean Connery; Charles Kettering; Bertrand Russell; Rossano Brazzi; Dave Garroway
WEAK: Auguste Rodin; Art Linkletter; Lance Reventlow; Charles Addams; R. D. Laing; Burt Reynolds; John Glenn; Drew Pearson
EVENTS: Chernobyl Nuclear Disaster; Bolsheviks Take Power; Wright Brothers First Flight; South Carolina Secession; (George Washington's Inauguration).

☉   Harry Shoaf; Rollo May; Carl Sandburg; Gregory Peck; Edouard Manet; Jean Paul Satre; Herman Melville

☽, ♄   Thomas H. Huxley; Marc Edmund Jones; Evel Knievel; Olga Worrall

☿   Jeddu Krishnamurti; Wright Bros. Flight; Ernest Pyle; Gianni Agnelli

♀   Franklin Roosevelt; Guglielmo Marconi; Johnny Carson; Sydney Omarr

♂   Sir Alexander Fleming; Wayne Gretzky; Anne Murray; Bertrand Russell; Ralph Nader; Jean Cocteau

♃   Tommy Smothers; Arturo Toscanini; Challenger Disaster; Edmund Halley; Sally Ride; Sir William Crookes

♅   Mick Jagger; Charles E. O. Carter; Lindburgh Lands; Jack Nicklaus; Cheiro; Paul Cezanne; Marc Edmund Jones

♆   Charles Kettering; Harry Shoaf; John McEnroe; Billy Rose; Arthur Rimbaud; Elton John; Manly Palmer Hall

♇   Laurence Olivier; Vittorio DeSica; Apollo 11 Moon Landing; Edna Ferber; R. D. Laing; Robin Williams

☊   Peter Max; Ernest Hemingway; Tom Jones; Apollo 11 Moon Landing

A   Claude Debussy; J. Von Ribbentrop; Jim Thorpe; Erwin Rommel

M   Benjamin Disraeli; Stonewall Jackson; Albert Schweitzer; Jack Paar

MOON/URANUS ☽/♅

Basic Ideas:

The melding of these two patterns helps to nurture an inner rebelliousness against maternal or traditional family roles. It can denote emotional detachment and an erratic restlessness. These motifs will both agitate your emotions and your sensitive or nurturing side, yet they also bring insight and perception with an intuitive flair. These planets can represent an innovative wizard without emotional stability, but who has an inventive faculty which comes from working with uncommon ideas or materials. Here is the person whose innovative insights are so far removed from the center of mankind that the person may be truly labeled 'an eccentric genius'. There is an impersonal sensitivity to tradition, as well as personal insights or uncertainties which breed nonconformity. Shown here is an unusual person whose insights into family needs can change the concept of life .

In Your Personal Life:

Thesis   You have a restlessness about family roles; inner pulls to balance nurturing and freedom needs; you gather impressions in an unusual way but can create objects appreciated by all; vulnerability vs. detachment.

Anti   You are a brooding person who wrecks emotional havoc, especially on the lives of people close to you; you are a person whose emotional war within affects the lives of others too; you easily disrupt family life.

In Your Relationships:

Thesis   You are attracted to people who are emotionally sensitive but erratic; your relationships are based upon giving trust and caring to another person regardless of how well they can control their emotional life.

Anti   You find it difficult to understand how your partner cannot control all parts of life; you only offer conditional nurturing or care based upon others curbing their emotions; you are intolerable of spontaneity.

With Body or Mind:

Stomach spasms; extremes of eyesight (good or bad); changes in the body's acid/ alkali balance; disruptions in female organs or ovaries; the stress of family life.

In Politics or Business:

Thesis   An enterprise with great insight into the needs of its people, yet one which has a very unusual way for showing care and appreciation toward its population; unconventional rulers with an emotional flair.

Anti   Leaders who rule at whim, with little sense of how their enterprise is seen by the rest of the world; an emotionally immature person placed in an important and visible leadership role.

MOON/URANUS with Planets and Points

☉   Family and family concerns come first in your life despite an inability to feel comfortable or satisfied with your family role; sharp innovative insight; mechanical adeptness; effective insight into family dynamics.

☿   Education to gain electrical, mechanical, or astrological skills; sharp ability to express innovative insights to others in a convincing manner; flexibility in achieving solutions; dexterity with tools and implements.

♀   A softness and lovingness in your ideas about how to act within family situations or roles; you recognize internal but old rhythms and melodies which you express in unusual ways or in more modern fashions.

♂   Actively creating labor saving objects for the household; added efforts put into unconventional approaches to solving ordinary problems; agitation for alterations and improvements in cars, motors, etc.; mechanical skills.

♃   Becoming more aware of the political skills required to market your ideas; luck and skill when promoting your ideas; misjudging the utility or worth of ideas you contribute ; success through inventive efforts.

♄   Acquiring a discipline to look upon failure of projects or ideas as a further stepping stone toward your goals; frustration at not being able to produce simple innovations; control over fluctuating emotions.

♆   Creativity and insight added to a budding but unconventional genius; the use of questionable methods to produce results; others steal your ideas or products; deceitful people who drain you of ideas or time.

♇   Tremendous changes wrought in society through your insights; faulty parts analyzed and repaired; improved methods for processing human or common trash or waste; extracting parts of matter as a source for invention.

☊   The ability to attract the correct people to listen to your ideas or insights; meeting and working with others who have similar genius-like inclinations; creativity and inventiveness as a primary purpose in your life.

A   Focusing on solving the problems to which you apply yourself; impressions from others on their appraisal of your family role; seeking attention from those you meet; affecting your role within family groups or orientations.

M   Growth of self as a person and recognition for creating things for others; the stature you gain from your inventiveness and ingenuity; the expertise and notoriety you are able to acquire through application of your practical skills.

MOON/URANUS CONCEPTS

Temporary Peculiarities	Romantic Surprises	Feels Adversity
Abrupt Accumulations	An Aloof Collector	Senses Discontent
Feminine Progress	Emotional Variation	Protects the Curious
Receptive to Uniqueness	Fickle Contrariness	Assists Novelty
Alters Individuality	Emotional Surprises	Feels Disruption
Receptive to Disruption	Illogical Disorder	Intuitive Insight
Novel Rhythms	Fosters Innovation	Subdued Deviation
Off and On Discontent	Intuits Indifference	Innovative Women
Discreet Regulation	Everyday Dissatisfaction	Senses Novelty
Inconsistent Differences	Maintains Peculiarities	Creates Emotions
Maternal Innovation	Rhythmic Variations	Subtle Apathy
Deviates from Habits	Fosters Discontent	Fickle Insight

Unconventional Compassion	Modest Experimentation
Common Peculiarity	Dissatisfied with Caring
Secluded Progress	Compassionate Insight
Maternal Dissatisfaction	Defends Differences
A Sentimental Agitator	Moody Discontent
Modern Sentiments	Psychological Indifference
Family Disruptions	Drawn to Contrariness
Uncertain about Regulation	Disregards Changes
Fosters Restlessness	Habitual Contrariness
Cares about Independence	An Unruly Parent
Provincial Oddities	Changes and Revisions
Imagines Contrariness	Insane Disorganization
An Astrological Imagination	Emotional Indifference
Off and On Deviations	Everyday Adjustments
Imaginative Regulation	Psychic Insight
Receptive to Astrology	Instinctive Individualism
Imaginative Revisions	A Surprising Collection
Common Adjustments	Novel Prophecies
Moody and Contrary	Lunar Astrology
Ineffective Opposition	Insular Eccentricity
Symbolic Regulation	Responds to Disruptions
Uncertain Peculiarities	Feels Indifference
Protects Indifference	Original Rhythms
Arbitrary Impudence	Peculiar Sensitivities
Illogical Regulation	Everyday Idiosyncrasies
Discovers Sentiment	Inconsistent Self-Reliance
Isolated Dissatisfaction	Novel Protection
Deviates from Common Styles	Discreet Surprises
Imaginative Innovation	Sensitive to Upsets
A Peculiar Imagination	Varieties of Parenting
Uncertainty and Variety	Dubious Revisions

MOON/URANUS With Itself

☽ A need for careful and cautious approaches to family problems which are not easy to solve or discuss; feeling ineffective about solving the problems you face in day-to-day life; feelings of wanting to isolate self.

♅ Seeing that an extreme approach to solving sticky everyday problems may be the only practical solution; a restlessness about the current state of affairs involving your family, home, or personal life; unexpected family roles.

Significant Examples of People and Events Using Moon/Uranus

General: **STRONG:** Bob Newhart; Richard Byrd; R. D. Laing; Ralph Nader; John Fremont; Sir Alexander Fleming ; Sydney Omarr; Billy Rose; Israel Regardie; Franklin Roosevelt; Ivar Kreugar; Willie Mays; Paul Joseph Goebbels
WEAK: Arnold Schwarzenegger; Joachim Von Ribbentrop; Stephen King; Georges Seurat; Vida Blue; Steve Wozniak; Sandy Koufax
EVENTS: First A-Bomb Explosion; Watergate Burglary; Chernobyl Nuclear Explosion; Kent State Shootings; (Woman's Suffrage Passed).

☉ Kareem Abdul-Jabbar; John Fremont; Jack Nicklaus; Liberace; Edouard Manet; Thomas H. Huxley

☽, ♅ Bob Newhart; Van Cliburn; Ida Rolf; Maurice Ravel; Ivar Kreugar

☿ Ralph Nader; John Denver; Elton John; John Glenn; Willie Brandt

♀ Vittorio DeSica; Robin Williams; Mark Spitz; John Glenn; Elvis Presley

♂ Harry Belafonte; Gus Grissom; Glen Campbell; Jean Cocteau; Stonewall Jackson; Franklin Roosevelt

♃ Jean Houston; Jim Thorpe; William Butler Yeats; Ervin Nyiregyhazi

♄ Sydney Omarr; Chernobyl Nuclear Disaster; Edgar Degas; Mary Martin

♆ Willie Mays; Jonathan Winters; Yehudi Menuhin; Rudolph Bing

♀ Olga Worrall; Vittorio DeSica; Muhammad Ali; Moshe Dayan; Benjamin Disraeli; Jean Houston; Ralph Nader

☊ Paul Gauguin; Ivar Kreugar; Jack Schwartz; Charles Gordon; Israel Regardie; Carl Sandburg

A Pearl Harbor Attack; Elton John; Carl Sagan; Muhammad Ali; Kareem Abdul-Jabbar; Earl Warren

M RMS Titanic Hits Iceberg; Gustav Dore; Arthur Rimbaud; Ulysses S. Grant; Edmund Halley

MOON/NEPTUNE   ☽/Ψ

Basic Ideas:

Sentiment and impression combine with dreaminess and illusion in a blending of similar motifs, as many qualities presently attributed to Neptune were assigned to the Moon in more ancient times. These planets symbolize carelessness and periods of neglect in your protection and safekeeping of the people, animals, or possessions entrusted to you. You see yourself acting with deeply felt sentiment about the things you love, but others see your inner yearnings as irregular and uncertain creations from a confused and dreamy person. This combination implies an increase in the sensitivity of your intuition, but you may lose your idea of reality in the dreams and fantasies you constantly build. Your imagination is heightened, and your ability to dream and see the future is enhanced. You may become a more sensitive person and find new ways of using mystical thinking to answer questions.

In Your Personal Life:

Thesis   You have good insight into the emotions behind people's sentiments, but find it difficult to separate your feelings from theirs; you have great feelings to nurture and care for others, and are inspired by their love.

Anti   You find it difficult to separate your dreams from the events of the real world; weakened faith in others as you see their shortcomings; receptivity to the potentials of situations as opposed to the reality of people.

In Your Relationships:

Thesis   You have the highest of internal and ideal love for your partner; your ability to create tender feelings for another is helped with this pairing; you have strong needs to show protection and care

Anti   You may not easily verify if your partner shares your feelings; you know that your love compensates for any neglect of your partner, but your partner has other views about how to share.

With Body or Mind:

Ulcers; nervous stomach; reactions thru a sensitivity to drugs; sensitivity to pollen, dust, etc.; tiredness due to emotional strain; female problems.

In Politics or Business:

Thesis   Production of chemicals, oil, food, or manufactured goods; dreams about agricultural produce, production, or policy; a leadership which heeds the opinions and emotional climate of its constituents.

Anti   Delusion about the popular support for current policies; an inability to utilize information about the moods of the people when setting the courses of action; scandals involving production or other quotas.

MOON/NEPTUNE with Planets and Points

☉ Strengthened inner devotion; authority to nurturing instincts; original and creative ways of showing how you care for others; the commitment you bring to mothering; impressive insights into people or events.

☿ Articulating dreams received about future or past themes of living; a study of the occult or magic; ingenuity in being able to express or relate inner feelings about people or things you encounter or experience.

♀ Femininity and charm added to your devotion and ideal feelings of others; enjoyment when sharing feelings of mystical contact; heightened needs to show love to others, or to share love with another.

♂ Increased impetus to rely on feelings and not on observations; feelings of anger and rancor from others; the energy and activity put into your dreams and fantasies; protests against physical activity or exertion.

♃ Enhanced ability to read people's motives and put these into a political context; enlarged need to dream and fantasize; increased needs for stimulants or drugs to enable functioning in the physical world.

♄ Caution and reserve when you start to neglect the things you care for; grounding your fantasies about what life should be; prolonging your indecisiveness, and thus increasing your disappointments.

♅ Working with modern equipment as part of your dreams for the future; an enhanced focus on developing new ideas about how the world should grow; an interest in astrology as a way to learn about others and how they differ.

♀ Increased needs for revenge against those who injure or hurt you in any way; added ferment and seething to emotions which you create within your dreams for escape from reality; a need to escape from confining ways.

☊ Kinship you feel with others who share your dreams and support your ideas about the future; meeting others who share your dreams; support from groups or associations for your visions and fantasies.

A Enhanced abilities to focus on people and read their states of mind or feelings as opposed to their stated intentions; increased needs to share your visions and fantasies about life and the world with others.

M The notoriety you gain about your ability to visualize and explain future options to others; personal guarantees you give and then cannot fulfill because you dream away your ability to fulfill your commitments.

MOON/NEPTUNE CONCEPTS

Incomplete Miracles
A Sensitive Imagination
Receptive to Ambiguity
Undecided about Ideals
Maternal Atonement
Uplifted Feelings
Neglects Intuition
Receptive to Disguises
Hesitates over Frivolity
Instinct for Mystery
Submits to Parenting
Avoids Changes

Temporary Shabbiness
Defends Vagueness
Touchy about Omission
Escapes through Moodiness
Sentimental Musings
Intuits Neglect
Imagines Counterfeits
Unhappy with Misuse
Fosters Daydreams
Emotional Inspiration
Imperfect Crabbiness
A Mother's Release

Common Disguises
Everyday Confusion
Defends Fraud
Irregular Losses
Illusive Consolation
Dubious Escape
Subtle Emotions
Vague Perplexities
A Mystical Home
Remembers Amends
Sensitive Release
Protects an Illusion

Imagines Sensitivities
Conflicting Inspirations
Uncertain Misunderstandings
Inconsistent Foolishness
Psychological Escape
Alters Disguises
Accumulates Alcohol or Drugs
Maternal Shoddiness
Sentimental Sanctity
Jittery Compliance
Uncertain Pretenses
Romantic Fantasies
Imperfect Illusion
Fabled Compassion
Illogical Musings
A Temporary Submission
Mystical Feelings
Weakens Sensitivities
Off and On Neglect
Imaginative Theatrics
Idealized Mothering
A Feeling for Disguises
Uncertainty and Confusion
Fosters Imperfections
Remembers Nonsense
Commonplace Dilapidation
A Basic Omission
Subtle Alterations
Erratic Holiness
Instincts for Illusion
Confused Crowds

Confusion amidst Changes
Holds on to Subservience
Illusion about Motherhood
Careless Hesitations
Provincial Costumes
A Common Omission
A Basic Lack of Practicality
Emotional Fantasies
Touchy about Dependence
Warns about Oversight
Protects Inefficiency
Instinctive Inadequacy
Maternal Inspiration
A Hidden Mystery
Touchy about a Weakness
A Secluded Sanctuary
Conceals Uncertainty
An Idealized Romance
A Confused Parent
Wavers over Faithfulness
Irregular Omission
Escapes through Mothering
Mysterious Protection
Subtle Sensitivities
Irregular Weakness
Feels Confined
The People's Imagination
Neglects Protection
Receptive to Make Believe
Drawn to Laxity
Fosters Illusions

MOON/NEPTUNE With Itself

☽   An increased ability to relate to the feelings of others in a mystical and otherworldly way; retreating from pressures to a more secluded and tranquil location; romantic feelings about the nature of caring.

♆   Escaping to places where there is water; feelings that your life has parts which are unreal or vague; deception about the intentions or feelings of others; a need for a study of or exposure to occult or mystical ideas.

Significant Examples of People and Events Using Moon/Neptune

General: **STRONG:** Dr. Sam Sheppard; Albert Camus; Paul Cezanne; Giacomo Puccini; Rollo May; O. J. Simpson; Jack Paar; Edmund Halley; Dustin Hoffman; Jerry Rubin; Joseph Joffre; Kareem Abdul-Jabbar
WEAK: Sandy Koufax; Nikola Tesla; Georges Seurat; Ellen Burstyn; Ritchie Valens; Edna Ferber; Bob Dylan; Burl Ives
EVENTS: Alaskan Earthquake; Challenger Explosion; First A-Bomb Explosion; James Meredith Enrolled; (Ramstein Airshow Disaster).

☉   Al Unser; Jerry Reed; Rollo May; J. Von Ribbentrop; Charles Addams

☽, ♆   Dustin Hoffman; R. D. Laing; Bob Fosse; John Denver; Mark Spitz

☿   First Medicare Patient Accepted; Carl Sagan; Benjamin Disraeli; Franklin Roosevelt; Ada Lovelace Byron

♀   Henri Toulouse-Lautrec; First A-Bomb Explosion; Mario Andretti

♂   Charles Steinmetz; Burl Ives; Edgar Degas; Sydney Omarr; Ervin Nyiregyhazi; Sam Sheppard

♃   Steve Wozniak; Jerry Rubin; Harry Shoaf; Lindburgh Lands in Paris; Lance Reventlow; Jack Nicklaus

♄   Francisco Franco; Robin Williams; Auguste Rodin; Hank Williams

♅   Jack Paar; Richard Byrd; Herman Melville; Melvin Belli; Sir Laurence Olivier; Mick Jagger; Johann Von Goethe

♇   Steve Allen; Edouard Manet; Challenger Explosion; Robert DeNiro

☊   Jeddu Krishnamurti; Erwin Rommel; Merv Griffin; John Dillinger

A   Stephen Sondheim; Edmund Halley; Dustin Hoffman; Sam Sheppard

M   Scott Carpenter; Carl Sagan; Jacques Cousteau; Drew Pearson; Walt Whitman; Arthur Godfrey

MOON/PLUTO   ☽/♀

Basic Ideas:

Intense transitions or reversals combine with cool, ordinary, maternal and instinctive qualities to bring quiet revolutions to life. The dominant role of an opinionated woman (perhaps your mother) affects your life. Your imagination wanders from morbid thoughts to romantic extremes. You find a sensitivity to extremes of change. You may sterilize or use extreme cleanliness to eliminate impurities. Your attitudes or sentiments toward the role of punishment fluctuates. You desire to accumulate power or control over all ordinary activities of life, especially those governed by your inner instincts. Your intuition may help you easily find hidden things, bring sympathy for those who monopolize or centralize powers, spur your attempts to avoid or clean out elements of corruption, and bring you compassion for the victims of immoral practices or criminal elements.

In Your Personal Life:

Thesis   Developing feelings for people who can not remove themselves from oppressive forces or situations; a preoccupation with the cleanliness of your home, yard, or work areas; a powerful female figure guides you.

Anti   An obsession with the hoarding of trash or debris; a touchiness about how others evaluate your sliding or degradation in certain areas of life; conflicting feelings about the use of violence as a means of control.

In Your Relationships:

Thesis   A depth of feeling and a need for romance prompt relationships; added maternal needs for compassion from others; a preference for strong or passionate romances; wanting to hold on too long to your partner.

Anti   Elements of clinging or vacillation about breaking up destructive relationships; uncertainty about relations with women in general in your life; a sterility or barrenness when trying to express your sentiments.

With Body or Mind:

Activities of the endocrine and pituitary glands; pressures in body cavities caused by toxemia or pus; cancer indications; large fluid accumulations.

In Politics or Business:

Thesis   The people's opinion about subjects like crime, war, or internal secrecy; the role of women in controlling self-destructive impulses; popular promises concerning an end to war, waste, etc. in appeals to the people.

Anti   Encourages violence or crime; people become doubtful about how to exert the proper controls on criminal or terrorist elements; obsessions which bring a misuse of the resources available for country or business.

MOON/PLUTO with Planets and Points

☉   Corrupting elements influence everyday situations; determination to end the obsessions your feelings or sentiment arouse within you; changing attitudes about the people you meet; emotional uplifting.

☿   Discussing the role of feelings and concern for others; thinking about the role of uncertainty; swings of public mood which bring shifts of power or control; bringing your unconscious insights into reality.

♀   Taking delight in the rituals of psychological purification; gaining enjoyment in the practices of punishment; a fascination with the elimination of maternal instincts in your life; a new delight in deep emotional situations.

♂   Uses force to achieve changes in corrupt practices; active in assuring that promised protection is delivered; participates in any clamor as a part of emotional intensity; deep irritation from delays in any form.

♃   Success when eliminating maternal or emotional dependencies; generous protection offered to criminal elements; success in cleaning up liquid pollutants; wise and powerful female authority figures.

♄   Avoiding the need to look at what parts of your inner self must change; realism about how to handle gloomy or morbid thoughts; secret grief about disciplining others; parents who have a profound effect.

♅   Becoming agitated or emotionally upset over vacillation; strange ways of eliminating unwanted items from the household; unique ways of hiding or eliminating suspicions; problems with electrical water-carrying systems.

♆   Confusion over the role of death or sex; using the occult to explain the mystical; lack of clairity from inner feelings; seeks miracles as a rescue from immediate problems; heightened mystical experiences.

☊   Finding others who share ideas for eliminating toxins from the body; rituals which serve to rid the body of impurities; sexually drawn to women of power or wealth; unexpected help from women who hold real power.

A   A strong personal focus on the need to eliminate habits or moods that interfere with life; contrasts ideals within against the reality of the world; many private moods and feelings; keeps thinking of another's problems.

M   Gaining positive psychological growth by analyzing and evaluating mood variations; fulfilling your personal inner aims through conquering emotionally based tendencies; successful handling of the moods of others.

MOON/PLUTO CONCEPTS

Receptive to Corruption
Uncertain using Force
Intense Rhythms
Hesitates over Perversion
Concentrates on Collecting
Emotional Suspicion
Intensely Compassionate
Formidable Inconsistencies
Deep Emotions Everywhere
Fosters Transitions
Commonplace Criminals
Drains the Imagination

Incomplete Vengeance
Unpredictable Intensity
Imagined Severity
Uncertain Ownership
Supplies Destruction
Vague Reproof
Imaginative Endings
Temporary Cessation
Ordinary Immorality
Condemns Foreboding
Uncertain about Power
Assists in Punishment

Intuits Dismissals
Fears Punishment
Common Reductions
Powerful Women
Feels Constraints
Holds Hatred
Feels Ruthlessness
Basic Obsessions
An Infrequent Fanatic
Protects Power
Fosters Suspicion
Wants Pure Supplies

Sensitive to Abnormalities
Maintains Compulsions
Defends Defeats
Changes of Ownership
Alters by Condensing
Eliminates Uncertainties
Secluded Breakdowns
Passing Obsessions
Punishes with Compassion
Reverses Tradition
Parental Denunciation
Ambivalent about Purification
Wavers over Destruction
Provincial Rejection
Illogical Hiding Places
Psychological Purification
Reduces Craziness
False Memories
Off and On Corruption
Common Waste Products
Receptive to Discipline
Hoards Ordinary Products
Psychological Criminals
Holds Back on Emotions
Imagines Violence
Feels Intensity
Emotional Constraints
Obsessed with Mother
Occasional Abnormalities
Receptive to Destruction
Relentless Discovery

A Complex Home
Uncertain over Discipline
Irregular Prosecution
Uneasy about Concealment
Eliminates Food
Slurs on the Family
Extreme Family Needs
Water Distillation
Excessive Moodiness
Common Deterrents
Rhythmic Subversion
Uncertain Suspicions
Compulsive Sympathies
Female Breakdowns
Relentless Opinions
Modest Duress
Discarded Feelings
Irregular Reversals
Modest Fixations
Temperamental Searches
Eliminates Mothering
Relentless Dejection
Troubles with Tradition
Depressed Women
Rejected Females
Accumulates Rancor
Punishment from Women
Expends Sympathy
Intense Nurturing
Maternal Remorse
Unhappy with Violence

MOON/PLUTO With Itself

☽   Additional deep feelings with whatever activities you are engaged in at the moment; added intensity in your emotional involvement and ability to convey feelings; vacillating needs to discard previous work.

♀   Added feelings that you must fight against whatever evils there are in life, even if you must drastically alter or rearrange your living circumstances to do this; feelings which are deep and personal; drastic mood variations.

Significant Examples of People and Events Using Moon/Pluto

General: **STRONG:** Stephen Sondheim; Alexis Carrel; Rupert Murdoch; John Denver; Ivar Kreugar; Robert DeNiro; Ernest Hemingway; F. Scott Fitzgerald; William K. Douglas; Robert Redford; Steve Allen; Winston Churchill
WEAK: Steve Wozniak; Albert Camus; Benjamin Disraeli; Sean Connery; Rollo May; Rossano Brazzi; Steven Spielberg; John Fremont
EVENTS: Apollo 11 Moon Landing; Lee's Surrender at Appomattox; George Washington's Inauguration; Woman's Suffrage Amendment Passed; (Alaskan Earthquake).

☉   Alexis Carrel; Earl Warren; Bobby Fischer; Johann Von Goethe; Sydney Omarr; Giacomo Puccini

☽, ♀   Willie Mays; Elton John; Stephen Foster; John Lennon

☿   Stephen King; John Glenn; Jim Thorpe; Sandy Koufax

♀   Washington's Inauguration; Pearl Harbor Attack; Moshe Dayan; Wayne Gretzky; Bjorn Borg; Thomas H. Huxley

♂   Paul Cezanne; Robert DeNiro; FDR Wins; Mario Andretti; J. F. Kennedy

♃   Thomas H. Huxley; Arthur Rimbaud; Apollo 11 Moon Landing; Harry Shoaf; Stephen Sondheim; Robin Williams

♄   Dave Garroway; Alan Leo; Al Unser; Willie Brandt; Abraham Lincoln

♅   Apollo 11 Moon Landing; Stephen Sondheim; Cheiro; J. Krishnamurti

♆   Francisco Franco; Arthur Ford; Jean Houston; Ralph Waldo Emerson

☊   Peter Max; H. G. Wells; Erwin Rommel; F. Scott Fitzgerald; Grant Lewi; Fidel Castro; Ervin Nyiregyhazi

A   Rex Harrison; Alan Leo; Helen Reddy; Arturo Toscanini

M   Charles Addams; Ferdinand Foch; Richard Alpert; Benito Mussolini

MOON/NODE   ☽/☊

Basic Ideas:

This combination represents an inner need and preoccupation for seeking and finding people who can help you with your tasks, questions, or problems. Your ability to nurture affiliations and ties to others, variations in your ability to progress toward meeting any spiritual or physical goals for personal growth or development, and your ability to relate to the public at large all begin here. Your ability to relate to people in groups or crowds, your indecision about calling or meeting friends, the quality of advice you receive from others, the help you seek from others, and your inner sensitivity to a destiny or plan for your life are also shown here. Your ability to nurture a relationship with the public at large, the hesitations you have when meeting new people, and your ability to demonstrate emotions before the public or during meetings, are also heightened here.

In Your Personal Life:

Thesis The personal attention you give to attracting people or groups; the temperament you develop for finding people who share a similar destiny; an increased cultivation of friendships.

Anti Illogical goals or methods for allying with others; a hit or miss process for finding people willing to help you; uncertainty toward the people with whom you associate; a focus on your sensitivities toward others.

In Your Relationships:

Thesis Learning to use or recognize the qualities or assets others may bring into your life; associating with people who may further your goals and interests; paths which lead you to people beneficial for you to meet.

Anti An inability or unwillingness to allow yourself to meet or associate with people who can help you; irrational fears that others will interfere with your routines or habits; social immaturity and barriers.

With Body or Mind:

The lymphatic system; any passages, tubes, or channels associated with internal organs; vision or eyesight difficulties; allergies and sensitivities.

In Politics or Business:

Thesis The production of goods for trade or commerce; measurements of productivity; foreign trade and the channels or means for conducting trade: ports of entry; roadways, canals, transit systems, etc.

Anti Common people involved in the conduct of foreign trade; the opinion of women in the conduct of trade or agriculture; agricultural failures or blockages at ports of exit or entry; public opinion about foreign trade.

MOON/NODE with Planets and Points

☉ The effectiveness or personal power you show when meeting people who may help you in life; the encouragement you receive from others who help you meet your personal, business, and social obligations.

☿ Adapting to events and communicating effectively; your education and how it opens opportunities for you; relating from your personal experiences to the needs of others; group discussions of emotions.

♀ The intimacy and rapport you develop through meeting others; people who bring their artistic talents to you or who come to you for your artistic talents; your charm and manners when meeting others.

♂ The energy you put into finding others and soliciting their advice and opinions; increased sexual stimulation and excitement; business acquaintances joining together for their own enhancement.

♃ Meeting others who share a similar philosophical sense about how life works; conviviality and joviality during meetings with others; studies of social theory or social psychology; sales meetings or presentations.

♄ Older and wiser people who give you sound advice about your life's direction; frustrations in trying to set up meetings or to meet honest and frank people; parents who prepare you for life's trials; lasting emotional ties.

♅ An unusual approach to meeting people who can help you understand life; meetings with astrologers to obtain counseling; innovative ideas during meetings with inventive or unique people; unusual emotional ties.

♆ People who give you false or inaccurate advice; lax or loosely structured ties to groups which are inspiring or ideal, but which have little practical advice for you; inefficient use of your connections or ties to others for advice.

♀ Censuring associates you thought would be helpful to you; the revenge that you or others take at meetings; ties to those who have great power and are able to give you emotional or other support for your efforts or goals.

A Concentrating on developing the connections you need; focusing on the various qualities of people or groups you associate with; the importance of privacy during meetings; emotionally charged meetings.

M Success through meeting or allying with those who share your interests and goals; recognition by influential people; learning and growing from your connections; the security felt by mastering emotions.

MOON/NODE CONCEPTS

Private Episodes
Ineffective Criticism
Protects Ties to Others
An Illogical Runaround
Dubious Acquaintances
Instincts for New Habits
Attracts Opportunities
Intuits Karmic Duties
Drawn by Ties to Others
Basic Delaying Tactics
Fosters Partnerships
Discovers New Friends
Sensitive about Supporters
Maintains Divisions

Isolated Appointments
Protects Sources
Intuits Separations
Touching Opportunities
Meetings among Females
Varies Presentations
Instinctive Kinship
Imagines Attachments
Receptive to Supporters
Drawn to Publicity
A Common Life's Aim
Ambivalent Interchanges
Fosters a Life's Aim
Sterile Presentations

Intuits Sexual Ties
Fosters New Habits
Disposes of Collections
Off and On Delays
Promotes Mergers
Drawn to Alliances
Incomplete Results
Sensitive Episodes
Fosters Alliances
Promotional Displays
Ordinary Habits
Ineffective Barriers
Everyday Disposal
Conceals Separations

Emotional Meetings
Sensitive to Bureaucratic Delays
Instincts for Ties to Others
Commonplace Evolution
Emotional Supporters
Resourceful at Meetings
Receptive to Sexual Liaisons
Uncertain Coalitions
Incomplete Separations
Illogical Interchanges
Average Backers
Sexual Ties with Fickle People
Unpredictable Affiliations
Karmic Ties about Parenting
Drawn to Meeting Others
Provincial Preoccupation
Attracts Sentimental People
Hesitates over an Annulment
Sympathetic Discourses
Experiences Barriers
Varies Approaches
Sensitive Cooperation
Imaginative Presentations
An Irregular Sense of Destiny
Imaginative Ties to Others
Temporary Interchanges
An Irregular Idea of Karma
Familiar Uncertainties
Touchy about Life's Aim

Unpredictable Presentations
Instincts for Attracting Others
Changes with Runaround
Nurtures Meetings with Others
Needs to Attract Others
Common Acquaintances
Unhappy with Associates
Off and On Joint Ventures
Receptive to Alliances
Sensitive to Attracting Others
Everyday Meetings with Friends
Protects Acquaintances
Maternal Sense of Destiny
Uncertainty about Disposal
Erratic Ridding
Ordinary Ties to Groups
Supports the Bureaucracy
Secluded Supporters
Feels a Sense of Destiny
Inner Desires to be a Parent
Fundamental Preoccupation
Spontaneous Ties to Others
Everyday Delays
Infrequent Cooperation
Emotional Alliances
Foresees the Runaround
Cares about Obligations
Receptive to Opportunities
Ties to Groups of Women

MOON/NODE With Itself

☽   Changes you encounter in your life's direction due to the influence others have on your course of life; your instincts for judging people to bring the right kind of influences; your unease when meeting audiences.

☊   The bonds you develop with those who influence your emotional growth; a meeting which opens opportunities for you to present ideas to your public; backers who help you overcome uncertainty when facing life's destiny.

Significant Examples of People and Events Using Moon/Node

General: **STRONG:** Jack Schwartz; Dave Garroway; Guglielmo Marconi; Stephen King; Bob Hope; Stephen Sondheim; Arthur Ford; Alexis Carrel; Stonewall Jackson; Robin Williams; Marlon Brando; Jean Francoise Millet
WEAK: Marc Edmund Jones; David Frost; Pierre Teilhard de Chardin; Henry Winkler; Auguste Rodin; Ernest Hemingway; Percy Bysshe Shelley
EVENTS: Apollo 11 Moon Landing; Watergate Burglary; Alaskan Earthquake; South Carolina Secession; (Lee's Surrender at Appomattox).

☉   Lawrence Welk; Alexis Carrel; Enrico Fermi; Friedrich Nietzsche

☽, ☊   Bob Hope; Mark Spitz; Step'n Sondheim; Dave Garroway; Carroll Righter; Robert Redford; Rudolph Bing

☿   Mary Martin; Kent State Shootings; Sam Sheppard; Benjamin Disraeli

♀   Norman Mailer; Tommy Smothers; Robin Williams; Elton John

♂   Carl Sagan; John Paul I; Al Unser; Stephen Sondheim; Harry Shoaf

♃   Arturo Toscanini; Jacques Cousteau; Louis Pasteur; Guglielmo Marconi

♄   Edgar Degas; Wayne Gretzky; Johann Von Goethe; Wright Bros. Flight

♅   Pierre Renoir; Vida Blue; Walt Whitman; Hermn. Goering; Jack Nicklaus

♆   H. G. Wells; Robert DeNiro; Edgar Degas; John Denver; Giacomo Puccini; Paul Cezanne; Vida Blue

♇   Lindburgh Lands; Challenger Explosion; FDR Wins First Election; Guglielmo Marconi; Robert Redford; Carroll Righter

A   John Glenn; Erwin Rommel; Claude Debussy; Al Unser; Jack Paar

M   Vincent Van Gogh; Jacques Cousteau; Nikola Tesla; F. Scott Fitzgerald

MOON/ASCENDANT ☽/A

Basic Ideas:

This combination represents your potential as a protective and sensitive person aware o f your immediate surroundings and the roles different people play. It mirrors your perception of others' personal styles, and fosters a sensitivity to the dispositions people have. A sentimental inner focus may cause you to nurture and cherish the attention you receive. You may receive subtle impressions from others, become more aware of the inner and personal fears from elements or people around you, have others see you as a somewhat fickle person, or show an inner restlessness which is activated by changes or alterations in your daily routine. An element of moodiness may affect the way you approach life, and you may vacillate as you try to address the cares and concerns of others. Your intuition and non-sensory hunches are accented, and you may learn to pay attention to them.

In Your Personal Life:

Thesis   A sensitive and caring person who is quick to notice the needs and care demanded by others; sensitivity to the reality of another's psychological space; you cherish the attention you receive and are sensitive to others.

Anti   Others get the impression that you do not give compassion; changing your views of others more than is needed; secret, irrational fears brought into focus; personal insecurity noted.

In Your Relationships:

Thesis   You become more aware of your partner's moods and need for personal space; you seek out others who are receptive to the attention and personal concern you give; attention to your partner's demands.

Anti   Moody indecision about relationship choices available to you; a crabby crankiness to your general disposition which makes it difficult for others to give you the kind of comfort and support you wish to have.

With Body or Mind:

Sinus sensitivities or infections; emotions held in check due to social or environmental pressures; sensitivity to dust or other allergens; emotional states.

In Politics or Business:

Thesis   How others view the disposition of the population; the effect that the women have in forming opinion or determining priorities; production goals met by workers; emphasis on immediate needs and quotas.

Anti   Causes for concern raised on behalf of the common people; an environmental study which affects the welfare of all; problems with the production of goods as seen by allies; raising of environmental causes.

MOON/ASCENDANT with Planets and Points

☉   Effecting major changes in relating to others; determination in caring for those important to you; showing a more successful picture of your willingness to help; concentrating on your role as a caring person.

☿   Thinking about how you can protect and nurture others; needs for educating yourself about the psychology of caring; a better understanding of the motives of people who offer you support in life, or to whom you offer support.

♀   Projecting a kindness toward others who are uncertain about their life's situations; admiring people despite their dependency needs; a softness to your mannerisms when offering to help or assist others.

♂   An irritation and impatience with those who interfere with your procedures; quickly receiving impressions or feelings from others close to you; a unique personal style of caring and concern.

♃   Placing emphasis on your observations of how others interact; exaggerated self-importance while relating to others; refining your insight into the emotional states of others; a need for recognition of self.

♄   A blocked perception of the emotional attitudes of others; discipline in your emotional state when directly relating to others; added perceptions of sternness apparent to others in interpersonal relationships.

♅   Abrupt reception of emotional reactions from others; staying aloof from the uncertainty or emotional states aroused by others; unusual sentiment in your mannerisms; an aura of being different even when you try to blend in.

♆   Becoming more sensitive to others; confusion about how other's feelings mix with yours; becoming lax about caring for others when you should be more vigilant; pretensions of concern; misreading another's emotions.

♇   Abnormal feelings of gloom or despair felt from others; eliminating awareness of needs for others; concentrating on self, excluding others; an emotional need to gain power or prestige at the expense of others.

☊   Finding people who are very sensitive and aware of the needs of others; seeking others to help heal your emotional wounds; circumstances where you may have to leave those you once cared for; outward emotional effects.

M   Attaining positions or power due to your ability to read and satisfy the needs of others; the experience you gain in understanding the emotional side of the many people with whom you work or have day-to-day interactions.

MOON/ASCENDANT CONCEPTS

A Sensitive Personal Focus
Emotional Expressions
Active Nurturing
Normal Convictions
Perceptive of Others
Receives Psychic Impressions
Variable Impressions
Ungraceful Reactions
Illogical Convictions
Protective of Environment
Fluctuating Sense of Style
Moody and Seeks Attention
Conceals Impressions
Notices Emotions

Sulky Mannerisms
Maternal Settings
Mood-Based Perceptions
Recognizes Self-Instincts
Surrounded by Defenses
Common Attitudes
Sensitive Perceptions
An Emotional Disposition
Emotional Reactions
Provincial Demeanor
Reacts to Changes
Sensitive Attitudes
Passing Rejoinders
Intuitive Leanings

Unspoken Attitudes
Protects Self
Alert to Imagination
Receptive Attitudes
Conflicting Sensations
Kindly Settings
Supportive Mannerisms
Inhibits Feelings
Needs to Feel Protective
Tender Disposition
Reacts to Protection
A Need for Privacy
Fancy Notions
Everyday Settings

Changes in How You Relate
Unhappy with Interpersonal Roles
Uncertain about Sensations
Represses Sensitive Feelings
Fickle about Grabbing Attention
Committed to Comforting Others
Fragmentary Concentration
A Sentimental Point of View
Receives Everyday Impressions
Compassionate Relating to Others
Understands Emotional People
Does not Need an Elaborate Place
Isolated Conditions
Notices How Others Parent
Sentimental Characteristics
An Altered Awareness of Self
Sentimental Portrayals
Sympathetic Responses
Uncertain of Responses
Ambiguous Interpersonal Roles
Unsure of Impressions Received
Inhibits Another's Reality
Fulfills a Consoling Role
Isolated Surroundings
Notices Motives
An Illogical Conception
Defends Environmental Conditions
Emotional Personal Responses
Needs a Family Environment

A Supportive Personal Style
Receives Impressions by Instinct
Fosters Perceptions
A Receptive Demeanor
Defensive Attitudes
Temporary Attention Seeking
Fosters Interpersonal Roles
Temporary Recognition
An Invented Sense of Style
Sensations Caused by Mood Swings
Relates to Others in Simple Ways
Fluctuating Mannerisms
Incomplete Assessments
Represses Emotions Easily
Sensitive to the Moods of Others
A Romantic Presence
Impressions which Fluctuate
A Basic Understanding of Others
Impressions in a General Context
Uncertainty Shows in Mannerisms
Ineffective Personal Responses
Impressions of Romance
Unsteady Understanding
A Cultural Environment
Nurtures Impressions Received
Changes Perceptions
Imaginative Personal Style
Rhythmic Reactions
Compassionate Reactions

MOON/ASCENDANT With Itself

☽   Your personal sensitivity about picking up emotional states of people near to you; your instinct for judging the mood of people from their body language and postures; support received from being with others.

A   An enhanced ability to read the mood and emotions of those around you; the other than verbal convictions you receive about the moods and attitudes of people you contact; an emphasis on emotional responses.

Significant Examples of People and Events Using Moon/Ascendant

General: **STRONG:** Sean Connery; Melvin Belli; Richard Strauss; Charles Steinmetz; Lawrence Welk; John McEnroe; Ira Progoff; Steven Spielberg; Erwin Rommel; Jacques Cousteau; Audie Murphy; Billy Rose; Shirley Jones
WEAK: Sandy Koufax; Stephen King; Audrey Hepburn; Manly Palmer Hall; Henry Mancini; Elton John; Art Linkletter; General Charles Gordon
EVENTS: USS Maine Explosion; South Carolina Secession; Chernobyl Nuclear Explosion; Ramstein Airshow Disaster; (Alaskan Earthquake occurs).

☉   Jack Schwartz; Ernest Pyle; George Patton; Jean Paul Satre; Gianni Agnelli

☽, A   Dustin Hoffman; Benjamin Disraeli; Joseph Joffre; Jean Paul Satre

☿   Dr. Tom Dooley; Benjamin Disraeli; George Patton; Rex Harrison

♀   Jack Nicklaus; Arthur Rimbaud; Lee's Surrender at Appomattox; First Medicare Patient Accepted

♂   Bob Dylan; Tom Jones; Charles Steinmetz; John F. Kennedy

♃   Mark Spitz; Charles E. O. Carter; USS Maine Explodes; Johnny Carson

♄   Chernobyl Nuclear Explosion; Toulouse-Lautrec; Emperor Hirohito; Richard Strauss; Vida Blue; Olga Worrall

♅   Edmund Halley; Nixon's Resignation; Abraham Lincoln; Helen Reddy

♆   Paul Joseph Goebbels; Steve Allen; Lawrence Welk; Dane Rudhyar

♇   Thomas H. Huxley; Bob Fosse; Stephen Sondheim; John F. Kennedy

☊   Edmund Halley; Erich Maria Remarque; Richard Chamberlain; Willie Brandt; Guglielmo Marconi; John McEnroe

M   Richard Alpert; Cheiro; Paramhansa Yogananda; South Carolina Secession; Gianni Agnelli; Jean Cocteau

MOON/MIDHEAVEN   ☽/M

Basic Ideas:

These points denote your capacity to combine qualities such as mothering, caring, sensitivity, support, and sympathy into your overall personal development and behavior. Your uncertainties over how to mature and grow independently, how to gain respectability from others, how to improve your reputation, and what your personal rules of conduct and behavior may be, are mirrored here. When these points are activated you again feel the strong maternal-like influences which originated in your childhood, and from these experiences remember and expect continuing motherly protection and sympathy as life's cares press you, even after you have reached adulthood. You show a sensitivity toward understanding your life's purposes, become emotional when having to cope with external stresses, and may be inconsistent with your emphasis in developing internal self-sufficiency.

In Your Personal Life:

Thesis   You recognize a need to better balance your feelings of caring, sympathy, and self-consciousness; your mother was a strong positive influence in your early experiences; you strive to be like mother's ideal.

Anti   You do not cope well with problems and have weak and varying ideas about who you are as a person or what you should do with your life; you mature through emotional attitudes and neglect reasoned analysis.

In Your Relationships:

Thesis   Seeking a partner who is sensitive to your needs and who is similar in nature to your mother; finding someone with whom you have excellent rapport so you can easily share your tender and inner feelings.

Anti   Mother's attitudes were very harsh and demanding and it is difficult to adjust to being intimate and close with others; it is difficult to decide what you want from others because of unresolved family bonds.

With Body or Mind:

Family genetic patterns of craving for or sensitivity to certain drugs; heredity patterns concerning acid-alkaline balance; stomach disorders.

In Politics or Business:

Thesis   The involvement of the common people with politics; women and their movements having influence on policies; production of basic materials or commodities raised as an issue of emotional concern.

Anti   The opinion of a minority of concerned people influencing policy; food production curtailed due to poor long-range planning; natural disasters which cause much concern and interrupt long-range policies or goals.

MOON/MIDHEAVEN with Planets and Points

☉ Defining your own character and growing beyond early family influences; the purpose and determination you set for yourself in defining who you are and what you will do with your life; the importance of family identification.

☿ Your ability to mentally adapt and conform to the pressures your family or mother placed on you; ideas you receive from your maternal influences; analyzing or discussing your family's self-concepts.

♀ The role of feminine values or virtues in your life, and how you express these through the person you are becoming; your desire to be protective of your status, career, or personal values; your ability to accept parenting as a goal.

♂ Anger you experience due to pressures to conform to maternal rules which others impose; insistence that you adopt maternal roles in life; persistence that others show in pushing on you their ideas of how you should develop.

♃ Opportunities which allow you to develop and be the person you want, as opposed to how your family feels you should grow; excessive maternal influence during your formative years; mother's ideas.

♄ Retards or delays your ability to develop independently away from maternal influences imposed in your early life; a lasting dependency on mother; plain and prudent ideas from mother about how you should organize your life.

♅ Sudden or unexpected disruptions in your affiliation with maternal imaging; peculiar ideas from mother about what you should be or how you should develop in life; a strong inner interest in computers or astrology.

♆ Idealistic or unclear images about who you are or how you can grow; confusion over your role in supporting others ; questions about where your identity begins and where the person mother wants ends.

♇ Extreme pressure to conform to mother's rules about how you should conduct your life's affairs; drastic measures to ensure your conformity to maternal roles; alteration of self-projection through such orders.

☊ Finding people other than your biological mother to fill your maternal needs; people who help you mature emotionally through accepting responsibility; groups which address family-based dependencies.

A Personal motivations to be like (or opposite to) mother, and to adopt (or discard) the family values acquired earlier; your drive to understand others through the role models your mother provided you.

MOON/MIDHEAVEN CONCEPTS

Fosters Protection
Average Fulfillment
Incomplete Self-Discipline
Cares about Conduct
Incomplete Self-Integration
An Ordinary Start in Life
Uncertain about Principles
Provincial Standards
Average Family Reputation
Unsteady Coping
Conflicting Aptitudes
Receptive to Safety

Emotional Outcomes
Sensitive Conforming
Unfulfilled Expertise
A Need for Coping
Fluctuating Assurances
Drawn to Experience
Intuits Self-Restraint
Emotional Guarantees
Sentimental Objectives
Experiences Caring
Everyday Defenses
Maternal Self-Restraint

Common Principles
Intuits Outcomes
Uncertain Results
Hidden Purposes
Family Roots
Protects Feelings
A Vague Expert
Timid Conduct
Romantic Methods
Emotional Coping
Fosters Security
Supports Purposes

Temperamental Conduct
Adheres to a Personal Code
Receptive to Integration
Touchy about Competence
Sensitive Learning and Growing
Imaginative Security Seeking
A Woman's Reputation
Sees a Parent as Weak
Has an Intuitive Capacity
Temporary Self-Restraint
Unsure of Life's Direction
Alters Basic Principles
Sensitive to Public Projection
Supplies Trustworthiness
Changes through Personal Growth
Matures through the Use of Intuition
New Ideas on Security Seeking
Inconsistent Self-Confidence
Dubious Corroboration
Modest Personal Assurances
Matures Emotionally
Fosters a Need for Standing
Uncomplicated Maturing
Receptive to Authentication
Common Persevering
Hesitates over Conclusions
Inconsistent Conduct
Wavering over Confirmation
Family-Oriented Development
Undecided Resolution
Alters Career Directions

Everyday Safekeeping
Occasional Persevering
Projection into the Public
Passing Recognition
Touchy about Purposes
Illogical Guiding Principles
Unhappy about Consequences
Protects Family Heritage
Ordinary Objectives
Learns to Live with Ambition
Feels Constrained by Career
An Expert on Compassion
Alters Context of Origins
Feels the Outcomes
Hides Family's History
Conflicting Personal Principles
A Temporary Honor
Provincial Mannerisms
Unsure of Personal Training
Temporary Workmanship
Uncertain about Credentials
Infrequent Authorization
Unhappy with Security Seeking
Imaginative Training
Emotional Fulfillment
The Expert who Changes Career
Maternal Security Seeking
Temporary Protection
Instincts for Stature (Standing)
Fosters Self-Restraint
Uncertain Intentions

MOON/MIDHEAVEN With Itself

☽   Focus on the role that family plays in giving you direction and impetus in life to achieve your goals; support for preparing yourself for the positions wanted; indecision about career direction or change.

M   Need for recognition and security thru position and prominence; clearing your concepts about who you are and where you want to go with your life; fostering the trust of the people; romantic experiences.

Significant Examples of People and Events Using Moon/Midheaven

General: **STRONG:** Drew Pearson; H. G. Wells; Marc Edmund Jones; Jack Nicklaus; Ellen Burstyn; Albert Speer; Dave Garroway; Ivar Kreugar; Johann Von Goethe; Alan Alda; Bob Dylan; Henri Toulouse-Lautrec; Lance Reventlow
WEAK: Kareem Abdul-Jabbar; Glen Campbell; Walt Whitman; Edouard Manet; Charles Kettering; Paramhansa Yogananda; Richard Strauss
EVENTS: Kent State Shootings; Lewis & Clark Expedition; Lee's Surrender at Appomattox; Apollo 11 Moon Landing; (Alaskan Earthquake occurs).

☉   Laurence Olivier; Liberace; Stephen Foster; Muhammad Ali

☽, M Rosanno Brazzi; Marc Edmund Jones; Watergate Burglary

☿   Carroll Righter; Ellen Burstyn; John F. Kennedy; Georges Seurat

♀   Ernest Pyle; Bertrand Russell; Jean Cocteau; Ralph Waldo Emerson

♂   USS Maine Explodes; Bob Fosse; Jim Thorpe; Olga Worrall; Jack Nicklaus

♃   Hermann Goering; Dave Garroway; Lewis & Clark Exped.; John Glenn

♄   Jerry Rubin; Marc Edmund Jones; Edna Ferber; Jack Nicklaus; Carl Sandburg; Burt Reynolds; Henri Matisse

♅   Mario Andretti; Robert Redford; Paul Joseph Goebbels; Jean Francois Millet; Edgar Degas; Marc Edmund Jones

♆   Edward R. Murrow; Burl Ives; Merv Griffin; Lee's Surrender

♀̲   Ira Progoff; J. Krishnamurti; Stephen King; Ivar Kreugar

☊   Dustin Hoffman; Paul Cezanne; Jean Cocteau; Jack Nicklaus; Thomas H. Huxley; Marlon Brando

A   Gustav Dore; Enrico Caruso; Al Unser; Jack Nicklaus; Bob Hope; Earl Warren; Ernest Pyle; Tom Jones

MERCURY/VENUS ☿/♀

Basic Ideas:

Versatility and shrewdness combine with charm and allure to bring you an appreciation of clever ideas, or methods of verbal or written expression. Your satisfaction and pleasure from learning something new is heightened, you find joy when words or ideas are expressed beautifully, and thoughts about satisfying others are prompted. You may think a lot about relationships, reason yourself out of appeasing another's interests, and have ideas on clever ways to indulge yourself at another's expense. Your love for the sound of language is augmented, and notions about how to tease or tempt others arise. Studies on how to use charm and beauty to attract the things you want, research on the role of glamor and allure, and an education about using personal beauty aids is also emphasized. You may feel some nervousness when having to express feelings of affection for another.

In Your Personal Life:

Thesis   You become familiar with the use of beauty in form and setting as a way of bringing enjoyment to self and others; you gather information on beauty and love, in order to apply this.

Anti   You talk much about your desire for affection in your life but tend to be only superficially interested in true love and sharing with others; you talk about emotions and depth of character, but do not experience it.

In Your Relationships:

Thesis   Your ability to discuss the depths of feelings and attachment to another is increased; love and communications play a central role in your sense of relationships; you enjoy bringing pleasure to your partner's life.

Anti   Your discussions about love are only superficial; you find it hard to identify your own feelings, and can not identify at all with another's feelings; you think that talk and discussion replace intimacy in love.

With Body or Mind:

Oxygen levels in the blood; the efficiency of lungs; food allergies and reactions; ability to assimilate oxygen; veins which oxygenate your brain.

In Politics or Business:

Thesis   Social communication; social psychology, or the study of people, their reactions, and their relationships; a mixture of business and society; beautification programs for highways; news about the status of wealth.

Anti   Propaganda about the ease and quality of life; a business sector at odds with society; speeches which emphasize economic facts; a transportation system which places beauty over function; debates on added costs.

MERCURY/VENUS with Planets and Points

☉   Determination to effectively use your physical assets to appear more attractive to others; convictions which convey love or affection; satisfaction with the person you are; humorous forms of expression.

☽   Expressions of (so-called) "feminine" values in life; feelings for what forms of pleasure another will accept; increased sensitivity toward the affection and pleasure others desire; discussions on love and romance.

♂   Assertion and assurance in your expressions of love and affection; conveying these in ways which please others; a sharpened speech which irritates others, especially in romantic situations; using loud music to heighten love.

♃   Assumptions and opinions about how to love; augmented thinking and exaggerated speech when expressing affection and love; success when expressing your values; a lot of talk about love and affection.

♄   Shortened talk when discussing your affections and love for another; accepting rejections of love calmly; caution in expressions of love; you do not obligate yourself to romance easily; long discussions on love.

♅   Upsetting news about a lover; an unusual person who tells you of feelings of love and affection; sudden feelings of love for another or an urge to tell that person; detached feelings when talking about love.

♆   Heightened appeal and allure, and a desire to make another's love a subtle reality; creating an image of a fragile and delicate self; being more open to dreams or vague visions about the nature of love; idealized ideas of love.

♇   Intensified desires to use others for the pleasures they may give; going to extremes with the thoughts of pleasure you may derive from another; verbalizing and sharing ideas on what love can be.

☊   Increased ability to attract others into your life for romance and love; an encouraging association with groups for opportunities and meetings with others; meeting others to share romantic kinship.

A   Assessing the sentiments of others and judging their ability to express their love and feelings for you in positive ways; emphatic responses received from others when discussing affections; a setting showing love and beauty.

M   Feeling increased pleasure and love for self as you age and become more comfortable with telling others of your affection for them; the pleasure you derive from receiving recognition for your cherished speeches and writings.

MERCURY/VENUS CONCEPTS

Talks about Affection
Backhanded Compliments
Graceful Illustrations
Bargains for Contentment
Explains Satisfaction
Talks about Beauty
A Skillful Pacifist
Quick Respect
Fidgety with Affinity
Questions Appreciation
Learns about Appreciation
Many Different Pleasures

Educated Composure
Dual Tenderness
Enjoys Notifications
Talks of Composure
Intimate Discussions
Discusses Inducements
Expresses Favoritism
Jealous Responses
Flattering Gestures
Intellectual Satisfaction
Tender Suggestions
Charming Evasiveness

Rapid Enjoyment
Hints of Favors
Rapid Politeness
Observes Charm
Sly Jealousy
Notices Courtesy
Enjoys Talking
Perceives Politeness
Fond of Bargaining
Swift Satisfaction
Poetic Language
Fast Smiles

Thinks about Consideration
Many Forms of Temptation
Interprets Artistic Endeavors
Captivating Discussions
Appeals to Dishonesty
A Talent for Composure
Reasons about Attraction
Varieties of Consideration
Knows about Pleasures
Informed about Beauty
Knows about Tantrums
Clever using Beauty Accents
Convenient Skills
Studies Pacification
Hints of Selfishness
Researches Intimacy
Hints of Infatuation
Pleasing Language
Shrewd Deference
Attentive to Glamor
Adapts despite Temptations
Expresses Vanity (Conceit)
Observes Peacefulness
Reasons about Fascination
Talks of Embellishment
Restless Satisfaction
Graceful Ambidexterity
Appreciates being Articulate
Notices Serenity
Articulates on Apathy
Expresses Gratitude

Questions Embellishment
Composed Expressions
Likes to Manipulate Others
Restless with Compliments
Shrewd with Preferences
Attentive to Quiet Persuasion
Easily Sidesteps Vanities
Nervous about Preferences
A Love of Knowledge
Nervous Composure
Beautiful Pronunciation
Likes Poetic Expressions
Thoughts of Enjoyment
A Love of Discussion
Recalls Enjoyment
Knows about Attraction
Questions Luxury
Shows Varying Composure
Expressions of Jealousy
Notices Relaxation
Glamorizes Pleasure
Crafty Forms of Satisfaction
Informed on Tenderness
Requires Rapid Satisfaction
Reveals Temptations
Adept with Compliments
Glamorous Illustrations
Observes Tranquility
Evades Intimacy
Enjoys Asking Questions
Cultural Discussions

MERCURY/VENUS With Itself

☿   Ideas about writing on love, beauty, and their effects on you or others; a need for additional education in the arts, and practice with an appropriate music or art medium; a lovely handwriting; writing music or poetry.

♀   Composure when addressing others, especially in formal settings; consciousness of the mechanics of music or art; a versatility with the forms of expression or technique used in specific modes of art or music.

Significant Examples of People and Events Using Mercury/Venus

General: **STRONG:** Paul Newman; Olga Worrall; Amadeo Modigliani; Evel Knievel; Steve Wozniak; F. Scott Fitzgerald; Albert Camus; George Patton; Anne Murray; Rollo May; Jackie Robinson; Elvis Presley
          WEAK: Alan Leo; R. D. Laing; Claude Debussy; Edmund Halley; Johnny Carson; Ernest Hemingway; Drew Pearson; Sally Ride
          EVENTS: Woman's Suffrage Amendment Adopted; Bolsheviks Seize Power; First Atomic Bomb Explosion; Apollo 11 Moon Landing; (Pearl Harbor Attack).

☉   Challenger Explosion; Lawrence Welk; Audie Murphy; Albert Camus; Chernobyl Nuclear Explosion

☽   Jackie Robinson; First A-Bomb Explodes; Jean Paul Satre; Marlon Brando

☿, ♀   Olga Worrall; Ama. Modigliani; Mary Martin; Paul Newman; Rollo May

♂   Audie Murphy; First A-Bomb Explodes; Olivia Newton-John; Bertrand Russell; Dave Garroway

♃   Herman Melville; Melvin Belli; James Meredith Enrolls at U. Miss.; Kareem Abdul-Jabbar

♄   Gen. Joseph Joffre; Stonewall Jackson; Louis Pasteur; Lewis & Clark Expedition starts; Sir Alexander Fleming

♅   Woman's Suffrage Amendment Passes; Al Unser; Ira Progoff; Billy Rose; Ernest Hemingway

♆   Kent State Shootings; Earl Warren; Sam Peckinpah; Burt Reynolds

♇   Ira Progoff; Anne Murray; Arturo Toscanini; Enrico Caruso; Elvis Presley; Edgar Degas; Charles Kettering

☊   Wayne Gretzky; F. Scott Fitzgerald; Liberace; Paramhansa Yogananda; Albert Speer; Steve Wozniak

A   Steve Allen; George Patton; Charles E. O. Carter; Robert McNamara

M   Bob Dylan; Dustin Hoffman; Jean Cocteau; Arthur Ford; Jerry Rubin

MERCURY/MARS ☿/♂

Basic Ideas:

These planets symbolize thinking or reasoning as you move or work. You may make rapid observations, have clever ideas about how to direct your activities, and receive aggravation from two directions. Here you find anger which arises quickly, an ability to argue a question or point from either side, and observations of agitated or disorderly actions. Enlivening your delivery of any communications, such as your lecturing or writing is also highlighted. You may put activity and motion into all means of expression, talk about your anger or personal internal struggles, encounter a deceptive competitor, or stimulate flows of information. You may hear noises which occur suddenly or loudly, stimulate your mental activity, remember aggravation caused by others, receive loud arguments back in response to carefully thought out or reasoned facts, and encounter a lot of mental pressure to perform.

In Your Personal Life:

Thesis   The thoughts you apply to your actions or activities; adapting to situations or presentations from others; versatility when handling irritations or complaints; getting rapid questions.

Anti   Increased nervousness when there is activity by others that you can not accept; giving into impulses to steal or be deceptive, tricky, or deceitful; expressions of anger shown in your speech or actions; crafty denials.

In Your Relationships:

Thesis   Increased ability to talk about and discuss your passions with your partner; a capacity to express feelings of mutual attraction; an ability to communicate sexually-based feelings of attraction.

Anti   Added intensity of any discussion when talking about inner feelings; raises arguments about basic communications; irritation with a partner who can't understand your ideas; rushed thinking on relationships.

With Body or Mind:

Hormone levels which affect your energy levels; convulsions caused by self-exhaustion; a hypersensitive sense of sense of smell; lung inflammations.

In Politics or Business:

Thesis   Travel by the military; an emphasis on the manufacture or production of military hardware; news of riots, fires, or warfare; the military occupying the attention of the news media; blasts from hot, dry winds.

Anti   Censorship of military news; news blackouts of disasters or wars; crime or criminals in the news; violence shown as part of the news; propaganda which distorts the news of the day; the transmission of energy.

MERCURY/MARS with Planets and Points

⊙   Emphasizing the importance of news activities; talks of an urgent nature by distinguished people; a preference for loud and showy announcements or proclamations; displays which involve great dexterity of movement.

☽   An accumulation of reasons for the use of force; defensive tactics against an usually communicative person; irregular observations of impatience or irritation; loud talk on family or home matters; verbal and active women.

♀   An appeasing element amidst talk on the use of force; self-satisfaction gained from thoughts of stimulation; intimacy following discussions of sexual activity; delight received from activity or athletic practices.

♃   Abundant talk about the use of force or might; too much commotion among many correspondents; permission granted for talks on the use of energy or force; generosity while educating those who have many questions.

♄   Avoiding discussions about force or might; frustrations with efforts to compromise during negotiations about noise or struggles; negotiations which endure loudly for a very long time; an old argument is debated.

♅   Unusual approaches to arguments which irritated people in the past; unexpected outcomes from talks involving activity of self or others; insightful gossip about energy sources; revision of ideas on noise.

♆   Expressions of anger which do little to clarify situations; a misuse of clever ideas in business or military strategy; neglecting complaints about irritating noises; frustrations at not being able to convey hostility.

♇   Compulsive, continuous talk which irritates others; discussions about any suspicions which arise on the activities; angry communications from bosses about your writing, business, or educational capabilities.

☊   Acquaintances who have an irritating style to their speech; how communications with associates can initiate their activity; people with similar interests in the expression or teaching of competitive practices.

A   A strong personal focus on the need to communicate with people who have a decidedly angry approach or demeanor; attitudes which show others that you can be limber, shrewd, or practiced in the use of your strength or might.

M   Working to fulfill personal goals by addressing life's problems more directly and completely; exerting control over others through discussions; striving to achieve completion and competence despite earlier incomplete actions.

MERCURY/MARS CONCEPTS

Raises Questions
Restless Aggressiveness
Variable Agitation
Observes Commotion
Decides on Indignation
Rapid Curiosity
Clever and Brave
Talks of Courage
Antagonistic Discussions
Cunning Arguments
Thinks of Courage
Describes Action/Activity

Reveals Initiative
Energetic Notifications
Describes Hostility
Swift to Anger
Ingenious Defiance
Offensive Ideas
Swift Commotion
Clever Animosity
Sneaky Aggravation
Shrewdly Shows Anger
Discusses Initiatives
Activates Dexterity

Notices Urgency
Two-way Energy
Sly Haste
Angry Thoughts
Discusses Duress
Speaks Loudly
Talks of Anger
Crafty Initiative
Rapid Complaints
Fidgety Rushing
Adapts Rapidly
Discloses Movement

Reasons on the Use of Force
Stimulates Information
Asks about Antagonism
Protests against Memorizing
Restless Action/Activity
Memorizes Arguments
A Spontaneous Mimic
Swift Animosity
Analyzes Annoyance
Rousing Discussions
Nervous Courage
Talks of Animosity
Reports about Complaints
An Irritating Interpretation
Versatile Anger
Talks of Action/Activity
Educated Aggressiveness
Initiates an Expression
Questions Asked in Haste
Alert to Urgency
A Fast Memory Recall
Defies Informed Sources
Forces a Discussion
Ingenious Indignation
Versatile Stimulation
Clever Impulsiveness
Crafty Stimulation
Able to Argue Either Side
Expresses Aggressiveness
Exciting Narration
Questions Animosity

Questions Urgency
Addresses Motion
Thinks of Aggression
Conversant with Force
Stimulates Thinking
A Hostility to Ideas
Recalls Complaints
Explains Excitement
Swift Aggressiveness
Nervous Arguments
Educated in Athletics
Writes about Struggles
Shrewd Courage
An Ambidextrous Fighter
A Talent for Stimulation
Hasty Thoughts
Talks about Commotion
Clever Arguments
Initiates Rumors
Versatile Complaints
Intellectual Arguments
Expresses Animosity
Crafty Complaints
Restless Commotion
Cunning Defiance
Scrutinizes Action/Activity
Interprets Impatience
Energetic Discussions
Varieties of Violence
Skillful Defiance
Observes Haste

MERCURY/MARS With Itself

☿   Increased awareness of the mental preparation necessary when competing against others; conversations on subjects having to do with athletics or the military; developing skills with weapons; an added insistence on analysis.

♂   Needs for communications about athletics or the military; an inner desire for mental conditioning prior to competitive events; courage for defiant attempts; revelations about attempts to prove bravery.

Significant Examples of People and Events Using Mercury/Mars

General: **STRONG:** John Fremont; Hermann Goering; Paramhansa Yogananda; Vincent Van Gogh; James Earl Carter; Jack Paar; Franklin Roosevelt; Burt Reynolds; Manly Palmer Hall; Nikola Tesla; Cheiro; Jack Nicklaus
WEAK: Ervin Nyiregyhazi; Arthur Ford; Dr. Francis Regardie; Willie Brandt; Johann Von Goethe; Yehudi Menuhin; Mark Spitz
EVENTS: Mt. St. Helens Explosion; Washington's Inauguration; Transcontinental RR completed; First A-Bomb Explodes; (Woman's Suffrage Amendment Passed).

☉   Lance Reventlow; Jonathan Winters; Paul Joseph Goebbels; Bob Hope

☽   Steve Allen; Sam Peckinpah; Jacques Cousteau; Arnold Schwarzenegger; Rosanno Brazzi

☿, ♂   Glen Campbell, David Frost, Franklin Roosevelt; Carroll Righter

♀   Neil Diamond; Merv Griffin; Francisco Franco; Claude Debussy

♃   Cheiro; Louis Pasteur; Nikola Tesla; Stv Allen; Jean Cocteau; Jimi Hendrix

♄   John Dillinger; Rosanno Brazzi; Georges Seurat; Edgar Degas; Rupert Murdoch; Friedrich Nietzsche

♅   Steven Spielberg; Transcontinental RR completed; Jean Paul Satre; Edward R. Murrow; Tom Jones

♆   Komar; Sydney Omarr; Paul Joseph Goebbels; Jerry Rubin; Art. Toscanini

♇   Grant Lewi; Mt. St. Helens Explosion; East Coast Power Blackout; Sir Laurence Olivier; Lord Byron

☊   Henry Kissinger; Burt Reynolds; Grant Lewi; Tom Jones; F. D. Roosevelt

A   H. G. Wells; Ralph Waldo Emerson; Alexis Carrel; Ernest Hemingway

M   Helen Reddy; Walt Whitman; Jean Francois Millet; Paul Gauguin

MERCURY/JUPITER   ☿/♃

Basic Ideas:

Needs for thinking and communicating combine with formal or learned education to show how persuasion in communications, writing, or speaking may be enhanced. These themes suggest that you work to expand your knowledge in areas like business, education, knowledge, travel, opportunities, law, or religion. You may increase your desire to notice and observe events unfamiliar to you, discover enrichment through new concepts and studies, and add enthusiasm to your discourses. Luck and success with communications in general, encouragement from siblings, and studies in politics or the law, may follow from these themes. They symbolize your ability for the rapid comprehension of situations, and for an enthusiasm which may cause you to be less than careful with the facts, and may impart a tendency for cheerful thievery or plagiarism to your disposition.

In Your Personal Life:

Thesis   Your ability to expand and broaden your outlook in life through education, self-study, and communications; practice in politics or the law; a swift and agile mind; the ability to think on your feet; optimistic thoughts.

Anti   Too much information; not being able to use or adapt to the knowledge you presently have available; erroneous interpretations of the facts; devious ways of presenting data; an excess of theoretical thinking.

In Your Relationships:

Thesis   Growing together thru educational and travel pursuits; an abundance of talent which you work to develop together; realizing and developing your partner's skills; successful communications with your partner.

Anti   Reason which overrides feelings in mutual discussions; too much flexibility and not enough substance or direction in the relationship; a misrepresentation of statements; a partner who is arrogant or mouthy.

With Body or Mind:

Excessive fat in the blood; inability to absorb sugars in the blood; weakness in the lung or oxygen exchange systems; sciatica; nervous disorders.

In Politics or Business:

Thesis   Communication about plans for expansion or growth; neighbors who want to expand transportation systems; discussions about business or legal affairs; communication on religious or philosophical ideals.

Anti   A budget strained by too much expansion or inflation; legal decisions which affect the commerce or transportation; religious leaders who have desires to assume political power; religion censuring scholarship.

MERCURY/JUPITER with Planets and Points

☉ Bringing personal influence to efforts to educate others about your interests; basic opinion which you restate as facts; the decisiveness with which you are able to present your information and ideas.

☽ Protecting your information and sources of data; your sentiments about how you use your formal education; the imagination you have when presenting researched or studied opinions, findings, and facts.

♀ Using your experience in music or the arts to create new compositions or studies; the pleasure you derive from study and education; the acclaim you receive for your efforts to expand artistic or religious talent in self or others.

♂ The effort and energy you put into pursuing various types of knowledge or education; the force to continue communicating with others about your experiences; using knowledge of military law to advantage.

♄ Discipline and persistence in correlating large amounts of information or news; constraints and boundaries to theories of intelligence flow; a lot of communication with disappointing news; business cycle study.

♅ Breakthroughs in communication or scientific theory; sudden development of radical new means of increasing capacities for data transmission; the study or expansion of theories concerning astrology, computing, or science.

♆ Too much faith in theories which are still confusing or poorly explained; erroneous thinking, or knowledge which persists or which is resurrected; theories on the parapsychological or mystical side of life.

♇ Immense criticism or rebuffs for theories which are inadequately presented; the repression of wise discourses or thinking; the elimination of discussions or books on religious or philosophical topics.

☊ Finding associates or groups who share similar philosophical or religious ideas; attending meetings with persons or groups who share philosophical and educational interests with you; links to people who publish ideas.

A A focus on presenting information from your accumulation of knowledge; increased ability to be flexible when presenting your findings and research to others; the repression of opinions; discussions about how to communicate.

M Finding a way to use your knowledge and education to enhance your life and gain recognition in your field(s) of endeavor; the sense of fulfillment received through recognition of your works or principles.

MERCURY/JUPITER CONCEPTS

Astute Assumptions
Attains Flexibility
Allows Mental Restlessness
Insight into Information
Recalls Experiences
Boasts about Education
Expresses Satisfaction
Clever Promises
Skills which are Satisfying
Promising Discussions
Maneuvers to Expand
Attentive to Luck

Satisfying Discussions
Skillful Estimates
Reasons on the Law
Shrewd Conjectures
Promises of Dexterity
Well-Reasoned Theories
Erroneous Reasoning
Rapid Misjudgments
Discussions about Errors
Swiftly Derived Principles
Intellectual Summation
Expresses Confidence

Questions Luck
Spoken Opinion
Hints of Bias
A Lot of Ideas
Sincere Imitations
Shrewd Forecasts
A Lucky Swindler
Recalls Sincerity
Adaptable Humor
Dual Assumptions
Adapts to New Beliefs
Uneasy with Theory

Opinion as Information
Stated Assumptions
Information about a Windfall
Amplifies Restlessness
The Principle Observation
Swift Comprehension
Inquires about Estimates
Optimistic Information
Knows How to Phrase Questions
Confident Considerations
Satisfaction from Writing
Understands Data
Inclined to Think
Ingenious Counsel
Enthusiastic about Knowledge
Thoughts which bring Luck
Knows about Influence
Questions Sincerity
Two-way Expansion
Optimistic Communications
Speaks about Honesty
Believable Information
Sly Expansion
Notices Expansion
Expresses Theory
Observes Philanthropy
Skilled at Laughter
Observes Assumptions
Luck in Many Forms
Information about Expansion
Inclined to be Cunning

Clever Proposals
An Increase in Illustrations
Develops a New Theory
Suggestions of Sincerity
Cheerful Conjectures
Witty Propositions
Rapid Understanding
Practices Foreign Languages
Promises Versatility
Cagey Inclinations
Expands Discussions
Opinionated Thinking
An Edgy Outlook
Swiftly Acquired Beliefs
Opinions on Handiwork
Talks about Beliefs
Expands Versatility
Expounds on Happiness
Intellectual Sincerity
Takes either Side
Varies Expectations
Hints at Satisfaction
Flexible Understanding
Increases Examination
Restless over Errors
Discusses Tendencies
Reveals Optimism
Considers Philosophy
Restless Expansion
Observes Faith
Discloses Principles

MERCURY/JUPITER With Itself

☿   Enhanced ability to be articulate and persuasive thru advertising, public relations, speech, or writing; gathering information on the use of communications to reach others effectively; popular writings.

♃   Additional insight and comprehension to efforts for motivating and influencing the opinions of others; success with plans to induce others to adopt your methods; further luck with gambling schemes; religious studies.

Significant Examples of People and Events Using Mercury/Jupiter

General: **STRONG:** Grant Lewi; Ernest Hemingway; William Butler Yeats; Henry Kissinger; Jonathan Winters; Carroll Righter; Franklin Roosevelt; Rossano Brazzi; Jean Cocteau; Sandy Koufax; Gregory Peck; Richard Chamberlain
           WEAK: Willie Mays; Walt Whitman; Tom Smothers; Arthur Rimbaud; Benito Mussolini; Paramhansa Yogananda; Art Linkletter; R. D. Laing
           EVENTS: Kent State Shootings; RMS Titanic Hits Iceberg; Bolsheviks Seize Power; President Nixon's Resignation; (First Medicare Patient Accepted).

☉   Alan Leo; Ellen Burstyn; Ernest Hemingway; Giacomo Puccini; Dave Garroway; Robert Redford

☽   Jean Cocteau; Steve Rosenbloom; Laurence Olivier; Arthur Godfrey

☿, ♃   Audie Murphy; Rudolph Bing; Arnold Schwarzenegger; John F. Kennedy Shot; Scott Carpenter

♀   Ritchie Valens; Dr. Tom Dooley; Steve Wozniak; Edouard Manet

♂   Pierre Renoir; Benjamin Disraeli; Komar; RMS Titanic Hits Iceberg

♄   Sydney Omarr; Melvin Belli; Ralph Nader; Stephen Foster; H. Kissinger

♅   Van Cliburn; David Frost; Glen Campbell; Giacomo Puccini; Stephen Sondheim; Hugh Downs; Edna Ferber

♆   John Lennon; Bob Hope; Alan Alda; Alan Leo; Moshe Dayan; Bob Newhart; Francisco Farnco

♀   Albert Speer; Olga Worrall; Stephen Crane; Al Unser; Henry Kissinger

☊   Rosanno Brazzi; Franklin Roosevelt; Ervin Nyiregyhazi; Mary Martin

A   Erwin Rommel; Kent State Shootings; Edward R. Murrow; W. Gretzky

M   Mick Jagger; Grant Lewi; Johnny Carson; Francisco Franco; U. S. Grant

MERCURY/SATURN   ☿/♄

Basic Ideas:

Controlling communications, simplifying thought and logic processes, training to become a disciplined observer, or perhaps some thoughts of despair may appear with these themes. Developing ideas cautiously, organizing your reasoning, and showing caution about how you prepare your information are also represented. Serious delays in talks or negotiations may arise, business dealings underway could be concluded or ended, or discussions about the stability of your workers could arise. These planets indicate shortened messages, but also indicate a hesitation or nervousness when speaking before others. These motifs show rigidity in thinking, the formulation of serious inquiries, and naivete or ignorance of the facts. You may develop a sense of loyalty to business or commercial enterprises with this combination and take information more seriously.

In Your Personal Life:

Thesis   Developing a more factual mentality; observing the mistakes of others; maintaining discipline about information entrusted to you; enjoyment with manipulating numbers, calculations, or doing mental puzzles.

Anti   Pursuit of dreary thoughts which invade your mind and lower your self-esteem; you enjoy thinking alone, and can take this to an extreme; hesitation in your speech or discussions; a restless wasting of time.

In Your Relationships:

Thesis   Serious discussions with your partner; talk which carries a sense of duty and realism; approaching and discussing difficult subjects with your companions; plans for joint projects or mutual activities.

Anti   Delays when discussing items of mutual importance; disappointments from others with your ideas, communications, or thoughts; increased rigidity to the ideas or views of others; discouraging talks with partner.

With Body or Mind:

Cataracts or similar blockage of senses, nerves, or nerve endings; breaks in mental activities; the quality of eyesight; clear thinking; nervous strain.

In Politics or Business:

Thesis   Caution or frustration during mutual planning or discussions; simplified means of communicating with the media; directness or forthrightness in a leader's reasoning; computer programming methods.

Anti   Treaties which are difficult to compromise or debate; leaders who take their time when responding to demands; impasses reached in negotiations, talks, or discussions; delayed or hindered discussions.

MERCURY/SATURN with Planets and Points

☉　Sharpens your mind when your will is applied to serious communications; increased effectiveness in thinking; determination in getting your ideas directly and clearly across; serious tones to news items.

☽　Sensitive communications; thinking about your parents; care and discipline applied when releasing information; intuitive feelings about the data you receive in business settings; silent thinking or analysis on female matters.

♀　Appreciating how others think and/or show logic; pleasures derived from rigorous thinking or problem solving; simple ideas about how to charm others with your views; placing melody or word to music.

♂　Tough-minded negotiations in business or personal matters; energy used in the production of exacting or serious information; hasty yet simple communication; simple or sparse, yet troubling information.

♃　Additional ideas which form the basis for serious discussions; generosity shown with helping others align their thoughts; idealistic but simple reasoning about philosophical or religious matters.

♅　Innovation from scientific research; irregular communication or disruptions in information processing; indifference to formal ideas and the ways they are presented; messages delayed by mechanical failures.

♆　Inspired thoughts for avoiding serious delays in analyzing facts, data, or other communications; breakdowns in logical processes; serious errors in official news sources; misleading items deliberately presented as facts.

♇　Serious incidents provoke questioning official communications; compulsion in ensuring that information is correct; the ending of business with others due to serious breakdowns in your communications.

☊　Others who come to assist you with serious communication secrets or tasks; connections to groups which are able to provide scientific or thoroughly researched information on areas of interest to you; attracting deep thinkers.

A　Meetings with people who are disciplined thinkers; a sharp sense of reality; an ability to clearly understand your local environment; a serious and thoughtful personal style; a cautious seeking of attention.

M　Adds to your wisdom and maturity as you accumulate and use your knowledge; discussions about how you intend to live, or grow as a person; finding principles which help you develop a better and a meaningful life.

MERCURY/SATURN CONCEPTS

Simple Thoughts
Frustrating Information
A Pessimistic Description
Rumors of Dishonor
A Disciplined Mind
Sneaky Restrictions
A Persisting Imitation
Observes Curtailment
Calls for Patience
Silent Memorizing
Moderates Depictions
Restrains Swiftness

Avoids Discussions
Describes Discipline
Rigid Scrutiny
Talk of Holding Back
Pessimistic Thoughts
Frustrated Reasoning
Simple Variances
Many Faceted Durability
Talks of Restraint
Cautious Thinking
Versatile Reserve
Flexible Constraints

Restrains Thinking
Swift Dejection
Two-way Pessimism
Rapid Restraint
Nervous Anxiety
Swift Commitment
Expresses Caution
Clever Recall
Cagey Older People
Swift Silence
Sharp Objections
Nimble Durability

Disappointing Thoughts
Notices Pessimism
A Cold Conversation
Suggests Curtailment
Suspended Information
Talks about Discipline
Observes Dejection
Rumors of Restrictions
Pessimistic Questions
Objections to Information
Expresses Simplicity
Receives a Suspension
Adapts to Inflexibility
Simple Flexibility
Inquires about Obstacles
Expresses Frustration
Proficient at Difficult Tasks
Discussions in Isolated Places
Frustrating Discussions
Disappointing Debates
Two-way Commitment
Rigidity during Talks
Intellectual Commitment
Cautious with Knowledge
Dual Tragedies
Explains Precautions
Discloses Decisions
Ignores Communications
Blocks Information
Talks about the Use of Time
Asks about Burdens

Curtails Talent
Disobedient Researchers
Restrains Reasoning
Skilled Precautions
Observes Restraint
Varies Commitment
Adapts to Pessimism
Nimble Restraint
Reveals Caution
Organizes a Discussion
Shifty Persistence
Blocks Ambidexterity
Annoying Accuracy
Explains Postponements
Thoughts which Last
Describes Uneasiness
Frustrating Speeches
Hints of Restrictions
Examines Solitude
Receives a Rebuff
Attentive to Performance
Inadequate Acumen
Examines Conscience
Observes Objections
Expresses Pessimism
Remembers Respect
A Silent Interrogation
Ingenious Simplicity
Cunning which Persists
Asks for Permanence
Hears about Rebuffs

MERCURY/SATURN With Itself

☿ A focus on the analysis of old or difficult to comprehend data; an agility or cleverness about how to interpret and present common information; serious discussions about findings; formal statements of rumors or gossip.

♄ Conservative views when presenting findings; respect for your reputation as a serious or responsible person with facts; rebuffs about work results; disobedience obeying instructions on how to behave.

Significant Examples of People and Events Using Mercury/Saturn

General: **STRONG:** Emperor Hirohito; Ralph Waldo Emerson; John McEnroe; Richard Byrd; Ida Rolf; Wayne Gretzky; John Fremont; Ernest Pyle; David O. Selznik; Amadeo Modigliani; Bobby Fischer; Edouard Manet; Helen Reddy; Muhammad Ali
WEAK: Harry Belafonte; Ulysses S. Grant; Sir Laurence Olivier; Tom Jones; Komar; Olga Worrall; Audie Murphy; Jean Paul Sartre
EVENTS: Lewis & Clark Expedition starts; USS Maine Explosion; Pearl Harbor Attack begins; Lindburgh Lands in Paris; (First Medicare Patient Accepted).

☉ Wayne Gretzky; Mark Spitz; Harry Shoaf; Jean Paul Satre; Herman Goering; Jackie Robinson; Richard Strauss

☽ Ralph Waldo Emerson; Vincent Van Gogh; Robert Redford; Stephen King

☿, ♄ Jean Houston; Jerry Reed; Sir Wm. Crookes; Albert Einstein; S. Spielberg

♀ Sally Ride; Robin Williams; Bolsheviks Take Power; Marlon Brando

♂ Alexander Graham Bell; Pearl Harbor Attack; F. Scott Fitzgerald; Giacomo Puccini; Jean Houston; Rex Harrison

♃ Gianni Agnelli; USS Maine Explosion; Dick Gregory; Albert Speer

♅ Auguste Rodin; Adolf Hitler; John F. Kennedy; Ervin Nyiregyhazi

♆ Winston Churchill; Abraham Lincoln; John Lennon; David O. Selznik

♇ John Denver; Erich Maria Remarque; William Butler Yeats; Sir William Crookes; Sally Ride; Bobby Fischer; Jacques Cousteau

☊ Edouard Manet; Paul Newman; Jonathan Winters; Jack Nicklaus

A Rudolph Bing; Challenger Explosion; Henri Toulouse-Lautrec; Richard Byrd; Edward R. Murrow

M Mary Martin; Erich Maria Remarque; Dustin Hoffman; Johnny Carson

MERCURY/URANUS ☿/♅

Basic Ideas:

This combination symbolizes expressing opinions while you remain emotionally detached and aloof from the subject matter. These themes prompt you to express ideas in clever ways, bring knowledge of and insight into mechanical or electrical methods, and allow you to understand information flows and processes, such as those used in computer or systems work. They heighten your interest in astrology and its application, and you may find yourself doing research or classifying information to see how or why technology works. You may quickly observe ways of doing things, and intuit how different procedures can be shortened or improved. Impertinent ways of expressing opinions, and a quick and ready wit which others may find abrasive are also indicated. You do your best work alone, but you also need friends and companions for the input and personal stimulation they provide.

In Your Personal Life:

Thesis   You work well with numbers and data, and understand electrical and mechanical concepts; you enjoy classifying information, and are known as a 'jack-of -all-trades'; you excel at revising another's work.

Anti   You have a brilliant but eccentric mind; your sarcasm and wit disturb others; you do not care for people as much as you care for numbers and data; you are quick to argue over the smallest details; a dry personality.

In Your Relationships:

Thesis   You and your partner establish and keep psychological boundaries between you; you accept another's individuality and need for space in a relationship, but ask that yours also be respected.

Anti   You have such a need to express your self-identity that you do not care about the feelings of others; you find it difficult to express your feelings about the relationship; you disturb others with your independent ways.

With Body or Mind:

Intestinal and stomach gas; sensitivities to certain food groups (milk, wheat, etc.); nervousness and restlessness as a personal trait; easily stressed by others.

In Politics or Business:

Thesis   Breakthroughs in the communication or transmission of information; modernization of transportation networks or policies; business groups which form to help initiate policy; labor coalitions or unions at work.

Anti   Rebellions or riots which start because information on goals is not well explained or defined; reform which causes disruptions in the transportation network; use of propaganda during emergencies.

MERCURY/URANUS with Planets and Points

☉   Orienting your life toward the upgrade of mechanical, electrical, or information processes; added determination to use all resources to improve existing methods; implementing rapid means for modernizing older techniques.

☽   An intuitive understanding of mechanical, electrical, and information processes; meeting women who encourage your tinkering or restlessness; deep emotion or sentiment in an otherwise dry personality.

♀   Your love for mechanical and abstract objects outweighs your love of people and their contributions; you enjoy beauty and comfort, but demand great freedom and do not easily commit yourself or realize your inner feelings.

♂   Quick and sharp of mind and wit; abrasive when addressing others; very restless, but a need to be active; you balk at allowing others to commit time or resources; insightful thinking is hastened.

♃   Increased need for freedom and demands to be independent; a sharp mind which sees and judges the legal implications of all events quickly and precisely; added quickness to grasp the potential of new technology.

♄   Slows your mind; caution about what you say; a need for solitude; enhanced abilities to repeat monotonous tasks without complaint; pessimism about the state of events in your life; practical ideas.

♆   Carelessness in your work or speech; sloppy habits to your eccentricity and aloofness; an ability to visualize and dream about how to create a better lifestyle; an irresponsible attitude toward organizing work.

♇   Enhanced ability to design and be creative with potentially important items; an interest in how to re-cycle and re-use waste products; added slurs and vulgarities in your speech; you attract sudden reverses or complications in life.

☊   Meeting people who inspire you and help you move toward your life's destiny; eccentric; an ability to cut others off from your mind if you do not care for their reactions or opinions of your work.

A   Concentrating on your work, while giving greater attention to remaining aloof from others; adds to your image of brilliant eccentricity; increased needs for privacy and being away from emotionally upsetting situations.

M   Increased recognition received for your contributions; an ability to cope with those who are not able to grasp your concepts; curbed wit; a more mature insight on how to present others with what they need.

MERCURY/URANUS CONCEPTS

Adapts to Discontent
Knowledge of Revisions
Skillful and Innovative
Expresses Indifference
Questions Contrariness
Rapid Opposition
Description of a Misfit
Varieties of Debates
Ingenious Disturbances
Notices Disorganization
Unique Notification
Two-way Regulation

Unusual Information
Disrespectful Restlessness
Cunning Friends
Two-way Novelty
Regulates Information
Talks of Novelty
Rumors of Deviation
Two-way Rebelliousness
Conveys Detachment
Thoughts of Discontent
Discovers by Observing
Hints of Peculiarity

Original Talent
Notices Deviations
Observes Insight
Swift Eccentricity
Contrary Questions
Unique Discussions
Cunning Insight
Fast Computations
Clever Insight
Observes Novelty
Depicts Detachment
Reveals Uniqueness

Clever Forms of Uniqueness
Hails Breakthroughs
Indifferent to Education
Sneaky Revisions
Disputes Innovation
Friendly Disclosures
Expresses Peculiarity
Multifaceted Variations
Agile with Expressions
An Educated Heretic
Indifferent Reasoning
A Friendly Description
Surprise Scrutiny
Shrewd on Exceptions
Analyzes Collections of Data
Peculiar Descriptions
Modifies Questions
Asks Scientific Questions
An Exceptional Illustration
Agile and Restless
A Peculiar Suitability
Remembers Rebelliousness
Reveals Surprises
A Surprising Imitation
Describes Independence
Revisions to Information
Recalls Novelty
Bargains for Exceptions
A Variety of Questions
Puts Astrology into Words
Clever Deviation

Peculiar Thoughts
Disrupts Discussions
Innovative Reasoning
Thoughts of Regulation
Adapts to Obstinacy
Tells about Disruptions
Skillful Manipulation
A Talent for Peculiarity
Adapts to Idiosyncrasies
An Informed Defector
Innovative Versatility
Questions Uniqueness
Novel Probing
Disruptive Questions
Indifferent to Memorization
A Clever Variation
A Talent for Unpredictability
Information about Reforms
Notices Disclosures
Unexpected Information
Novel Forms of Memorizing
Astrological Research
Describes Differences
Unexpected Discussions
Disrupts Thinking
Expresses Surprise
Talks of Progress
Clever Expressions
Expresses Regulation
A Deft Substitution
Learns about Disruptions

MERCURY/URANUS With Itself

☿   A clever and quick way of thinking; emphasized observation of facts and classification of ideas; noticing how things work, and placing an emphasis on analytical processes; scientific data or information.

♅   Insight into mechanical or engineering processes; added discontent about how the world operates and the role that people play in running your life; novel insights into the use and application of computers or astrology.

Significant Examples of People and Events Using Mercury/Uranus

General: **STRONG:** Winston Churchill; Burt Reynolds; Jackie Robinson; John Fremont; Henri Matisse; Jack Schwartz; Johann Von Goethe; Yehudi Menuhin; Henry Kissinger; Liberace; Grant Lewi; Earl Warren; Giacomo Puccini; Benito Mussolini
WEAK: Charles Kettering; Norman Mailer; Paul Gauguin; Lance Reventlow; Ira Progoff; Robert DeNiro; Pres. Jimmy Carter; Gregory Peck
EVENTS: South Carolina Secession; East Coast Power Blackout; John F. Kennedy Shot; James Meredith Enrolled; (Lewis & Clark Expedition starts).

☉   Stephen Sondheim; Jackie Robinson; Stonewall Jackson; Richard Byrd

☽   Alan Leo; Arthur Rimbaud; Dustin Hoffman; Jackie Robinson; Jack Schwartz; John F. Kennedy; Manly Palmer Hall

☿, ♅   Henri Matisse; Jimi Hendrix; Burt Reynolds; John F. Kennedy Shot; Friedrich Nietzsche; Moshe Dayan; Jonathan Winters

♀   Ritchie Valens; Ernest Pyle; Stonewall Jackson; Albert Einstein; Burt Reynolds; Georges Seurat; Sam Sheppard

♂   Edgar Degas; Johnny Carson; Erich Maria Remarque; Alexis Carrel

♃   Nixon's Resignation; Johnny Carson; Jean Francois Millet; H. Goering

♄   Alexis Carrel; Earl Warren; Vida Blue; Paul Cezanne; Param. Yogananda

♆   Sam Sheppard; Drew Pearson; Henry Mancini; Percy Bysshe Shelley

♇   Peter Max; Neil Diamond; Moshe Dayan; Muhammad Ali; Vincent Van Gogh; Bob Fosse; Tommy Smothers

☊   Franklin Roosevelt; Jacques Cousteau; Jackie Robinson; Neil Diamond

A   Ernest Pyle; Winston Churchill; George Patton; John F. Kennedy Shot

M   First Medicare Patient; Harry Shoaf; Willie Mays; Winston Churchill

MERCURY/NEPTUNE   ☿/Ψ

Basic Ideas:

Inspiration expressed through communications, increased interest or fascination with mystical subjects, confusion in everyday thinking or reasoning, and the origin of unsound ideas, are all themes contained in this combination. These motifs highlight your deftness with performing deceptions and illusions, allow you to see both sides of the question even with incomplete reasoning, and add to your impulses to let obligations slide. These themes show inspired thinking and the expression of ideas in poetic ways using music, words, symbols, or foreign languages. Your nervousness when you are being evasive, your neglect of communications, your swift interpretations of dreams and visions, the use of your mental faculties to visualize thoughts and ideas, and your methods for creating machine-aided reasoning are also symbolized within this combination .

In Your Personal Life:

Thesis   Expressions of insight into mystical subjects; logical thinking about procedures for solving problems which are difficult to visualize; clever thinking and deductions about nebulous ideas or spurious subjects.

Anti   A restless mind which creates delusions of how the world and people work; confused thinking and communications; weak or spurious observations; shrewd use of mysticism or deception for your purposes.

In Your Relationships:

Thesis   Building an inner ideal about your partner; measuring your partner against your needs; good feelings of mystical oneness with your partner; inspired communications with your partner.

Anti   Illusions about how another person should be rather than how they are; added confusion about your feelings for another; finding that you are not above deceiving your partner about yourself.

With Body or Mind:

Drug reactions affect the nervous system; weakened lungs; vivid dreaming; weakness in the nervous system; a stroke; nervousness, in general.

In Politics or Business:

Thesis   An enterprise which visualizes and debates its future; leaders with the ability to communicate their visions of progress and growth; a legislature which controls the excesses and dreams of its leaders.

Anti   An inability to bring reality into planning and productivity; weak or artificial plans which must be rethought or redesigned; a leader who mesmerizes people with delusions of possible progress or growth.

MERCURY/NEPTUNE with Planets and Points

☉   Energized psychic reasoning; evaluation of hunches as a means for finding answers to problems; feelings of fullness and completion as dreams materialize; effective creative mental visualization.

☽   Increased sensitivity to thoughts or ideas about how the mystical or spiritual realms work; opened receptivity to channeling information from non-physical sources; intuitive thoughts which bring confusion and questions.

♀   Idealistic thinking about beauty and its role in life; idealizing love and affection, especially in an intellectual way; you have many ways of expressing vanity; increased mental appreciation of music or the arts.

♂   Energizes dreams and ideas, and breathes real life into them; confusion about how to mentally prepare self for exercise or combat; anxieties may reflect themselves in dreams about violence or anger.

♃   Increased dreams and visions on how the future should be; insight into using meditative faculties to understand that which troubles you; elusive thoughts about an ideal society; new patterns of metaphysics.

♄   Increased restraint shown about the use of intuition vs. logic; a need for confirming mystical impressions and observations with facts from the physical world; persons who have psychic gifts disappoint you.

♅   Increased ability to gain inspiration by using rational analysis along with psychic help; using astrology as a means for understanding different parts of life; unusual friends who have good psychic skills; a sudden lack of ideas.

♇   An obsession with using psychic or dream material as a means for determining physical reality; a termination of contacts with spiritual realms; learning and practicing purification rituals to rid self of mystical influences.

☊   Attracting people who tune into other forms of information in or out of this world; encounters with groups of people who are very prescient; sexual ties with psychic persons; alliances with mentalists; karma with psychics.

A   Tuning into events occurring around you on a level deeper than the physical; added impressions which come in mentally but not verbally from those around you; identifying and finding people with psychic powers.

M   Using mental images of your past experiences to help you to mature; developing psychic abilities to help you read others; added ability to work with psychic persons for mutual growth and self-development.

MERCURY/NEPTUNE CONCEPTS

Inspires Questions
Fraudulent Research
Artificial Intelligence
Fantastic Descriptions
Garbled Announcements
Confused Thinking
Omits the Reasons
Shoddy Handicrafts
A Sharp Imagination
Subtle Expressions
Questions an Omission
Conveys Capitulation

Expressions of Frivolity
Thoughts of Escape
Talks of Mysteries
Versatile with Disguises
A Shrewd Fraud
Observes Compliance
Notices Dilapidation
Two-way Inspiration
Adept at Amends
Sneaky Disguises
A Talent for Costumes
Talks of Reparation

Clever Camouflage
Mythical Variations
Tricky Confusion
Talk of Submission
Rumors of Neglect
Recalls Weakness
A Swift Escape
Thinks up Fantasies
Avoids Talking
Reveals Deceit
Studies Flaws
Sly Subtlety

Skilled with Fantasies
Cunning Mysteries
Reasons on Subtlety
Information on Miracles
Inefficient Interrogation
News of Complications
Recalls Indifference
A Swift Imagination
Interprets Dreams
Mysterious Restlessness
Hidden Information
Neglects Logic
Careless in Different Ways
Depicts Redemption
Remembers Counterfeits
Questions Neglect
Discloses an Image
Rumors of Escape
Skilled at being Vague
Imaginative Questions
A Clever Imagination
An Omitted Observation
Garbled Information
An Imperfect Imitation
Considers Deception
Imitates Holiness
Nimble in Escape
Talks of Inspiration
Hints of Complications
Inspired by Observations
Weak Thinking

Swift Concealment
Clever Fantasies
Thinks up Mysteries
Informed about Drugs
Impractical Questions
Thinks of Shoddiness
Forgotten Information
Misunderstood Expressions
Swift Inspiration
Contrives Reasons
A Deft and Able Liar
A Weak Memory
Imagined Observations
Limber Mystics
Misunderstood Suggestions
Notices Counterfeits
Shoddy or Weak Reasoning
Observes Weakness
Thinks about Giving Up
Expresses Weakness
Mysterious Variations
Whimsical Explanations
A Notice of Capitulation
A Confusing Notice
Cunning Subtlety
Lies about a Theft
Revealing Submission
Debates a Hypothesis
Garbled Hints
Vague Scrutiny
An Intellectual Fraud

MERCURY/NEPTUNE With Itself

☿   Increased awareness of the subtle forces and activities of life over which science has no explanation or control; inquires designed to occupy your time and resources, but which have no reality behind them.

Ψ   Added dreaminess in your thinking and reasoning; contriving ideas and solutions which may seem impractical at first, but which have an underlying basis for approaching your problems in new ways.

Significant Examples of People and Events Using Mercury/Neptune

General: **STRONG:** Steve Wozniak; Tom Jones; Stephen Sondheim; Marc Edmund Jones; Olga Worrall; John McEnroe; Carl Sandburg; Stephen Crane; Elvis Presley; Dave Garroway; Paul Joseph Goebbels
WEAK: Albert Speer; Robert McNamara; Arturo Toscanini; Yehudi Menuhin; Albert Camus; Sally Ride; Ernest Pyle; Gianni Agnelli
EVENTS: Lewis & Clark Expedition; Washington's Inauguration; Alaskan Earthquake; USS Maine Explosion; (Woman's Suffrage Amendment passed).

☉   Alex. Graham Bell; Norman Mailer; O. J. Simpson; Erwin Rommel

☽   Sir Alexander Fleming; James Meredith Enrolled at U. Miss.; Mary Martin; Sir Laurence Olivier

☿, Ψ   Erich Maria Remarque; Gustav Dore; Tommy Smothers; Apollo 11 Moon Landing; Richard Strauss

♀   Jerry Rubin; Audie Murphy; O. J. Simpson; Jacques Cousteau; Billy Rose; Johann Von Goethe; Burl Ives

♂   Bob Fosse; Wayne Gretzky; Sandy Koufax; Charles Kettering; Amadeo Modigliani; Thomas H. Huxley

♃   G. Washington's Inaug.; Elvis Presley; David O. Selznik; H. Kissinger

♄   Carl Sandburg; Marc Edmund Jones; Robert DeNiro; Adolf Hitler

♅   Jean Paul Satre; Jim Thorpe; Dave Garroway; Shirley Jones; Edward R. Murrow; Arthur Ford; Richard Chamberlain

♀   Ralph Waldo Emerson; John McEnroe; Enrico Caruso; Billy Rose

☊   O. J. Simpson; Jean Francois Millet; Grant Lewi; Sigmund Freud

A   East Coast Power Blackout; USS Maine Explosion; Jack Nicklaus; Gregory Peck; Steve Wozniak; Erwin Rommel; Sandy Koufax

M   Stephen King; Marc Edmund Jones; Stephen Foster; Olivia Newton-John

MERCURY/PLUTO   ☿/♀

Basic Ideas:

You may debase your thinking in ways that are subtle but important. Through these themes you can gain an obsession with reasoning and thinking which leads you into intense and drastic experiences where you will your ambitions to dominate another's wishes. These themes indicate extreme thoughts about using death or destruction as an implement for control, a duality in your approach to sexual expression, and fanatical speculation and reasoning which takes into you areas beyond normal social acceptance. These planets symbolize desires to imitate people who have achieved power and control. You may think little of using and abandoning others, or taking revenge on those who have not followed your orders or instructions. You may have many secrets you are willing to discuss with others, and may consider injuring others to obtain needed information.

In Your Personal Life:

Thesis   Ambitions to perform more precise research; you can be ruthless in the ways you pursue sources of information; becoming obsessed with informing on others who tell secrets; learning how to interrogate.

Anti   You have a paranoia about secrets and their disclosure; you can be very unforgiving with people who have not followed your rules; you are not above punishing others; acquiring very clever and cunning styles.

In Your Relationships:

Thesis   You attach yourself to another only after much thought, and when you give another your loyalty you expect the same in return; you have great depths of passion, and enjoy talk about the most intimate subjects.

Anti   Stimulation from erotic literature and pictures; gaining enjoyment from bisexual sharing; need to have control over your partner's activities; consideration of using others for sex.

With Body or Mind:

Pituitary or endocrine glandular imbalances are highlighted; breakdown of body tissue caused by toxins; degenerative nerve diseases; toxins in the lungs.

In Politics or Business:

Thesis   High security communications and intelligence activities; political talk which offers abrupt changes to some functions; communications satellites; news of space exploration, orbital weapons, or toxic gases.

Anti   Secrets concerning the business community or transportation systems; communications within the intelligence gathering agencies; self-destructive impulses in business; breakdowns in the road networks.

MERCURY/PLUTO with Planets and Points

☉   Conviction and determination to use force to locate or obtain information; added commitment to bisexual feelings; enhanced authority or prestige among people who control important information or news.

☽   Diminished capacity for enjoying sex with one partner; mood swings when you can not obtain your way with others; sensitivity to the sexual and intellectual needs of others; obsessive needs for privacy or power.

♀   Ruthlessness in desires to control others; seeking control over sources of artistic information and using these to your advantage or to increase your position; a desire for intellectual gratification from the arts.

♂   Aggressiveness and persistency in quests for sexual power and control; an untiring energy in your search for information; demands that information be used in the ways you plan; mental preparation before difficult exercise.

♃   Need to control publishing sources and the presentation of material and information to the public; increased public relations or advertising expertise; a bias about what information you release to others.

♄   Disappointment when releasing information which you feel is secret; delays in your plans to exert control over knowledge; added efficiency to your ruthlessness in pursuing sources of data or rumors.

♅   Remaining aloof from others who do your bidding to obtain data in any way possible; an interest in using research to study the validity of astrology; great understanding of engineering processes; unusual scientific insight or ideas.

♆   Mystical insight into where and how to get the information you need; using deception and concealing information; an inefficient or messy researcher; the disappearance or falsification of experimental data.

☊   Contacts with people who help you obtain information or news; a need to share secret information with allies; emotional separation from the desires of others; contacts with powerful criminal elements.

A   Once you have decided what it is that you want, this contact allows you to go after your goals in a persistent and dedicated way; intensifies your search and desire to control information, its sources, and its dissemination.

M   Added needs to grow and develop through what you learn about life; receiving recognition from others for your achievements; altering your behavior so others can notice that you have more importance than before.

MERCURY/PLUTO CONCEPTS

Shrewd Corruption
Thinks about Vengeance
Researches Purification
Considers Cleansing
Crafty Morbidity
Calls for Constraints
Reflects on Violence
Debased Thinking
Informed of Corruption
Crafty Dishonesty
Extreme Ingenuity
Obsessive Thoughts

Learns about Power
Nimble when Destroying
Chaotic Planning
Stealthy Tyranny
Reasons on Elimination
Obsessed with Intellect
Clever Restitution
Hints at Poisoning
Swift Punishment
Compulsive Questions
Reasons on Obsession
Thinks of Restitution

Swift Restitution
Clever Elimination
Compulsive Trickery
Clever Dilution
Observes Corruption
Discloses Defeat
Sneaky Crimes
Subtle Remorse
Adapts to Chaos
Fidgety at Funerals
Hasty Vengeance
Varies Obsessions

Reveals a Rejection
Informed on Coercion
Condenses Information
Nimble with Punishment
Questions Admonishment
Cagey Ways of Eliminating
Suggests Dishonesty
Conceals Restlessness
Information on Shortages
Revenge on Informed Sources
Disapproves of Reasoning
Questions Restitution
Skilled with Using Force
Relentless Restlessness
Information which is Suspect
Insidious Punishment
Ceases to be Eloquent
Observes Restitution
New Data on Degradation
Can Destroy in Many Ways
Punished for Information
Destroys Information
Inquires about Monopolies
Drastic Gestures
News of Death
Retaliates with Letters
Talk of Destruction
Agile Oppression
Interrogates Criminals
Restless for Vengeance
Suspicious of Education

Talks of Fixations
Describes Destruction
Questions Contamination
Eliminates Inquiry
Intense Discussions
Shrewd with Concealment
Observes Dishonor
Two-way Condemnation
Many Ways of Purifying
Obsessive Questions
Spoken Curses
Contempt for Duality
Questions Vengeance
Inquires about Fanaticism
Flexible Dismissal
Tells Secrets
Reveals Duress
Hidden Reasoning
Talks of Elimination
Versatile Prosecution
Notices Suspicion
Corrupts Expressions
A Shortage of Information
A Morbid Analogy
Adept with Dismissals
Troubles with Speech
Skillful Retaliation
Compulsive Talking
Observes a Breakdown
Knows about Depression
Subversive Thinking

MERCURY/PLUTO With Itself

☿   Creates a mental curiosity within you that can lead to obsessions about accumulating or correlating facts and data as a definitive information source; adds to your need for intellectual stimulation and enhancement.

♀   A ruthlessness when seeking whatever information you desire; increased needs to hide your actions and activities from others; increased likelihood of hearing depressing information; the end of discouraging information.

Significant Examples of People and Events Using Mercury/Pluto

General: STRONG: Mark Spitz; Dr. Francis Regardie; Lord Byron; Adolf Hitler; Ivar Kreugar; Art Linkletter; John Glenn; Dane Rudhyar; Norman Mailer; Gregory Peck; Burl Ives; Hank Williams; Stephen King; Pierre Teilhard de Chardin
WEAK: Arthur Ford; Gustav Dore; Jack Schwartz; Edgar Degas; Melvin Belli; Jack Nicklaus; Lawrence Welk; Richard Byrd
EVENTS: Apollo 11 Moon Landing; Alaskan Earthquake; FDR's First Election; East Coast Power Blackout; (Bolsheviks Take Power).

☉   Art Linkletter; Sigmund Freud; Lord Byron; Alan Leo; Watergate Burglary Discovered; Pierre Tielhard de Chardin

☽   Georges Seurat; Herman Melville; Jean Houston; Henry Kissinger

☿, ♀   F. D. Roosevelt; Helen Reddy; Earl Warren; Norman Mailer; Albert Einstein; George Washington's Inauguration

♀   John Dillinger; Carl Sagan; Neil Diamond; Cheiro; Steve Allen; R. Bing

♂   Transcontinental Railroad completed; Jack Schwartz; Teilhard de Chardin; Lance Reventlow

♃   Lewis & Clark Expedition starts; USS Maine Explosion; Lord Byron; Helen Reddy; Arthur Ford; John Dillinger

♄   Henri Toulouse-Lautrec; Ralph Nader; Bjorn Borg; Neil Diamond; Jerry Reed; Sir Alexander Fleming

♅   Gregory Peck; Carroll Righter; Albert Camus; Earl Warren; F. Nietzsche

♆   Steven Spielberg; Edna Ferber; Carl Sagan; Arthur Rimbaud; Jean Francoise Millet; Amadeo Modigliani

☊   Willie Brandt; Liberace; Laur. Olivier; Tommy Smothers; Sean Connery

A   Marlon Brando; Transcon. RR done; Jean Houston; Steven Spielberg

M   Wayne Gretzky; Merv Griffin; First Medicare Patient; Alaskan Earthquake; Maurice Ravel; Earl Warren

MERCURY/NODE   ☿/☊

Basic Ideas:

Thoughts on how to meet, coordinate, and communicate with people who think like you are central to these themes. There is an added emphasis on the content of your messages. Pursuing connections to others who provide information or fill gaps in your knowledge is also shown. Research which requires help from others, and finding and locating the people you need for specific tasks or for general assistance in meeting goals, is also shown by these themes. How you gather information or conduct your investigations, your research on or observances of sociological connections among people, quick or versatile reactions to the needs and requirements of others, or how you evaluate your relationships with others, are also mirrored here. Your nervousness before others, observations about group politics, or fated ties to people you have previously known, are also indicated.

In Your Personal Life:

Thesis   Highlights communication and interaction with others; aware-ness of how to present information so that you can attract and keep attention; researching sociological data.

Anti   Pursuing ties to others solely for sexual means; curiosity about concepts which you need to attract others; use of trickery or cunning to attract others to your ideas; a rapid presentation of data; nervous when alone.

In Your Relationships:

Thesis   Ideas you have and the research you do to meet and to attract compatible people to you; alliances and ties to others; the ability to attract the right types of people to your life; sharing your thoughts with partner.

Anti   Using questionable or shady means to attract others for your needs; discussions with others solely for the purpose of sexual liaisons or ties; habit patterns which involve some waste of information resources.

With Body or Mind:

Assimilation of food unable to get to the body parts needed due to broken or blocked channels or passages; connecting tissues for nerves; a blocked tongue.

In Politics or Business:

Thesis   The creation of new corridors for transportation; enhances the connection between people and goods; enabling business to ship or transport merchandise; joint efforts which are well-thought-out and coordinated.

Anti   The use of transportation facilities for smuggling or similarly unlawful means; the theft of material or information on trans-portation capabilities or policies; ineffective efforts to coordi-nate transportation options.

MERCURY/NODE with Planets and Points

☉　Efforts made toward enhancing interpersonal communications; added personal emphasis and focus on the effectiveness and the importance of the message presented; well-coordinated personal ventures.

☽　Sensitive reactions about how others use information presented; a tradition of using associates to research or pass on information and communication; locating people to gather information; details meant for the general public.

♀　Rapport developed thru meetings with people interested in banking or the arts; appreciation for how friends or allies can help communicate your messages; communicating messages of beauty to friends.

♂　Competitive efforts to exert influence thru ideas; struggles to effectively relate ideas; movement or activity generated while speaking or lecturing; the transmission of ideas; anger conveyed by thoughts.

♃　Reasoning about the ethics of group communications; exhibiting communication equipment designed for enhancing exchanges among religious or philosophical coalitions; advertising, marketing, or promotional successes.

♄　Disciplined thoughts on effectively getting your message across; the lasting bonds and ties you have developed through groups of friends; ties to conservative organizations; fated talks on personal destiny.

♅　Manipulating allies to carry your messages to others who need to listen to them; indifference to groups who work to communicate your ideas; disruptions or upsetting events at sessions where you are lecturing.

♆　A weakening of the ties you have established with others through a lack of proper communications; visions of how to improve your communications potentials when meeting with others; clever deceptions when passing data.

♇　Suspicions about leakages thru spies; removing massive amounts of data through groups of closely working companions; drastic measures taken to present your ideas to acquaintances; provocative data.

A　Creating conditions to facilitate the exchange of data and information; concentrating on the need for communicating to and thru others; reactions to how information is transmitted to or received by groups.

M　Development of an understanding of how those who share similar interests are able to assist you in enhancing your prestige; the use of groups who can help you grow in stature and reputation; your intentions for giving data.

MERCURY/NODE CONCEPTS

Removes Information
Smart Exhibitors
A Skillful Sexual Liaison
Talks to New Friends
Fidgety Acquaintances
Intellectual Karma
Questions Supporters
Skillful Discourses
Calls on Relatives
Observes Group Sociology
Informed about Alliances
Thinks of Sexual Ties

Different Pathways
Nimble Ways of Ridding
Intelligent Friends
Questions Life's Aim
Shrewd Discourses on Life
Reasons about Life's Aim
Learns Cooperation
Swift Separations
Clever during Meetings
Restless with Life's Aim
Varies Criticisms
Talks about Separations

Rapid Attraction
Notices Alliances
Nervous at Breaks
Reasons on Ridding
Dual Sexual Ties
Informed on Events
Questions Bonds
Duality in Life's Aim
Crafty about Allying
Thinks about Support
A Talent for Alliances
Clever with Mergers

Talks about Attracting Others
Sources with Information
Keeps Tabs on Associates
Two-way Sense of Destiny
Astute Associates
Details on Joint Ventures
Interviews which Educate
Ideas during Meetings
Reveals a Joint Venture
Discussions about Karma
Sidesteps a Separation
Learns to Attract Others
Demonstrates Reasoning
Details about Obligations
Wonders about Cooperation
Thinks about Associates
Occasional Versatility
Expresses a Need for Groups
Discussions during Meetings
Links to Neighbors
Hails Others at Gatherings
Inquisitive at Meetings
Discusses Needs for Exchanges
Restless during Meetings
Disputes Layoffs
Dishonest Companions
Two-way Discussions
Talks about People Delays
Responsive at Meetings
Talented Acquaintances
A Talent for Friendships

Quick Answers to Questions
Skilled Information Exchanges
A Flexible Attitudes
Thinks about Attracting Others
Expects to Locate People
Presents Two Subjects
Reads on a Sense of Destiny
Eloquent Interchanges
Restless over Partnership
Thinks about Dismissals
Inquires about Delaying Tactics
Researches Life's Direction
Explains New Habits
Clever Use of Ties to Others
Informed on Confederates
Educational Conference
Comments on Preoccupation
Two-way Separations
Fast Friendships
Clever Reasoning on Karma
Thinks of New Habits
Debates with Acquaintances
Adaptable with Life's Aim
Notices Ties to Others
Observes Bureaucratic Methods
Talks of Separations
Reads about Kinships
Finds Solutions to Delays
Agile Accomplices
Expresses a Need for Alliances
Easily Lets Go of Another

MERCURY/NODE With Itself

☿   Communicating with people who have ideas and talents similar to yours; discussing your ideas or work with others becomes important; making shrewd observations about how others react to situations or information.

☊   Enhanced need to seek feedback or approval from people on your work or ideas, and to associate with professional acquaintances; luck in finding meetings where people are receptive to your ideas.

Significant Examples of People and Events Using Mercury/Node

General: **STRONG:** Benito Mussolini; Sir Laurence Olivier; Jerry Rubin; Bob Hope; Jack Schwartz; Alexander Graham Bell; Sydney Omarr; Helen Reddy; Robert Redford; Paul Gauguin; Ira Progoff; Dave Garroway; Willy Brandt
WEAK: Sam Peckinpah; Richard Strauss; Liberace; Bjorn Borg; Stephen King; Walt Whitman; Elvis Presley; Albert Schweitzer
EVENTS: Pearl Harbor Attack; Lindburgh Lands; South Carolina Secession; Kent State Shootings; First A-Bomb Explosion; (Apollo 11 Moon Landing).

☉   Vincent Van Gogh; Paul Gauguin; Abraham Lincoln; Herman Melville

☽   R. D. Laing; Percy Bys. Shelley; Vittorio DeSica; Pearl Harbor Attack

☿, ☊   Bob Hope; Ira Progoff; Paul Joseph Goebbels; Ritchie Valens; Pierre Gauguin; Franklin Roosevelt; Alexis Carrel

♀   Ernest Pyle; Merv Griffin; Mary Martin; Robert Redford; Stephen Sondheim; David O. Selznik

♂   Pierre Renoir; J. Von Ribbentrop; Burt Reynolds; Jackie Robinson

♃   Melvin Belli; Franklin Roosevelt; Henri Matisse; Jerry Rubin; Burl Ives

♄   First Medicare Patient accepted; Kareem Abdul-Jabbar; Stephen Foster; Lawrence Welk; Jean Cocteau

♅   Peter Max; Nikola Tesla; A. Schwarzenegger; Tommy Smothers

♆   Willy Brandt; Dane Rudhyar; John McEnroe; Mark Spitz; Sir William Crookes; Alexander Graham Bell

♀   Jack Schwartz; Rudolph Bing; Hugh Downs; Ervin Nyiregyhazi; S. Allen

A   Paramhansa Yogananda; Ernest Pyle; Pierre Teilhard de Chardin; Pearl Harbor Attack begins; Henri Matisse

M   Arnold Schwarzenegger; Wayne Gretzky; Anne Murray; Gus Grissom

MERCURY/ASCENDANT   ☿/A

Basic Ideas:

An increased awareness of the world around you, the people in it, and how these people react to you and you to them is central to these themes. You may spend much time noticing the reactions of others, or focusing on the roles that others play in their lives or in your life. Through this motif you receive impressions about people and how they respond to life's situations, and notice what their postures, pretenses, and reactions are to you, others, or the world in general. These themes bring a restlessness to your concentration, and you may additionally develop the means to mentally follow several thoughts at once. They may symbolize a loss of concentration, or becoming restless or bored with the stimulation you receive from others. You prefer a changing environment. You become very informed about others and what they need or want from other people in life.

In Your Personal Life:

Thesis   You become a thinking person who relates to others through observing how they react; focusing on your reactions to others, or how they react to you; people's reactions become important to you; criticizing others.

Anti   You spend a lot of time talking and boring others with your observations of them, their moods, and disposition; you may sum others up so quickly that you lose sight of many different deeper qualities they have.

In Your Relationships:

Thesis   Enhanced mutual understanding and communication between partners; a better understanding of your partner's motivations; relating to the concerns and interests of other people.

Anti   Studying and analyzing the motives and intentions of another person; an increased nervousness when you are not able to understand another's communications; shutting out the ideas of another person.

With Body or Mind:

The effect of your mental attitude on your health; intestinal gas from the stress of having to relate to others; your speech organs and their functioning.

In Politics or Business:

Thesis   Desires to communicate with friends or allies; the importance placed on clearly communicating intentions to others; an emphasis on efficient and reliable transportation systems; rapidly disseminated news.

Anti   Weather, and weather-related phenomena; business and government unable to communicate their concerns and mutual interests; a transportation system supported or run by business interests or powers.

MERCURY/ASCENDANT with Planets and Points

☉   Emphasizing how to speak and relate to others; noticing another's reactions to your ideas or thoughts; encouragement from others for your ideas; added importance in your communications; determination to get your ideas out.

☽   Sensitivity and awareness when judging the reactions of others and their responses to your ideas; sensitive, moody reactions when stimulated by certain people; irregular communication attempts or patterns.

♀   Softness of speech, and a need for using correct manners and politeness when relating to others; emphasis on your personal importance in relationships, and how you may react to others you encounter.

♂   Emphasized need to mentally understand people and their reaction to you and the world; observing the reactions of others and learning about what motivates them; energetic mannerisms while speaking.

♃   Increased need for social contacts; observing or evaluating others for their political or personal potential to you; thinking about why others behave as they do; philosophical ideas about people, their motivations, or their needs.

♄   Disciplined observations help you shorten how you classify and categorize the reactions of others; added realism to your view of what motivates others; you need less time to communicate with others.

♅   You are introduced to the potential astrology or science has in helping you to understand other people and how they live; others get the idea that you have eccentric or singularly-focused ideas or views on life.

♆   Confusion about the motivations and intentions of others; you relate to others through intuitive senses, and not just through observing their physical reactions; a laxity or looseness in how you see or record events.

♇   Insight into understanding yourself as a person, and the role that other people play in your life; added urges for you to study interpersonal psychology; rejection or dismissal of your ideas and communications.

☊   Initiating observations of other people, and evaluating the roles they may play in your life; contact with others who have ideas similar to yours about observing and understanding people; meeting people for whom you have kinship.

M   Realizing the role and contributions of others in your life, especially as you mature; coping with the difficulties, and placing these into a better perspective on life, its turns, and meanings; education as a step to fame.

MERCURY/ASCENDANT CONCEPTS

Inquires about Others	Disposed to Education	Adapts to Settings
Describes Current Conditions	Reveals Mannerisms	Skilled Perceptions
Notices Surroundings	Two-sided Demeanor	Recalls Pretenses
Knowledge taken in Context	Thinks about Attitudes	Sudden Viewpoints
Analyzes Relating to Others	Sly Perceptions	Either-way Attitudes
Discusses Another's Style	Describes Mannerisms	Skillful Rejoinders
A Restless Nature	Quick Mental Focus	Discusses Reactions
Notices Restlessness	Two-way Sense of Style	Hints of Inhibitions
Tricky Personal Style	Discusses Experiences	Inquisitive Habits
Interprets Observations	Versatile Reactions	Clever Attitudes
Reasons on Sense of Reality	Inquisitive Mental Focus	Swift Reactions
Flexible Disposition	Questions Attitudes	Disputes Reality

Adaptable Personal Beliefs	Thoughts on Diverse Ideas
Shifting Sensations	Views Others as Restless
Knows about Repressing Ideas	Expresses a Sense of Reality
Swift at Understanding Others	Scrutinizes Personal Style
Asks about Attention Seeking	Intelligent Cognizance
Adapts well to Conditions	Flexible about what Reality is
Appears Restless	Examines Surroundings
Addresses Attention Seeking	Reasons about Mannerisms
Variable Points of View	An Intellectual Impression
Disputes Conceptions	Variable Personal Style
Describes Reactions	Expresses Perceptions
Writes about their Reality	Discussions on Consciousness
Observes Inhibitions	Questions an Assessment
Detects Another's Cleverness	Explores Surroundings
Questions Relating to Others	Clever at Reading People
Skilled with Rejoinders	Adaptive Mannerisms
Information on Experiences	A Reasonable Mental Focus
Sees Interpersonal Boundaries	Represses Another's Ideas
Gains News from Introspection	Swift Perceptions
Expresses Interpersonal Roles	Sly about Attention Seeking
Quick Recognition	Ingenious Ways of Relating
Restless Demeanor	Thinks about the Present
Versatile Tone (Attitude)	Notices Interpersonal Roles
Attentive to Consciousness	Observes Reactions
Notices Another's Personality	Studies Mannerisms
Thinks about Perceptions	Writes with a Personal Flair
Thoughts on Getting Attention	Clever Ways of Relating
Reasons about Inhibitions	Recalls Personal Style
Sly Ways of Relating to Others	Receives Multiple Impressions
Questions Reality	Thoughtful Mental Focus
Variable Sense of Reality	Two-way Interpersonal Roles

MERCURY/ASCENDANT With Itself

☿   Interpretation of verbal and similar information from people you meet; making important points with an emphasis which comes from the result of educated conviction; flexibly adapting to another's needs.

A   Experiences which cause you to notice how others react and function within their environment; understanding yourself better because you have learned about yourself by observing how others react and function in life.

Significant Examples of People and Events Using Mercury/Ascendant

General: **STRONG:** R. D. Laing; Paul Newman; David Frost; Herman Melville; Peter Max; Bjorn Borg; Jim Thorpe; Grant Lewi; Albert Schweitzer; Paul Joseph Goebbels; Maurice Ravel; F. Scott Fitzgerald; Benjamin Disraeli
WEAK: Ida Rolf; Robert Redford; Ada Lovelace Byron; Ernest Pyle; Audie Murphy; Paul Cezanne; Jean Cocteau; Muhammad Ali
EVENTS: Bolsheviks Take Power; Alaskan Earthquake; Mt. St. Helens Explosion; South Carolina Secession; (George Washington's Inauguration).

☉   Thomas H. Huxley; Paul Joseph Goebbels; South Carolina Secession; Fidel Castro; Maurice Ravel; Ralph Waldo Emerson

☽   Bob Dylan; Watergate Burglary; Jackie Robinson; Edgar Degas; Anne Murray; Marc Edmund Jones; Drew Pearson

☿, A   Paul Newman; Jim Thorpe; A. Schwarzenegger; Bjorn Borg; Maur. Ravel

♀   Carl Sagan; Peter Max; Stephen Sondheim; East Coast Power Blackout

♂   R. D. Laing; Ritchie Valens; Mick Jagger; Shirley Jones; Liberace; Vittorio DeSica; Arthur Godfrey

♃   Gen. Joseph Joffre; Evel Knievel; H. G. Wells; Francisco Franco; Jack Nicklaus; Norman Mailer

♄   Peter Max; Hank Williams; Jerry Rubin; Carroll Righter; Erwin Rommel

♅   Bolsheviks Take Power; Benjamin Disraeli; Edward R. Murrow; C E Carter

♆   Jerry Reed; John Paul I; Arthur Godfrey; Helen Reddy; Bob Newhart

♇   Apollo 11 Moon Landing; Alexis Carrel; Albert Camus; Ira Progoff

☊   Apollo 11 Moon Landing; East Coast Power Blackout; Georges Seurat; Liberace; Lawrence Welk; Jack Nicklaus

M   RMS Titanic Hits Iceberg; Rudolph Bing; Albert Schweitzer; H. Mancini

MERCURY/MIDHEAVEN ☿/M

Basic Ideas:

These themes, combined, symbolize how you apply your education and intellect toward achieving your potential in life. They suggest developing the potential for which your education and family environment have prepared you. They represent your ability to adjust the mental image you have about your life's objectives, your willingness to work for educational and job related credentials, and the training you put yourself through to improve your position or stature in life. The ways you apply your creativity, the recognition you receive for your accomplishments, and how you use your native faculties to help you mature as a person are also represented. Your inner image of what you can achieve as a person, your mental preparations in developing an ability to cope with life, and your efforts to play out life's various roles and scripts are also shown through these themes.

In Your Personal Life:

Thesis   The personal growth and maturing you experience as a result of your encounters with different situations in life and how you are able to adapt with these; the intelligence behind your psychological defenses.

Anti   Finding that fabrication and cunning are good cover-ups for mistakes in life; adopting dishonest means to enhance personal progress; lying or distortion as a way of life; innocent thievery or crime.

In Your Relationships:

Thesis   Learning to grow and appreciate your partner for the qualities they may develop in you; insights from others which can change your life for the better; helps you work together with another to appreciate life together.

Anti   Increased inability to cope with any problems your partner brings; you tend to misjudge another's good or bad intentions and do not learn or grow from experiences in relationships, family, or early life.

With Body or Mind:

Genetic deficiencies or strengths concerning lungs, breathing, etc.; family history of asthma or bronchial problems; nervousness which is inherited.

In Politics or Business:

Thesis   Effective communication about the policies and goals; setting transportation policies; bringing the goals of businesses and manufacturing together with the aims and policies of the legislative arms of the state.

Anti   Any miscommunication which prevents the executive from being able to gain support for policies; ineffective or poorly planned transportation or communication networks; weakened communications.

MERCURY/MIDHEAVEN with Planets and Points

☉   The prominence and renown you achieve through hard work and your personal will and determination to develop into a better person; the self-confidence you build as you mature; a positive picture of self.

☽   The uncertainty and vacillation that creeps into your assessment of how life treats you; using intuition and impressions of life to grow as a person, rather than study, work, and research; inconsistent thoughts on maturing.

♀   Developing a softness to your personality as you mature; a satisfaction about the person you are becoming; self-contentment with your stature and recognition; a deceitful trend creeps into your aims in life.

♂   Added energy and activity for the efforts you go through to mature and develop; the importance of working out anger accumulated from situations or people; courage to progress toward and work for goals.

♃   A successful quality to your writing and speeches; gaining recognition for your work; understanding and forgiving others for deeds done; publicity and recognition for work accomplished or completed.

♄   A sternness or sense of austerity to your demeanor and selfhood; the sense of obligation to work hard and become someone important in life; commitments you make to self about completing and finishing.

♅   Manipulating position and friends to gain respect and regard for personal attainments; sudden or unpredictable events which affect your stature or standing; unique ways to show your personal maturity and individuality.

♆   Personal or self-deceptive practices or habits confuse your judgment about situations or people; a laxity in the attention you give to projects; using education or research aptitudes in a very mature way.

♇   Urges hard work to correct defects in your personal attitudes; the extremes you go through to reconcile and integrate your principles of work and life; the personal intensity you bring toward gaining any recognition due you.

☊   Associations with different people who can help you to gain stature and recognition in life; the kinship you feel with your family; paths which open and allow you to make the most of opportunities in life.

A   Observations made about people and how they help you grow or mature; characteristics of personality you develop through your education, thinking, or writing which help you to advance and grow.

MERCURY/MIDHEAVEN CONCEPTS

Talks of Self-Restraint	Informed of Outcomes	Shrewd Behavior
Informed on Safekeeping	Wandering Intentions	An Adaptable Infancy
Two-way Security Seeking	Thinks of New Methods	Reasons on Origin
Conveys Self-Restraint	Schemes for Outcomes	Calls for Standards
Self-Taught Integration	An Anxious Beginning	Considers Constancy
Talks about Origins	Thinks of Intentions	Swift Mastery
Ingenious Accomplishments	Skillful Perseverance	Learns Expertise
Standardizes Information	Reasons out Results	Thinks of Coping
Astute on Starting in Life	Slyly Seeks Security	Clever Protection
Rapid Personal Training	Expresses Integrity	Observes Principles
Thinks of Seeking Security	Talks on Objectives	A Talent for Rank
Swift Self-Restraint	A Versatile Expert	Rapid Respectability
Intellectual Distinction	Persists in being Shifty	Well-Schooled Conduct

Knowledge of Consequences	Confirms Rumors
Educated with Self-Restraint	Clever with Principles
Explains Self-Concepts	Remembers Outcomes
Questions Objectives	Thinks of Public Projection
Restless Personal Development	Many Faceted Intentions
Rapid Safekeeping	Two-way Attainment
Knows about Maturing	Swift Protection
Discusses Personal Code	Describes Beginnings
Reveals a Need for Security	Nervous Confidence
Describes How to Mature	Shifts Ideas on Schooling
Learns by Observing	Evasive Self-Concepts
Reasons on Objective	Observes Integration
Recalls Personal Guarantees	Thinks about Corroboration
Alert to Maturation Processes	Speaks on Intentions
Talks of Learning and Growing	Restless Integration
Ages and Acquires Knowledge	Expounds on Integrity
Information on Self-Becoming	Examines Authorization
Talks of Aging Gracefully	Bargains for Protection
Questions Security Seeking	Well-Thought-Out Results
A Flexible Sense of Fairness	Questions about Coping
Studies for Gaining Stature	Clever Ways of Feeling Secure
Perceives Intentions	Skillful Expertise
Nervous about Consequences	Writes about Self-Concepts
Versatile when Growing	Illustrates Principles
Memorizes Behavior Patterns	Rumors about Plans
Depicts Uprightness	Discussions of Intentions
Expresses Intentions	Informed on Self-Concepts
Intends to Act Cleverly	Observes Ambition
Outcomes which Change	Questions about Origin
Information Methods	Inquiries for Confirmation

MERCURY/MIDHEAVEN With Itself

☿   Strong ability to extract information from data, and present it to others in coherent ways; examining your progress with life, and where you want to go or what you want to accomplish with your aptitudes.

M   Added pride taken with your work and your feelings about a completed product; enhanced self-discipline and pride for doing your tasks well and producing finished work which needs no further embellishment.

Significant Examples of People and Events Using Mercury/Midheaven

General: **STRONG:** Benito Mussolini; Paramhansa Yogananda; Steve Allen; Hermann Goering; Lawrence Welk; Jean Paul Sartre; Henry Winkler; Earl Warren; Henri Toulouse-Lautrec; Jerry Rubin; Bob Dylan; Rupert Murdoch; Carroll Righter
WEAK: Olivia Newton-John; Sigmund Freud; Dane Rudhyar; Friedrich Nietzsche; Albert Camus; Gregory Peck; Franklin Roosevelt; Enrico Fermi
EVENTS: Lee's Surrender at Appomattox; First Atomic Explosion; James Meredith Enrolled at U. Miss.; George Washington's Inauguration; (USS Maine Explosion).

☉   Richard Alpert; Albert Einstein; Walt Whitman; Carroll Righter; B. Borg
☽   Ervin Nyiregyhazi; Richard Byrd; Joachim Von Ribbentrop; Sean Connery; Richard Chamberlain
☿, M   Lance Reventlow; Liberace; Wm. Butler Yeats; Henry Winkler; Carl Sagan
♀   First A-Bomb Explosion; Dick Gregory; Bertrand Russell; Marlon Brando; Jonathan Winters; Lord Byron
♂   Bolsheviks Take Power; Sydney Omarr; Grant Lewi; Rupert Murdoch
♃   Charles Steinmetz; Van Cliburn; Fidel Castro; Robert McNamara
♄   Gus Grissom; Sam Peckinpah; Earl Warren; Bob Dylan; Carroll Righter
♅   Rosanno Brazzi; Rex Harrison; Paramhansa Yogananda; Hermann Goering; Ira Progoff; Ralph Waldo Emerson
♆   Jean Francois Millet; Stonewall Jackson; Mario Andretti; Albert Einstein
♀   John Denver; Ira Progoff; Stephen Crane; Paul Gauguin; Auguste Rodin
☊   Albert Schweitzer; Arthur Rimbaud; Yehudi Menuhin; Kent State Shoot.
A   Burt Reynolds; Bob Dylan; James Meredith Enrolled at U. Miss.; Marc Edmund Jones; Elton John

VENUS/MARS ♀/♂

Basic Ideas:

Tenderness encounters impulsiveness, rage feeds on irritation, vanity meets force, and jealousy finds stimulation. The primary female and male planets introduce very different themes as the push and pull of the sexual archetypes unite in this combination. While Venus charms the Martian aggressiveness, Mars' need for action counters by stimulating Venus to move beyond its lethargy. These motifs may arouse your jealousies, as well as impel you into recognizing the beauty in self or others. They activate the pleasure you derive from haste, danger, and recklessness. They highlight the enjoyment you get from the activities you pursue. They slow and charm your haste, while inflaming your temptations. You may find you are quick to become envious, or hasty in your attachment to the beauty of the person or place at hand. You actively display your wealth or beauty.

In Your Personal Life:

Thesis   Enjoying the pleasures which others introduce to you; impulsive attachments to the energies of another person; the beauty of an exciting location; enjoyment or gratification from the courage others show.

Anti   Coincident stimulation and gratification; impulsive affections given and then withdrawn; anger which builds quickly; impulses or temptations to delight in the problems of others; jealousy which builds fast.

In Your Relationships:

Thesis   The heat and passion of the moment buried in the pleasure of your activity; the innocent compliment meets the assertive argument; an appreciation of your partner's charms after physical activity or efforts.

Anti   A noisy argument about your partner's devotions; aggravated dormant jealousies; compelling forces which push to the breaking point; sexual gratification tied to battles or arguments.

With Body or Mind:

Sexual pleasure; haste in sexual release; relaxing muscles; the muscle tone of your body; fevers which start with blood problems; forced sexual activity.

In Politics or Business:

Thesis   Courtesy shown to adversaries by a combatant; a ruler with martial skills, charm, and diplomatic tendencies, too; scenery where natural beauty is evident for all to see and enjoy.

Anti   A ruler who will not let others enjoy or indulge in risking the beauty or resources available; making a spectacle of prowess in martial arts or competitive sports; satisfaction derived from fighting or recklessness.

VENUS/MARS with Planets and Points

☉   Vigorous and lively pleasure from your activities; an active need for approval after athletic activities; mastery of graceful movement and motion, and a tendency to be proud of activities.

☽   Maternal feelings aroused from your affections and activities; satisfaction from activities where you can show concern; increased enjoyment from household activities; adds to your love of home or family.

☿   Discussions about your need for satisfaction from love and sex; communication about male and female roles in life; dialogues on the beauty of speed or acceleration; you to find pleasure in observations.

♃   Appreciating the beauty demonstrated in contests of strength or mastery of skills; an excess of musical noise which some find beautiful; exaggerated pleasures from intimate contacts with another person .

♄   Inhibited direct pleasure derived from the opposite sex; respect or admiration gained from exercise; a conservative side to displays of affection or admiration; a diminished attraction for competing.

♅   An upsetting or unusual movement when showing grace during action; expressing beauty in motion in unusual or extreme ways; erratic shows of angers; a need for independence in any relationship.

♆   Added need for escape during passionate moments; the use of drugs to heighten sexual response; weakness shown in a beauty competition; subtle, inner delights from activities also bring pleasure.

♇   Extremes of passion or envy; stealth in satisfying the need for stimulation or excitement; using sex for power; condemning those who have satisfied their anger on self or others; intensifies envy in those having strength or courage.

☊   Meeting people who bring pleasure and enjoyment to your activities; associations with others who enjoy similar forms of music or performing arts; a feeling that it is your destiny to enjoy reckless activities.

A   Focusing on activities which bring relaxation and pleasure; any awareness of your effects on others and how you use this to heighten pleasure in people; disputes about pretenses which bring enjoyment to you.

M   Fulfillment of your need for pleasure from another; the experience of being able to enjoy yourself with another person; the pleasure experienced in returning to your family origins; placing personal controls on rage or anger.

VENUS/MARS CONCEPTS

Admires Initiative
Insists on Consideration
Relishes Panic
Loves Excitement
Attracts Action/Activity
Satisfies Aggression
Admires Commotions
Polite Coercion
Rushes to Luxury
Apathetic Defiance
Balks at Charm
Hasty Satisfaction
Desires Commotion
Appeases Aggression

Envies Defiance
Initiates Satisfaction
Satisfies Urges
A Charming Initiative
Enjoys Loud Music
Pleasurable Urges
Excited by Beauty
Defies Temptations
Delights in Insistence
Delicate Initiative
A Pleasant Commotion
Charming Coercion
Attached to Exertion
Beautiful Advances

Jealous Anger
Proud Defiance
Charms Animosity
Graceful Strength
Favors Haste
Attracts Pursuit
Energy for Loving
Elegant Exertion
Civilized Anger
Polite Complaints
Delights in Struggles
Urges for Vanity
Favors Violence
Respects Courage

Enjoys Acceleration
Sensual Action/Activity
Considers Stimulation
Glamorizes Exercise
Irritation with Beauty
Quiet Disturbances
Appreciates Commotion
Entices Brutality
Indulges in Disturbances
Repays with Defiance
Amorous Arguments
Grateful for Heroism
Clamors for Consideration
Defies Convenience
Considerate of Aggression
Appreciates Initiative
Sweet Vindictiveness
The Courage to Love
Argues for Consideration
Envious of Competitors
Beautiful Action/Activity
Attracted by Muscular Bodies
Envious of Aggressiveness
Delights in Anger
Frenzied Disturbances
Gentle Excitement
Satisfies Complaints
Affectionate Animosity
Kind to Pushy People

Pleasing Arguments
Polite Aggressiveness
Beautiful Protests
Complains about Affection
Charming Stimulation
Courteous Arguments
Delightful Defiance
Appeases Disputes
Satisfies Anger
Civilized Indignation
Satisfying Stimulation
Loves Anger
Tender Virility
Appreciates Haste
Enjoys Defiance
Pleasurable Animosity
Spectacular Excitement
Beauty in Motion
Enjoys Stimulation
Rushes into Affection
Compulsive Vanity
Appreciates Sexuality
Pleased by Stimulation
Struggles with Charm
Forces Pleasures
Modest Bravery
Polite Action/Activity
Flatters Vigor
A Beautiful Combatant

VENUS/MARS With Itself

♀ Deriving enjoyment from exercise or movement; charming others as a form of sexual arousal; immediate attractiveness; movement in art or music; the tranquility and inner peace which follows exertion.

♂ Added immediacy for fulfillment of pleasures; yielding to impulses to find enjoyment in recklessness or activities where speed and agility are emphasized along with elements of danger; a need to race, to win, to covet a prize.

Significant Examples of People and Events Using Venus/Mars

General: **STRONG:** Bob Hope; Claude Debussy; Sir Alexander Fleming; Dr. Francis Regardie; Hermann Goering; Rex Harrison; Stephen Sondheim; Jean Paul Sartre; Richard Strauss; Carl Sagan; Jack Paar; R. D. Laing
WEAK: Alexander Graham Bell; Jim Thorpe; Dick Gregory; Komar; Jimi Hendrix; Henri Toulouse-Lautrec; Steve Allen; Bob Fosse
EVENTS: East Coast Power Blackout; Kent State Shootings; Apollo 11 Moon Landing; Challenger Explosion; (Woman's Suffrage Amendment Passed).

⊙ Vittorio DeSica; Amadeo Modigliani; George Patton; Mount St. Helens Explosion; Gustav Dore; Richard Strauss

☽ Walt Whitman; Ida Rolf; Gregory Peck; Rupert Murdoch; Drew Pearson; Charles Kettering; Shirley Jones

☿ Erich Maria Remarque; Evel Knievel; Jerry Rubin; Gregory Peck

♀, ♂ Tom Jones; Adolf Hitler; J. F. Kennedy Shot; Ivar Kreugar; W. Mays

♃ F. D. Roosevelt Wins; East Coast Power Blkout.; Krishnamurti; Millet

♄ Johnny Carson; Johann Von Goethe; Francisco Franco; Sally Ride

♅ Jean Cocteau; F. Scott Fitzgerald; Dr. Tom Dooley; Stonewall Jackson

♆ Dustin Hoffman; Erich Maria Remarque; G. Seurat; A. Schwarzenegger

♀ Rudolph Bing; Hugh Downs; Johnny Carson; Bert. Russell; Chernobyl

☊ Charles E. O. Carter; Merv Griffin; Israel Regardie; Challenger Explos.

A James Meredith Enrolled; Giacomo Puccini; Jerry Rubin; F. Nietzsche

M Jonathan Winters; Ernest Pyle; Burl Ives; Jean Francois Millet; J. Reed

VENUS/JUPITER ♀/♃

Basic Ideas:

These planets symbolize showing grace when giving opinions, urge you to gain appreciation for the wisdom you encounter from others, and stimulate you to increase your manners and politeness when dealing with all people whatever the circumstances. Through these themes you can derive pleasure and delight from opinions, religion, legal matters, ethics, or philosophy, and find joy and harmony in promoting optimism. These combinations show an increase in your finances, satisfaction from using and trying your luck, and opportunities and chances which are fortunate. They enhance the softness, femininity, or mildness of your disposition, and your urges to expand your participation with cultured and sophisticated styles. They can also symbolize your capacity for envy or jealousy, and the temptations which lure you away from work or obligations you have made.

In Your Personal Life:

Thesis   Expanding on your pleasure in creating opinions in law, ethics, religion, or philosophy from your studies; softening your approach to others thru improving your manners and politeness.

Anti   You take pleasure in giving too much opinion without adequate fact; an increased conceit about your abilities; becoming prone to erroneous assumptions; need for excesses of placating.

In Your Relationships:

Thesis   Expanding on your partner's pleasure; increasing your delight in social events or sporting activities enjoyed with your partner; happiness and joy felt from loving; enjoyment from your sexual activities.

Anti   Feeling that consistent routines will increase relationship pleasures; you experience good feelings with your partner but neither of you work to balance all parts of your relationship in the same way.

With Body or Mind:

The effects of indulgence on your body; accumulations of body fat; wasted muscle; acid accumulations due to dietary imbalances, sweets, or inactivity.

In Politics or Business:

Thesis   Periods of prosperity and growth; an expansion in the economic and general outlook; increased processing of legal cases; many new laws; attraction of foreigners to an enterprise; foreign capital investments.

Anti   Expansion of religions and their interference into the justice system; an expansion of social culture which affects all aspects of life; foreign raids on the treasury; an inability to defend values or symbols of enterprise.

VENUS/JUPITER with Planets and Points

☉   Understanding the importance of social activities with new manners and politeness; increased feelings of luck and pleasure from taking chances; added importance given to politics, social opinion, and expectations.

☽   Fundamental fears about current social philosophy and its effect on home or the family; conflicting sentiments which lead to errors in the judgment of values; arbitrary quality or evaluation methods.

☿   Emphasized education in areas of philosophy, religion, ethics, etc. investigation of new systems of thought in economics, culture, religion, markets, etc.; ability to speak or write on similar subject areas.

♂   The energy and forcefulness you put into your convictions about life and its events; irritation you have with those who do not understand the ideas behind the topic; aroused desires to pursue further studies.

♄   Increased caution or care about opinions or advice given to others; an emphasis on the seriousness behind your intentions and principles; guarded statements about your stand on issues; an interest in business methods or cycles.

♅   Sudden or unexpected events which propel you to think about new ways of coping; original thoughts in philosophical areas; an expanded role of astrology or computers in your life; exceptional new thoughts.

♆   The inflation or expansion of any current process; weakening of limitations which are imposed; expanded illusions about your welfare or health in general; confusion as a factor to delaying your progress.

♇   Extreme reactions to opinions which others feel damage their areas of interests; your need to investigate and research facts to back up the development of ideas; hidden resources you have which help correct errors.

☊   Making the proper connections with people able to support your ideas or causes; joining groups where your opinions are valued; meetings where you receive feedback or input about your doctrines or ideas.

A   Concentrating on presenting ideas and opinions about your values or ethics; a softness in your personal style pleases others and adds to your image of being a gentle, cultured, or refined person.

M   How you learn to overcome and soften behavior patterns which annoy your friends; the recognition you receive for the elaboration of your ideas on social justice, philosophy, etc.; the consequences of your ideas on pleasure.

VENUS/JUPITER CONCEPTS

Delights in Assumptions	Values Expectations	Charming Opinions
Graceful Optimism	Relaxes with Religion	Quiet Sincerity
Glamorizes Doctrine	Rages if not Satisfied	Softens Opinion
Appreciates Opinions	Kind and Sincere	Promises Sensuality
Cherishes Boasting	Tranquil Persuasion	Enjoys Luck
Resents Guesses	Desirable Promotions	Polite Assumptions
Indulges in Generosity	Admires Approximations	Pampers Theory
Embellishes Errors	Pleasurable Expansion	Satisfying Promises
Glorious Attainment	Attached to Inaccuracy	Cordial Opinions
Modest Commitments	Values Theory	Mannerly Studies
Courteous Satisfaction	Rages over Beliefs	Enjoys Philosophy
Mellows Beliefs	Inclined to Charm	Polite Optimism
Envies Expansion	Delights in Pomposity	Embellishes Beliefs
Mismanages a Beauty	Satisfying Cheerfulness	Lucky in Love

Satisfied with Estimates	Pleasing Sincerity
Glamorizes Wisdom	Agreeable Cheerfulness
Appreciates Foreign Things	Values Discernment
Discreet Promises	Appreciates Expansion
Expanding Affection	Polite Guesses
A Captivating Doctrine	Delights in Theory
Theorizes on Love	A Large Reimbursement
Attached to Expectations	Indulges in Sincerity
Delights in Promises	Beautiful Improvements
Inclined toward Delight	Upholds Assumptions
Captivating Enthusiasm	A Flattering Proposition
Pleased with Attainment	Gentle Mismanagement
Charming Conjecture	Believes in Beauty
Satisfies Expectations	Modest Errors
Attached to Sincerity	A Promise of Harmony
Supplementary Sensations	Softens Expectations
Feminine Beliefs	A Satisfying Suggestion
Assures Encouragement	Appeases Errors
Satisfied by Promises	Quiet Expansion
Softens Optimism	Tactful Frankness
Potential for Pleasure	Appreciates Beliefs
Attracted to Frankness	Enjoys Assumptions
Gratifying Laughter	Luxurious Expansion
A Respect for Honesty	Favors Boasting
Laid-back Cheerfulness	A Discreet Concession
Expands Thinking on Affection	Attached to Theory
Delightful Counsel	Admires Wisdom
Enjoys Understanding	Delights in Promotions
Amusing Adornments	Values Principles

VENUS/JUPITER With Itself

♀ Finding favor with people who hold strong attitudes about feminine temperaments; being easily lulled by flattery; additional satisfaction when you hit a lucky streak; increased sensuality and charm.

♃ Increased understanding of the effects of beauty, and the value of proper clothes and appearance; increased opportunities for contacts and success in music, finance, banking, or the arts in general.

Significant Examples of People and Events Using Venus/Jupiter

General: **STRONG:** Lawrence Welk; Bobby Fischer; Henry Winkler; Joachim Von Ribbentrop; Alan Alda; Hank Williams; Sam Peckinpah; E. Rommel; Ada Lovelace Byron; Willie Brandt; Elton John; Erich Maria Remarque
WEAK: Benjamin Disraeli; Gustav Dore; Albert Speer; A. Schwarzenegger; Jerry Reed; Dr. Francis Regardie; Kareem Abdul-Jabbar; Nikola Tesla
EVENTS: Bolsheviks Seize Power; Ramstein Airshow Collision; First A-Bomb Explosion; George Washington's Inauguration; (Alaskan Earthquake occurs).

☉ Rex Harrison; Audie Murphy; Watergate Burg.; D. Pearson; E. Rommel

☽ Arthur Godfrey; Ralph Nader; Apollo 11 Moon Landing; Bob Fosse; Hank Williams; Jack Paar; Art Linkletter

☿ Wm. Butler Yeats; John Lennon; Ervin Nyiregyhazi; Steve Wozniak

♀, ♃ Henry Winkler; Ada Lovelace Byron; Johann Von Goethe; B. Fischer

♂ R. D. Laing; David O. Selznik; Vincent Van Gogh; Bob Dylan; R. Valens

♄ Stephen Sondheim; Apollo 11 Moon Lndg.; Moshe Dayan; M. E. Jones

♅ Joachim Von Ribbentrop; Jack Schwartz; Ramstein Crash; Cheiro

♆ Edward R. Murrow; Lord Byron; Jimi Hendrix; J. F. Kennedy Shot

♀ Olga Worrall; Paul Newman; Nixon's Resignation; Apollo 11 Landing

☊ Hugh Downs; Charles Gordon; Rudolph Bing; Mary Martin; S. Wozniak

A Ernest Hemingway; Auguste Rodin; Robert DeNiro; Paul Gauguin

M Lee's Surrender; Mt. St. Helens; Guglielmo Marconi; Benito Mussolini

VENUS/SATURN   ♀/♄

Basic Ideas:

These themes indicate lessened or blocked enjoyment from activities designed to bring love, pleasure, or relaxation to your life. They symbolize working for satisfaction, adding caution to your desires for affection, and realism or innocence to your desire for respect. Through these motifs you gain lasting enjoyment despite setbacks, acquire pleasure from silence, and discover brief temptations. You may impose discipline on your jealous tendencies, find that your desire for affection or love becomes more serious and stable, and show a polite and mannered disposition when necessary and proper. You may also find that you are disappointed with the gratification you receive, become inflexible about how you will accept or show luxury, and suffer some temptations in solitude. These themes can also show restrictions in your love life, and an isolation from admirers.

In Your Personal Life:

Thesis   You learn to gain enjoyment even through restrictions on your activities; you find that the simple pleasures in life bring great enjoyment; you become pleased with the way the pleasures you experience are lasting.

Anti   The enjoyment you hope to receive is diminished, and you are disappointed with the value you receive from your entertainment; you are forced to suffer silently as you can not express your affections openly.

In Your Relationships:

Thesis   The love you share with your partner is simple but enduring; you derive great sensual pleasure from a partner, but these periods are brief and inadequate; your partner's sense of luxury is subdued and serious.

Anti   You find difficulty relating to your partner's passions; satisfaction feels blocked; you become disappointed with the value of your partner's affections, feeling a cool reserve toward you.

With Body or Mind:

Diminishes sense of smell and taste; restricts passages in the throat; poor blood supply to the joints encourages calcium and other deposits; arthritis.

In Politics or Business:

Thesis   Restrictions on wealth or income; law enforcement avoiding difficult or cumbersome issues; changes forced on enterprise by new social, artistic, or musical values; building the value of the enterprise.

Anti   Restrictions on the way society is able to function; elderly people in the enterprise who have artistic tendencies; a law enforcement bureau which derives pleasure from restricting the movement of the people.

VENUS/SATURN with Planets and Points

☉   Distinguished, older people who are serious artists enter your life; your tastes remain simple, but you still enjoy extravagant displays of beauty; honors received in later life from artistic or musical skills.

☽   Your instincts about a simple life vacillate, and you are inconsistent between demanding luxury and seeking solitude; your pleasures often feel incomplete; you console those who find little or no love.

☿   Studying the effects of beauty and charm, and how to enhance these qualities within you; delayed enjoyment from your experiences with education; creating lasting and enjoyable communications; messages of lasting love.

♂   Enhanced impulses to quickly receive pleasure in short bursts from your activities; enjoying traditionally male oriented activities; complaints against restrictions which curtail loud music; lasting get-rich quick schemes.

♃   Increased enjoyment of the more modest pleasures of life; makes a simple lifestyle more complicated and demanding; support and approval from areas or people which you may not have anticipated.

♅   Resentment over disappointments which diminish your enjoyment or appreciation of activities or objects; rebellion over circumstances which force you to conform to certain styles of dress or behavior.

☊   Enhanced abilities to produce artistic works which bring pleasure to others, but only those few who are serious in their appreciation of your work; adds mystery and charm to simple or plain objects of beauty.

♀   Increased intensity of your need for simple pleasures in life; trouble with the ways you show appreciation to others; retaliation from people who feel you have restricted or curtailed their love.

☋   Meeting serious, older but charming people who can help you find answers to your problems; you find the right kind of business people to help you through your present situations; strong karmic attraction to an older person.

A   Concentrating on using charm and manners in social situations where decorum and sophistication is required; considering the impact of your need for pleasure on others; a sterile beauty in your present surroundings.

M   Maturity and understanding of how you can relax amidst the demands of a pressure building life-style; enhanced needs to be noticed for your enduring financial contributions to important causes or efforts.

VENUS/SATURN CONCEPTS

Prolongs Love
A Serious Artist
Cautious Satisfaction
Satisfies Restrictions
Delights in Boycotts
Accepts Burdens
Attached to Simplicity
Obstacles to Appreciation
Restrains Affection
Holds Back on Payments
Delights in Objections
Accommodates Shyness

Prefers Plainness
Indulges in Caution
Deliberate Delicacy
Softens Frustration
Grateful for Durability
Charming Restraint
Polite Rigidity
Repays with Efficiency
Polite Objections
Values Constraints
Enjoys Innocence
Attracted by Humility

Stable Affections
Enjoys Frustration
Values Austerity
Fitting Silence
Upholds Defense
Pampers Old Things
Humors Rigidity
Values Objections
Enjoys Decorum
Admires Simplicity
Respects Modesty
Cold Politeness

Committed to Indulgence
Appreciates Silent Beauty
Rages over Postponements
A Pleasant Burden
Adores Discipline
Delays in Showing Beauty
Feminine Burdens
Confessions of Appreciation
Admires Commitment
Appreciates Simplicity
Attached to Discipline
A Love of Restrictions
Disappointing Affection
Feminine Modesty
Delights in Berating
Bears Burdens Quietly
Restricts Appreciation
Attached to Silence
Indulges in Austerity
Resents Work
Disappointed with Beauty
Satisfies Frustrations
Cherishes Dedication
Invites Restrictions
Avoids Attachment
Very Little Enticement
Resents Restraints
Glamorizes Conformance
Indulges in Practicality
Continuing Sophistication
Humbles Venality

Desires Durability
Pessimistic about Pleasure
Enduring Art or Music
Admires Stability
Continuing Indulgence
Enduring Charm
Uneasy Touching
Frustration with Selfishness
Beautiful Old People
Highly Regards Discipline
Restricted Love
Repays with Dejection
Appreciates Self-Control
Pleased with Precautions
Uneasy with Glamor
Approves of Silence
Rages when Frustrated
Softens Restrictions
Satisfying Organization
Polite Commitment
Disappointing Pleasures
Committed to Pampering
Annoying Admiration
Spartan Politeness
Simple Indulgences
Stops Reimbursement
Cautious with Beauty Aids
Satisfies Older People
Softens Pessimism
Simple Sensuality
Indulges in Silence

VENUS/SATURN With Itself

♀   Satisfaction with various circumstances in your life despite worries, setbacks, or restrictions; an increased respect for planning or organizing pleasures; longer needs to withdraw and relax in comfort.

♄   An increased tendency to feel restricted or curtailed by the commitments you have made to console or provide for others; increased realism about the status of affections and appreciation received; smaller payments for artists.

Significant Examples of People and Events Using Venus/Saturn

General: **STRONG:** Rupert Murdoch; Jackie Robinson; Steve Rosenbloom; Willie Mays; Richard Strauss; Dane Rudhyar; Dr. Francis Regardie; Bobby Fischer; Richard Chamberlain; Willie Brandt; Paul Newman
WEAK: Tom Jones; Alan Alda; Burt Reynolds; Abraham Lincoln; Yehudi Menuhin; Bob Dylan; Marlon Brando; Stephen Crane
EVENTS: Transcontinental Railroad completed; East Coast Power Blackout; John F. Kennedy Shot; Watergate Burglary discovered; (Franklin D. Roosevelt Wins First Election).

☉   Ira Progoff; Earl Warren; John Denver; Mario Andretti; Marlon Brando

☽   F. Scott Fitzgerald; Komar; Richard Strauss; George Patton; G. Marconi

☿   John Fremont; John Denver; John Lennon; Laurence Olivier; A. Carrel

♀, ♄   Shirley Jones; Richard Chamberlain; Ida Rolf; Dustin Hoffman

♂   Jean Cocteau; Carroll Righter; Auguste Rodin; Richard Strauss; Elvis Presley; Sydney Omarr; Ada Lovelace Byron

♃   Kareem Abdul-Jabbar; Bob Newhart; Giacomo Puccini; Alan Leo

♅   Jackie Robinson; Erwin Rommel; Laurence Olivier; Friedrich Nietzsche

♆   Willie Mays; Steve Allen; Ada Lovelace Byron; Transcon. RR Done

♇   Robert DeNiro; Art Linkletter; Percy Bysshe Shelley; David Frost

☊   Dr. Tom Dooley; Cheiro; Gregory Peck; Paul Newman; John Paul I

A   Bob Newhart; Pearl Harbor Attack; Arturo Toscanini; Burl Ives; Israel Regardie; Louis Pasteur; Ada Lovelace Byron

M   Georges Seurat; Al Unser; Billy Rose; Steve Rosenbloom; Edmund Halley; Benito Mussolini; Muhammad Ali

VENUS/URANUS ♀/♅

Basic Ideas:

This combination shows methods of affection and loving that are both impersonal and independent. You find new ways of expressing your appreciation for what others do, develop a fondness for innovation or unpredictability, and get pleasure from surprising others with peculiar ways of expressing sophistication. You can show a politeness while disrupting and disturbing others, feel delight when seeking reforms, and discover pleasure while expressing new forms of antisocial behavior. Unique and unusual forms of entertainment attract you. You get sudden temptations which need to be satisfied, discover new ways of charming others, and create distinctive forms of dress or relaxation. You express unique ways of showing your affection, and a jealousy which is aroused in sudden and unusual ways. You may also have a love of mechanical and electrical objects,

In Your Personal Life:

Thesis   Encourages a stamp of personal individuality in the way you desire to show affection to others; beauty which is expressed in unusual ways; your ability to derive enjoyment through using or studying astrology.

Anti   An inability to derive satisfaction or pleasure easily; the restless feeling which accompanies your longing to find self-worth; a longing to appreciate who you are as a person or tangible things you can do for others.

In Your Relationships:

Thesis   A relationship where your partner finds your expression of uniqueness to be fulfilling and satisfying; affection expressed in unusual ways and yet appreciated by another; enjoyment you get from being different.

Anti   You keep finding partners who cannot accept the way you show love; you feel detached in your affection for another; indifference to the ways others express beauty or loveliness; sudden temptations which arise.

With Body or Mind:

Any unusual compositions in your blood; shock due to acid conditions in the body; abnormalities in female organs; sudden complications in the throat.

In Politics or Business:

Thesis   A treasury which shows unexpected rises and falls in its valuation; rulers using unusual means to develop the plant or tree resources available; a strange appreciation for financial assets or planning.

Anti   Distinctive settings which are suddenly exploited for development; the ruling bodies unable to cope with sudden infusions or lacks of financial resources; unpredictable vanity shown by leaders or executives.

VENUS/URANUS with Planets and Points

☉ Effective or reliable ways of showing unusual forms of beauty and appreciation; influencing standards with innovative music or art; unusual demonstrations of innovation in finance, music, or the arts.

☽ Unusual forms of beauty and art shown with compassion and sensitivity; appreciation of novel art forms created by ordinary people; uncertainty over how to present innovative charm or affection; novel forms of romance.

☿ Unusual forms of beauty and appreciation communicated, discussed and/or observed; thoughts of inspiration about new or unusual forms of loving or beauty; novels which express unusual forms of lovingness or satisfaction.

♂ Effort and energy placed into novel or unique forms of appreciation and/or satisfaction; sexual love tested in an odd or extraordinary manner; an emotionless way of throwing yourself into weird forms of art or enjoyment.

♃ Generosity shown toward those who express enjoyment in innovative ways; a fortunate acceptance of new or peculiar ideas in art, love, or finance; wisdom exercised with results of innovation.

♄ Moderation when demonstrating unusual methods of beautifying or embellishing self; caution taken with innovative forms of gratification; perpetuating new forms of expression involving art, finance, or music.

♆ Inspiration is added to innovation by developing new forms of pleasure; deception within new and different forms of art, finance, or music; confusing impersonal responses when demonstrating affection.

♀ Accusations, attack, or disruptions in seeking enjoyment or satisfaction; obsession with unusual forms of pleasing others; fanatical appreciation for haphazardly offered forms of enjoyment or affection.

☊ Connections to others who develop innovative and unusual forms of music or art; presentations showing unusual forms of entertainment; attention-getting methods which use disruptive forms of affection.

A Concentrating on innovative themes in music, art or finance; a heightened show of affection to those who have unusual talents in artistic fields; unusual delights received from enjoying your personal space.

M Developing an appreciation for the unusual in the worlds of music, art, and finance; family origins rooted in the pleasures of being a rebel; focus on and modernizing of your personal stylistic tastes as you mature through life.

VENUS/URANUS CONCEPTS

Resents Rudeness	Unique Gratification	Quiet Manipulation
Abnormal Temptations	Novel Privileges	Touching Variations
Attached to Disruption	Displeasing Oddity	Sudden Politeness
Resents Revisions	Scientific Preferences	Satisfying Politics
Tolerates Oddities	Gentle Adjustments	Admires Serenity
Pleasing Substitutions	Unusual Opposition	Novel Jealousy
Glamorizes Deviations	Innovative Pleasures	Upsets the Harmony
Indifferent to Satisfaction	Expensive Oddities	Admires Surprises
Sudden Impartiality	Enjoys Being a Renegade	Electronic Music
Values Friendliness	Delightful Insight	Courteous Compromise
Appreciates Peculiarity	Unique Kindness	Polite Reforms
A Lovely Idiosyncrasy	Rebels with Satisfaction	Appeals to Discontent

Indifferent to Temptation	Charming Innovation
Polite Rebellions	Erratic Attraction
Unstable Relaxation	Cherishes Peculiarity
Softens Unpredictability	Glamorizes Experiments
Mannerly Individualism	Envious of Contrariness
Irregular Loveliness	Appreciates Surprises
Envious of Innovation	Affectionate Insight
Disturbs Your Composure	Delightful Variation
Disrupts Satisfaction	Regulates Tenderness
Jealous Indifference	Impersonal Charm
Satisfies Opponents	Regulates Jealousy
Indiscriminate Politeness	Pleased with Revisions
Charming Disruptions	Unusual Compliments
Considers the Irregular	Jealous Rebelliousness
Revises Vanity (Conceit)	Polite Rulings
Unexpected Satisfaction	Tempting Deviation
Changes done with Love	Abrupt Consideration
Indiscriminate Enjoyment	Values Disruption
Charming Indifference	Unusual Jealousy
Indifferent to Affection	Attracted to Politics
Unprecedented Politeness	Enjoys Uniqueness
Unexpected Harmony	Peculiar Politeness
Cooperates with Scientists	Courteous Indifference
Unusual Consideration	Satisfaction from Astrology
Glamorizes Variations	Innocent Differences
Unpredictable Preferences	Jealous of Innovations
Envies Variation	Revises Compliments
Expensive Compromise	Sudden Jealousy
A Liberated Beauty	Envious of Insight
Prizes Insolence	Jealous Variation
Disruptive Envy (Coveting)	Flattery and Manipulation

VENUS/URANUS With Itself

♀ Newtemptationstoindulgeselfwhich mustbegratified now;increased respect from peers for unusual insight and clarification of existing work; impulses to start satisfying self in all areas of life and work.

♅ New disruptions in pleasurable feelings during passionate moments; increased harmony with rebellious or unusual people; you become upset by actions which show unexpected politeness in weird ways.

Significant Examples of People and Events Using Venus/Uranus

General: **STRONG:** Albert Schweitzer; Stephen Sondheim; Steven Spielberg; John F. Kennedy; Jerry Reed; Nikola Tesla; Lance Reventlow; George Patton; Erich Maria Remarque; Gianni Agnelli; Gregory Peck; Albert Camus; O. J. Simpson
WEAK: Sally Ride; John Paul I; Mick Jagger; Alan Alda; Marlon Brando; Arthur Rimbaud; Ervin Nyiregyhazi; Steve Wozniak
EVENTS: Pres. Nixon's Resignation; Alaskan Earthquake occurs; President John F. Kennedy Shot; First Medicare Patient Accepted; (Kent State Shootings).

☉ Jack Schwartz; Jimi Hendrix; Alan Leo; Erich Maria Remarque; Winston Churchill; Lawrence Welk; Steve Allen

☽ Walt Whitman; Wayne Gretzky; Charles Addams; Hank Williams

☿ Dick Gregory; Bob Newhart; William K. Douglas; Franklin Roosevelt

♀, ♅ Jackie Robinson; Stephen Sondheim; Albert Schweitzer; Joachim Von Ribbentrop; Robert Redford; Lance Reventlow

♂ Steve Allen; Jean Paul Satre; East Coast Blackout; J. McEnroe; Lord Byron

♃ Ritchie Valens; Ivar Kreugar; Erich M. Remarque; Carl Sagan; Rud. Bing

♄ Ellen Burstyn; Albert Schweitzer; Stephen Sondheim; Hugh Downs; East Coast Power Blackout; Cheiro; Enrico Caruso

♆ Pearl Harbor Attack; Audie Murphy; Edna Ferber; Benito Mussolini; Guglielmo Marconi; Alexis Carrel

♇ Stephen King; Glen Campbell; Franklin D. Roosevelt; Gus Grissom; Steve Rosenbloom; Neil Diamond; Cheiro

☊ Francisco Franco; Edna Ferber; Tom Jones; Henry Mancini; Elton John

A John F. Kennedy; Willie Brandt; Burl Ives; Yogananda; Mt. St. Helens

M Albert Speer; Joseph Joffre; Israel Regardie; Percy Bysshe Shelley; Melvin Belli; Charles E. O. Carter

VENUS/NEPTUNE ♀/Ψ

Basic Ideas:

These themes denote an appreciation of how dreams and visions can become the prototypes for future reality. You may feel delight in accomplishing a successful deception, gain enjoyment from the subtleness of creating beauty, or derive pleasure from the study and application of mysticism or magic. You may create subtle ways to display your jealousies, gain satisfaction from being evasive or illusive, and feel affection when you receive romantic gestures from another. These motifs may show weakness in your attempts at being more beautiful or lovely, confusion about using makeup or body ornaments, and false impressions about the admiration you show to others. You may be tempted to be lazy or indulge in pure sensual gratifications, earn appreciation from being more holy or obedient, delight in wearing creative disguises, or appease your yearnings for total personal freedom.

In Your Personal Life:

Thesis   Inspiration for creating new concepts in music or the arts; increased appreciation for subtle or devious means of enjoying reality; temptations to neglect resources; assets which are allowed to waste away.

Anti   Receiving pleasure when evading or deceiving others; envy felt when another is more romantic; laxity or looseness as a part of your personality; pleasure from causing confusion or loss.

In Your Relationships:

Thesis   Increased appreciation for the quality of romance that a good partner can bring to you; compassion shown for those you love; romantic feelings of love from those close to you; idealized love.

Anti   Deception through romance; an imperfect understanding of romantic love; nebulous promises of affection become easier to believe and cling to; neglect of your partner's satisfaction, or your partner neglects you.

With Body or Mind:

Inner reactions to drugs; weakness in kidneys or bladder; weakened senses in general; defects, poor storage, or chemicals which weaken blood supplies.

In Politics or Business:

Thesis   Appeals to the ideals of the people; an inflated treasury; use of inflation as a means for controlling or manipulating growth; wealth derived from gas, chemicals, or oil; exaggerates or misstates internal resources.

Anti   Scandals concerning the misuse of, or deceptive practices within, the treasury or internal resources; subversives who desire to gain access to finances; spies in the financial branches; monetary fraud; art deception.

VENUS/NEPTUNE with Planets and Points

☉ Presenting your innate beauty in more effective, if subtle, ways; prestige from association with film or artistic endeavors; increased influence in occult, mystical, illusion, or magic situations; a confused situation for many.

☽ Comforting those who delight in deceit, or escape from reality through drugs, self-delusion, etc.; feelings of romance; romantic notions about life; equating caring with love; dreams of romantic or escapist love.

☿ An exceptionally active mind able to create effective pretenses or delusions; added ability to detect pretenses or deceit; nervousness when confronting confusion; a study of effective disguises; thievery aided by deceptions.

♂ Actively pursuing deceptions and disguises as a way of life; courage when attempting to evade a situation, or escape from difficult surroundings; irritation with failures; rushed illusions done for gain.

♃ Openness to good advice on how to use makeup or adornments; excessive use of deceptive practices in financial or artistic endeavors; indulging in religious deceptions as a form of holiness.

♄ Admiration for the effects achieved in creating circumstances which appear to mirror reality; an effective special effects effort or delusion; brief shows of satisfaction with illusions or mysticism; no gain, or loss, through evasions.

♅ Producing unusual methods to convince others about what is real and what is not; extremes you are willing to try to inspire appreciation in others for artistic or musical creations; the politics of deceit and vanity.

♀ Suspicions felt about deceptive practices; disguising waste or unwanted products with artificial covers; power gained by continuing deceptive practices; criminals using elaborate cover-ups for fraud or deceit.

☊ Associations with others who are able to effect deceptions or illusions about reality or nonreality; situations where your talent for using artificial means for creating beauty or enjoyment for others are appreciated or glamorized.

A An appreciation of how reality can be altered for your own enjoyment; indulging in another's fantasy for personal gratification; perceptions about the illusions of how matter or form combine in the world.

M Learning to be effective in creating what others think they want to see and hear; a mature appreciation of the use of makeup or other artificial means for increasing personal appeal; inspired self-fantasies.

VENUS/NEPTUNE CONCEPTS

Pleasing Daydreams	Delicate Imagination	Subtle Pleasantries
Enjoys Shoddiness	Escapes a Rage	The Beauty of Fraud
Tempting Stimulation	Lazy Devotion	Modest Faith
Affectionate Submission	Enjoys Confusion	Subtle Selfishness
Favors an Omission	Neglects Manners	Supports the Occult
An Amorous Deception	Enticing Fantasy	Quiet Fantasies
A Weakness for Jealousy	Delights in Escapism	A Satisfying Illusion
Pleasure from Drugs	Artificial Charisma	Admires Atonement
Attached to Holiness	Mysterious Politeness	A Shabby Illusion
Sensual Mysteries	Admires Subtlety	A Beautiful Parable
Artificial Adornments	Weakens Jealousy	Shoddy Glamor
A Confused Romantic	Indulges in Folly	Tempted to Escape

Absent Appreciation	Gains Enjoyment
Enhances Fiction	Has a Subtle Beauty
The Pleasure of Freedom	Shoddy Luxury
Submits to Passion	Polishes Image
Inspired by Jealousy	Embellishes Fantasies
Tastefully Uses an Illusion	Mercenary Atonement
Satisfying Inspiration	A Glorious Reverie
Solicits Appreciation	Escapes into Luxury
Enjoys a Mystery	Tempting Imagination
Inspires Charming Behavior	Delights in Make Believe
Confused by Affections	Disguised Tantrums
Subtilely Affectionate	Tempted to Submit
Repaid with Shortcomings	Shoddy Materials
Dreams of a Life of Luxury	Senseless Pleasures
Delights in Shoddiness	Imperfect Satisfaction
Appreciates Fantasies	Neglects Affection
A Weakness for Vanity	Pretends to Holiness
Rants at Omissions	Submits to Love
Attracted to Indiscretion	Satisfied with Confusion
Gentle Forgiveness	Inspires Temper Tantrums
Pleasing Imagination	Neglects Adornments
Convenient Reparation	Disguises a Gift
Appreciates Mysteries	Artistic Inspiration
A Delusion of Kindness	Favors Laxity
Miracles of Beauty	An Art Fraud
Sensual Fantasies	Deceit and Greed
A Satisfying Romance	Indulges in Shoddiness
A Love of Escape	Appreciates Subtlety
Pleasant Perplexities	Cherishes Faults
Affectionate Compliance	Enhances Escapist Ideas
Considers Reparation	Entertains with Garbles

VENUS/NEPTUNE With Itself

♀ Pleasurable feelings when escaping through dreams or visions; added charm and sophistication for using beauty as a potent form of attraction; increased delight in escaping from reality through illusions.

Ψ Indecisiveness about your appearance; added need to relax and escape from the realities of the physical world; seeing defects in the composition of pretty objects; a shabbiness to physical objects of wealth.

Significant Examples of People and Events Using Venus/Neptune

General: **STRONG:** Enrico Caruso; Arnold Schwarzenegger; Dave Garroway; Erwin Rommel; Charles Addams; James Earl Carter; Olga Worrall; Abraham Lincoln; Rudolph Bing; Hugh Downs; Robin Williams; Gergory Peck; Cheiro
WEAK: Ernest Pyle; Edward R. Murrow; F. Scott Fitzgerald; Ritchie Valens; Melvin Belli; Benjamin Disraeli; Earl Warren; Burl Ives
EVENTS: Bolsheviks Take Power; Pres. Nixon Resignation; Pearl Harbor Attack; Lewis & Clark Expedition starts; (Georoge Washington's First Inauguration).

☉   H. G. Wells; Louis Pasteur; Nikola Tesla; Benito Mussolini; Rollo May

☽   Marc Edmund Jones; Ervin Nyiregyhazi; Yehudi Menuhin; Robert McNamara; Bertrand Russell; Ernest Pyle

☿   Bertrand Russell; Vida Blue; Stephen Sondheim; Albert Speer; Johann Von Goethe; Mark Spitz; Auguste Rodin

♀, Ψ   Teilhard de Chardin; Louis Pasteur; Enrico Caruso; Emperor Hirohito

♂   Elton John; Rosanno Brazzi; Jerry Rubin; Mark Spitz; Pearl Harbor Attack; Olivia Newton-John; Alexander Graham Bell

♃   Woman's Suffrage Amendment passed; Steve Wozniak; Erwin Rommel; Enrico Caruso; Abraham Lincoln

♄   Gus Grissom; Norman Mailer; R. D. Laing; Mick Jagger; Challenger Explosion; Sandy Koufax; Hermann Goering

♅   F. Scott Fitzgerald; Billy Rose; Lindburgh Lands in Paris; Willie Brandt; Pierre Renoir; Benito Mussolini; Israel Regardie

♀   Nixon's Resignation; Dave Garroway; Erwin Rommel; Mick Jagger

☊   Jimmy Carter; Watergate Burglary; Wm. Butler Yeats; John McEnroe

A   Dr. Tom Dooley; Friedrich Nietzsche; Van Cliburn; R. D. Laing; Guglielmo Marconi; John Denver; Anne Murray

M   Robert DeNiro; J. F. Kennedy Shot; Harry Belafonte; Jean Paul Satre

VENUS/PLUTO   ♀/♀

Basic Ideas:

The use of financial or personal resources to increase power or prestige, deriving satisfaction from punishing activities, and taking delight with hidden or concealed activities. These themes heighten needs to promise anything so personal power can be augmented. They denote an obsession with beauty and glamor, and symbolize throwing yourself wholeheartedly into passion. They show awareness of needs to purify or cleanse, reversals of rage or jealousy, and heightened pleasure from intense sexual activity. They may show a compulsive need to act in a civil manner, activate feelings of pleasure from destroying people or things, or hide intense and deep feelings of passion or attachment for another. They may symbolize extremes of passion or pleasure, urges to contaminate or ruin pretty places (by littering, defacing, etc.), or criminals hiding behind visions of luxury.

In Your Personal Life:

Thesis   Needs to experience depths or heights of passions and feelings; indulgence in your obsession to find extremes of anything; a compulsion to purchase almost any luxury or material item.

Anti   Hidden, angry, destructive impulses which force you to ruin or deface things; a blatant disregard for the possessions of others; temptations to alter or abuse that which brings delight to others.

In Your Relationships:

Thesis   Heightens the sexual satisfaction you can feel from your partner; adds to the extremes of passion you share with another; affection for a partner who can share your inner needs for sensual gratification.

Anti   Exposes you or your partner to a destructive inner rage; extreme reactions from another during sex; an obsession for having a partner with beauty, or material wealth; a partner with a sexually spread disease.

With Body or Mind:

Hyper or hypo-thyroidism; toxins which overwhelm the kidneys; tonsillitis with extreme infection; rare blood diseases; sexual diseases; kidney efficiency.

In Politics or Business:

Thesis   Extremes of private wealth hidden in secret places; attraction by those persons who wish to transform the natural beauty of a country; genetic alterations; model or beautiful waste processing or disposal systems.

Anti   Volcanic activity deep within the earth which causes great destruction of agricultural activities or financial centers; attracting elements of organized crime; a breakdown within the social fabric of a society.

VENUS/PLUTO with Planets and Points

☉ Mastering lower urges to be destructive; skills in demolition; achievements in extremely beautiful works of art; acts of elimination; delight with eliminating ego or pride; selfish acts involving sexual perversion.

☽ Amplified urges to destroy; taking pleasure in the arbitrary use of punishment; commonplace items used for waste receptacles; a need to glamorize self by creating glitzy gaudiness; popular forms of luxury.

☿ To study and understand the powers of destructive forces; education in subtle forms of terrorism; gaining extreme proficiency with exotic languages; media attention for waste or disposal processes; talk of sexual diseases.

♂ Armed struggles where destructive energy is directed against centers of finance or art; aroused temptations to initiate drastic depletion of personal reserves of cash, agriculture, etc.; potent sensual activation or inspiration.

♃ Propagation of destructive impulses; intense feelings of pleasure from activities of gratification, power, or destruction; studies of the ethics of appeasing destructive forces which can be used by self or others.

♄ Curbs on the use of destructive impulses or weaponry; less impact of destructive forces; an obligation or responsibility toward those who take pleasure in delivering restitution; less enjoyment from sex.

♅ Indifference to the destructive powers available for personal or political uses; compromises involving extreme uses of power; friends who find delight in receiving or engaging in unusual forms of punishment.

♆ Deception, inadequate threats, or punishment; illusions about practices of hiding or concealing financial assets; faulty security or planning involving the protection of personal assets or artistic articles.

☊ Associations where deep and intense love feelings are involved; demonstrations of powerful means for ensuring financial, monetary, or agricultural gains; the creation of financial or business panics.

A Concentrating on the need for a polite response to those who have a destructive or punishing intent; meeting people who delight in learning or hearing about ghastly facts; creating a false sense of glamor.

M Growing through destructive tendencies and overcoming obsessive habits which do little for your personal standing; creating some protection for self or family against large, destructive, natural or man-made forces.

VENUS/PLUTO CONCEPTS

Entertained by Devastation
Devoted to Corruption
Glories in Restitution
Fanatical Intimacy
The Destruction of Beauty
Satisfying Morbidity
A Love of Destruction
Innocent Injury
Loving Astral Entities
Gaudy Displays of Power
An Intense Artist
Pride in Wasting

Pleased with Losses
An End to Gratification
Gentle Purification
Pleased with Cover-up
Feminine Curses
Attentive to Depravity
Seething Jealousy
Extremes of Greed
Enjoys Depletion
Excessive Elegance
Values Vengeance
A Sensual Fixation

Gratifying Control
Enraged over Losses
Punished for Rages
Envious of Obsession
Pleasing Perversions
Pleased by Hatred
Rediscovers Love
Enjoys Using Poisons
Honors to a Tyrant
Delicate Morbidity
Morbid Pleasures
Intense Appreciation

Satisfied with a Conviction
Delights with Preoccupation
Pleasure from Punishment
Glamorizes Powerful Weapons
A Love of Condemnation
Controlled by Money and Luxury
Money from Criminal Activities
Intensifies Appreciation
Obsessed with Beauty
A Nicely Mannered Gangster
Appeals to Ownership
The Value of Purification
Satisfying Corruption
Undermined by Jealously
Depressed by Peacefulness
A Lowering of Self-Esteem
Condemned by Mannerisms
Enjoys Cleaning Up
Invites Catastrophes
A Convenient Distiller
Hidden Love for Another
Tempted to Dilute or Debase
Intensity with Affections
Satisfied with the Ending
Envious of Destruction
Glamorizes Sexuality
Hidden Jealousy and Rages
Delights in Destruction
Ceaseless Jealousy
Glamorizes Pollution
Beautifies Waste Products

Expensive Waste Disposal
Temptations to Destroy
Respect for a Monopoly
Reimbursed for a Funeral
Appreciates Corruption
Obsessed by Jealousy
The Power of Wealth
A Forced Satisfaction
Expensive Decadence
A Suspicion of Flattery
Calm Dishonesty
Fanatical about Innocence
Temptations to Debase
Intensifies Envy
Enjoys Taking Losses
Compulsive Rage
Degraded Respect
Tempted by Corruption
Resents Restitution
Jealousy which Destroys
Fixated on Wealth
Kinky Fetishes
Compulsive Charm
False Affections
Appreciates Ghastly Facts
Well Done Destruction
Softens Rancor
Concealed Envy
Delighted with Elimination
Savors Prosecution
Satisfied with Impurities

VENUS/PLUTO With Itself

♀   Softening of deep and powerful impulses which could be used for destruction;pleasures received from participating in activities which are very dangerous or reckless; a deeply satisfying attraction or love.

♀   Using power and prestige to enhance your position; a need to conceal people or activities; great changes in your wealth; openings to persons having immense wealth or power; extreme changes in your affections.

Significant Examples of People and Events Using Venus/Pluto

General: **STRONG:** Alexis Carrel; Jimi Hendrix; Sydney Omarr; Paul Newman; Sean Connery; Erwin Rommel; Melvin Belli; Jean Francoise Millet; Harry Shoaf; Marc Edmund Jones; Marlon Brando; Alan Alda; Gen. Ferdinand Foch
     WEAK: Emperor Hirohito; Rossano Brazzi; Charles Gordon; David Frost; Steve Wozniak; George Patton; John Fremont; Merv Griffin
     EVENTS: RMS Titanic Hits Iceberg; Pearl Harbor Attack; Ramstein Airshow Disaster; Women's Suffrage Passed; (J. Meredith Enrolled).

☉   Ida Rolf; Henry Mancini; Billy Rose; Bob Newhart; George Washington's Inauguration; Burt Reynolds

☽   Nixon's Resignation; U. S. Grant; Kent State Shootings; Muhammad Ali

☿   Edmund Halley; Paul Newman; Stephen Foster; Jean Francoise Millet; Henry Kissinger; Dr. Tom Dooley; Adolf Hitler

♀,♀   Liberace; Sydney Omarr; Wm. Butler Yeats; Gugli. Marconi; H. G.Wells

♂   Steven Spielberg; Ferdinand Foch; Willie Brandt; Ida Rolf; Rupert Murdoch; Melvin Belli; Georges Seurat

♃   Erwin Rommel; Marlon Brando; Ulysses S. Grant; Sam Sheppard; R. Bing

♄   Fidel Castro; Benjamin Disraeli; Jean Paul Satre; R. Strauss; Grant Lewi

♅   Edouard Manet; Alexander Graham Bell; Dane Rudhyar; Elvis Presley; Jack Nicklaus; Evel Knievel; Norman Mailer

♆   Jim Thorpe; Alaskan Earthquake; Erwin Rommel; Sean Connery

☊   Alexis Carrel; First A-Bomb Explosion; Ritchie Valens; Ernest Hemingway; Jean Paul Satre; Jeddu Krishnamurti

A   Paul Joseph Goebbels; Liberace; Rollo May; Paul Newman; Richard Byrd

M   Jean Houston; Kareem Abdul-Jabbar; Muhammad Ali; Richard Alpert

VENUS/NODE   ♀/☊

Basic Ideas:

The pleasure and cooperation received from acquaintances made or associations joined is shown here. These themes emphasize the delight experienced in being with people who share similar interests, the satisfaction derived from attracting and finding people who can help you with your interests, and the satisfaction received from identifying and correctly following your life's destiny. Any reimbursements delayed by bureaucratic shufflings, devotion given to groups with matching interests, and indulgence which arises from past habit patterns, also starts here. Affiliations with artistically creative persons, an ability to present yourself as a pacifist at meetings, presentations where recognition or monetary rewards for past activities is received, the use of bribes to acquire close access to others, and resentment over the conduct of meetings are also symbolized here.

In Your Personal Life:

Thesis   The cooperation given or received at meetings with associates; the joy or delight experienced from associating with friends; meetings or exchanges with others with similar ideas; links to people with money.

Anti   Feelings that your contributions to others are not adequate enough; recognizing the support extended by your friends; jealousy over the recognition given to others; resentment over any lack of cooperation.

In Your Relationships:

Thesis   Attracting the right type of partner into your life, especially through friends or groups; cooperation given to or received from those who try to help you; kindness from your associates; dating or friendship services.

Anti   Misuse of the friendship offered; karma and destiny linked with another whose friendship you refuse to acknowledge; separations from people who have given you support and backing.

With Body or Mind:

Your ability to relax with friends; associates who help you with your medical problems; muscle or ligament tears in the throat, larynx, or with the kidneys.

In Politics or Business:

Thesis   The role of society in shaping collective destiny; how social activities can help associations or treaties; the preference of leaders for alliances and treaties; cooperation given or received from like-minded friends.

Anti   An impetus where the social aspect of diplomacy outweighs legislative; desire to increase self-worth before the eyes of others; wealth which leaves the enterprise due to poor management or bungling.

VENUS/NODE with Planets and Points

☉   Pleasure from encouragement obtained at meetings with others; highlights meetings or encounters which make a notable impression on you, or where you have a strong effect on the other participants.

☽   Assistance or support you receive for your family through group or personal associations; basic changes in the way you approach others because of advice received; avoiding meetings not needed; popular peace coalitions.

☿   The presentation and acceptance of ideas at meetings; an adaptability to alter responses and respond quickly to the needs of others; quickness of mind and an ability to read the motives and intentions of others.

♂   Encounters others with whom you have sexual attraction; the assertion of your interests to others; persistence in your efforts to sustain your ideas and interests; demands for immediate gratification.

♃   The acceptance of your ideas or philosophies by others; advice given or received from those having similar interests; encountering pomposity or bombastic oratory; eases compliance with your reasoning.

♄   You temper ideas and thoughts so they are briefer; others judge you to be more organized than most people; continuing frustrations coming through others; ties to older people who have resources you need.

♅   Disruptions which occur suddenly at meetings you attend; unsettling news received from friends; pleasant meetings among those who share astrological or computer knowledge; polite indifference to ideas.

♆   Ambiguous results from others who share your interests; the artificial fronts others present when meeting with you; illogical or indecisive people you encounter; groups which mix astrology and the occult.

♇   Intensity by artists or financiers; the power that you or others bring or show to others; troubles which arise because others want the power without wanting to do the work required; deep and intense personal feelings.

A   Discussions of your personal beliefs; observing the demeanor and convictions of others when meeting with them; the way that you treat others at meetings; the pleasantness with which you greet others.

M   Learning and growing from your interactions with others; recognition of your accomplishments by friends; the conclusions and experiences gained from working with others; family life rich in values or wealth.

VENUS/NODE CONCEPTS

Beauty which Attracts
Appreciates Close Ties
Alliances for Beautification
Tranquil Supporters
Agreeable Separations
Assures Life's Aim
An Opportunity for Peace
Delights in Attracting Others
Satisfying Acquaintances
Layoffs which Go Pleasantly
A Feminine Confederation
Rages at Separations

Relinquishes Comforts
Charming Attachments
Delights in Groups
Innocent Sexual Ties
Polite Interviews
Honors Separations
Polite Demonstrations
Your Source of Desires
Amorous Sexual Ties
Tender Familiarity
Affection for Associates
Invites New Habits

Respects Connections
Pleased with Associates
Enjoys Bureaucracy
Cordial Distancing
Grateful for Alliances
Satisfying Life's Aim
Quiet Presentations
Assemblies with Beauty
Glamorizes Hallways
Cherished Allies
Polite Affiliations
Meets with Beauty

Reimbursed for an Interview
An Affectionate Attachment
Finds Others at Peace
Envious of Opportunities
A Harmonious Bureaucracy
Glamorizes Cooperation
Supports Associates
Sophisticated Occasions
Invites Appointments
Supports Bureaucratic Delays
Enjoys Connecting with Others
Attracts Envious People
Satisfying Presentations
Pleasant Exchanges
Indulges in Attracting Others
Satisfied by an Interchange
Charming Presentations
Jealousy Arises at Meetings
Sophisticated Performances
Affectionate at Meetings
A Conference on Femininity
Respects Alliances
Considerate of Connections
Appreciates Sexual Ties
Favorable Treaties
Preoccupied with Luxury
Attracts Artists
Envious of Ties to Others
Rages at Meetings
Delightful Interviews
Charming Associates

Values a Consolidation
Indulges in Kinship
Satisfied with Fate
Mannerly Preoccupation
Tempted to Find New Friends
Appreciates Ties to Others
Pacifies Acquaintances
Demonstrates for Peace
Appreciates Opportunities
Gentle Cooperation
Supports Ties to Others
Familiar Considerations
Learns about Jealousy
Harmonious Assemblies
Intimate Bonds
Polite Familiarity
Vain Acquaintances
Pleased with Ties to Others
Grateful for Conventions
Glamorizes Dissolutions
Politeness during Meetings
Indulges in Apportionment
Enjoys Alliances
Respects Associates
Delights in Discovery
Softens Demonstrations
Delays which Satisfy
Leaves Jealousy Behind
Pleased with their Destiny
Embellishes Walls or Hallways
Considerate of Alliances

VENUS/NODE With Itself

♀ Meeting people who are pleasant and charming, with whom you are able to enjoy friendship; charm and courtesy shown to others; enhancing spaces or offices used to meet and impress visitors or friends.

☊ Notable artists or musicians who enter your life; joining or associating with people who have the enhancement and promotion of beauty, pleasure, or art as a fundamental purpose; old lovers as new friends.

Significant Examples of People and Events Using Venus/Node

General: **STRONG:** Alexis Carrel; James Earl Carter; Moshe Dayan; Vittorio DeSica; Charles Addams; William K. Douglas; Wayne Gretzky; Ellen Burstyn; Bertrand Russell; Paul Joseph Goebbels; Sam Peckinpah; Sigmund Freud; David Frost
WEAK: Joachim Von Ribbentrop; Stephen Crane; Willie Brandt; Albert Einstein; Burt Reynolds; Herman Melville; Carroll Righter; Giacomo Puccini
EVENTS: Pres. Nixon's Resignation; East Coast Power Blackout; George Washington's Inauguration; Bolsheviks Take Power; (USS Maine Explosion).

☉ David O. Selznik; Thomas H. Huxley; Alexis Carrel; Steve Allen; Adolf Hitler; Scott Carpenter; Bertrand Russell

☽ Harry Shoaf; Franklin Roosevelt; Ellen Burstyn; Lord Byron; Glen Campbell; Paramhansa Yogananda; Moshe Dayan

☿ Jerry Rubin; Richard Strauss; Jimi Hendrix; Henry Mancini; Georges Seurat; Ira Progoff; Fidel Castro; John Fremont

♀, ☊ Enrico Fermi; Willie Mays; Alexis Carrel; Robin Williams; Melvin Belli

♂ Paul Gauguin; Bertrand Russell; Marc Edmund Jones; Vittorio DeSica

♃ Henri Toulouse-Lautrec; Chernobyl Nuclear Explosion; JeanPaul Satre; Gen. George Patton; Winston Churchill

♄ Yehudi Menuhin; Stonewall Jackson; Robert Redford; Scott Carpenter

♅ R. D. Laing; Ida Rolf; Grant Lewi; Charles Kettering; Ulysses S. Grant

♆ Komar; Friedrich Nietzsche; East Coast Blackout; Jacques Cousteau

♇ Arthur Rimbaud; Lee's Surrender; Ivar Kreugar; Charles Steinmetz

A Elvis Presley; Elton John; Gregory Peck; Sydney Omarr; Stephen Sondheim; Moshe Dayan; Ada Lovelace Byron

M William K. Douglas; Henri Matisse; Robert McNamara; Henry Mancini

VENUS/ASCENDANT   ♀/A

Basic Ideas:

This combination shows an added desire to be appreciated and liked by the other people you meet. When these themes are activated you find a strong desire to tell others what they want to hear and to act in ways that please them. You are motivated to bring pleasure to those you meet and to impress people with your charm and grace. Developing loving attitudes and intentions go far to give the impression that you are a polite and likeable person. You center your mind on peace and harmony and spend much time thinking about your appearance, your mannerisms, and what others think of you. However, you do not have any control in these matters, and you may dres sinappropriately or appear sloppy, although your ideals lie elsewhere on these subjects. You easily become aroused with jealousy when other people make a better impression than you do.

In Your Personal Life:

Thesis   Needs to become aware of self and your values in life on the subject of appearance, manners, etc.; you notice the appearance of others easily, and are quick to note their imperfections.

Anti   You think one way about pleasing people but act in a different way; you enjoy fine things and luxury but will not work hard to attain these; you love to have others indulge or pamper you; you greet others with love.

In Your Relationships:

Thesis   Enhanced ability to work with others as potential partners; an awareness of different ways to generate rapport; increased ability to please others as you want to become very aware of what delights them.

Anti   Your need for personal gratification is locked into one thing: you; other people find it hard to please you because you do not share your inner self easily; you are often disappointed with the way others treat you.

With Body or Mind:

Your ability to feel comfortable with the image you project; your psychological state and feelings about love and affection; a refined taste or smell.

In Politics or Business:

Thesis   Others become impressed with your wealth and the beauty of your home or surroundings; art which serves to inspire others; a society judged through the glamor of its mannerisms; focus on showing or displaying wealth.

Anti   A strong political focus on the natural resources or treasury; efforts to promote natural beauty or scenic areas; the effect of the opinions of others on trends in art or music; misusing art for shows of glamor.

VENUS/ASCENDANT with Planets and Points

☉   You show sincerity, charm and manners as you meet others; you feel impelled to maintain your appearance, and to appear as a loving and kind person to all; you become famous for your style.

☽   Enhanced concerns for your feminine traits and side; increased moodiness and variability; an ability to relate well to what others desire; satisfying and pleasing the people you choose to entertain or host.

☿   Noticing what others wear and how they present themselves to the public; a good fashion and style critic; enhanced needs to learn more about manners, charm, and how to use beauty to attract or please .

♂   Energy to use ideas about charm, style, and beauty in your life; becoming more aware of the sexual needs of others; an ability to please others with your sexuality; a harsher or rougher facade to your charm.

♃   Increased desire to notice fashion and style changes in society; an added ability to be recognized for your talents; expanded ideas or artistic qualities to present new social changes or directions to people or the world in general.

♄   Withdrawing from others; alone with self; finding that you will not be hurried or pushed; new barriers to the way you want life to go; not getting your way with others; shorter periods with charming people.

♅   You make your appearance distinct so that people will notice you; you have progressive ideas about style and manners; you may not be easily held down by others through outdated social rules; sudden jealousy from others.

♆   Adds a mystical quality to your appearance, expressions, and demeanor; you find that momentary stimulation from certain drugs helps you relate better to people; you are not above presenting false appearances.

♀   Pushing hard for your ideas to influence style and beauty; a heightened need for attention or flattery; finding ways to increase your personal or financial security thru others; surroundings of great natural beauty or wealth.

☊   An enhanced ability to find the right type of people for your social life; you meet others easily and impress them with your charm and sophistication; when you are sexually drawn to another, you get joy from pleasing them.

M   Compliments received about the way you conduct yourself in life; others admire you for your grace and charm, especially as you age; notable maturity and self-control in your youth.

VENUS/ASCENDANT CONCEPTS

Admirable Mannerisms
Charming Surroundings
Grateful Responses
Delightful Motivations
Gallant Sense of Style
Flattering Personal Style
Enjoys Circumstances
Loving Pretenses
Mental Focus on Beauty
A Joyous Inner Vitality
Mental Focus on Charm
Affectionate Reactions

Affectionate Demeanor
Concentrates on Glamor
Satisfying Perceptions
Charming Reactions
Amorous Attitudes
Sensations of Love
Appreciative Attitudes
Enjoys Experiences
Pleasing Sense of Reality
Vain Personal Style
Satisfying Attitudes
Softens Convictions

Softens Reactions
Modest Attitudes
Lovely Surroundings
A Focus on Vanity
Amiable Reactions
Enticing Settings
Gentle Perceptions
Sensual Leanings
Polite Demeanor
Glamorizes Self
Envious of Attitudes
Quiet Disposition

An Easy Person to Admire
Attracted to Recognition
Delightful Personal Responses
Enjoys Personal Attitudes
Sophisticated Characteristics
An Artistic Sense of Reality
Receives Discreet Impressions
Affectionate Pretenses
Sensitive to Feminine Views
Considerate of Others
Harmonious Mental Focus
Values Impressions Received
Satisfying Personal Style
Glorious Portrayals
A Graceful Demeanor
A Loving Personal Style
Conscious of Beauty
Alert to Showing Adornments
Lovely Settings
Surrounded by Love
Inclined to Music and Dance
Detects Beauty in Surroundings
Treats Others with Love
Sensual Rejoinders
Smiles at Others
Graceful Postures
Charming Personal Motives
Modest Personal Beliefs
Appreciates Reactions
Selfish Sense of Style
Considerate of Personal Style

Respectful Attention Seeking
Thinks Often of Others
Intimate Interpersonal Roles
Charms Others through Attention
Placating Sense of Style
Appreciative Personal Style
Luxurious Pretenses
Sensual Sense of Reality
Sophisticated Perceptions
Appreciates their Surroundings
Polite Introductions
Captivating Presence
Enjoys Attention Seeking
Innocent Peculiarities
Represses Vanity
Treats Others with Courtesy
Envy within Sense of Style
Innocent Sense of Reality
Impressed by Charm
Sensual Experiences
Delightful Perceptions
Conceited Introspection
Impressive Manners
Pleasing Postures
Values Attention Seeking
Seeks Beauty and Art Together
Polite when Listening
Affectionate Recollections
Surrounded by Beauty
Mental Focus on Affection
Treats Others with Gratitude

VENUS/ASCENDANT With Itself

♀   Your personality shows an air of being a civil and polished person; added cooperation and consideration; satisfaction with your interpersonal relations; you charm others with your abilities and ways.

A   Denotes how you present yourself and how people react to you; increased ability to notice the mannerisms or habits of others, and to observe how they conduct themselves; life in pleasant surroundings.

Significant Examples of People and Events Using Venus/Ascendant

General: **STRONG:** Paul Newman; Benito Mussolini; Glen Campbell; Jean Houston; Alan Leo; Moshe Dayan; Dr. Francis Regardie; Albert Speer; John Dillinger; R. D. Laing; Richard Alpert; Ida Rolf; Liberace; Dick Gregory; Sydney Omarr
WEAK: Sigmund Freud; Stephen Sondheim; Carl Sagan; Ralph Waldo Emerson; Sir Alexander Fleming; Alexis Carrel; Melvin Belli
EVENTS: John F. Kennedy Shot; Apollo 11 Moon Landing; George Washington's Inauguration; Lee's Surrender at Appomattox; (Wright Brothers First Flight).

☉   William K. Douglas; Glen Campbell; Vincent Van Gogh; Willy Brandt

☽   Maurice Ravel; Gus Grissom; Robert Redford; Al Unser; Arturo Toscanini; Bjorn Borg; Sally Ride; Sam Peckinpah

☿   Paul Newman; John Dillinger; John Fremont; Lance Reventlow; Louis Pasteur; John Paul I; Bobby Fischer

♀, A   Cheiro; Ernest Pyle; Liberace; Art Linkletter; Mick Jagger; Adolf Hitler

♂   H. Toulouse-Lautrec; John F. Kennedy; Mario Andretti; Apollo 11 Moon Landing; Enrico Fermi; Vida Blue

♃   Francisco Franco; Henry Mancini; Ritchie Valens; Richard Chamberlain; Jack Nicklaus; Al Unser; Dick Gregory

♄   Earl Warren; Paul Newman; John McEnroe; H. G. Wells; Cheiro

♅   Herman Melville; Henry Mancini; Benito Mussolini; Wm. K. Douglas

♆   Peter Max; Ralph Waldo Emerson; Steve Rosenbloom; Benito Mussolini

♇   F. Scott Fitzgerald; Rupert Murdoch; Liberace; S. Carolina Secession

☊   Marlon Brando; Albert Speer; Maurice Ravel; Dave Garroway; Moshe Dayan; Mark Spitz; Charles Kettering

M   Merv Griffin; Israel Regardie; Jack Paar; Ira Progoff; Richard Alpert

VENUS/MIDHEAVEN   ♀/M

Basic Ideas:

This combination represents the appreciation you develop within yourself for the accomplishments and recognition you receive. Also here is your inner sense of gratitude and the feelings of self-worth you have about your choice of career, the positions you earn, your work proficiency, the cooperation you give to or receive from others, and the reimbursement you receive because of your qualifications. These themes also represent the way you integrate and relate to the feminine energies within yourself, and how secure you feel with the feminine side of your nature, regardless of your sex. These motifs depict your ability to mature thru the experiences you gain by understanding love, both giving and receiving, and in the romantic, family, global, and brotherly senses. They denote how you relate to and take advantage of beauty, art, or music in your home, professional, or inner life.

In Your Personal Life:

Thesis   Coping with what life returns to you from the efforts you give; growing through a use and understanding of the finer things in life; using beauty and harmony to achieve peace in life; pleasure with your life goals.

Anti   The difficulties you have in learning how to blend gifts of money or material possessions with the appreciation you receive from others; the lessons of learning how to treasure whatever returns to you in life.

In Your Relationships:

Thesis   Learning to both give and receive love; the role you want love to have in your relationships, and the inner peace you achieve through this; learning to love or to return the love of another.

Anti   Equating love given or received with material gifts or presents; the role that developing sophistication in love, beauty, or the arts takes in your life, and how you use these new talents to make your life harmonious.

With Body or Mind:

Difficulties in appreciating the value or contributions of family or others; gaining inner peace through romantic expressions; genetic blood disorders.

In Politics or Business:

Thesis   Wealth or resources accumulated to help achieve goals; the use of artistic works, or acclaimed artists, to enhance the image of an enterprise; a treasury bureau which sets important policy or trends.

Anti   A squandering of wealth on projects which do little to bring a return to the enterprise; an inability to find cooperation with others in the pursuit of common goals; creating superficial changes for visitors.

VENUS/MIDHEAVEN with Planets and Points

☉   Approval received from others for appreciation given; an important and significant artistic or financial event; learning to integrate and appreciate the role that love can play in life; working to integrate love as a personal trait.

☽   Separating nurturing needs from love or appreciation needs; becoming a more complete person as you grow from your family origins to your present position in life; coping with changes in the respect received from others.

☿   Education which helps you cope with or understand the importance of giving or receiving love; learning to communicate your true self to another; enhances artistic dexterity or technique; new schooling to appreciate values.

♂   Further forcefulness to gain a fair share for your efforts; using athletics or exercise as an art form; persistent activity to present self as excelling in life; the role of inner anger vs. acceptance and love as you evolve.

♃   Enjoyment from travel or religious experiences; increased understanding of loving intentions received for your efforts; expanded appreciation for beauty or love; adding love to one's philosophy.

♄   Appreciation of others is judged by their direct efforts for your causes; curbs on recognition received for efforts; added inflexibility to matters of compensation for work; less appreciation received for your efforts.

♅   Using automated or mechanical means to create beauty, music, or art; an inability to express emotions in romantic love; new ways of creating or performing in music or in art; disrupts love or beauty.

♆   Avoiding commitment in love; enhanced needs for artificial means of increasing beauty; self-delusion in what you are able to learn from loving another; a lack of respect for those who love you, or vice versa.

♀   A very strong appreciation for what beauty is and how to enhance the different forms it can take; an inner eye for the expensive and elaborate; you to rapidly deplete the resources of those who support you in life.

☊   Association with others who are able to teach you about love and the different types of beauty you encounter; familiarity with notable persons in the arts; the connections you develop to famous people in music or the arts.

A   A strong mental focus on the need for understanding the role of love and beauty in life; enhanced personal attitudes about the role of what is returned to you for what you have given to others for their work.

VENUS/MIDHEAVEN CONCEPTS

Appreciates Self-Restraint	Enjoys their own Efforts	Supports Outcomes
Respects Self-Concepts	Devoted to Origins	Delights in Coping
Courtesy as a Way of Life	Satisfies Intentions	Placates Expertise
Desires Security Seeking	Favors Protection	Enjoys Training
Agreeable Principles	Grateful for Principles	Peaceful Resolution
Mellows Expertise	Sophisticated Origins	An Envious Position
Envious of Reconciliations	Values their Start in Life	Polite Intentions
Encouraged by Experiences	A Charming Expert	Pleasing Behavior
Peaceful Confirmations	Vain Security Seeking	Tempting Objectives
Sophisticated Self-Restraint	Softens Integration	Respected Birthright
Convenient Safekeeping	Affectionate Early Life	Affectionate Origins
Embellishes Self-Concepts	Tranquil Outcomes	Joyous Principles

Feminine Trustworthiness	Convenient Corroboration
Considerate of Self-Restraint	Distinctive Composure
Grateful for Start in Life	Savors Recognition
Satisfying Personal Growth	Upholds Stature (Standing)
Glamorizes Stature (Standing)	Pleasing Self-Restraint
Enjoys Attainment	Considerate of Intentions
Convenient Experience	Experience with Beautifying
Pleases Others while Maturing	Supports Safekeeping
Gentle Consolidation	Tactful Rules of Conduct
Grateful for Self-Concepts	Appreciates Corroboration
Mercenary Work Habits	Loving Intentions
Upholds Learning and Growing	Admires Accomplishments
Matures with Honors	Temptations for Security
The Consequences of Envy	Satisfies Security Seeking
Personal Guarantees of Charm	Delightful Reconciliations
Drawn to Purposes and Goals	Charming Personal Reserve
Matures Gracefully	Enjoys Confirmation
Envies Self-Restraints	Devoted to Fulfillment
Delightful Experiences	Feminine Self-Concepts
Innocent Ways of Maturing	Appreciates Attainment
Appreciates Intentions	Treasures Security
Assured of Purposes	An Expert on Affection
Learns about Beauty	Supports Security Seeking
Satisfying Protection	Integrates Affections
Appreciates Upbringing	Principles involving Jealousy
Mannerly Sense of Fairness	Considerate of Outcomes
Satisfying Fulfillment	Softens Consequences
Delightful Self-Discipline	Principles involving Vanity
Attracted to Mature Conduct	Copes with Beauty
Cherishes Start in Life	Loving Protection at Home
Considerate of Family Roots	Respects Expertise

VENUS/MIDHEAVEN With Itself

♀   Increased appreciation for the efforts of others, and what they can contribute to your well-being or fulfillment; appreciation for the inner qualities and strengths you have developed; wealth and success accorded to your position.

M   Recognition for the importance of your contributions to life, and the impact of your efforts; increased support from family and siblings; achievement of standards or security from past efforts; confirmation for your contributions.

Significant Examples of People and Events Using Venus/Midheaven

General: **STRONG:** Abraham Lincoln; Charles Kettering; Arthur Ford; Manly Palmer Hall; Ira Progoff; Jack Paar; Merv Griffin; Georges Seurat; Alexis Carrel; Vida Blue; Mark Spitz; Francisco Franco; Art Linkletter; Rosanno Brazzi

               WEAK: Friedrich Nietzsche; Burt Reynolds; Albert Einstein; Franklin Roosevelt; Henri Matisse; Sir William Crookes; Rex Harrison; Vittorio DeSica

               EVENTS: Nixon's Resignation; First Medicare Patient Accepted; Lindburgh Lands in Paris; Ramstein Airshow Crash; (South Carolina Secession).

☉   John Denver; Jonathan Winters; Jas. Meredith Enrolled; Norman Mailer

☽   Johnny Carson; Dr. Tom Dooley; Stonewall Jackson; Jackie Robinson

☿   Dr. Tom Dooley; Adolf Hitler; Edgar Degas; Giacomo Puccini; J. F. Millet

♀,M   Ira Progoff; Bobby Fischer; Vida Blue; Georges Seurat; Abraham Lincoln; Enrico Caruso; Jim Thorpe

♂   Edmund Halley; Nixon's Resignation; Benito Mussolini; John Fremont

♃   Thomas H. Huxley; Bobby Fischer; Kareem Abdul-Jabbar; Arthur Rimbaud; Carroll Righter; Jim Thorpe

♄   Art Linkletter; Wm. Butler Yeats; Lord Byron; Emperor Hirohito

♅   Claude Debussy; Transcon. RR done; J. Carter; Vida Blue; J. Robinson

♆   Mary Martin; Tom Jones; Percy Bysshe Shelley; Shirley Jones; P. Renoir

♇   Sam Peckinpah; Alaskan Earthquake occurs; Ralph Waldo Emerson; Evel Knievel; Ervin Nyiregyhazi

☊   Sydney Omarr; Stephen Sondheim; Pierre Gauguin; Alan Leo; Art Linkletter; Jackie Robinson; Liberace

A   Neil Diamond; Pierre Renoir; Albert Speer; Harry Belafonte; Drew Pearson; Dr. Tom Dooley; Gen. Charles Gordon

MARS/JUPITER   ♂/♃

Basic Ideas:

These themes denote ample supplies of energy or courage at whatever level desired, and urge the wise use of your stamina for all reasons. A lot of drive for activity, or additional power is available to be called upon when needed. Understanding the competitive nature or side of life is encouraged, or assumptions about using activities or actions may be made. These motifs represent rash misjudgments about present circumstances, or misinterpretation of the amount of insistence or emphasis required to sustain efforts. They show luck in competitive undertakings, enhancd trust or faith in the use and application of your strength, and increased sincerity with which you approach life's struggles. Taking advice from persons considered to be 'hotheads', initiating actions against legal judgments, or receiving opinions or advice on your recklessness are indicated.

In Your Personal Life:

Thesis
Large amounts of activity; a very active person; a person who has large amounts of reserve energy; ample supplies of courage; stimulates your luck; initiates spirited philosophical or religious debates or teachings.

Anti
Irritation over the feigned sincerity of another; impatience with the opinions of others; errors or misjudgments in the use of force or power; boasts of strength or courage; rushes into new beliefs in ideas.

In Your Relationships:

Thesis
Having a partner who can participate with you in sports or out-of-doors activities; leading an active social life or religious life with your partner; a life with mutual activities or competition as a focus.

Anti
Quarrels experienced during competitive activities; meeting an overopinionated partner; errors in judging partner's determination; hasty judgments of others; rash assumptions about your partner's activities.

With Body or Mind:

Strength of limb; gross motor control; improving muscle tone; hypoadrenalism; aggravation of acute ailments; hip or liver surgery; major surgery.

In Politics or Business:

Thesis
Action taken in response to legal judgments; too much legal activity or opinions; advice which angers or inflame others; legislative actions concerning competitive sports activities; religious activities or festivals.

Anti
Judgment of enemies or those who seek to do battle; misuse of forces when engaging another; an expansion in military hardware; legal opinions or judicial cases which affect the military or metal industries.

MARS/JUPITER with Planets and Points

☉   Strong determination about life's objectives; the respect you receive; developing additional self-respect;   resolving to correct errors of judgment; efforts and energies placed in legal or religious defenses.

☽   Becoming more aware of your strength; encouraging physical activity or sports within the family; ebbs and flows on your energy levels; your activity to start a home life; public displays of courage.

☿   Efforts into more direct means of communicating; an energetic and enthusiastic speaker on subjects of foreign trade or religion; irritation with the way others present information; expressions or discourses on competitive sports.

♀   Admiring the ways you use your strength or force in general; a conflict between wanting to use guile or force when competing; the use of social energies to stimulate expression in others of fine arts or music.

♄   Dedication to expand self through application; a realistic view toward using restraint vs. force; lowered energy levels; despair caused by stronger forces; paying for excessive haste or a lack of planning.

♅   Ability to find the best political approaches during times of unrest; abrupt uses of social forces; changes in the rules for competitive sports; applying self to study and learn about people's motivations.

♆   Confusion over how to use the powers or forces available to you; your use of force to establish new religions or mystical insight; misstatements of doctrine or philosophy are spread; a draining of energy resources.

♇   An extreme or fanatical use of forces under your control; rebellious or vigilante activities which provoke legal action; added intensity within your activities; increased powers or forces for use against others.

☊   Increased ability to push your ideas and plans with others; attracting people who have similar ideas about the use of force in competitive activities; concerns about the disposal or disposition of spent energy resources.

A   Development of a personal style which includes the portrayal of your personal strength or energy; directing your consciousness toward your physical energies; repression of unwanted activities with others.

M   A personal growth and nurturing by using all forces or energy available; learning to structure activities in beneficial ways; gaining recognition or fame by using competitive activities as a starting point.

MARS/JUPITER CONCEPTS

Irritated Optimists	Reckless Assumptions	Noisy Blessings
Anger at Organized Religion	Bold Confidence	Hasty Promises
Troublesome Errors	Troubling Promises	Added Abrasiveness
Enlarges Disturbances	Influences Competitors	Theories on Noise
Irritating Boasting	Defends Morals	Earnest Competitors
Initiates Optimism	A Noisy Understanding	Speedy Expansion
Motivates Ideals	A Competitive Standard	Suggests Aggression
Forceful Opinions	Doctrinal Struggles	Begins with Promises
Defies Coincidences	Noisy Encouragement	Excites Attitudes
Vigorous Optimism	Loud Blunders	Vibrant Honesty
Hurried Beliefs	Aggressive Leanings	Persistent Bias
Anger toward Ideals	Activates Beliefs	Adds to Courage
Aggressive Expansion	Activates Sincerity	Sparks Ideals
Expands Exercises	Persists through Studying	Irritated by Theories

Initiates Conjectures	Arguments over Ideals
Comprehends Recklessness	The Propagation of Noise
Anger at Theory	Fortunate Progress
Expanding Irritations	Energizes Luck
Reckless Promises	Assertive Representations
Accelerates Errors	Armament Negotiations
Assumptions of Activity	Rushes into Expansion
Does not Fear the Law	Fights Errors
Stimulates Optimism	Mistakes due to Haste
Exaggerates Impatience	Awakens Faith
Forces (Pushes) Beliefs	Idealizes too Quickly
Optimistic Competitors	Balks at Studying
Put off by Studying	Struggles with Assumptions
Competes to Expand	Shouted Promises
Hurried Studying	Courage to Defend Principles
Persistent with Beliefs	Pushes Beliefs on Others
Expects Troubles	Clamors for Expansion
Sincere Annoyance	Provokes Moral Issues
Principles of Aggression	Arouses Opinions
Forces Expansion	Asserts Preferences
Sincere but Persistent	Insists upon Morality
Spirited Understanding	Luck within Competitions
Expounds upon Arguments	Activity which Expands
Luck which Persists	A Hasty Understanding
Enthusiastic Mayhem	Rapidly Developed Morals
Balks at Understanding	A Potential for Trouble
Stimulates Expansion	Angered by Promises
An Immediate Optimist	Competitive Justification
Studies Aggressively	The Courage to Assume

MARS/JUPITER With Itself

♂   An abrasiveness and roughness to the way you use your energy; a competitive edge in contact sports; a need to bully others and threaten them with your strength or physical ability; hasty expansion plans.

♃   More recklessness than usual; numerous physical encounters with others; allows the use of religious scruples as an excuse for using force; increased anger over the morals of others as they apply to you.

Significant Examples of People and Events Using Mars/Jupiter

General: <u>STRONG:</u> Alexander Graham Bell; Percy Bysshe Shelley; Emperor Hirohito; Joseph Joffre; Charles Gordon; Carl Sandburg; Glen Campbell; Albert Schweitzer; Ferdinand Foch; Ervin Nyiregyhazi; Edna Ferber
<u>WEAK:</u> Sir Alexander Fleming; Elton John; Edgar Degas; Merv Griffin; William K. Douglas; Stonewall Jackson; Ed. Halley; Ada Lovelace Byron
<u>EVENTS:</u> Challenger Explosion; Chernobyl Nuclear Explosion; Kent State Shootings; RMS Titanic Hits Iceberg; (Apollo 11 Moon Landing).

☉   John Dillinger; Rupert Murdoch; First A-Bomb Explosion; Evel Knievel

☽   Liberace; Joseph Joffre; Emperor Hirohito; Challenger Explosion; Paul Newman; Nikola Tesla; Enrico Fermi; Glen Campbell

☿   Jonathan Winters; Israel Regardie; John F. Kennedy; South Carolina Secedes from Union; Jerry Rubin; F. Scott Fitzgerald

♀   Carl Sandburg; John Paul I; Walt Whitman; Richard Alpert; A. Murray

♂, ♃   Percy Bysshe Shelley; Cheiro; Carl Sandburg; Willie Brandt; S. King

♄   Sean Connery; Bjorn Borg; Robin Williams; David O. Selznik; G. Lewi

♅   David Frost; Rollo May; Kent State Shootings; Bob Hope; Fidel Castro

♆   Charles Gordon; Edouard Manet; Lindburgh Lands; Paul Jos Goebbels

♇   Rupert Murdoch; Jack Schwartz; Ira Progoff; Wayne Gretzky; Ferdinand Foch; Alexis Carrel; Anne Murray

☊   Franklin Roosevelt; Sir William Crookes; Olga Worrall; Richard Strauss

A   George Washington's Inauguration; Joseph Joffre; Robert McNamara; Auguste Rodin; Arnold Schwatzenegger; Fidel Castro

M   Bob Dylan; Lawrence Welk; Lord Byron; Ferdinand Foch; Al Unser

MARS/SATURN   ♂/♄

Basic Ideas:

This combination of stop and go urges you forward, but then applies the brakes. You exercise restraint and self-control in your use of your force or energy, have great endurance through your personal strength, and encounter activity which persists. You place much emphasis on your physical abilities, and the throwing of caution to the wind as recklessness prevailing over caution is common. You encounter delays at the start of projects, dilemmas which are not psychologically easy to resolve, hard and rigid reactions from others, and a restlessness with self-discipline. You balance caution vs. action, violence vs. restraint, and experience controlled periods of noisy and energetic outbursts. You find activity which must be repeated monotonously (as in assembly lines), have trouble applying responsibility, and show anger when dealing with frustrations or limiting restrictions. You may become a cautious competitor.

In Your Personal Life:

Thesis   The cultivation of discipline in sports or physical training programs; an impulse to heat up a cold activity; obligations imposed to provide liveliness; ambition which is put into motion; serious efforts.

Anti   Activity frozen by restrictions or incompetence; prolonged struggles; lasting anger; the introduction of ignorance; persistant noise; the arousal of dormant frustrations; diminishing urges.

In Your Relationships:

Thesis   Increased ability to work out problems of activity vs. restraint and caution vs. recklessness in relationships; working out anger directed at you, or vice versa, into more positive activities.

Anti   Aroused irritation that you turn and direct at your partner; prompts you to see your faults and difficulties as being caused by your partner; you see your partner as a person who blocks your best efforts.

With Body or Mind:

High blood pressure; health problems caused by blockage of energy or emotion; hyper followed by hypo; frustration; muscles which weaken or wither.

In Politics or Business:

Thesis   Curtailing force or military power by authorities; enforcement of honor through the use of strife or struggle; wars which persist; frustrations imposed upon or by criminal elements; demands to halt armaments.

Anti   Military actions which continue under political or other restrictions; an obligation to use force when restraint is required; the ambitious taking of that which belongs to another; an older enterprise becomes angered.

MARS/SATURN with Planets and Points

☉   Progress in learning to control impulses; applying restraint to urges; leadership and roles of authority for older persons; determination to deliberately encourage active people with their progress; basic rules for competitions.

☽   Awareness of the need to restrain impulsive activity; an active or athletic mother; fluctuations in energy levels; development of strength or courage; anger over restrictions imposed by family or home.

☿   Communication with athletic or military personnel; angry talk in a hushed tone; education which slows development of your ability; loud shouting or noises at formal speeches; expressions which show regret.

♀   A softening to the hard edge of anger and irritation shown during active moments or in haste; admiration for those who train or practice well; a love of might or muscle developed thru work and application.

♃   An urge to overextend yourself during competitive practices; the personal inner struggles you must overcome to achieve your desired results; assures success when you prepare activities thoroughly.

♅   Sudden and unexpected interruptions carried out in a loud and brash way at or in formal settings; indifference to slow and arduous activity; impulsive behavior controlled by friends; astrological efforts or actions which persist.

♆   A weakening of well-prepared plans for the development of desires; defects in training regimens; pretenses or cover-ups about the state of preparedness or readiness of self or others; inefficient use of energy.

♇   Extreme measures taken to apply force or might directly to those who are no longer able to defend themselves adequately; intensely applying might or energy toward goals; respected activities are corrupted.

☊   Meeting others who are able to apply restraint to your impulses; encountering people who need the restraint you bring to their misdirected activities; group meetings about effective planning activities, or personnel resources.

A   Concentrating on bringing discipline or restraint to the various activities or contests you engage in; important military people or athletes who are close to you; your attitudes about disciplining yourself, and promoting practice.

M   Increases in the respect or personal stature you receive due to great efforts on your part to develop self slowly and in a mature fashion; learning the role of discipline and persistence in gaining expertise.

MARS/SATURN CONCEPTS

Dedicated Activity	Modest Efforts	Restrains Activity
Competitive Frustration	Fights Blockages	Immediate Austerity
Urges Dissatisfaction	Aggressive Old People	Irritating Pessimism
Forces (Pushes) Delays	Troublesome Delays	Pressure Begins
Arms Control	Quickly Restrained	Shouts of Misery
Persists with Restraint	Aggravating Pauses	Urges Shyness
An Enduring Competition	Angry over Repression	Excites Aloofness
Simple Competitive Plans	Exciting Obligations	Simple Shouts
Enforces Obligations	Balks at Discipline	Spirited Drills
Hurried Restrictions	Angry and Frustrated	Activates Rigidity
Insists on Constraints	Haste Makes Waste	Spirited Caution
Formal Competition	Impatience with Duties	Noise which Lasts

Restrictions in Battles	Inspires Embargoes
Sudden Disappointments	Maddening Abstinence
Irritating Caution	Short Periods of Curtailment
Bothersome Restraints	Combats Objections
Troubling Frustrations	Struggles with Pessimism
Initiates a Serious Tone	Threatens Scarcity
A Hasty Retreat	Disappointing Masculinity
Resists Rules and Regulations	Noisy Postponements
A Commitment to Fight	Balks at Commitment
Courageous Silence	Relies on Strength
Aggravating Delays	Simple Irritations
Angry with Restrictions	Argues over Inflexibility
Aggressive with Objections	Stimulates Skepticism
Shouts when Disappointed	Restraints on Aggression
Throws Caution to the Wind	A Durable Competitor
Courage which Endures	Fights Frustrations
Fights which Gain Nothing	Introduces Tension
Urgent Restrictions	Silent Energy
Initiates Brevity	Energy Restrictions
Competitive Failures	Persistent through Pessimism
Shouts of Commitment	Irritating Objections
The Courage for Duty	Monotonous Rigidity
Remains at Post	Stimulates Suspensions
Stimulates Objections	A Cautious Competitor
Loud Objections	Serious Obligations
Maddening Disappointments	Hasty Pessimism
Sudden Dejection	A Hasty Commitment
Disciplines Reckless People	Persists with Simplicity
Troubles which Last	Restrains the Competition
Persistent in Solitude	Retards Aggression
Stimulates Deterrence	A Lasting Exertion

MARS/SATURN With Itself

♂   Abrasiveness shown when pushing forward with efforts that should be halted; anger over delays caused by impulsive actions taken long ago; loud clamor for results from important efforts that are stalled.

♄   Deficiencies in planning due to an incomplete review of plans; a loss of momentum from a lack of drive by leaders; prudence and caution disregarded as pressure is brought for completing stalled work.

Significant Examples of People and Events Using Mars/Saturn

General: **STRONG:** Stephen Foster; Joseph Joffre; Anne Murray; Richard Strauss; David O. Selznik; Jean Cocteau; John Glenn; Arthur Ford; Paul Joseph Goebbels; Paul Newman; Ivar Kreugar; Alan Leo; Muhammad Ali
WEAK: Tom Jones; Ellen Burstyn; Drew Pearson; Erwin Rommel; Jackie Robinson; Sir William Crookes; Bertrand Russell; Henry Kissinger
EVENTS: Wright Bros. Flight; Transcontinental Railroad completed; Apollo 11 Moon Landing; John F. Kennedy Shot; (Pearl Harbor Attack).

☉   Jim Thorpe; Mick Jagger; David O. Selznik; John Denver; Rollo May

☽   Muhammad Ali; Vincent Van Gogh; Dane Rudhyar; Jean Cocteau

☿   Steve Rosenbloom; George Patton; Bjorn Borg; Ivar Kreugar

♀   Jack Nicklaus; Bob Dylan; Edouard Manet; John Denver; Elvis Presley

♂, ♄   Albert Schweitzer; Charles Gordon; Jean Houston; Richard Strauss

♃   Lindburgh Lands; Charles Gordon; Georges Seurat; Anne Murray

♅   Steven Spielberg; H. G. Wells; Albert Schweitzer; East Coast Blackout

♆   Georges Seurat; Burt Reynolds; Charles Gordon; William K. Douglas

♀   Edward R. Murrow; Teilhard de Chardin; Alan Leo; Paul Gauguin

☊   Kareem Abdul-Jabbar; Jimi Hendrix; John Fremont; Lindburgh Lands

A   Friedrich Nietzsche; Vincent Van Gogh; Erich Maria Remarque

M   Muhammad Ali; Merv Griffin; Richard Byrd; Rollo May; R. Valens

MARS/URANUS ♂/♅

Basic Ideas:

Energy and activity meet rebelliousness and independence, creating unpredictable or unusual activity. These themes stimulate and agitate, but do not allow tranquility or stability until some basic change has been effected. People who are impersonal competitors, who initiate changes in activities which trouble them, or who push for renovation or reform, all have this motif activated. When matters which irritate lie unchallenged, when interference starts noisy arguments, when anger arises rapidly or suddenly, when others label a person as having a 'short fuse', then these themes have been used. This blend suggests how to employ your energies quickly, or how to gain a grasp of the competitive nature of life's activities. Hostility against surprises, energy to push for basic research, or struggles against opposition to progress, are also denoted here.

In Your Personal Life:

Thesis	Your courage to persist with personal struggles against all opposition or despite the length of the struggle; your insistence on correcting what you perceive as a wrong; energy for scientific or astrological activities.
Anti	A busybody who interferes with other's lives and causes disruptions; a pushy troublemaker; a person with rebellious impulses who does not want society to impose rules of personal conduct; annoying impulses.

In Your Relationships:

Thesis	You are not one to allow any relationship to slip into routine; you seek a partner who brings an answer to your forms of excitement, both intellectual and physical; you admire people who are forthright.
Anti	Others find your demands for independence and freedom in a relationship difficult to bear; you show unpredictable outbursts of anger destructive to self and others; you find it difficult to relate to others.

With Body or Mind:

Muscle spasms; rapidly fluctuating energy levels; deafness from exposure to noise; sudden inflammation; unexpected penetrations, punctures, or fevers.

In Politics or Business:

Thesis	Reforming a military organization; changes within the armed forces of the nation; modernization of basic energy or steel industries; groups formed to use or exploit energy resources; unplanned military actions.
Anti	Malice or unrest accompanied by violence; using security forces to control strife; radical movements within the military; rebellions against modernization efforts; sudden attacks or outbreaks of hostility.

MARS/URANUS with Planets and Points

☉   Implementing needed corrections or changes effectively and with determination; fundamental rules of conduct which you will not allow others to transgress; personal influence with scientific persons.

☽   Enhances sensitivities to underlying rhythms of life; moods which ebb and flow with changes in life; behavior which makes you difficult to please; you are hesitant and indecisive but also are quick to anger or become aggressive.

☿   You find working with metal and mechanical objects interesting; you devote much energy to research, and are careful to present facts clearly and correctly; urges to action to have views debated and not set aside.

♀   Softens an otherwise harsh or unruly side of self; you to present your views, but in more polite and less blunt ways; you may be dogmatic with or insistent about your views, but you do try to please others too.

♃   Increased ability and desire to fight and win for your side; a leniency to your otherwise harsh views of what you will or will not allow in life; a good judge of aggressive and pushy scientific-type persons.

♄   You may be known as a rash and impulsive person, but you carefully examine all sides of an argument before you forge ahead with your views; loneliness and isolation and a need for more personal solitude.

♆   You may be pushy and impetuous, but you have a dreamy and intuitive side to you which will abandon fights or confrontations when you become bored; you want to push for change but you do not always understand why.

♇   Your efforts for change have more far-reaching effects than you plan; people get more fury than help from you; confronting or battling against more powerful forces; starting from a disadvantage; finishing fights to the end.

☊   Enhanced ability to be active with others; presenting views directly and clearly; facing down all opposition to your ideas; you have many ordeals with others on your views and do not avoid confrontations.

A   You may become verbal or abusive to those who do not share your ways, or who impede progress; you derive enjoyment from agitating or upsetting others; presenting an unusual appearance or mannerism.

M   Becoming more philosophical and mature in your ways; new approaches to effecting social changes or lifestyles; approval given for work done while pushing for modernization; recognition for scientific achievements.

MARS/URANUS CONCEPTS

Rushes into Modernization
Anger with Disruptions
Competitive Surprises
Innovative Forms of Energy
Defects to the Competition
Competitive Renegade
Irritates the Rebels
Loud Contradictions
Noisy Indifference
Bold Independence
Stimulates Regulation
Peculiar Movements

A Variety of Activity
Aggressively Regulates
Hasty Indifference
Spirited Disruption
Stimulates Surprises
Hot Tempered Politics
A Variety of Stimulation
Immediate Idealism
Fights Perversions
Unique Irritations
Hasty Rebelliousness
Balks at Novelty

Sudden Variations
Hasty Discontent
Anger at Novelty
Incites Dissidents
Stirs up the Misfits
Sudden Insight
Loud Curiosity
Noisy Revisions
Aggressive Reform
Boldly Revises
Fights Aloofness
Noisy Rebelliousness

Forces (Pushes) Surprises
A Peculiar Beginning
Has Unique Courage
Criticizes Contrariness
Forces (Pushes) Deviation
Troubled by Indifference
Instantaneous Science
Regulates the Competition
An Aggressive Rebel
Forces (Pushes) Disruptions
Surprising Persistence
Enlivens Differences
Begins by Being Contrary
Disturbed by Protests
A Rash Nonconformist
A Clamor for Novelty
Revises Competitive Rules
Persistent through Innovation
Surprised by Troubles
Spirited Rebelliousness
Introduces Progress
Stimulates Innovation
Participates in Politics
Rushes into a Defection
A Stimulating Politician
Immediate Disinterest
The Courage to be Different
Varieties of Combat
Insight into Anger
Aggressive Indifference
Angered by Regulation

Spirited Innovation
Sparks Indifference
Anger over Variations
An Unusual Competitor
Sexual Regulation
Combats Deviations
Energizes Rebelliousness
Balks at Innovation
Irritated at Astrologers
Awakens Troublemakers
Immediate Opposition
Balks at Regulation
Intolerable Peculiarity
Competitive Disarray
Unpredictable Troubles
Regulates Energy Sources
Disruptive Activity
Anger over Exceptions
Strong Peculiarity
An Insistent Misfit
Hasty Revisions
Irritated with Malcontents
Shouts of Discontent
Arouses Opposition
Courageous Insight
An Indifferent Athlete
An Exciting Heretic
Instigates Exceptions
Arouses Uniqueness
Strained to the Extreme
Persists in Trying Variations

MARS/URANUS With Itself

♂   Additional energy and activity to areas where you are discontented or in disagreement with others; feeling as if you must fight for your rights whatever the cost; added urgency to your demands for freedom.

♅   Increased discontent with the present way others are using your abilities and energies; a need for independence from any restrictions, and a willingness to fight for independence despite obstacles or costs.

Significant Examples of People and Events Using Mars/Uranus

General: **STRONG:** Bobby Fischer; Dick Gregory; Stephen King; Guglielmo Marconi; Paul Joseph Goebbels; Edna Ferber; Paramhansa Yogananda; Edouard Manet; Olivia Newton-John; Burl Ives; Rupert Murdoch
WEAK: Pierre Teilhard de Chardin; Ida Rolf; Manly Palmer Hall; William K. Douglas; Henri Matisse; Gustav Dore; Mario Andretti; Henry Mancini
EVENTS: First Medicare Patient Applies; Lewis & Clark Expedition; Women's Suffrage Amendment passed; John F. Kennedy Shot; (Franklin D. Roosevelt's First Election).

☉   Jack Nicklaus; S. Carolina Secedes; Jean Cocteau; Sir Laurence Olivier

☽   Bob Newhart; Cheiro; Charles Steinmetz; J. Von Ribbentrop; Burl Ives

☿   First Medicare Patient; Steve Allen; Sydney Omarr; Kent State Shootings

♀   Edmund Halley; R. D. Laing; Johann Von Goethe; Rupert Murdoch

♂, ♅   John Fremont; John Denver; Vida Blue; Bobby Fischer; John Paul I

♃   Steve Wozniak; Shirley Jones; Ivar Kreugar; Giacomo Puccini

♄   Ulysses S. Grant; Elton John; Albert Schweitzer; Dr. Tom Dooley

♆   Bobby Fischer; Alex. Graham Bell; Amadeo Modigliani; Stephen King

♇   Ernest Pyle; Jack Schwartz; Helen Reddy; Kareem Abdul-Jabbar; Auguste Rodin; Jean Cocteau; Wayne Gretzky

☊   Richard Strauss; Burt Reynolds; Tom Jones; Richard Byrd; Stephen King; Dick Gregory; Franklin Roosevelt

A   Ivar Kreugar; Norman Mailer; Sydney Omarr; Jimi Hendrix; Jack Paar

M   Arthur Ford; Alan Leo; Watergate Burglary; Ernest Hemingway; Alan Alda; Francisco Franco; Robin Williams

MARS/NEPTUNE ♂/♀

Basic Ideas:

These two very different themes denote the energy and enthusiasm to continue your devotions while stimulating your inspiration. They show impulses for continuing with deceptive practices, aggravation about confusing situations, or combativeness and belligerence when faced with neglect. They indicate degrees of subtlety to your manner of competing, prompt you to overlook that which is important to you, show openness to aggression, belligerence, or threats from metaphysical sources, and weakness or shunting aside of physical strength. They symbolize haste and urgency to abandon people or things, aggravating illusions and impatience over ambiguity. You are confronted with noisy ghosts, situations which propel you toward sanctity or holiness, arguments over idealistic principles, and arousal of your spirituality.

In Your Personal Life:

Thesis   The courage to continue on your way toward holiness; intensified feelings for enlightenment; added strength to combat any attacks which you receive from illusive, nebulous, or vaguely defined sources.

Anti   The haste with which you change or abandon principles of spiritual or metaphysical development; the illusion that you will continue with a task; the neglect of ongoing activities; irritation felt toward losses.

In Your Relationships:

Thesis   Increased passion with which you pursue romantic activities; idealistic views about your relationship(s); inspiration for continuing or expanding your interpersonal affairs.

Anti   Irritation at the way your partners or friends deceive you; feelings of ire at another due to an incompatible need for romance or fantasy; anger at ambiguous or deceptive demands for romantic attachments to others.

With Body or Mind:

Weakens your overall physical stamina; muscle weakness or atrophy; physical conditioning; hypoadrenal conditions; high fevers from unknown ailments.

In Politics or Business:

Thesis   The threat of war or force to be used against the ideals of the people, the country, or its rulers; the use of internal rebellion as a means of weakening the military; military rule as a form of national glamor.

Anti   Scandals involving the Armed Forces; the use of industrial espionage; fires in national hospitals; rioting over nationalized health care; delusion about the strength of the military; military spying or spies.

MARS/NEPTUNE with Planets and Points

☉ A distinguished and noted magician or mystic performs; added effectiveness to the impact of a deception or illusion; your ideas of the holy or divine forced on others; weakened intensity of influential people.

☽ Added apprehension to struggles you have with deceptive or misleading activities; subtle contention or belligerence in romantic situations involving other people; a fluctuating anger toward visions.

☿ The adaptability you show when taking the power of the visions or dreams you have to others; the energy you put into acquiring knowledge about the mystical or magical side of life; fast but angry encounters from holy people.

♀ The consideration you show others even when you are irritated with their impractical dreams and visions; appeasement of those who complicate your efforts; gratification of needs to practice religion superficially or quickly.

♃ Amplification of your dreams and visions and the power or force you use to bring them to reality; excessive or impractical planning for how you should spend your energy resources; theories about the energies that mystics use.

♄ Frustrations encountered when punishing those who deceive others; blockage of anger toward people who avoid reality; pessimism over arguments received from clerics or mystics; a yogi who is disciplined.

♅ Unusual stamina to speed up the outcome of activities; an unconventional approach to forcing idealism or socialism on others; a noisy rebellion against aggravating dreams or visions forced by others.

♇ Compulsion with finding the source of and using the available energies of mystical or unknown natures; an excessive amount of dreams containing violence or aggravation; severe stimulation of your need to go or fade away.

☊ Meeting or encountering people who have access to subtle or mystical energy forces; meetings with new people who try to deceive you about their stamina or competitive capabilities; punishing romances.

A A strong mental focus on the subtle ways you use to compel or coerce others into adopting your ideas; focusing attention on the causes of confusion which surround any tense conditions you encounter.

M Attaining an understanding of the subtle forces or energies which drive the nonphysical world; integrating the messages of your meditation or dreams to help you overcome anger or fear; success in pushing or prodding ideas.

MARS/NEPTUNE CONCEPTS

Persistent Flimsiness	Angry Dreams	Noisy Illusions
Hastens Inspiration	Argues against Psychism	Avoids Aggression
Noisy Complications	Indirect Aggression	Yields in Combat
Garbled Insistence	Pushed to Yield	Subtle Courage
Inspired Activities	Disregards Clamor	Avoids Combat
Disguises Stimulation	An Inefficient Fighter	Potent Drugs
Deceptive Aggression	Stimulates an Illusion	Fast Denials
Dreams of Confrontation	A Neglect of Energy	Noisy Submission
Neglect which Persists	Inspired to Avoid	Disregards Psychics
Pretenses which Anger	Bluffs in Battles	Hasty Submission
Complicated Aggressions	Activates Insecurities	Noisy Pretenses
Deception in Combat	Balks at Deception	Rousing Holiness

Forces (Pushes) Summaries	Pretends to be Courageous
A Strong Dependence	Initiates a Counterfeit
Incites (Goads) Mystics	Aggravating Avoidance
Insists on a Deception	Energizes Pretenses
Immediate Shortcomings	Angry and Confused
Pretends to be Aggressive	Confusion amidst Hostilities
Potent Guilt	Inspires Aggression
Illusive Troubles	Tolerates Frantic Activity
Argues for Atonement	A Mysterious Competitor
Stimulates Frivolity	Anger at Mystics
Troubling Complications	Avoids the Competition
Illusive or Subtle Forces	Sudden Ambiguities
Resents Carelessness	Dissipates an Explosion
Troubled with Subtlety	Anger over a Deception
Instigates Dreams	Inspires a Fantasy
Balks at Pretenses	Aggressive Mysticism
Persists through Confusion	Incoherent with Irritation
Courageous Deception	A Confusing Rescue
A Vision which Persists	Perplexed with Speed
Struggles with Abstraction	Disguises Masculinity
Agitates for Mysticism	Fights Illusions
Weakens the Energetic	Loses a Struggle
Irritated by Complications	Spirited Pretenses
Intensifies Ambiguity	Sudden Neglect
Complicates Activities	Actively Avoids (whatever)
A Release of Energy	Irritation with Flimsiness
A Disguised Threat	Courageous Avoidance
Troubled by Submitting	Stimulates a Mystic
Contrived Irritation	Speedy Redemption
Persistent Inspiration	Difficulty with Confusion
Dreams of being Competitive	Deceives Competitors

MARS/NEPTUNE With Itself

♂ Impulses for combativeness, irritation, or determination to forge ahead with projects and ideas even before you examine them for their soundness; increased feelings for hasty judgments of mystical persons.

♆ Finding a quiet place for examining your inner self; searches for different methods of mystical practices for gaining an inner control on your sexual and bodily urges; a need for meditation and yoga.

Significant Examples of People and Events Using Mars/Neptune

General: **STRONG:** Jimi Hendrix; Shirley Jones; Dane Rudhyar; Edna Ferber; Carl Sagan; John Denver; Harry Belafonte; Stephen Sondheim; Wayne Gretzky; Scott Carpenter; Steven Spielberg; Helen Reddy; Vittorio DeSica
WEAK: Anne Murray; John F. Kennedy; Robert DeNiro; Muhammad Ali; Mario Andretti; Alan Alda; Albert Camus; Marc Edmund Jones
EVENTS: Woman's Suffrage Amendment passed; Lewis & Clark Expedition starts; Wright Brothers First Flight; Pearl Harbor Attack; (Challenger Explosion).

☉ Robert Redford; Edgar Degas; Robert McNamara; Francisco Franco

☽ Stephen Crane; Friedrich Nietzsche; Chernobyl Nuclear Explosion; John Fremont; Carl Sagan; Peter Max; Moshe Dayan; Dick Gregory

☿ Olivia Newton-John; Helen Reddy; Edna Ferber; Scott Carpenter

♀ Jeddu Krishnamurti; Glen Campbell; Jack Nicklaus; Sigmund Freud

♂, ♆ Ellen Burstyn; F. Scott Fitzgerald; Bobby Fischer; Charles Gordon

♃ Charles Gordon; Scott Carpenter; Sir Alex. Fleming; Stephen Foster

♄ Charles Gordon; Maurice Ravel; Vittorio DeSica; Jimi Hendrix

♅ Bobby Fischer; Charles E. O. Carter; Bolsheviks Seize Power; Carl Sagan; Mark Spitz; Anne Murray; Sally Ride

♀ Maurice Ravel; Wright Bros Flight; Edouard Manet; Helen Reddy

☊ Henri Toulouse-Lautrec; Edgar Degas; Henry Winkler; South Carolina Secession; Gregory Peck; Melvin Belli

A Dick Gregory; Stephen Sondheim; Wright Bros. Flight; Alexis Carrel

M Joseph Joffre; U. S. Grant; Jimi Hendrix; S. Spielberg; J. F. Kennedy Shot

MARS/PLUTO ♂/♀

Basic Ideas:

Heated arguments, the courage to raise suspicions, and aggravation at polluting or contamination practices, are central to these themes. Here you find the energy to purify or change that which is undesirable or imperfect; the stimulation to be deceptive, corrupt, or degenerate; and a loosening of your destructive tendencies. These motifs show endurance and energy for fights or battles, to overcome any obstacle, to control aggression, and to be put in situations where you are forced to retaliate or punish others. They show increased sexual passions, extremes of irritation or displeasure, and the courage to reverse or overthrow that which is corrupt or needs drastic change. They indicate provoking struggles or battles against evil forces, and the energy or will to set out after furious disputes to correct that which you feel needs reversal or adjustment despite the opposition.

In Your Personal Life:

Thesis   Courage or energy to pursue the most difficult or goals or challenges; sticking through to the end despite encountering the most dire or dreadful circumstances; impulses to correct wrongs; steady applications of effort.

Anti   Base feelings which push you to prolong gratification from practices which deplete people or resources; raising the heat of battle, or retaliating; aggravation over corruption or waste of people or resources.

In Your Relationships:

Thesis   Mean emotional reactions from others; turning emotions around and working with your partner in business or social schemes; counters the suspicions of others with suggestions for better planning or approaches.

Anti   Giving in to the lowest forms of pornographic or deviant behavior; provoking arguments for the sheer enjoyment of battle; stimulates passions through using lewd or profane remarks, gestures, or activities.

With Body or Mind:

An overproductive pituitary gland; active cell regeneration or production; rectal irritation; tumors; toxemia or diseases in the sexual organs; massive fevers.

In Politics or Business:

Thesis   Security forces allied with the military; conducting clandestine operations; using police or military against criminal elements; energy to clean up surroundings; attacks using powerful forces and weaponry.

Anti   A police state with rigid military controls; the use of suppression and torture as a means for enforcing policy; exporting upheaval and political theory to others as an objective; wars, rape, mayhem, chaos.

MARS/PLUTO with Planets and Points

☉   Effectiveness in imposing your will and theories upon others; forcing ideas upon others; a strong and unyielding will; one who is pushy and demanding; achievements attained by superior technique or endurance.

☽   Strong impulses to proceed with your ideas; habits which force you to use whatever means are necessary to achieve your tasks; an off and on temper or self-control; using traditional means of power to meet goals.

☿   Using foul or abusive language to bring attention to yourself; techniques which transfer energy from other places; discussions or descriptions of powerful weapons or great destruction; noises with carnage or battle.

♀   Softened approach when using harsh or repulsive tactics; great projects to increase wealth or power; the attainment of pleasure or luxury as a goal for acquiring power; art or music featuring death or morbidity.

♃   Increased destructive powers; the use of powerful forces to highlight conditions; the ethics of propagating powerful destructive forces or urges; a fortuitous outcome when activating extreme measures.

♄   Endurance and persistence used in the services of others for personal gain; frustration in achieving goals despite inner fortitude and persistence; a forceful, hard-driving personality; lessened personal power.

♅   Use of whatever power or means you have available to reform, disrupt, stir-up or otherwise alter conditions; inner interests for doing research in the mechanical, electrical, computing, or astrological fields.

♆   Illusions about what the use of power can do for you; deception by others in the form of lies, flattery, etc.; weakness in will to proceed with unpleasant tasks; powerful romantic or sexual fantasies; drug-induced delusions.

☊   The drive to find others to help you use power or aggressive tendencies to achieve goals; close ties to the powerful and/or the rich; channels open for you to achieve your goals; connections to the infamous.

A   Concentrating on using whatever means of control or will you have available to achieve your ends; a need to focus on your local environment and keep it clear and free of clutter; a coercive demeanor which intimidates.

M   Learning how to gain control of and use powerful or extreme measures for increasing your stature or standing; fulfillment of certain ambitions by attaining recognition and influence; principles which propel you to success.

MARS/PLUTO CONCEPTS

A Hurried Reversal
Troubling Corruption
Fights for Purification
The End of Aggression
Hidden Deletion
Pushes Poisons
Persistently Depletes
Obsessed with Competitors
Anger and Violence
The Courage to Punish
Shouted Suspicions
Secret Excitement

Active Disapproval
Loud Cursing
Fights a Dismissal
Sudden Reconstitution
Instigates a Reversal
Quick Rejection
Gruesome Competitors
Rapid Destruction
Fights Hatred
Nefarious Competitors
Energizes Passions
Depletes Energy

Noisy Punishment
Spirited Destruction
Active Retaliation
Clamors for Power
Activates Dying
Hasty Bankruptcy
A Driven Fanatic
Defames an Athlete
Angry and Distrusting
Destructive Battles
A Strong Monopoly
Blatant Rejections

Courage to Raise Suspicions
Persistent Movement
Suspicious of Using Force
Introduces Dishonesty
Struggles against Depravity
Spirited Purification
Difficulty at Funerals
Offensive Corruption
Initiates Oppression
Provokes an Expulsion
Compulsive Persistence
Turns Situations Around
Struggles with Transition
Rash Retaliation
Struggles to Recondition
Intense Spiciness
Instigates a Death
Extreme Exertions
Irritates Guilt Feelings
Rediscovers Persistence
Hasty Concealment
Rapid Dishonesty
Hastens Fermentation
Fights Crime
Pursues Purification
Activates Carnage
Angry over Dismissals
The Courage to Fight Corruption
Troubled by Devastation
Provokes Condemnation
Pushy and Willful

Removes Impulsiveness
Troubled with Power
Fights Obsessive Activities
Strains against Morbidity
Combative Intensity
Conceals Aggression
Arouses Ruthlessness
Prosecutes the Belligerent
Eliminates Assertiveness
Contests to Punish
Constrains Aggression
Fixes upon Activity
Obsessed with Haste
Immediate Revenge
Fights Oppression
Disturbed over Impurities
Suspicious of Spirits
Condemns Struggles
Hasty Corruption
Loud Dying
Heated Punishment
Arouses Suspicion
Punishes Competitors
False Insistence
Energetic Intensity
Fights Punishment
Punishing Battles
Death and Destruction
Forces (Pushes) Fetishes
A Quick Death
Persists with Adulteration

MARS/PLUTO With Itself

♂   Anger and impulsiveness added to an already 'short fuse' in your temper; impulses to hide your activities from others even further; needs to fight against the activities and intentions of people in general.

♀   An impulse to lower yourself and your status in life; an obsession for doing vengeance against others who harm or impede you; debases your standards of living and overall responses to others in life.

Significant Examples of People and Events Using Mars/Pluto

General: **STRONG:** Arthur Ford; Bob Hope; Earl Warren; Joseph Joffre; John McEnroe; Franklin Roosevelt; Emperor Hirohito; Marlon Brando; Marc Edmund Jones; Stephen Sondheim; Ada Lovelace Byron; Alexander Graham Bell; Stephen Crane
WEAK: Arthur Rimbaud; Edouard Manet; John Glenn; Audie Murphy; Henri Toulouse-Lautrec; Herman Melville; Albert Camus; Mary Martin
EVENTS: First Medicare Patient Accepted; Lewis & Clark Expedition starts; Kent State Shootings; Lee's Surrender at Appomattox; (James Meredith Enrolled at U. Miss.).

☉   Jerry Reed; Marlon Brando; Apollo 11 Moon Landing; Steve Allen
☽   Ada Lovelace Byron; George Washington's Inauguration; Rudolph Bing; Vittorio DeSica; Steve Wozniak
☿   First Medicare Patient Accepted; Ernest Pyle; Harry Shoaf; Gen. Ferdinand Foch; Arthur Godfrey; Charles Steinmetz
♀   John Lennon; Ferdinand Foch; Transcon. RR Done; Marlon Brando
♂, ♀   Arthur Ford; John McEnroe; John Paul I; David Frost; Harry Belafonte
♃   Jean Francois Millet; Guglielmo Marconi; Audrey Hepburn; J. Carson
♄   Bob Hope; Alexander Graham Bell; Benito Mussolini; Tommy Smothers; Stephen Sondheim
♅   Sam Sheppard; Olivia Newton-John; Bob Hope; Glen Campbell
♆   Henry Mancini; Carl Sandburg; Stephen Crane; Charles Steinmetz
☊   Auguste Rodin; Bob Fosse; USS Maine Explosion; Ellen Burstyn
A   Marc Edmund Jones; Vida Blue; Watergate Burglary discovered; Amadeo Modigliani; Jean Houston; Grant Lewi
M   Albert Speer; Van Cliburn; Bob Fosse; Ernest Hemingway; David O. Selznik; Burl Ives; Paul Cezanne

MARS/NODE ♂/☊

Basic Ideas:

The activity and emphasis you place on finding new friends or people who can help you achieve your aims in life, your insistence on having your way during meetings, and your haste and impatience with delaying tactics and bureaucracies are all found as part of this pattern. The noisy and persistent criticism you attract, the initiatives you take with any potential offered you, and the trouble and reversals you face from friends are also found here. Insistence and clamor unite with the potential or encouragement you receive through others in a unique combination of powers which induce you to activate new friendships and associations to help you with your work and its recognition or correction. Your progress due to help or advice from others, arguments which force you to retreat and then attack, and your battles against forces which divide are found within these themes.

In Your Personal Life:

Thesis   Your ability to control and bend the will of others so that they work for your ideas; your persistence in following through and pursuing your ideas during meetings; your haste to find new friends who can help you.

Anti   Your impatience with bureaucracy and delays; your need to forge ahead with your ideas; the friends you call on for help and the stimulation of ideas which you have; your irritation with criticism received.

In Your Relationships:

Thesis   Enhanced needs for having the dominant sexual position in a relationship; increased drive to find new friends after you have discarded old companions; your physical strength and sexual drive in love.

Anti   Arguments because neither person wishes to consider another's point of view; your irritation and insistence on having only your way in a relationship; the criticism you give another because they are not you.

With Body or Mind:

Tears and rips of muscles or ligaments which hold any body tubes, like the intestines; energy levels which are affected by stress induced from others.

In Politics or Business:

Thesis   An ability to attract or to sell military might from others; the use of mercenaries; allies who send military help in times of need; energy or military hardware which is provided for by friends or treaty.

Anti   The dispersal of military weapons or resources without safeguards or intention from others that they will pay for these; aggressive actions against the nation by hostile countries; treaties broken by warlike acts.

MARS/NODE with Planets and Points

☉ A need to dominate during meetings where your views are presented for comment or criticism; the personal command and presence you bring before others; enhanced ability to lead others to your ideas.

☽ The inner apprehension and fear you develop about the acceptance of your ideas and your insistence on staying with them despite opposition; inconsistency and indecisiveness of attitudes which seem fixed.

☿ Articulating your needs and views to others; mental agility to field questions and present forceful, direct answers which close debate on issues; lifelong friends who meet during sport activities at school.

♀ Soften presentations which make your views seem less harsh and more acceptable; manners and consideration in the insistence that your views shall predominate; attraction to another met by chance.

♃ You read the politics which occur at meetings or among friends and use this to advance your interests and causes; increased desires to study law or to associate with people having similar interests.

♄ You gain perspective on business and financial aspects of how groups can help you, or vice versa; you have less need for feedback from others and are more insistent on your ideas; you sustain your friends.

♅ Sudden disruptions when meeting with friends; accidental breaks in the thrust or tensions of important meetings; emotionless and disinterested presentations where you are able to present findings and information.

♆ Insight into how others can help you, but also false promises of help and followthrough ; increased confusion at meetings with friends and assistants; visualizations on how to guide and direct groups.

♇ Increased needs to be in control of groups and associations which wield influence in your professional areas of interest; need to be in control in sexual liaison; deters others from competing against you.

A Focusing on the need for bringing others into your life to develop your ideas and information; insight into the needs of others and their behavior in professional groups, activities, or during meetings.

M The recognition you achieve with your ideas, and the help you have from groups and associates in achieving distinction; your experience and maturity at being able to control and direct the will of the collective masses.

MARS/NODE CONCEPTS

Establishes Connections
Energizes Life's Aim
Asserts Ties to Others
Arouses Sexual Ties
Induces Karmic Acts
Clamor at Presentations
Irritating Separations
Initiates Sexual Ties
Stimulating Exhibitions
The Karma of Mistreatment
Spirited Ties to Others
Competition as a Life's Aim

Irritating New Habits
Hostile to the Familiar
Initiates Appointments
Hasty Separations
Noisy Interviews
Activates Karma
Explosive Splits
Urgent Interchanges
A Competitor's Layoffs
Immediate Separations
Tempestuous Supporters
Fast New Friendships

Aggressive Allies
Anger over Fate
Hasty Presentations
Noisy Removal
Loud Meetings
Reckless Removals
Begins with Delays
Spirited Sexual Ties
Noisy Separations
Speeds Evolution
A Powerful Destiny
Attracts Backers

Angry with Cooperation
Rash Joint Ventures
Fights those who Divide
Hostile to Appointments
Thrilling Meetings
Activates Segmentation
Irritating Criticism
Initiates Events
Troubled by Layoffs
Forceful Familiarity
Prompts Acquisitions
Stimulates Group Connections
The Courage to Face Others
Resents Alliances
Rapid Layoffs
Hostility toward Mergers
Persistent Ridding
Energetically Attracts Others
Unbearable Associations
Energizes Assemblies
Rushes into Relationships
Persistent in Attracting Others
Assertive Colleagues
Impatient to Separate
A Show of Aggression
Fights with Supporters
Tempestuous Meetings
Criticizes Interviewers
Enlivens Group Allegiances
An Aggressive Presenter
Exciting Familiarity

Hurried Ties to Others
Irritation at Conventions
Noisy Meetings with Others
Introduces New Habits
Impulsive Alliances
Argumentative Supporters
Immediate Cooperation
Sexual Connections
Presents a Bold Front
Forces a Separation
Disturbed by Interchanges
Competition among Partners
Explosive Karma
Activates Fated Meetings
Makes New Friends Fast
Belligerent Friends
Rushes into Attachment
Masculine Kinship
Hasty Sense of Destiny
Fights the Bureaucracy
Competes to Attract Others
Demonstrates Aggression
Energetic Acquaintances
Threats to Connections
A Noisy Sexual Liaison
Karma Concerning Noise
Hostile Presentations
Prompts Separations
Criticizes Masculine Habits
Spirited Separations
Urgent Sexual Ties

MARS/NODE With Itself

♂ Gathering with friends in loud and noisy celebrations; impulses for you to meet new people or to work with others who can help you find fulfillment; competitive activities which help you show your abilities.

☊ Impels you to spend much time in soliciting others for their opinion and help with your ideas in life; tracing other people who have resources you need or will find helpful in your work or assignments.

Significant Examples of People and Events Using Mars/Node

General: **STRONG:** Lawrence Welk; Franklin Roosevelt; Ida Rolf; Steve Allen; Giacomo Puccini; Grant Lewi; Al Unser; Bob Hope; Evel Knievel; Hank Williams; Paul Joseph Goebbels; Sigmund Freud; Robin Williams
WEAK: Komar; Peter Max; Arthur Ford; Charles E. O. Carter; Emperor Hirohito of Japan; George Liberace; Jack Paar; Stephen Foster
EVENTS: Alaskan Earthquake; Ramstein Airshow Disaster; First Medicare Patient Accepted; (Chernobyl Nuclear Plant Explosion).

☉ Apollo 11 Moon Landing; Bob Hope; Hermann Goering; Adolf Hitler
☽ Stephen Crane; James Meredith Enrolled at U. Miss.; Stephen Sondheim; Edward R. Murrow; Hugh Downs; Ernest Hemingway
☿ Mary Martin; Richard Strauss; Tommy Smothers; Vittorio DeSica
♀ Edmund Halley; Ulysses S. Grant; John Paul I; Arturo Toscanini; Henry Winkler; Francisco Franco
♂, ☊ Bolsheviks Seize Power; Hank Williams; Benito Mussolini; Robert McNamara; Rupert Murdoch; Franklin Roosevelt
♃ Grant Lewi; Steve Rosenbloom; Franklin Roosevelt; Henry Winkler
♄ Francisco Franco; Rupert Murdoch; Neil Diamond; Toulouse-Lautrec
♅ Jack Nicklaus; Giacomo Puccini; Paul Newman; Benito Mussolini; Alan Alda; Bob Hope; Carl Sandburg
♆ Paul Jos. Goebbels; Alaskan Erthqk.; Transcon. RR Done; Steve Wozniak
♀ Jacques Cousteau; Ernest Pyle; Erich Maria Remarque; Marc Edmund Jones; Audie Murphey; Ivar Kreugar
A Paul Gauguin; Jerry Reed; Lord Byron; Albert Speer; Manly Palmer Hall
M Steve Allen; Lindburgh Lands; John Denver; Bob Dylan; Dick Gregory

MARS/ASCENDANT ♂/A

Basic Ideas:

This combination shows an energetic concentration upon the common daily events of life which occur around you. You have life in your personal style, you blend your energy into those activities occurring in your immediate environment, and you emphasize your attitudes through activity, and your enhanced ability to notice and observe. These points help bring an awareness that the energy of the Universe is without limit and is available as from a cosmic storehouse. When you become physically tired a rest to recharge yourself (whether five minutes or ten hours) makes you ready for new activity and challenges. With this combination you need activity, you have a restlessness to your body, and you center on your approach to people. These themes indicate that you focus, either directly or subconsciously, on using the vitality which permeates your entire life system.

In Your Personal Life:

Thesis   A stimulating personal environment; an awareness of the competitive factors at work within your interpersonal activities; increased observation of events and people near you.

Anti   An irritation with people who are slower, or who block or impede progress; forcing your will on others; emphasized impulsive reactions to whatever the needs of the moment are; becoming bored with routine.

In Your Relationships:

Thesis   Urge to find a partner with a high energy state who can match your energy levels; you evaluate others for their ability to keep up with you physically; a focus on sharing experiences with another.

Anti   Urge to show anger toward others; an inner urge to keep your moods inside and block your outward going feelings; an impulsive shifting mental focus from event to event; scattered energies.

With Body or Mind:

Pressure or heat within the ocular fluids; elevated blood pressure caused by your environment; a need to maintain body heat when our in the elements.

In Politics or Business:

Thesis   Keeping military forces in a state of readiness for activity or movement; a well-trained military and an active armament industry; an ability to focus sharply on the business needs of industry.

Anti   A poorly prepared defense or war making capability; leaders who don't have the will or energy to mobilize their resources productively; focusing the efforts of an enterprise upon its energy or armament needs.

MARS/ASCENDANT with Planets and Points

☉   The personal belief that you have sufficient energy to succeed in any endeavor; the development of your personal or attitudinal strength; the enlivened force of your personality; your focused will power.

☽   Vacillation or hesitation when trying to see yourself as a unique individual; consoling those around you who have inner conflicts; indecision about how to get others to react with you or for you; females with intensity and energy.

☿   Highlights your need to verbalize your feelings about life or events which occur around you; emphasizing the psychological attitudes of self or others and how these blend and interact within patterns of life.

♀   Softens any combative or loud noises which may arise; shows tenderness and compassion before arguments arise; a need for pleasant settings; enjoying the rest which can follow activity; others who love your energy.

♃   Increased emphasis for developing the metaphysical or religious from your activities; emphasized inner energy and activity; a lot of noise around you; spotlights aspects of sociology or psychology for you; exaggerated loud talk.

♄   You directly meet any immoderate haste; decreased ability to express yourself gracefully through movement; the dramatic exposure of an arrogant or superior attitude; emphasizes planning and preparation.

♅   Urges to surprise or upset others through activities or attitudes which startle; upsetting others with practiced activity; a need to express your uniqueness through your dress, personal habits, or interests.

♆   Depletes your energy more quickly than you expect; brings a naive understanding of others; an unexplained lack of activity; misleading perceptions about anger or irritation; uncommon measures of progress.

♇   An urge to motivate others through the force of your personality; a need for you to have a deep and thorough understanding of the motives of others; you show irritation with people who block you.

☊   You to seek those who are similarly active and energetic; you find friends who share your attitudes and opinions and will work with you to develop these; you have a need to understand motives.

M   Confirmation of impressions you receive about the attitudes and inclinations of others; experience in tempering your energy so that you can accomplish all of your goals; validation of your attitudes and impressions.

MARS/ASCENDANT CONCEPTS

Activates Awareness
A Masculine Style
Spirited Mannerisms
Energetic Ways of Relating
Stimulates Mental Focus
A Pushy Disposition
Persists with Attitudes
Energetic Disposition
Driven to Seek Attention
A Spirited Presence
Abrasive Attitudes
Aggressive Personal Style
Active Introspection
Strong, Quick Rejoinders

Rapidly Senses Reality
Disturbing Masquerades
Bewildering Perceptions
Angry Mannerisms
Reckless Pretenses
Stimulates Portrayals
Noisy Recognition
Spirited Reactions
Defends Responses
Energetic Personal Style
Perceives Irritations
A Combative Tone
Strains to Perceive
Combative Personal Ways

Noisy Perceptions
Hasty Reactions
Represses Irritations
Rapid Opinions
Hasty Mannerisms
Stimulates Attitudes
Abrasive Reactions
Realizes Anger
Pushes Viewpoints
Quick Observations
Forces Attitudes
Noisy Mannerisms
Impatient Attitudes
Troubling Reactions

Fights Intrusions
Rash Perceptions
Quickly Forgets Ideas
Consistently Seeks Attention
Excited by What is Seen
Begins to Understand Others
Pushes Others Around
Forced to Join into Battles
Anger at Competitors
Clamors for Experiences
An Active Need for People
Exudes Boldness
Energizes Others at Meetings
A Strong need to See Things
Troubled by Another's Traits
Receives Lasting Impressions
Annoying Mental Habits
Annoyed by Conditions
A Continuing Presence
Activates Assessment
Hampers Personal Style
Forces Interpersonal Roles
Anger from Impressions
Troublesome Perceptions
Balks at Relating to Others
Insulting Rejoinders
Persistent Personal Style
Assertive Point of View
Receives Competitive Ideas

Energizes the Surroundings
Struggles with Perceptions
Argues for Privacy
A Courageous Tone (Attitude)
Rapid Sensations
Instigates Inhibitions
Rushes into a Setting
Irritating Characteristics
Reckless and Rash Responses
Disturbing Mannerisms
A Stimulating Personal Style
Forces Relating to Others
Fights Unreal Perceptions
Pushy Mannerisms
Impatient Personal Ways
Energetic Reactions
Argumentative Leanings
A Competitive Personal Style
Fights Understanding Others
Argues over what Reality is
Aggressive Ways of Relating
Strong Sensations
An Aura of Personal Boldness
A Competitive Environment
Focuses on the Competition
Spirited Disposition
Understands Others Fast
Actively Defends Personal Space
Forces Self into Surroundings

MARS/ASCENDANT With Itself

♂   A quick defense of personal situations or attitudes; clashes over any intrusion upon of your personal space(s); argument over questions on personal attitudes; a recognition of the need for movement or exercise.

A   Emphasized need to understand others and their reactions to you or life in general; highlight s the surroundings and settings for events and their circumstances as they occur; urges to spend time observing life.

Significant Examples of People and Events Using Mars/Ascendant

General: **STRONG:** Henry Mancini; Rupert Murdoch; Willie Brandt; Vittorio DeSica; Paul Cezanne; H. G. Wells; Richard Chamberlain; Edgar Degas; Alexis Carrel; Robert McNamara; Bobby Fischer; Dr. Francis Regardie
WEAK: Merv Griffin; F. Scott Fitzgerald; Jean Francoise Millet; Enrico Fermi; Ada Lovelace Byron; Fidel Castro; Harry Shoaf; Walt Whitman
EVENTS: Lindburgh Lands in Paris; RMS Titanic Hits Iceberg; Challenger Explosion; Bolsheviks Take Power; (East Coast Power Blackout).

☉   Charles Kettering; Rex Harrison; Bjorn Borg; Dick Gregory; Robert McNamara; Henri Matisse; Guglielmo Marconi

☽   S. Carolina Secedes; Charles Kettering; Henri Matisse; Stephen Sondheim

☿   Erwin Rommel; Jacques Cousteau; Apollo 11 Moon Lndg; L. Reventlow

♀   Paramhansa Yogananda; Robert DeNiro; Grant Lewi; Alexis Carrel; Alexander Graham Bell; Helen Reddy

♂, A   The Lewis & Clark Expedition Starts; Bobby Fischer; Richard Chamberlain; Pierre Teilhard de Chardin

♃   Alan Leo; Arthur Ford; Ritchie Valens; K. Abdul-Jabbar; J. Krishnamurti

♄   Olga Worrall; Mark Spitz; Audie Murphy; Titanic Hits Iceberg; H. Mancini

♅   Claude Debussy; Peter Max; Paul Jos Goebbels; Bjorn Borg; Sally Ride

♆   Apollo 11 Moon Landing; Steve Wozniak; Edward R. Murrow; Arthur Rimbaud; Arturo Toscanini; Dane Rudhyar

♇   Paul Cezanne; William K. Douglas; John Denver; Melvin Belli; W. Brandt

☊   Rupert Murdoch; David O. Selznik; Erich Maria Remarque; Rollo May

M   Evel Knievel; Charles Gordon; Ralph Nader; H. G. Wells; Albert Schweitzer

MARS/MIDHEAVEN ♂/M

Basic Ideas:
This combination symoblizes your awareness of the need for personal development and integration as you struggle with the competitive battles of life. You
begin to learn that your best personal progress comes by being insistent with your
ideas, and responding immediately to all challenges. 'The best defense is a good
offense' is a lesson which you learn through this combination. You develop a
persistence for pushing your interests, you learn to create energy and power when
battling for your principles, and you practice not being afraid when insisting on
your personal rights. You can use this blend to push for personal recognition and
to ensure that the security you or your family need is achieved. These themes
denote persistance with personal growth, making the most noise and getting the
most attention, and discovering that it is only through insistence that you achieve
the recognition you want.

In Your Personal Life:
Thesis   Tough competitive spirit; personal drive combined with inner
determination to progress in life; competing in life and forging
ahead despite opposition; inner toughness brings success.

Anti   Realizing that bluff and bravado are all a part of life; developing
aggressive skills as a means for obtaining your goals; a realization
that personal strength and fighting skills can always be improved or helped.

In Your Relationships:
Thesis   Emphasizing your need to grow and develop with another;
seeking a person who can be your real life hero; persistence for
working through the needs of a relationship, and coping with
reality.

Anti   New or additional anger that your partner brings out in you;
realizing that noise and bravado must be controlled within any
successful relationship; struggles for self-identity which involve
both people.

With Body or Mind:
Emphasizes your personal maturity and the energy you place into becoming
psychologically whole; brings a need to be active in defining your inner self.

In Politics or Business:
Thesis   The development of a military capability for both safety and
defense; a use of natural energy sources to help in development;
using created enemies of the state as targeted examples or focus
objects for hate.

Anti   The fostering of paranoia for political control of the people; a
fear of foreign domination and preparation for same; legislative bodies which order arming as a means of protecting the
borders or rights.

MARS/MIDHEAVEN with Planets and Points

☉   Better understanding of self and how you can use your inner strength to define who you are as a person; adds to the importance you place on allowing yourself to mature in life; helps direct your attitudes.

☽   Realizing that you have emotions and the role these can play in making you a unique person; an emphasized inner need to develop the maternal qualities of caring, sympathy, and understanding for others.

☿   Highlights your need to use your innate intelligence and inner gifts to progress in life; you realize your spiritual origins and the need to develop your attitudes and efforts to conform to these inner principles.

♀   Appreciation of the personal growth and development process; generating beauty and serenity in your surroundings for growing and becoming; using charm and politeness when stimulating maturing and/or coping with life.

♃   The role that religion or philosophy play in helping you to become a better and different person; your susceptibility to or use of persuasion in seeking the principles which can make you more well-rounded as an individual.

♄   Restraining personal ambitions and realizing the role that others can play in your life; a need to succeed in life and make a definitive mark upon the world which others recognize and praise; pursuit of rewards.

♅   Realizing how you are unique as a person and what you can do to show others this personal uniqueness; a need for you to examine unusual methods and philosophies for understanding people.

♆   Realizing that life is more than what appears in the physical world; an inner need to understand yourself in the context of the universe at large, or through a religion with its ceremony and doctrines; ideals gone astray during life.

♇   Desire to be noticed for the abilities you have, and the urge to apply yourself more forcefully and directly to your tasks; a deep inner need to be recognized and appreciated as a person.

☋   Contacts through others which help you develop your interpersonal capabilities; increased needs to use force or noise so that others will take notice of you; an irritation with how others seem to get all of the breaks in life.

A   Reflecting on your perceptions of how others change as they grow in life; an emphasis on the importance others have in allowing you to grow and mature as a person and thus gain recognition for your efforts or position.

MARS/MIDHEAVEN CONCEPTS

Persists thru Consequences
Fights for Conclusions
Competitive Fulfillment
Rushes into Assurances
An Apt Competitor
Persistent by Birthright
Knows How to Fight
Continues Self-Integration
Aggressive Protection
Motivates Competence
Fights for Certification
Accelerates Maturing

An Impulsive Expert
Hostile Intentions
Anger with Origins
Clamors for Results
Hostile to Objectives
Learns to Work Hard
Hot Tempered Behavior
Activates Experiences
Excited by Principles
Stimulating Start in Life
Rapid Reconciliation
A Lively Expert

Insists on Protection
Noisy Adjustments
Irritating Outcomes
Stimulates Results
Asserts Standards
Hurried Morals
Heroic Attitudes
Begins with Capacity
Forceful Reactions
Intolerable Outcome
Pushy Conduct
Reckless Methods

Begins with Self-Guidance
Stimulates Inner Growth
Troubled with Experts
Speedy Public Projection
The Courage to Develop
Learns and Grows through Battles
Arguments over Consequences
Persistent Personal Growth
Aggressively Seeks Recognition
Gains Skill as a Competitor
Overcomes Annoyance
Fights for What is Right
Competes for Certification
Matures through Mastering Tasks
Forces (Pushes) Self-Restraint
Gains Stature through Competing
Aggressive Personal Training
Forceful, Pushy, Behavior
Hastens Ambition
Forces Self to Seek Security
Persistent Self-Restraint
Experience through Progressing
Fights Life's Battles
Hampers Career
Troubled with Intentions
Forces (Pushes) for Outcomes
Copes with the Competition
Rushes into Developing Self
Energetic Persevering
Urgent Self-Restraint
A Constant Battle to Mature

Spirited Learning and Growing
Fights Past Difficult Beginnings
Integrates Aggression
Restrained Competition
Defends Self-Concepts
Moves toward Intentions
Irritating Personal Growth
An Aptitude for Impatience
Guarantees to Excite
Restrains Self-Aggression
Has Expertise in Fighting
Advances through Performance
Knows How to Compete
An Insistent Conscience
Threats to Reputation
Balks at Learning and Growing
Proficient at being Reckless
Lively Ways of Maturing
Activity to Achieve Goals
Persists through Coping
Hastens Self-Concepts
Initiates Self-Restraint
Aggressive Intentions
Exciting Goal Seeking
Protection from Competitors
Hastily Conceived Self-Concepts
Pushes for Recognition
Struggles to Gain Proficiency
Gives Trust Impulsively
Stimulates Career Options
Pursues Rewards

MARS/MIDHEAVEN With Itself

♂ Fighting for what you want in life and also taking pains to protect your gains from those who covet them; your anger when others question your status or gains; your excitement about competitive activities.

M You bring more energy and emphasis to attaining career status than personal status; you work very hard and long to achieve expertise and recognition for your efforts; you tend to fight to defend your code of ethics, or family.

Significant Examples of People and Events Using Mars/Midheaven

General: **STRONG:** Albert Camus; Jack Paar; Steven Spielberg; F. Scott Fitzgerald; John McEnroe; Jack Nicklaus; Evil Knievel; Ritchie Valens; Ulysses S. Grant; Gianni Agnelli; Alan Leo; Edna Ferber; Johnny Carson
WEAK: Edward R. Murrow; Richard Strauss; Mick Jagger; William Butler Yeats; Robert McNamara; Paul Joseph Goebbels; Elton John
EVENTS: RMS Titanic Hits Iceberg; George Washington's Inauguration; John F. Kennedy Shot; Transcontinental Railroad completed; (Bolsheviks Seize Power).

☉ Israel Regardie; Lance Reventlow; Edmund Halley; Tommy Smothers

☽ Steve Rosenbloom; Alan Alda; Walt Whitman; Rex Harrison; David O. Selznik; Olivia Newton-John; Benito Mussolini

☿ Dick Gregory; Edward R. Murrow; F. Scott Fitzgerald; William K. Douglas; Jacques Cousteau; Paul Cezanne

♀ Melvin Belli; Laurence Olivier; Rudolph Bing; Carl Sandburg; Alan Leo

♂, M Ramstein Airshow Crash; Gianni Agnelli; Maurice Ravel; Dane Rudhyar; Albert Speer; Bjorn Borg; Paramhansa Yogananda

♃ Ulysses S. Grant; Friedrich Nietzsche; Norman Mailer; Shirley Jones

♄ Woman's Suffrage Amendment passed; Ernest Pyle; Charles Kettering; Kareem Abdul-Jabbar; Ritchie Valens; Ralph Nader

♅ Marlon Brando; David Frost; John McEnroe; Benj. Disraeli; Elton John

♆ Wright Bros. Flight; Norman Mailer; Tom Jones; Steven Spielberg

♇ Enrico Fermi; Johnny Carson; Joachim Von Ribbentrop; J. Krishnamurti

☊ Stonewall Jackson; Jack Nicklaus; Billy Rose; Ernest Pyle; Dane Rudhyar

A Edmund Halley; Wright Brothers First Flight; Jerry Reed; Stephen Foster; Olivia Newton-John; Charles Steinmetz

JUPITER/SATURN   ♃/♄

Basic Ideas:

These planets show cycles of expansion and contraction within all the varieties of lifestyle and activity which you experience. They represent your personal ambitions, the expansion of your thinking with successful work ideas, or symbolize what you can or cannot accomplish with your time and resources. They denote that you exercise caution or restraint with your opportunities, focus your thinking with simple and quiet directness, and accept guidance about your life. You may find that they symbolize a lessened interest in pursuing religious or philosophical ideals. You state your opinions more cautiously, and gain an increased understanding of how you can progress with your life. You may find a greater number of disappointments or delays, discover a lot of pessimism, and become frustrated when you rely too much on the opinions or promises of others.

In Your Personal Life:

Thesis   Setting realistic goals and plans for your time and energy; gaining realism about advice offered; an idealist with your feet on the ground; adding to resources to increase future security.

Anti   Increased pessimism about your ability to cope with the future; feeling inadequate when comparing yourself to others; glossing over the real reasons for present or past failures; numerous failures with businesses.

In Your Relationships:

Thesis   A serious outlook about your partner and your mutual potential; a preference for a serious person who has a true desire for travel and adventure; seeing your partners for the people they are.

Anti   A lack of realism in assessing the talents you and your partner have together; added rigidity when discussing moral or religious issues together; feeling that your partner doesn't know your potential.

With Body or Mind:

Inflammation of the joints; calcium deposits in the liver or hip joints; fluid on the knee; less acid or fat in the body; inefficient glucose producing mechanisms.

In Politics or Business:

Thesis   The serious side of justice and the law; processes concerning checks and balances; changes in the governmental, religious, or social orders; an expansion within the rocks in the ground; repression based on morality instituted by law or religion.

Anti   Too many restrictions on the operation of justice; a judicial system at its breaking point; pessimism about the ability of the police to control lawbreakers; leniency and harshness vie for balance within the overall social and economic systems.

JUPITER/SATURN with Planets and Points

☉   Dreaming of a potential for actuality; feeling that you can positively influence social change; boasting a lot; an increase in self-pride and your ability to demonstrate positive leadership before others.

☽   Planning for cyclical ups and downs; extending influence over business or social activities involving the public; a tendency to overestimate your remaining personal inventory or commodities reserve.

☿   Communicating effectively about planning and organization for all activities; using the media to publicize your ideas and aspirations; information which is contrary to knowledge available in general.

♀   Increased appreciation for the value of planning and organization in the arts, etc.; learning new ways of showing affections, or developing social manners and grace; jealousy due to the social recognition given to others.

♂   New efforts to effect positive changes in your social life through sports or competitive activities; introducing duress as a means for forcing social change; added irritation over delays for new beginnings.

♅   Creating a lifestyle where you have more freedom to choose your activities; freedom from the shackles of a demanding job to pursue more leisurely and personal activities; quick changes abruptly introduced to your lifestyle.

♆   Ideas for a more perfect society; dreams about changes you need to implement in your life or business; added needs to avoid change even when needed; disillusionment about the relative pace of progress.

♇   You may have a total reversal to plans previously made; extremes in the changes you implement in your lifestyle; transforming personal ideas about the future into the today's reality; intense business activity.

☊   Finding and associating with people who help you build and progress through the cycles of life; help from influential persons in effecting social or personal changes; new ideas or people contacts which broaden your life.

A   Changes on how you observe or react to others; new ways you judge or reflect on your personal relationships; increased awareness of coping with the forces of change encountered daily; cycles of expansion or contraction.

M   Maturing by accepting and integrating changes which occur in your life; coping with social and personal change and being able to grow with this change; new outlooks for personal refinement and growth.

JUPITER/SATURN CONCEPTS

Honest Respect	Glaring Ignorance	Delayed Success
Studies Restrictions	Exaggerated Findings	Enlarged Obstacles
Expanding Boredom	Wrong Types of Realism	Too Much Gloom
Convinced of Limitations	A Lot of Discipline	Excessive Caution
A Persuasive Confession	Enlarges on Failure	Expands Dishonor
Studies in Silence	Sincere Modesty	Fortunate Times
Prefers Reliability	Aspires to Silence	Widens Self-Control
Additional Admiration	Augments Concessions	Ample Rebuffs
Mistaken Discipline	A Successful Assignment	Enjoys the Stillness
Increased Stoppages	Restrained Wisdom	Lots of Skepticism
Furthers Durability	Glaring Inadequacy	Accepts Despair
A Realistic Assumption	Prudent Restrictions	Too Much Rigidity

Lasting Satisfaction	Cheerful Caution
Wise Silence (Meditation)	Potential through Organization
Increases Responsibility	Flagrant Rebuffs
Additional Commitment	Magnifies Responsibilities
Simple Generosity	Burdened with Inaccuracy
Accepts Postponements	Increases Commitment
Prefers Monotony	Understands Moderation
Wise Caution	Accepts Restrictions
Abstains from Aspirations	Wise Practicality
Extensive Stability	Simple Wisdom
Augments Monotony	Successful Business Planning
Modest Happiness	Comprehends Obligations
Boasts about Postponements	Boasts about Patience
Sufficient Shyness	Enough Pessimism
Prefers Silence	Extensive Tragedy
Frustrating Beliefs	A Fortunate Commitment
Recommends Austerity	Lenient Determinations
Additional Realism	Assists in a Failure
Disciplines Wisely	Numerous Old People
Furthers Humility	Untimely Acceptance
Sufficient Reserve	Ponders on Commitment
Cautious Persuasion	Increases Burdens
A Simple Misjudgment	Satisfied with Conclusions
A Sensible Influence	Great Postponements
Too Much Pessimism	Allows a Commitment
Lessens Generosity	Inclined to Introspection
Abundant Dejection	Magnifies Monotony
Assumes Heartaches	A Lot of Despair
Exemplary Silence	Loosens Restrictions
Idealistic Realism	Expects Severity
Disappointing Theories	Accepts Imposed Restrictions

JUPITER/SATURN With Itself

♃   Need to apply principles of hard work and dedication toward goals set; generosity shown toward others; difficult assignments performed with ease; delays when producing publications; many obstacles.

♄   Abbreviated comprehension understanding life's situations; added constraints on time or resources available; disappointment from products not built to last; a lack of honesty in business negotiations; a scarcity of wisdom.

Significant Examples of People and Events Using Jupiter/Saturn

General: **STRONG:** Carl Sandburg; Willie Brandt; Johnny Carson; Bob Hope; Alexis Carrel; Paul Joseph Goebbels; Edmund Halley; Henry Kissinger; Neil Diamond; David Frost; Joseph Joffre; Cheiro; Ida Rolf; John Denver
WEAK: Kareem Abdul-Jabbar; Bobby Fischer; Jack Nicklaus; Tom Jones; Jean Francoise Millet; Enrico Fermi; Arthur Ford; Dustin Hoffman
EVENTS: John F. Kennedy Shot; Transcontinental Railroad Completed; Titanic Hits Iceberg; First Atomic Bomb Explodes; (Apollo 11 Moon Landing).

☉   Arthur Ford; U.S. Grant; Ritchie Valens; Jimmy Carter; F.D. Roosevelt

☽   Carl Sandburg; Paul Cezanne; Carroll Righter; Manly P. Hall; Bob Hope; Ralph Waldo Emerson; Abraham Lincoln

☿   First A-Bomb Explosion; Adolf Hitler; Charles Addams; John Denver

♀   Ervin Nyiregyhazi; J. Meredith Enrolled; Jimmy Carter; Mick Jagger

♂   Ada Lovelace Byron; Jerry Rubin; Henry Kissinger; Stonewall Jackson

♃, ♄   John Lennon; Charles Gordon; Ed. R. Murrow; Bob Fosse; A. Modigliani

♅   Lewis & Clark Exped.; Sir Wm. Crookes; Rosanno Brazzi; Carl Sagan

♆   Bob Dylan; Komar; Mark Spitz; Edouard Manet; Henry Kissinger

♇   Vida Blue; Ferdinand Foch; Bob Newhart; Franklin D. Roosevelt Wins First Election; Edmund Halley; Steven Spielberg

☊   Carroll Righter; Evel Knevel; Albert Schweitzer; Bob Hope; Paul Joseph Goebbels; Jim Thorpe; Charles Kettering

A   Rudolph Bing; Cheiro; Rosanno Brazzi; Jean P. Satre; Apollo 11 Moon Landing; Alexis Carrel; Harry Shoaf

M   John Glenn; Chernobyl; Ivar Kreuger; Willie Brandt; Helen Reddy

JUPITER/URANUS ♃/♅

Basic Ideas:

These themes denote discontent with legal, religious, and philosophical matters. They represent added internal unhappiness when encountering indifference toward new ideas, or when there is an extension of feelings of detachment about matters of life which were once important. Assertions about the progress of past activities may cause you to seek new prospects or opportunities which will take you through realms that are unique, different, and surprising. The philosophy of life you build about using scientific or labor saving devices; additional studies you undertake in science, computing, or astrology; your opinions on improving the efficiency of existing political, social, or legal methods; or inclinations to learn the principles of astrology all begin with these motifs. They allow added opportunities to alter your discontent with situations in original or revolutionary ways for you.

In Your Personal Life:

Thesis   Shows ways to understand life and living; opens you to new opportunities in science, engineering, or astrology; gaining publicity from experiments which use extraordinary ideas; unpredictable aspirations.

Anti   Focusing upon change for change itself, or because you feel others need to be shaken from complacency; an exaggerated ability to make or produce objects; added rudeness toward others; increased restlessness.

In Your Relationships:

Thesis   Socializing in unusual ways, or with partners who open you to ideas beyond those normally encountered; the potential of you and your partner to express uniqueness in your relationship.

Anti   Promises about adapting to partner and how this potential is developed; change as an excuse for not focusing on growth opportunities in a relationship; preferences for new freedoms.

With Body or Mind:

Abnormalities in the body caused by excess of fat in the blood; upsets to your glucose metabolism; deafness from not wanting to hear others' opinions .

In Politics or Business:

Thesis   The application of legal methods against breakdowns in order, revolutions, or strikes; growth following periods of reform; opportunities for modernization which accompany new labor-saving inventions.

Anti   Reform which originates in religious principles; government where no expansion due to modern principles is allowed; civil war or unrest due to a legal or religious system which stifles justice for common people.

JUPITER/URANUS with Planets and Points

☉ The decisiveness you bring to changing from the ordinary or common-place to the modern and new; changes in outlook or perspective which help you understand the role of incorporating new ideas in life.

☽ Sensitivity for the need to transform your life through a change of religion, moral principles, philosophy, etc.; your inconsistency in dealing with the forces of change and revolution which occur daily.

☿ Recognizing the improvements that change can bring, and your dexterity with creating mechanical objects to effect this change; thinking on the need for change in your life, and how you can effect this.

♀ An attraction to novel forms of art or beauty which introduce the latest fads to your life; your charm when forcing the new upon others; the satisfaction you get from creating the new to improve life overall.

♂ Feverish haste to produce new or different forms of things; difficulties you surmount in producing new objects; the impatience you have with the parts of daily life which do not offer you sufficient or varied forms of excitement.

♄ Enhanced ability to work slowly and patiently toward your goals; increased resistance to change; the disappointments you encounter during your efforts to bring new life to old methods or habits.

♆ Delusion about improving life through constant modernization; avoiding reality in the pursuit of your dreams; the visualization of new ideas or products which you feel will make the world a better place.

♀ Extreme efforts to produce novel or original changes in life; devices with potential to transform the world; extreme reworking of your designs or ideas to ensure they will work properly and be received correctly.

☊ Making connections to people who can provide you with the support you need; groups of people who recognize the importance of your ideas; barriers to progress from schooled but unqualified people; old ideas reworked.

A Added mental persistence or focus to your ideas for the new; eccentric mannerisms or dress in a flashy way; a personal sense of style that includes a focus on changes in life; seeking others to support your ideas for change.

M Receiving recognition for the improvements you created because you were dissatisfied with parts of life; the personal rewards you gain from seeing the effects of changes you have initiated or promoted in life.

JUPITER/URANUS CONCEPTS

An Ideal Revolution
Exaggerates Disruption
Accepts Variations
Aspires to Computers
A Lot of Peculiarity
Happy with Friends
Various Misjudgments
Allows Disarray
Sufficient Indifference
Aspires to Different Versions
Promises Regulation
Increases Deviation

Excessive Leniency
Forgives Infractions
Additional Restlessness
Sincere Uniqueness
Unexpected Explanations
Brings Sufficient Insight
Prefers Rebelliousness
Presupposes Antagonism
Wisely Indifferent
Extensive Revisions
Accepts Contrariness
Happy with Discontent

Easy Obstinacy
Amplifies Novelty
A Lot of Insight
A Wise Malcontent
Magnifies Rudeness
An Erroneous Revision
Generous Friends
Encourages Surprises
Adds to Uniqueness
Unusual Sincerity
Various Preferences
A Lot of Misfits

Unpretentious Agitator
Understands Discontent
Alludes to Experiments
A Surprise Recommendation
A Peculiar Suggestion
Influences Indifference
A Flagrant Transgression
Unique Opportunities
Novel Forms of Persuasion
Peculiar Ideas on Philosophy
Indifferent to Persuasion
Opposes Idealism
A Larger Computer
Additional Indifference
Totally New Mistakes
Accepts Deviation
Peculiar Opinions
Increases Discontent
Inspires an Agitator
Further Regulation
Sufficient Impertinence
Freedom from Endorsements
Aspires to be Disruptive
Advice on Individualism
Notorious Insolence
Boasts about a Discovery
Augments Restyling
Additional Insight
Supports a Call for Change
A Sincere Defector
Additional Surprises

Misjudges Innovation
Opinions on Cleverness
Extensive Indifference
Assists with an Innovation
Insight from Studying
Impartial to Theory
Peculiar Forms of Generosity
Improves through Manipulations
Surplus Revisions
A Lot of Regulation
Likes Many Surprises
Antagonistic toward Mistakes
Many Astrologers
A Successful Rebellion
Too Many Revisions
Errs in Accepting Deviations
Fortunate Breakthroughs
Novelties which bring Laughter
Enhances Variations
Rebels against Understanding
Increases Contrariness
Widens Self-Reliance
Happy-go-Lucky Surprises
Much Innovation
Laughs over Unpredictability
Furthers Waywardness
Jovial Rebelliousness
Genuine Peculiarities
Many Disruptions
Unique Aspirations in Life
Believes in Indifference

JUPITER/URANUS With Itself

♃ A restlessness about the status of ideas and concepts and a need to change these for more modern doctrines; increased ability or need to boast or give opinions where you have little skill or expertise; many forms of peculiarity.

♅ Realizing that your present status of life must change, and that you may be the only person pushing for such change; stepping aside from the ordinary mold of life; freedom from religious promises.

Significant Examples of People and Events Using Jupiter/Uranus

General: **STRONG:** Ralph Nader; R. D. Laing; Stephen Crane; Charles Gordon; Sigmund Freud; Henry Mancini; Stephen Sondheim; Bob Fosse; Richard Chamberlain; Henri Toulouse-Lautrec; Alexander Graham Bell
WEAK: Kareem Abdul-Jabbar; Jean Cocteau; Winston Churchill; John Lennon; Nikola Tesla; Claude Debussy; Richard Byrd; Lawrence Welk
EVENTS: James Meredith Enrolled; Lindburgh Lands in Paris; Bolsheviks Seize Power; Apollo 11 Moon Landing; (George Washington's Inauguration).

☉ Arthur Ford; Bob Hope; Bob Newhart; Rosanno Brazzi; Olga Worrall
☽ Albert Speer; Sam Peckinpah; Edgar Degas; Mark Spitz; Anne Murray
☿ Jacques Cousteau; Pearl Harbor; East Coast Blackout; Sam Sheppard
♀ Sam Peckinpah; Edna Ferber; Yehudi Menuhin; Glen Campbell; Neil Diamond; Ralph Waldo Emerson; Robin Williams
♂ Paul Cezanne; Car. Righter; Wm. Butler Yeats; Emp. Hirohito; E. Rommel
♃, ♅ Apollo 11 Moon Landing; J. Von Ribbentrop; Ritchie Valens; H. Mancini
♄ Audrey Hepburn; Bolsheviks Seize Power; Paul Newman; John Dillinger; Bob Fosse; Challenger Explosion
♆ Stonewall Jackson; John Glenn; Ira Progoff; Ed. Manet; Stephen Crane
♀̤ Richard Chamberlain; Shirley Jones; J. Von Ribbentrop; Arthur Godfrey
☊ Paul Newman; Jimi Hendrix; Henri Toulouse-Lautrec; Enrico Fermi; Mick Jagger; Tom Jones; Ralph Nader; USS Maine Explosion
A Marc Edmund Jones; Woman's Suffrage Amendment Passed; Shirley Jones; Henry Kissinger; John Paul Satre
M Alaskan Earthquake Occurs; Stephen Crane; Transcontinental Railroad Completed; Ralph Nader; Charles Kettering

JUPITER/NEPTUNE ♃/♆

Basic Ideas:

Expansiveness and wholesome joviality combine with confusion and neglect to expand upon or elaborate daydreams or visions, a better comprehension of the mystical or unknowable side of life, and a belief that goals and obligations can be explained away as you tire of meeting them. These themes denote success in understanding miracles or events which have no explanation in physical reality, an aspiration for a study and understanding of the occult, and complications in affairs you had hoped to publicize. They mirror thoughts on what an ideal combination of circumstances and situations may bring, visions of how to effect totally different directions to life, generosity with the attention disadvantaged people receive, and studies concerning drugs, alcohol, or rehabilitation. These motifs are also concerned with how dreams influence society, or with worn-out or inefficient forms of publicity.

In Your Personal Life:

Thesis   Sympathy for people at a disadvantage; honest preferences for understanding people from an intuitive view; a strong association with depictions of life which emphasize unreality.

Anti   An urge to make excuses for failures or the noncompletion of obligations due to occult happenings; excessive idealism when reality is needed; errors in hiding that which requires comprehensive analysis.

In Your Relationships:

Thesis   Feelings of mystical oneness in a relationship; good feelings at an intuitive level between partners; overlooking faults within others; the role of forgiveness within relationships; overlooking partner's faults.

Anti   Spending too much time making vague excuses for actions which anger partner or you; a lot of confusion about the current state of affairs in the relationship; a failure to understand partner's visions or values.

With Body or Mind:

Fatty deposits in body caused by stress or weakness; not enough exercise or body care; abnormal levels of glucose; problems with B vitamin absorptions.

In Politics or Business:

Thesis   Expansion and elaboration of ideals or dreams; policies of expansion and growth; ideals mirrored in a religious context; churches espousing a moral philosophy for all; foolish or unfounded legal situations.

Anti   Scandals about growth, values, or belief systems; hypocrisy growing as a form of internal policy; a legal system where ethics and morals are based upon favors and payoffs; degradation in systems of justice.

JUPITER/NEPTUNE with Planets and Points

☉   Emphasized use of daydreams and visions to enhance personal capability; purpose and confidence in areas where confusion or deception exists; the prestige you lend to efforts which can help others.

☽   Instincts which lead you to seek a mystical explanation for all that occurs; fundamental assumptions about how the supernatural pervades all of life; uncertainty about what is real and what is unreal in life.

☿   Analysis and discussion about the effect of the supernatural in reality; skills with deceptive practices; misleading or misdirecting the attention of others; self-study in areas of magic or mysticism; speaking for the deprived.

♀   Pleasant feelings obtained by escape from reality; delight thru using substances or methods to allow an escape from mental or physical pain; satisfaction from attempts to understand the mystical side of life.

♂   Defiant or hostile reactions to explanations about delays, confusion, or laxity in meeting obligations; warnings against acceptance of theories about mystical events; courage to defend your explanations of reality.

♄   Looking at both the mystical and real side of life; combining the real with the unreal in activities; disappointment with mystical explanations of reality; curtailed occult practices of little or no scientific basis.

♅   Disruptions by events which have no real explanation; basing decisions on odd or unusual theories about the effects of the supernatural; impersonal treatment for those who have drug dependencies; unaccustomed confusion.

♀   Condemnation or suppression of theories about the mystical or occult; the development or use of weapons based upon esoteric principles; application of ideas gained from dreams or visions to control waste or pollution.

☊   Affiliations among people who share a mystical rapport; meetings where the subject matter turns to aspects of nonphysical reality; encounters which cause people to give up on a mystical or magic approach to explanations.

A   Situations or people with explanations for life which go beyond physical reality; interpersonal roles which add to a sense of the unreal; a shoddiness to the way you dress or to your appearance.

M   The personal gains you muster in life from an understanding of a nonphysical reality; experience you gain with magic or mysticism; the role of politics as a means of gaining in stature or standing in your life.

JUPITER/NEPTUNE CONCEPTS

Propitious Musings
Glaring Craziness
A Well-Timed Illusion
Hidden Assumptions
Assists with Confusion
Exaggerated Holiness
Favors Trickiness
Flagrant Flimsiness
Additional Inspiration
Amplifies an Illusion
Mistaken Pretenses
Magnifies Imperfections

Emphasizes Carelessness
Inspires Confusion
Increases Perplexities
Sincere Inspiration
A Notorious Capitulation
Judicious Impasses
Happy Compliance
Cheerful Compassion
Happy with Subordination
Discreet Opinions
A Preference for Subtlety
Delicate Assistance

Deceptive Influences
Astute Deceit
Prudent Doubts
An Improved Illusion
Inspired Wisdom
Further Inaccuracies
Abets Pretenses
A Wise Withdrawal
Satisfying Mysteries
Benefits Daydreams
Wise Diversions
Joyous Skepticism

Plenty of Confusion
Magnifies Nebulousness
Finesses Optimistically
Complicated Theories
Mistaken Guilt
Increases Complications
Ideal Compliance
Extensive Avoidance
Allows Shoddiness
Further Fantasies
Elaborates on Guilt
Influences Fraudulent Activity
Ineffective Persuasion
Encourages Inspiration
Prefers Complications
Convincing Dreams
A Lot of Indecisiveness
Additional Musings
A Wise Psychic
Convincing Mystical Thoughts
Inordinate Disregard
Theories with Shortcomings
Foolish Surmisings
Improves a Religious Miracle
Deceived by Dogma
Impractical Promises
A Successful Release of Ideas
Beneficial Inspiration
Accepts Pretenses
Utopian Illusions
Widens Reparation

Accepts Condensations
Plenty of Evasion
Errors in Submissions
Delusions of Success
Excessive Compliance
Prompts a Disguise
Deceptions Performed Happily
Acceptance of Psychism
Condones Worthless Work
Excessive Neglect
A Neglect of Ethics
Errors and Confusion
Honest Carelessness
A Belief in Occult Practices
Favorable Blunders
Subtle Authorization
Senseless Doctrine
Confused Presumptions
Increases Daydreaming
Genuine Neglect
Positive Diplomacy
Additional Subtlety
A Successful Deception
Furthers Needs for Salvation
Propagates Make-Believe
Lots of Dreams
Cheerful Disguises
Excessive Mysticism
A Lack of Comprehension
Permits an Oversight
Sufficient Confusion

JUPITER/NEPTUNE With Itself

♃ Studies to understand religious or mystical beliefs or events; a need to study and expound on theories of the occult or unknown; added need to remain positive about life; prefers feigned or staged performances.

♆ Seeing events with a religious or holiness perspective; promoting inner ideas with theories which are strange or unclear; efforts to show others that there is a spiritual side to life, and a life beyond physical or earthly reality.

Significant Examples of People and Events Using Jupiter/Neptune

General: **STRONG:** Edmund Halley; Albert Einstein; Sir Laurence Olivier; Benjamin Disraeli; Tom Jones; Rudolph Bing; Mario Andretti; Erwin Rommel; Marc Edmund Jones; David Frost; Burl Ives; Scott Carpenter; Alan Alda; Calude Debussy
WEAK: Sally Ride; Tom Smothers; Carl Sandburg; William Butler Yeats; Joseph Joffre; R. D. Laing; Enrico Fermi; Bjorn Borg
EVENTS: East Coast Power Blackout; RMS Titanic Hits Iceberg; First Medicare Patient; Alaskan Earthquake; (USS Maine Explosion).

☉ Sam Peckinpah; Liberace; John F. Kennedy; Norman Mailer; Francisco Franco; Thomas Huxley; Earl Warren; Ernest Hemingway

☽ Ramstein Airshow Crash; Jeddu Krishnamurti; Rudolph Bing; Richard Alpert; Peter Max; Edgar Degas; Bob Fosse

☿ F. Scott Fitzgerald; Albert Einstein; Rosanno Brazzi; Johann Von Goethe; Gregory Peck; Marc Edmund Jones

♀ RMS Titanic Hits Iceberg; Albert Camus; Johann Von Goethe; Tom Jones; Albert Schweitzer; Lindbergh Lands in Paris

♂ Gen. Charles Gordon; Transcon. RR Done; Van Cliburn; Gregory Peck

♃, ♆ Sir Laurence Olivier; Sydney Omarr; Erwin Rommel; Jim Thorpe; Georges Seurat; Rosanno Brazzi; Benjamin Disraeli

♄ Gen. Ferdinand Foch; East Coast Blackout; Kareem Abdul-Jabbar; Al Unser; Paramhansa Yogananda; Steve Rosenbloom

♅ Alan Alda; First Medicare Patient; Titanic Hits Iceberg; Ritchie Valens

♀ First Medicare Patient Accepted; Mark Spitz; Erwin Rommel; Jean Francoise Millet; Lawrence Welk; Jacques Cousteau

☊ Winston Churchill; Merv Griffin; Jimi Hendrix; A. Einstein; Vida Blue

A John Lennon; Dick Gregory; Stephen Crane; Carl Sagan; Lord Byron

M Olga Worrall; Charles Addams; Pearl Harbor Attack; Dr. Tom Dooley

JUPITER/PLUTO ♃/♇

Basic Ideas:

These themes symbolize developing understanding about and involvement with extremes (of anything), such as the correction of unbearable conditions, the cleansing of impurities, or the use of force. Your beliefs in using sex as a form of service, or using people in ways that degrade their self-image or force them to be viewed as objects instead of humans, may also begin here. With this combination you reach for great public renown, and use your official powers and connections to attain added personal prestige and recognition. You may have a reputation for generous help of disadvantaged persons (especially those willing to help themselves), or in working with groups to rehabilitate drug users, care for the terminally ill, feed the hungry, etc. You may find success by surmounting bad habits acquired in the past, such as obsessions or fetishes which control parts of your life.

In Your Personal Life:

Thesis   You have a need for power and control over others, but are able to keep this obsession within socially acceptable bounds; you use your position to make your opinions known, and to help disadvantaged persons.

Anti   You find it easy to use and discard people; your need for power grows to become an obsession; you are quick to destroy anything that lies in your way; you enjoy corrupting the morals and ethics of others.

In Your Relationships:

Thesis   Outdoor activities, travel, and adventure play a big part in the way you relate to others; you like a partner who shares mutual interests; you have needs to be noticed with others by society and the influential.

Anti   You find it easy to use and discard potential partners; you may be ruthlessness in social priorities; you do not hesitate to use force, or threats to keep your partner under personal control.

With Body or Mind:

Possible cancer indicator; tends to accumulate fat and poisons in the body; inefficiencies in elimination; breakdown of cells from bad eating habits.

In Politics or Business:

Thesis   Relations or pacts with foreigners on the use of force or weapons; the growth of security or spy agencies; greater powers for religious leaders; a society which wields much influence; extreme depletion of resources.

Anti   Self-destructive forces which stem from official corruption or moral laxity within society; extremely potent natural disasters; criminal elements with great social influence; destruction of legal documents.

JUPITER/PLUTO with Planets and Points

☉ Accumulation of personal power and influence; a fundamental need to grow in power and prestige in society and be noticed; a focus on the gathering of acclaim; efforts to be less compulsive personally.

☽ Your quest to reach the top of your society may take many turns; an inconsistency in pursuing power goals; a powerful female influence; added insecurity about self or family; changes in family influences.

☿ Articulating and expounding upon your needs, goals, or opinions; an obsessive need for studying how to isolate yourself physically from others; you often feel you are above the law; thoughts on eliminating offensive ideas.

♀ Added social charm; willingness to give attention to other people you want to impress with your manners and sophistication; pleasure from music and the arts; enjoyment of artistic notoriety at some level.

♂ Fighting others for your rights; a controlling or ruthless purpose in life; using others to fight your physical battles or to protect you; asserting yourself; feeling diminished or insecure before others.

♄ Shortened need to expound upon all subjects; a conservative flavor to a liberal person; hindrances in quests for both fame and privacy; delayed plans for advancement; lessens the focus on destruction.

♅ Sudden and unexpected interference to plans for advancement; the exceptional and unusual situation may occur to you; you rebel against society and seek to start your own clique of influential friends.

♆ Using drugs to enhance escapes from reality or pressure; being drawn to mystical religions and abstract ideas to explain what life is about; unclear goals in life; confused thoughts, goals, or plans.

☊ Increased needs to be the center of attention within your circle of friends or audience; you easily break ties with others after you have used them and their services; cooperation becomes an important issue.

A Focusing your personal opinions about how to use and discard others; added self-importance and focus on concerns and ego definition; ability to read other people and their intentions, especially if they also seek power.

M A powerful influence in early life who pushed you to excel in all areas; developing a code of ethics and rising beyond petty ideas and inclinations; recognition and respect from others for great accomplishments in society.

JUPITER/PLUTO CONCEPTS

The End of Influence
Destructive Erasures
Extensive Punishment
Endures Penalties
Dilutes Influence
Copious Pollution
Exaggerates Force
Slants Evolution
Obsessed with Errors
Potential for Destruction
An Extensive Bankruptcy
Wastes Potential

Supports Reconstitution
Accepts Corruption
Favors Fanaticism
Successful Punishment
Potential Corruption
Excessive Killing
Eliminates Influence
Suspicious of Potential
Magnifies Intensity
Publicizes Denunciation
A Notorious Prosecution
Too Much Scandal

Exaggerates Damage
Permits Obsession
Too Much Waste
Genuine Shortages
Lots of Control
Honest Infatuation
Possible Punishment
Favorable Rebirth
Gives Pursuit
Studies Tyranny
Misplaced Suspicion
Supports Violence

Presupposes Squandering
Numerous Constraints
Large Amounts of Disapproval
Conceals Liberalism
Potential Termination
Extensive Devastation
A Potential for Concealment
Purifies Opinions
Propagates Curses
An Expanded Funeral
Hidden Publications
Increases Compulsion
A Generous Termination
Glaring Infection
Inaccurate Defamation
Increases Suspicion
Accepts Dismissal
Extensive Cleansing
Understands Termination
Intensely Generous
Publicizes Condemnation
Excessive Reversals
Extracts an Improvement
Erroneous Punishment
Numerous Poisons
Increased Purification
Influences Reconditioning
A Potential for Retaliation
Understands Corruption
Promises which Undermine
A Convincing Overhaul

Promotes Passions
Compelled to Excess
Sincere Denunciation
Opinions on Reform
Studies Concealment
Furthers Rediscovery
Counsel on Ownership
Promotes Purification
Learns about Purification
Misjudges Ruthlessness
Excessive Suspicion
Sufficient Controls
Publicizes Suspicions
A Happy Ending
Inordinate Recrimination
Helps with Restitution
Understands Phobias
Inspires Manias
Understands the Use of Force
Furthers Stealth
Permits Intensity
Excessive Constraints
Support for Suspicions
Induces a Transition
Corruption of the Honest
Publicizes Destruction
Laughs over Ejection
Increases Scarcity
Sincere Cleansing
Emphasizes Cessation
A Lot of Publicity

JUPITER/PLUTO With Itself

♃   Awareness of underlying conditions which need correcting or adjustment; freedom to reverse practices which are oppressive or trying; chances to correct extreme biases or beliefs; an overloaded system.

♀   Seeking a legal redress for wrongs imposed; an understanding of the power of the forces of destruction and how to use or subjugate with these; increasing needs to control and eliminate forces of great destructive powers.

Significant Examples of People and Events Using Jupiter/Pluto

General: **STRONG:** Henry Mancini; Johnny Carson; Jackie Robinson; Vittorio DeSica; Jack Schwartz; Ervin Nyiregyhazi; Joseph Joffre; Richard Strauss; Jonathan Winters; Erwin Rommel; Robert DeNiro; Emperor Hirohito
WEAK: Teilhard de Chardin; Nikola Tesla; Lord Byron; Benito Mussolini; Dr. Francis Regardie; Jeddu Krishnamurti; Al Unser; Steve Allen
EVENTS: First A-Bomb Explodes; Ramstein Airshow Disaster; George Washington's Inauguration.; USS Maine Explosion; (Apollo 11 Moon Landing).

☉ Elton John; Ralph Nader; Winston Churchill; Peter Max; Neil Diamond

☽ Stephen Crane; Amadeo Modigliani; Glen Campbell; Neil Diamond

☿ Herman Melville; Willliam Butler Yeats; H. G. Wells; Billy Rose; Harry Belafonte; East Coast Power Blackout; Rosanno Brazzi

♀ Arturo Toscanini; Stephen Sondheim; Bobby Fischer; Arthur Ford

♂ Gen. Joseph Joffre; Al Unser; Kar. Abdul-Jabbar; Stephen Foster; A. Alda

♃, ♀ Charles Kettering; Erwin Rommel; Ralph Nader; Mark Spitz; Mick Jagger; Jean Houston; Bjorn Borg; Burl Ives

♄ Stonewall Jackson; USS Maine Explodes; Erwin Rommel; Percy Bysshe Shelley; Marlon Brando; Jack Paar; Melvin Belli

♅ Melvin Belli; Richard Alpert; F. Scott Fitzgerald; Willie Mays; FDR Wins

♆ John Glenn; Hugh Downs; Billy Rose; Earl Warren; Ramstein Airshow Disaster; Erwin Rommel; RMS Titanic Hits Iceberg

☊ Pierre Renoir; Robert McNamara; Rupert Murdoch; A. Schwarzenegger

A Anne Murray; Bolshevik's Take Power; First A-Bomb Explodes; Alexander Graham Bell

M William Butler Yeats; Fidel Castro; Lance Reventlow; Elton John; Arthur Rimbaud; Gustav Dore

JUPITER/NODE   ♃/☊

Basic Ideas:

Luck in meeting the right people, an ability to expand or increase ties to friends, and a talent for using the resources acquaintances innately have is shown through these themes. With these motifs you formulate and present ideas well when meeting or conversing with others, make effective or promising contacts through groups and associations, and show a sense of humor and laughter at appropriate times during gatherings. Boasting about friendships which may not exist, assuming closer ties to others than were intended, and exaggeration over who has more influential contacts, are represented within these themes. You find times when errors in judgment prevail, or when you bring the wrong kind of people into your confidence, but your good fortune with contacts persists, and your ability to use personnel resources wisely continues and is enhanced.

In Your Personal Life:

Thesis   Ability to forge ties to the right kinds of people; insight into who brings the right kind of assistance; the opportunities which close friends offer; expanding social contacts thru friends.

Anti   You are prone to judge some people incorrectly; when you make errors in judgment you persist with these, even when they are obvious to all; boasting about friendships or connections which do not really exist.

In Your Relationships:

Thesis   A most fortunate contact between you and another person; denotes a relationship which is beneficial for both persons; added happiness, laughter and joy with good feelings; expanded sexual enjoyment.

Anti   Too many contacts with partner; confusion over too many partners; eased times of separation and parting; two people who are loose and free with each other in relationships.

With Body or Mind:

Expansion in the joints or connecting tissue; swelling of the joints; stretching of ligaments or tissue; fats accumulate in joints or connections of the body.

In Politics or Business:

Thesis   Matters concerning the legal consequences of treaties with allies; religious leaders who have an opinion on legal matters expressed through friends; a focus on imports which are disrupting the trade or business.

Anti   An excessive amount of interference from religious groups through a legal process; the system of legal justice bound and hampered by erroneous decisions about the status of groups or parties; closed legal societies.

JUPITER/NODE with Planets and Points

☉   Ease in contacting important people; access to people who wield influence and power; joining or benefiting from powerful and distinguished societies, clubs, or associations; efforts to keep ties with cronies.

☽   Important women who help you; increased uncertainty to feelings about contacts with or seeking help from others; an increased ability to read the intentions or motives of others; respect from the common people in life.

☿   Expressing your opinions more clearly to influence others; increased desires to do research in the legal, political or religious fields; further pursuit of educational oportunities; discussions of opportunities.

♀   Added charm and grace with manners or movements; others see you as a gentle and refined person in social capacities; contacts among those who have authority in the artistic, financial, or musical fields.

♂   Added intensity to an already forceful personality; energy and enthusiasm for the efforts given toward meeting or working with others; an urgency for keeping contacts and communications open; completing plans at meetings.

♄   Emphasis on the business aspects of life; contacts with helpful friends or groups; some disappointments through contacts or associates; delays in receiving help from friends or associates; a lessening of control over others.

♅   Being impersonal with contacts; places the contributions of others to your goals in better perspective; fortunate contacts with astrological groups; peculiar views cause you to pursue erroneous goals.

♆   Others see you as more mysterious and mystical than intended; being deceived by the promises or intentions of friends; errors of judgment about the desires or needs of associates; need for religious contacts.

♇   There is a chance that you could make contacts who have shady or criminal intentions, and will hold you responsible for whatever help they give you; you could use your contacts to gain enormous benefits.

A   Focusing on the reality of what other people offer you, or can do for you; insight into another's psychological needs or purposes; increased ability to find and locate people; responses to those who have separated from you.

M   Adds to your reputation and renown because of an ability to make the right contacts and be a member of the proper groups; increased rank or recognition within groups; others see your views as seasoned and mature.

JUPITER/NODE CONCEPTS

Successful Sexual Ties
Perfects Persuasion
Comprehends Life's Aim
Boasts about Opportunities
Biases Presentations
Open Alliances
Potential with the Familiar
Fortunate Relationships
Sincere Attachments
Affirmative Friendships
Assists Ties to Others
Easy to Attract People

Supplements Removals
Sincere Separations
Happy Ties to Others
Misjudges Life's Aim
Assumes Sexual Ties
Abundant Ridding
Excessive Bureaucracy
Positive New Habits
Benefits Acquaintances
Wise Acquaintances
Aspires to Mergers
Expands on Life's Aim

Happy Karma
Allows Barriers
Proposes Alliances
Accepts Associates
Familiar Boasts
Favors Kinship
Joy at Separations
Accepts Alliances
Prefers Treaties
Laughs over Delays
Successful Passages
Increases Alliances

Idealistic Joint Ventures
Errors at Meetings with Others
Increases Separations
Persuasive about Life's Aim
Aspires to Meetings with Others
Understands Sense of Destiny
Too Many Ties to Others
Ideal Partnerships
Assumes Relationships
Assumptions during Meetings
Widens Life's Aim
Sincere Meetings with Others
Amplifies on Course of Destiny
Persuasive at Meetings
Ambitious Appointments
Aspires to Joint Ventures
Idealistic Attraction
Laughter during Meetings
Understands Bureaucratic Channels
Advocates Publicity
Bolsters Ties to Others
Additional Interviews
Errors during Presentations
Improves Opportunities
Accepts Group Connections
Too Much Consolidation
Attracts the Wrong People
Increases the Bonds to Others
Aspires to Attracting Others
Direct Connections with Groups
A Fortunate Childhood

Furthers Sexual Ties
Mistaken Separations
Wise Partners
Aspires to Cooperation
Exaggerated Familiarity
Fortunate Performances
Persuasive on Alliances
Mistakes by the Bureaucracy
Jovial Sense of Destiny
Propitious Destiny
Suggests Separations
Adds to that which Connects
Advice on Presentations
Misjudges Criticism
Numerous Ties to Others
Added Opportunities
Successful Cooperation
Luck with Dismissals
Accepts Appointments
Increases Acquaintances
Loosens Sexual Ties
Locates the Wrong People
Fortunate Alliances
An Honest Attraction
Assists Bureaucratic Delays
Innumerable Splits
The Philosophy of Karma
Boasts of Familiarity
Additional Criticism
Misjudges Relationships
Mistaken Supporters

JUPITER/NODE With Itself

♃   Interest in the social aspects of how people are motivated and function together; a need to expand your circle of friends, and to reach those who can help you; approval from friends or those you trust or endorse.

☊   Increased need to have others as friends with whom you can share ideas and ideals; a need to contact or maintain friendships with important people; added need to understand group or personal karma and its effects.

Significant Examples of People and Events Using Jupiter/Node

General: **STRONG:** Dr. Francis Regardie; Bjorn Borg; Franklin Roosevelt; Paul Joseph Goebbels; Lawrence Welk; Arthur Ford; Mick Jagger; Bertrand Russell; Manly Palmer Hall; Charles Kettering; Jackie Robinson; R. D. Laing; Paul Cezanne
WEAK: Robert Redford; Ervin Nyiregyhazi; Lance Reventlow; Mario Andretti; William B. Yeats; Steve Wozniak; William K. Douglas; Jerry Reed
EVENTS: Kent State Shootings; Mt. St. Helens Explosion; South Carolina Secession Passed; Wright Brothers First Flight; (Bolsheviks Seize Power).

☉   Wright Bros. Flight; Jean Houston; Mt. St. Helens; G. Washington's Inaug.

☽   John F. Kennedy; Nikola Tesla; P. Yogananda; Jack Paar; Watergate Burgl.

☿   Hank Williams; Mick Jagger; Fran. D. Roosevelt; E. R. Murrow; Alan Alda

♀   Alan Alda; R. D. Laing; Olga Worrall; Ritchie Valens; John F. Kennedy

♂   Sir Laurence Olivier; Franklin Roosevelt; Dave Garroway; Henry Mancini; Benito Mussolini; Liberace; Rupert Murdoch

♃, ☊ Audrey Hepburn; Bob Dylan; Paul Joseph Goebbels; Vincent Van Gogh; Tom Jones; Rudolph Bing; Alexander Graham Bell

♄   Friedrich Nietzsche; Arthur Ford; Paul Jospeh Goebbels; Ralph Nader; Mick Jagger; Albert Einstein; Paul Cezanne; Jerry Reed

♅   Arthur Ford; Lawrence Welk; USS Maine Explosion; Manly P. Hall; Vittorio DeSica; Anne Murray; Arnold Schwarzeneggger

♆   Albert Speer; Bob Hope; Al Unser; Jn. McEnroe; Edgar Degas; Steve Allen

♇   Claude Debussy; Rudolph Bing; Bobby Fischer; Harry Shoaf; Bob Fosse

A   O. J. Simpson; Giacomo Puccini; R. Brazzi; Mary Martin; Lewis & Clark Ex.

M   Edouard Manet; Richard Strauss; Louis Pasteur; Henry Kissinger; Gen. Joseph Joffre; John Lennon; Cheiro

JUPITER/ASCENDANT ♃/A

Basic Ideas:

These themes denote an inspiring mannerism, or a cheerful front filled with sincerity which is loved by those you meet. Through these motifs you may develop your ability to inspire others, make too many assumptions about another's needs or wants, or devise a lot of arrogant convictions. You may become a sincere and genuine person able to read and manipulate the motivations of others, an optimist who is always ready with a kind word or a generous and hearty greeting, or a pleasing and cordial person. You may develop a knack for meeting others easily and leaving them with warm and sincere feelings about your intentions. You may develop added insight about the motives of others, and learn to read the inner objectives or intentions of the people you meet. You learn to grow beyond immediate limitations through inspiring positive responses in others.

In Your Personal Life:

Thesis   An affable, well-meaning person who has a sharp eye for the political needs of others; an opportunist who is able to capitalize on the needs and desires of others and turn them to advantage.

Anti   You boast too much and easily fool yourself about correctly reading the needs of others; ignoring things or people which you find unpleasant; accepting the words of others too easily; overly optimistic attitudes.

In Your Relationships:

Thesis   Your happy mannerism attracts similarly sincere and contented people; you have a way of exuding joy to those you are with, and they respond in kind; generosity with your partners and friends; a happy couple.

Anti   Your boasting repels those who have affection for you when it becomes excessive; you fool yourself easily about the intentions of others who appear to be well-meaning; you are not able to read clever people well.

With Body or Mind:

Acid accumulations from an excessive social life; the tendency to add too much body fat; attraction to alcohol and similar drugs; large hips or buttocks.

In Politics or Business:

Thesis   Others who notice your intentions; a strong but sluggish legal or justice system; legal maneuverings or changes in laws; emphasizes relations with foreign or religious interests; an expanding government.

Anti   Highlights legal affairs or interests of foreign countries or businesses; a mixture of religion and politics; prompts a morality or ethics which helps form the basis for common law or judicial decisions.

JUPITER/ASCENDANT with Planets and Points

☉   A strong personality with much affability and charm; interest in the welfare of others; added charm and superficiality; a sincerity to the way you greet and understand others; an effective politician or leader.

☽   Showing sensitivity or emotion before others; enhanced acting abilities; added receptivity to the emotions of others; reading emotional reactions at subtle levels; kind women with political or social acumen.

☿   A gift for oratory, or the ability to make speeches which evoke strong emotional reactions; listening to what others are saying and reading the political or personal aspirations behind their words; a learned professor.

♀   A relaxing, calm mannerism which inspires others thru your ability to mix good humor and wise sayings; music or art which arouses the emotions and spirits; others like you for the true person you are.

♂   Being sharp and loud when you greet people; greeting others with hail and heartiness; much activity and motion when meeting or introducing others; strong desire to be around and with others.

♄   Reserve and caution in an otherwise affable personality; caution when meeting others at first, but then sincerely opens up; shows an interest in people but will hold back impressions until these have been evaluated.

♅   Bursts in on others and greets them loudly or in unusual ways; suddenly comes upon people who need help and a kind word; unique ways of making others feel comfortable when in your surroundings; many friends.

♆   Presenting a dreamy and unreal personal quality, and inducing people with your ideas of life; a superficial interest in the needs and wants of others; an astute politician but one with little practical sense.

♇   Not afraid to use political ambitions as a means to meet the powerful and rich; uses others for their own ends; becomes involved in large legal or judicial battles; decadence caused by corrupt or socialized political leanings.

☊   Ability to attract and meet the right people; a sense of destiny which includes attracting others who are right for you; presentations which are well received; sexual encounters with social or political hopefuls.

M   A more mature self which grows through the years as an ability to read the political needs and intentions of others is sharpened and used; increased political awareness; learning to read and react to the needs of other people.

JUPITER/ASCENDANT CONCEPTS

Successful Perceptions	Augments Recognition	A Wise Demeanor
A Fortunate Personal Style	Reacts to Aspirations	Prolific Pretenses
Prefers to be with Others	A Liberal Mental Focus	Erroneous Attitudes
Happy with Surroundings	A Lot of Attention	An Improved View
Persuasive with Reactions	Potential Reactions	Acceptable Reactions
Gives Adequate Attention	Notices Many Things	Lenient Attitudes
Wise Personal Demeanor	Honest Mannerisms	Helps Reactions
A Favorable Tone (Attitude)	Observes Preferences	Sincere Mannerisms
An Understanding Environ	Magnifies Conditions	Fortunate Settings
An Ideal Mental Focus	Increases Reactions	Widens Reality
Improved Observations	Much Experience	Furthers Portrayals
A Jovial Sense of Style	Lots of Personal Style	Wise Attitudes

Further Represses Ideas	Promising Personal Style
Auspicious Conditions	Sincere when Relating
Brings Happiness to Others	Benefits Observations
Appears as a Generous Person	Reacts as if All is Ideal
An Impression of Sincerity	A Location with Prestige
Conveys Ideal Concepts	Misjudges Reactions
Warm, Hearty Greetings	Treats Others Optimistically
Able to Spout Philosophy	Numerous Experiences
Works on Personal Style	Pompous in a Peculiar Way
Increases Impressions Received	Sees Reality in the Best Light
Has Ideas which are too Lofty	An Ability to Read People
An Encouraging Disposition	Notices what is Going on
Pompous Notions	Always Ready to Speak
Aspires to Relate to Others	Seeks Much Attention
An Ability to Portray Others	People Like to be with You
Easily Misjudges Intentions	Accepting of Surroundings
A Need to Interact with People	Many Portrays of Reality
Assumes Numerous Ideas	Improves Personal Style
Desires a Lot of Attention	Increases Mental Focus
Has a Lot of Wisdom	Jovial Reactions
Accepting and Positive	Accepting of Self
Sees the Best in Everything	A Lenient Disposition
Stresses Understanding Others	Increases Personal Responses
Adapts Self to Attitudes	Receives Happy Greetings
Seen as Magnanimous	A Philosophical View
Develops a Sincere Attitude	Genuine Personal Reactions
Fortunate Ways of Relating	Additional Mannerisms
Favorable Impressions	A Pompous Personal Style
Always Seeking Attention	Errs in Selecting Surroundings
Confident of Understanding	Has a Wise Mental Focus
A Persuasive Style	Wise in Judging People

JUPITER/ASCENDANT With Itself

♃ Increased need to be with others; giving people responses they want; expanded needs to study people and their political motivations; political promises; preaching the gospel of your latest convictions.

A Increased ability to remember names and faces of people; any inflation of your self-worth and ability; expands your gullibility about people and their intentions, how you feel you can use them, or vice versa.

Significant Examples of People and Events Using Jupiter/Ascendant

General: **STRONG:** Jacques Cousteau; Dustin Hoffman; Maurice Ravel; Benjamin Disraeli; Jim Thorpe; Ivar Kreugar; Steve Rosenbloom; Vittorio DeSica; Bob Newhart; Alexis Carrel; Fidel Castro; Georges Seurat; Stephen Crane
WEAK: Ernest Pyle; Tom Jones; John Fremont; John F. Kennedy; Richard Byrd; Winston Churchill; Auguste Rodin; Burl Ives
EVENTS: Lindburgh Lands in Paris; Chernobyl Nuclear Explosion; First Medicare Patient Accepted; Bolsheviks Seize Power; (Wright Brothers First Flight).

☉ RMS Titanic Hits Iceberg; Alex. Graham Bell; Stephen King; S. Peckinpah

☽ Evel Knievel; Transcon. RR Done; Hank Williams; Yehudi Menuhin

☿ First A-Bomb Explosion; Rudolph Bing; Thos. H. Huxley; Dane Rudhyar

♀ Charles E. O. Carter; Georges Seurat; Sam Peckinpah; Lord Byron; Gianni Agnelli; Mario Andretti; Gustav Dore

♂ Moshe Dayan; O. J. Simpson; Ada Lovelace Byron; F. Nietzsche; Jos. Joffre

♃, A Enrico Fermi; Jacques Cousteau; Bob Newhart; Neil Diamond; Steve Allen

♄ Stephen Foster; Georges Seurat; F. Scott Fitzgerald; Enrico Caruso; Paul Gauguin; Komar; Jimi Hendriz; Evel Knievel

♅ Audrey Hepburn; Mary Martin; Cheiro; Ritchie Valens; Richard Alpert

♆ Benjamin Disraeli; Ralph Nader; Jean Houston; Mount St. Helens Explosion; Abraham Lincoln; Manly Palmer Hall

♇ Kareem Abdul-Jabbar; John F. Kennedy Shot; Pierre Teilhard de Chardin; Charles Addams

☊ Lord Byron; Norman Mailer; H. G. Wells; Jean Paul Satre; Nikola Tesla

M Charles Steinmetz; Charles Gordon; Jacques Cousteau; John Paul I; Mary Martin; Georges Seurat

JUPITER/MIDHEAVEN   ♃/M

Basic Ideas:

These themes represent the importance of cultivating a social or political life, and the role that being a leader in society can have on your goals, hopes, ambitions, and self-image. These motifs show an inner personal wisdom through your family and early life experiences. Here begin the rules of personal conduct you adopt to enhance your reputation, the religious or philosophical theories you accept and practice to enrich your personal development, and the optimism you learn to show as part of your life's guiding principles. Expanding your overall knowledge and acquiring experience from life; developing an understanding of people and how to motivate them effectively; learning to be forgiving about mistakes, omissions, or intolerances; and developing a respect for conscience and its role in helping you become a more morally and ethically responsible person, begins here.

In Your Personal Life:

Thesis   The pursuit of ethics, philosophy, or morality as a fundamental goal of life; expansion of your early learning to include concepts that are far beyond previous experiences; success due in part to credentials earned.

Anti   You may become so theoretical that you cannot accept fundamental changes to the way you conduct your life; an inability to accept any philosophy or set of guiding principles in life, as you try many of them.

In Your Relationships:

Thesis   Increased ability to relate and grow through the various experiences your partners provide for you; aspirations to expand your social life, sports, travel, and philosophy with or through a partner in a significant way.

Anti   Finding that you are less than honest about what you contribute to your partner; failing to develop potential with another; neglect of social chances with your partner due to misunderstandings.

With Body or Mind:

Genetic patterns or abnormalities from gracious living, or from being unable to cope with social or peer pressures; a family history of drug dependencies.

In Politics or Business:

Thesis   Plans set forth by the executives for future guidance; recognition or reward given for past work or accomplishments; political maneuverings and posturings within society; situations with distant people.

Anti   A legal system which sets restraints on how the executive is able to fulfill its plans for the future; religious principles which set overall policy; questions about the morality or intentions of the leadership.

JUPITER/MIDHEAVEN with Planets and Points

☉   Added confidence built within self as you cope and adjust to different circumstances; building moral principles within self as you mature; emphasizing the role of ethics or personal scruples as you develop.

☽   Realizing there are additional ways you can develop potentials; assessing the impact your feelings have on your personal development; receiving or giving consolation to increase your self-esteem or worth.

☿   Enhanced ability to verbalize and discuss aspects of personal growth; explaining to yourself or others the effect of the inner changes you undergo after studying new philosophies, religions, or ideas of others.

♀   A need to bring various forms of relaxation and introspection into your life as part of your learning and growing process; realizing the importance of cooperation given to or received from others in life.

♂   Exerting your will over life's circumstances and becoming more persistent with self-growth and maturity; anger about any lack of progress toward your personal objectives or needed successes; recognition for sports proficiency.

♄   Personal restraint and tolerance when accepting various pitfalls in life; meticulous and exacting experiences for you to examine and thus learn more about your inner self; a loss of personal prestige or morals.

♅   Growing and maturing despite upsets or surprises which offer new insight into people or self; personal growth and insight achieved through the study or application of science or astrology; disruptions to your needs for security.

♆   Illusions and deceptions about ability to cope with life's problems; lack of progress in expanding horizons thru study or travel; a need for poetry and music; motivation gained from studying the occult.

♇   A turnaround in your outlook on life due to the study and application of philosophies which differ from those of your childhood; troubles come to you, but you survive them and grow as a person.

☊   Ties and connections to others who teach you important lessons of life; helps open you to new ideas; traveling with others for education and experiences; closeness to friends who show added interest in your welfare.

A   You focus on the need to absorb life's lessons; you gain from your daily experiences; enhanced needs to understand the motives and intentions of others; reminders that you must work with people in life.

JUPITER/MIDHEAVEN CONCEPTS

Ambitious Guiding Principles	An Expert is Wrong	A Happy Person
A Social Stature (Standing)	Boasts about Experience	Accepts Origin
Wisdom from Living Life	Fortunate Conclusions	Honest Conduct
Opinions on Self-Restraint	Wise Approvals	Liberal Methods
An Ideal Childhood	Amplifies Capacities	Plenty of Defenses
An Enhanced Conscience	Additional Life's Choices	Copes Well in Life
A Potential for Distinction	Encourages Schooling	Positive Effects
Credentials which Benefit	Successful Birthright	A Favorable Career
Errors in Self-Concepts	Elaborates on Recognition	A Wise Expert
Expands Competence	Expands Trustworthiness	Has Safety in Life
Idealistic Intentions	Assumes Success in Life	Expands Plans
Develops Personal Sincerity	Expanded Integrity	Learns to be Happy

Extensive Evolvement	Increases Self-Restraint
Theories of Personal Development	Aspires for Self-Restraint
Increased Learning and Growing	Develops a Happy Personality
A Lot of Experiences	Assists with Attainments
Wise Learning and Growing	Augments Success of Outcomes
Favorably Provides for Family	Promises with Guarantees
Prefers Self-Development	Inaccurate Workmanship
Happy with Life's Progress	Augments Personal Security
Inclined to Fulfill Goals	Loosens Self-Restraint
Accomplished Discernment	Coping with Optimism
Enhanced Personal Rewards	Increasing Distinction
Furthers Efforts to Persevere	A Potential for Resolution
Errors during Development	Increases Expertise
Encourages a Sense of Fairness	Inflates Credentials
Emphasizes Personal Standards	Furthers Purposes
Adds to Respectability	Assumes Expertise
Encouraging Validation	A Reputation as a Happy Person
Approval as You Mature	Proficient with Promises
Brings Fortunate Recognition	Opinions on Self-Discipline
Elaborates on Personal Goals	Corroborates Generosity
Widens Personal Development	Wise Family Standards
Gains Experience and Knowledge	Supplementary Standards
Prefers Personal Growth	Fortunate Early Beginnings
Happiness in Old Age	Aspirations for Recognition
An Increased Need to Mature	Errors Learned as a Child
Misjudges Objectives	Increases Potential
Fortunate Resolutions	Summarizes Results
A Belief in Respectability	Assures with Guarantees
Learns about Assumptions	Generous with Expertise
Aspires to Become Self-Made	A New Philosophy in Life
Supplements Fairness	Magnifies Attainments

JUPITER/MIDHEAVEN With Itself

♃   Successes derived from situations with travel, foreign influences, or religious exposure; publicity from those who like your role in life; added potential to learn from different ideas or philosophies in life.

M   The reputation you develop by your ability to explain life's processes and implications to others; receiving recognition for proficiency in your work or for principles you set; the consequences of various activities and aspirations.

Significant Examples of People and Events Using Jupiter/Midheaven

General: **STRONG:** Bobby Fischer; Paul Newman; Richard Byrd; Johann Von Goethe; Ernest Pyle; Drew Pearson; Stephen Crane; Erich Maria Remarque; Moshe Dayan; John Dillinger; Jimi Hendrix; Jean Paul Sartre; Nikola Tesla
            WEAK: Gustav Dore; Alexander Graham Bell; Mary Martin; Rollo May; Carl Sandburg; John Denver; Vincent Van Gogh; Benito Mussolini
            EVENTS: Wright Brothers First Flight; Alaskan Earthquake; Challenger Explosion; USS Maine Explosion; (Mt. St. Helens Explosion).

☉   Johnny Carson; Chernobyl Explosion; Ralph Nader; Muhammad Ali

☽   Jim Thorpe; Erwin Rommel; Helen Reddy; Willie Brandt; Carl Sandburg

☿   Steve Rosenbloom; Arthur Ford; Louis Pasteur; Charles E. O. Carter

♀   Vittorio DeSica; Elton John; Ralph Nader; Transcon. RR Done; S. Spielberg

♂   Charles Kettering; Carl Sandburg; Ida Rolf; Norman Mailer; John Dillinger; Erwin Rommel; Paul Newman

♃, M   David Frost; Carl Sandburg; Kent State Shootings; Steven Crane; J.acques Cousteau; Bobby Fischer; Olivia Newton-John

♄   Jimi Hendrix; Mick Jagger; Bolsheviks Seize Power; Sir William Crookes

♅   Wayne Gretzky; Dane Rudhyar; Ervin Nyiregyhazi; Hank Williams

♆   Chernobyl Nuclear Explosion; Cheiro; Edward R. Murrow; Jackie Robinson; Charles Addams; Sydney Omarr

♇   Lewis & Clark Expedition Begins; Edouard Manet; Mick Jagger; Shirley Jones; Dustin Hoffman; John Paul I

☊   Robin Williams; Ida Rolf; Tom Jones; Charles Addams; Arthur Ford

A   Shirley Jones; Ellen Burstyn; Alan Leo; Sydney Omarr; Arthur Ford

SATURN/URANUS ♄/♅

Basic Ideas:

These themes symbolize the tension between maintaining traditional methods and introducing innovative techniques when facing life's alternatives. Here your need to balance new ideas with conservative objectives begins. You may find that restrictions arise suddenly and without warning, encounter rigidity which leads to rebuffs, or find a commitment to reach for distinctive or unique goals. You may find your insight into new methods of problem solving is diminished, receive disappointments from unexpected sources, or have to tread carefully when introducing new ideas. Revisions which are changes to procedures but simplify your work, the compromise which exists between those of the "old school" and those with "fresh ideas," and pessimism which is broken by unpredictable circumstances can also be found here. These motifs also mirror the conflict between old ways and new ideas.

In Your Personal Life:

Thesis   Increased desire to break barriers with innovation and insight; demands for further controls and planning; needs to properly, carefully, and correctly present deliberately imposed changes.

Anti   May bring prohibitions on methods of modernization; alteration of circumstances caused by manipulations of traditional methods of accomplishing tasks; delays caused by unexpected substitutions.

In Your Relationships:

Thesis   Balancing the role of friendship between partners who want more commitment from you; allows others to express who they are or what they believe in even though their ideas are different from yours.

Anti   Personal frustrations at coping with ideas from others which run counter to your own; retards friendships which have existed because of political alliances; indifference or odd reactions from reliable friends.

With Body or Mind:

Calcium deposits arise from nervousness or reactions to stress; arthritis in the knees or ankles; unexpected ailments; aging problems; spasms in joints.

In Politics or Business:

Thesis   Legislative processes able to temper traditional needs to new ideas; interaction of legislative and executive bodies; balancing conservatives and progressives; counter-revolutionary rule.

Anti   Restrictions on personal contacts due to political situations which are beyond an enterprise's jurisdiction; control of access to political dissidents; sudden indifference by people to traditional mores or laws.

SATURN/URANUS with Planets and Points

☉ Finding effective means of reconciling forces for change with demands to uphold tradition; determination to introduce the new to those who remain conservative; prestige acquired thru invoking radical reforms.

☽ Protection of traditional procedures from radical changes; new ways of protecting family or home traditions; rebellion against traditional methods of raising children; fickleness over innovative work.

☿ Educational reforms which break accepted barriers; new ways of communicating radical changes to traditional workers; innovative words appearing in language to describe new or different activities; monotonous politicians.

♀ Introducing change in a more acceptable way; satisfaction with new ways of showing affection; indulgence for unusual changes to traditional roles in finance; appeasement of those demanding changes.

♂ Increased irritation with changes which alter conservative traditions; impatience with radicals who insist upon new ways; struggles which impose changes upon people who show loyalty to traditional methods.

♃ Opinion and advice on how to effect change to traditional ways; many suggestions on how to impose progressive modifications; traditional politics shattered by new and unexpected practices; conservatives vs. radicals.

♆ Weakened or masked changes designed to break traditional roles; the delusion that change will operate to improve upon the traditional methods; visions or insight on how to impose conversions in an unhurried manner.

♇ Concealing changes to activities; termination of extreme practices which have been hindering progress; drastic changes in a previously liberal atmosphere; rigid inflexibility replaces adaptation.

☊ Attracting people who help move traditionalists toward new ideas; locating associates who share similar views toward effecting needed changes or holding down discontent; increased needs to rid groups of divisive radicals.

A Sudden focus upon forces for change which had been abruptly halted due to traditional influences; public attitudes about the institution of change for traditional procedures; less attention given to agitators.

M Accepting change, removing old habits, and yet benefiting from this as a person; altering your personal goals and aspirations due to changes in society or at work; releasing old ideas which no longer work.

SATURN/URANUS CONCEPTS

Brief Disruptions
Frustrated at Revisions
A Respect for Oddities
Careful Restyling
Restricts Rebelliousness
Discourages Innovation
Depressing Indifference
Tests for Self-Control
Inflexible Instructions
Continues with Obstinacy
A Justifiable Disclosure
Prolongs Eccentricity

Varieties of Ignorance
Deviates from Restrictions
Boring Aloofness
Definite Unpredictability
Silent Breakthroughs
Delayed Surprises
A Respected Troublemaker
Dependable Astrologers
Careful with Rudeness
Unyielding Waywardness
Prolonged Impartiality
A Little Contrariness

Quiet Alterations
Unique Rebuffs
Lessens Disarray
Limits Disobedience
A Few Variations
Little Novelty
Simple Variations
Stops Modernization
Cautious Deviation
Stifles Surprises
Hinders Reform
Precise Computers

Discontented with Restraints
Obvious Eccentricity
Restrained by Friendliness
Continues with Originality
Indifferent to Rebuffs
Restrains Cleverness
Unstable Conservatives
Unhurried Changes
Independent Justification
Continuous Surprises
Deliberate Erratic Actions
Silent Indifference
Halts Innovation
Continuing Instability
Pessimistic Friends
Real Astonishment
Simply Overwhelms
Restrained by Impartiality
Lasting Pessimism
Postpones Independence
Unchanging Discontent
Regular Revisions
Dissatisfied with Respect
Cautious Indifference
Unyielding Politics
Curtails Liberty
Banishes Originality
Cautious Rebelliousness
Insufficient Audacity
Progressive Postponements
Simple Abstinence

Relentless Disinterest
Responsible for Instability
Continuing Regulation
Only a Little Defiance
Hinders Experimentation
Distressing Insurgence
Innovative Restraint
Discourages Surprises
An Honorable Defector
Dissatisfied with Sparseness
Discourages Contrariness
Unique Distress
Simple Indifference
Unmistakable Idiosyncrasies
Prohibits Noncompliance
Constant Disregard
Novel Estrangement
Insufficient Substitutes
Restricts Uniqueness
Weakens Adversity
Delays Insight
Little Innovation
Continual Variations
Realistic Insight
Functional Modifications
Silent Surprises
Discourages Disruptions
Boring Experiments
A Regular Renegade
Varieties of Restrictions
Diminishes Disclosure

SATURN/URANUS With Itself

♄ Order and respect in a rebellious and impertinent nature; a dreary air in activities designed to break old habits; plain and simple changes to daily routines; subdued calls for improvements in procedures.

♅ Desires for change and innovation in areas which have been neglected or hidden away; increased restlessness for independence and deviation from accepted norms of practice; a prompt to seek more freedom.

Significant Examples of People and Events Using Saturn/Uranus

General: **STRONG:** Vittorio DeSica; Arthur Ford; Jacques Cousteau; Joseph Joffre; O. J. Simpson; Albert Schweitzer; Jean Paul Sartre; Burt Reynolds; Olivia Newton-John; Lord Byron; Jackie Robinson; Henry Kissinger; Arnold Schwarzenegger
WEAK: Carroll Righter; Jack Nicklaus; Ernest Pyle; John McEnroe; Bobby Fischer; Sir Laurence Olivier; Jack Paar; Percy Bysshe Shelley
EVENTS: Wright Bros. First Flight; Ramstein Airshow Crash; Pres. Nixon's Resignation; First Medicare Patient Accepted; (Apollo 11 Moon Landing).

⊙ Ritchie Valens; O. J. Simpson; Jim Thorpe; Thomas H. Huxley; Olga Worrall; Anne Murray; Sally Ride; Bjorn Borg

☽ Titanic Hits Iceberg; Mt. St. Helens Explosion; Enrico Fermi; Jeddu Krishnamurti; Charles Addams; Erwin Rommel

☿ Arnold Schwarzenegger; Ramstein Air Crash; Willie Mays; Hugh Downs; Elton John; Bolshevik's Seize Power; Franklin Roosevelt

♀ Gustav Dore; Fidel Castro; Adolf Hitler; Burl Ives; Anne Murray

♂ Albert Schweitzer; Ellen Burstyn; Erwin Rommel; Adolf Hitler

♃ Ralph Waldo Emerson; Arnold Schwarzenegger; Dane Rudhyar; Jack Schwartz; Elvis Presley; Charles E. O. Carter

♄, ♅ Arthur Ford; Albert Schweitzer; Ferdinand Foch; Sir Alex. Fleming

♆ Franklin D. Roosevelt Wins First Election; Ellen Burstyn; Yehudi Menuhin; Bertrand Russell; Francisco Franco; Mt. St. Helens Explosion

♀ Gen. Joseph Joffre; Ralph Nader; Arturo Toscanini; Robin Williams

☊ Al Unser; Richard Strauss; John Fremont; Albert Einstein; Hugh Downs

A Ada Lovelace Byron; Drew Pearson; Edouard Manet; Willie Brandt

M Vittorio DeSica; Audie Murphy; Jack Schwartz; Cheiro; Jackie Robinson

SATURN/NEPTUNE   ♄/♆

Basic Ideas:
Caution, pessimism, and rigidity meet evasion, dreaminess, and inefficiency in themes which allow you to fool others with delusions of personal integrity. Any deceptive practices in progress are extended, and restrictions for past activities can be avoided. These motifs mirror neglect which has persisted over long periods, confusion or denials about responsibility for present conditions, and disappointment over a general lack of accountability. These topics represent control over your dreams and visions, which helps you alternate between an ever illusive reality and the presence of illusions. They denote weakness in any areas of personal discipline or wariness. Subtle hints of pessimism can creep through facades, and caution is encouraged for those who attempt deceptive practices. These planets favor lasting spiritual inspiration and long-lived mystical persons.

In Your Personal Life:
Thesis   Applying caution to overcome the practices of carelessness which have been ongoing; replacing your musings or mind wanderings with carefully analyzed research; restricting, defining, or uncovering frauds.

Anti   Continuing with practices which are detrimental; finding that restrictions imposed are substantially weakened; finding it easy to abandon or neglect responsibility toward previously important matters.

In Your Relationships:
Thesis   An older partner may bring mystical and romantic feelings of caring into your life; you find that you enjoy planning and dreaming with others but also that you need the realism they may offer you.

Anti   You can purposely deceive others about your intentions and go to elaborate means to ensure that your lies are not discovered; you meet responsibility silently; dreams about how your relationship will last.

With Body or Mind:
Difficult-to-diagnose diseases of a long-lasting nature; weakened bones and cartilage; anemia from drug reactions, fungus, or lack of exercise.

In Politics or Business:
Thesis   Delusions among the real leadership; long lived programs which have no real purpose; policies which restrict spies; misusing law officers; inefficient use of capable expert advice; mistaken religious leaders.

Anti   Leaders deceive about the exercise of control; deficient business practices exposed; respected persons involved in questionable practices; reliable equipment failures; a leader capitulates.

SATURN/NEPTUNE with Planets and Points

☉   Initiating effective deceptive practices; a weakness of character not immediately evident; new confidence to overcome nervousness in life's situations; drama and flair added to displays of illusion.

☽   Hesitation about replacing that which no longer functions as intended; activities which serve no real purpose and seem to come and go; increased dependency on drugs to escape harsh realities of living and responsibility.

☿   Studies to correct deficiencies in business or commerce; skill at correcting long-standing disputes; information on weakness of character; discussions which bring lasting motivation or inspiration.

♀   Choosing correct forms of relaxation; deception about values being presented; inspiration for repackaging older forms of music or art; decreased values for goods or wealth; disappointing values for expensive items.

♂   Accelerated haste and thus potential neglect of people or situations you encounter; defending shabby practices; enlivening drab rituals which rely on ancient fantasies or myths; an old, active, mystic.

♃   Expanded ideas that reality is just a vision; deceptive practices which are further concealed by religious ceremony or implication; fortunate answers and inspiration from meditation or inner deliberation.

♅   Uncommon or unexpected recoveries from weaknesses which surface after a dormant period; a new discipline which adds astrology to religious and mystical practices; indifference to decay in older buildings or structures.

♇   Punishment for those who have allowed decay and decadence to persist; the rejection of responsibility and denial of guilt from responsible people; new ideas on evolution which upset long-held but weaker historical theories.

☊   Attraction to groups or people who feel that neglect in society is acceptable; ridding yourself of practices detrimental to your reputation and work; joint efforts to reverse decay and corruption in life.

A   Noticing the pretenses or false intentions of others; inhibitions about correcting long standing areas of disappointment; easing your mental focus when revising past errors or practices which have become lax.

M   Taking a definite stand on practices which lessen the quality of life; your reputation for correcting such practices; using shortened, inefficient methods when tough, dedicated, and completed work is needed.

SATURN/NEPTUNE CONCEPTS

Simple Shoddiness
Restrained Compliance
Relentless Mystery
Disciplined Subservience
A Painstaking Capitulation
Uninteresting Devotion
Discourages Escape
Sustained Carelessness
Postpones Salvation
Hypothetical Realism
Sustains Imperfection
Endures despite Weakness

An Abbreviated Vision
A Usable Counterfeit
Senseless Justification
Frustrating Complications
An Erosion of Respect
An Honorable Poet
A Simple Folly
Efficient Concealment
Stifles the Imagination
Postpones an Escape
Depends on Isolation
A Deliberate Omission

Discourages Illusion
A Selective Oversight
Discourages Subtlety
Silent Neglect
Boring Mysteries
Deliberate Misuse
Limits Laxity
Isolated Confusion
A Distracting Illusion
Limited Submission
Halts Garbles
Restrained Musings

Old and Abandoned Issues
Inadequate Holiness
Inspired to be more Dependable
Discouraging Breakdowns
Complicates Enduring
Frustrating Carelessness
Persistent Vagueness
Brief Compassion
Perpetuates Fantasies
Stifles Inspiration
Responsible for Laxity
Stops Hiding
Curbs Disappointments
Dilapidated Restraints
Silent Fantasies
A Disguised Reputation
Lasting Perplexities
Shortens Complications
Responsible for an Omission
Restricting Confinement
Reticent about Escape
An Illusion of Respectability
Sustained Inspiration
Distressing Inefficiency
Denies Carelessness
Frustrating Foolishness
Inadequate Piety
A Rigid Imagination
Shoddy Precision
Undisguised Vagueness
Silent Inspiration

Monotonous Subservience
Distressing Confusion
Endures with Mysticism
Simple Imagination
Sustains Disregard
Ancient Shortcomings
Stifles Fantasies
Persists with Drugs
An Illusion of Frugality
Shoddy Discipline
Distressing Neglect
Prohibits the Occult
Discourages Imagination
An Old Ambiguity
Infrequent Dreams
Selective Disregard
Restrains Visions
A Little Carelessness
Avoids Loneliness
Restrained by Illusions
Weakness in Rigid Structures
Delays from Complications
Selective Misunderstandings
Realistic Disguises
Utilitarian Subordination
Prudent Inflexibility
Simple Mysteries
Postpones Temptations
Little Subtlety
Perplexed with Pessimism
Not Many Miracles

SATURN/NEPTUNE With Itself

♄   Cutting thru confusion or deception and getting to the heart of matters; relying on people who have other than sensory means of obtaining information; added toleration for performing tedious tasks.

Ψ   Breaking thru rigid patterns; presenting newly visualized views of reality or the future; dissolving rigid or outmoded structures; inspiration derived from drugs; illusive heightened awareness using escape.

Significant Examples of People and Events Using Saturn/Neptune

General: **STRONG:** Lance Reventlow; Paul Joseph Goebbels; Albert Camus; Edmund Halley; Richard Chamberlain; Dave Garroway; John Fremont; Adolf Hitler; Henry Kissinger; Dr. Tom Dooley; Jonathan Winters; Carroll Righter
WEAK: Ellen Burstyn; Cheiro; Norman Mailer; Jean Paul Sartre; Sean Connery; Claude Debussy; Albert Speer; Peter Max
EVENTS: Pres. Nixon's Resignation; Lee's Surrender at Appomattox; Chernobyl Nuclear Explosion; RMS Titanic Hits Iceberg; (Kent State Shootings).

☉   William K. Douglas; Enrico Fermi; Peter Max; Ivar Kreugar; Bob Newhart; Jack Nicklaus; John McEnroe

☽   Dane Rudhyar; Stephen Foster; Scott Carpenter; Adolf Hitler; William Butler Yeats; Elton John; Arthur Ford; Burl Ives

☿   Mick Jagger; Israel Regardie; Robert Redford; Kent State Shootings

♀   Jonathan Winters; Mary Martin; Sam Peckinpah; Komar; Art. Rimbaud

♂   Charles Gordon; Willie Mays; John Paul I; Moshe Dayan; Gus Grissom

♃   Sandy Koufax; Olivia Newton-John; J. Von Ribbentrop; Charles Gordon

♄, Ψ   Charles Gordon; Ernest Pyle; Ralph Nader; Gianni Agnelli; Henri Toulouse-Lautrec; Steve Allen; Earl Warren

♅   Chernobyl Nuclear Explosion; Challenger Explosion; William K. Douglas; Joachim Von Ribbentrop

♇   Stephen Foster; Lindburgh Lands; John Paul I; Drew Pearson; Transcontinental Railroad Completed; Joachim Von Ribbentrop

☊   First Medicare Patient Received; Elton John; Evel Knievel; Earl Warren

A   Alexis Carrel; Bob Hope; Rex Harrison; John Lennon; Ferdinand Foch

M   Edouard Manet; Guglielmo Marconi; Henry Kissinger; David O. Selznik; John Dillinger; Erich Maria Remarque

SATURN/PLUTO ♄/♀

Basic Ideas:

These themes denote organizing and planning work needed to meet your obligations. Adopting a more realistic attitude toward defining your motives, methods for developing the discipline you need to meet personal goals, and tight or unyielding deadlines which are only met through much hard work or extreme pressure are also indicated. This combination shows your ability to restrain or discipline extreme desires, correct the effects of past excesses, and then organize a turnaround from old reversals. Your desires to replace past rigid habit patterns with more progressive and needed actions, your determination not to be swayed from your inner goals, and your obligations to employ stealth can also start here. Your emphasis on any continuing depletion of resources, or your ability or failure to adequately provide for conditions of future reversals is also represented.

In Your Personal Life:

Thesis   Reorganizing your priorities; the setting of more realistic goals; careful preparations for limiting the suspicions of others; endurance of activities designed to curb or correct past excesses or extreme practices.

Anti   Disappointment with prior preparations; taking back commitments made previously; a loss of control or intensity; setting more rigid procedures with better official controls; despair over secret work.

In Your Relationships:

Thesis   Destroying habit patterns which hinder your relationships; a sense of seriousness in your sexual desires; a need for mutual self-discipline within the relationship; adding intensity and loyalty to commitment.

Anti   Loss of intensity or desire between partners; anguish in relating to partner, or vice versa; strong tendencies toward miserliness or unwillingness to share equally within the relationship.

With Body or Mind:

Loss or lessening of sexual desire; lowering of functions from the pituitary gland; intensive pain or discomfort in joints; shrinks hemorrhoids or piles.

In Politics or Business:

Thesis   Use of secret police or military agencies; restraints on destructive weapons; earth blocks sewage systems; upsets in existing checks and balances; turmoil in any rigid or older structure.

Anti   Keeping affairs private or not open to scrutiny; secret preparations for future restrictions; hoarding resources for potential future disasters; lengthy consideration of methods of removal or destruction.

SATURN/PLUTO with Planets and Points

☉   Dominating others thru strong will and determination to be better thru competent application; leadership based upon effectiveness of plans and thoroughness of preparation; important denials of extremes.

☽   Identifying and controlling emotions as you push toward goals and objectives; an inconsistency in your work, achievements, or records; strong urges to work with women who have power; strong control over people's habits.

☿   Mental shrewdness toward efforts to meet your goals; communicating intentions to proceed with dangerous or difficult tasks; curiosity which spurs you to research items further; difficult or long studies.

♀   Softening excessive restrictions; delays in the destruction of things which have value or desired beauty; deriving pleasure from organizing your work; a deep love of certain art forms or traditional music.

♂   Activating plans for much destruction or upheaval; energy to continue restraining activities which contaminate, adulterate, or otherwise poison; a need to use whatever means or power is available to continue working.

♃   Favorable outcomes in the use of large expenditures of resources or energies; people who have leadership and power to dispense; opinions about how to reclaim the use of waste products for other activities.

♅   Sudden changes or upsets in plans which have been made concerning very important activities; reforms in the way punishment is given for important crimes; the erratic or uneven use of retaliatory measures.

♆   Defects in the planning for large and important activities; improbable effects from excessive activities of the past; neglect of important methods for preserving or caring for waste treatment processes; disguised uses of power.

☊   Associating with those who plan and work hard before they proceed with important work; identifying paths to those who have power or influence to wield or sell; a destiny about holding or abusing power.

A   Concentration upon important matters which lie before you; assessments of how to work with those who have power or influence; an environment which gives you the impression of silent power or continuing influence.

M   Knowledge of how to acquire, use, and wield the types of power which can make significant changes to society; the acknowledgement from others that you have such power or prestige in your field of expertise.

SATURN/PLUTO CONCEPTS

Continuing Removals
The Degeneration of Respect
Concentrates on Loyalty
Downgrades Responsibility
Postpones Death
Distressing Restitution
Continues with Defamation
Monotonous Punishment
Undisguised Retaliation
Cautious Purification
Restrains Compulsions
Retards Restitution

Unseen Contamination
Cautious Cover-ups
Destructive Rebuffs
A Single Accusation
A Corrupted Reputation
Limits Concealment
Realistic Elimination
Relentless Retaliation
Practical Destruction
Insufficient Morbidity
A Simple Obsession
Silent Elimination

Persisting Dispersal
Lasting Poisons
Lessens Extremes
Rigid Controls
Delays Vengeance
Deters Reduction
Inferior Corruption
Persists with Rancor
Destroys Rigidity
Rejects Suspicions
Diminishes Rigidity
Lessens Corruption

Holds Back on Obsessions
Restrained by Suspicions
Undisguised Condemnation
Rediscovers Realism
A Contempt for Corruption
Continues with Obsessions
A Compulsion for Dishonesty
Unhurried Conclusions
Continuing Vengeance
Suspicious of Discipline
Monotonous Destruction
Terrible Pollution
Postpones Obliteration
Renounces Corruption
Simple Dishonesty
An Undisguised Defeat
Relentless Vengeance
Limits Ownership
Discourages Duress
Unending Punishment
Practical Reforms
Restrains Corruption
Abbreviated Purification
Responsible for Transformation
Terrible Secrets
Silent Vengeance
Disciplined Concealment
Ceases to be Dependable
Restricts the Prosecutor
Justifiable Extraction
Simple Contamination

Enduring Punishment
Gives up on Decadence
Hates Pessimism
Legitimate Punishment
Restricts Compulsions
Discourages Vengeance
Persists with Fanaticism
Lessens Punishment
Unhurried Use of Force
Discourages Punishment
A Silent Infatuation
Abnormal Construction
Denies Devastation
Rediscovers Honor
Careful Eradication
Halts Disintegration
Perpetuates a Falsity
Denies Concealment
Responsible for Retaliation
Cautious and Stealthy
Builds to a Conclusion
Sparse Restitution
Time Consuming Prosecution
Monotonous Prosecution
Only a Little Destruction
Constant Suspicion
Obvious Elimination
Hidden Corruption
Realistic Restoration
Sustains Wilfullness
Continuing Amends

SATURN/PLUTO With Itself

♄   Becoming realistic about the good and bad in life; an increased need to question what can be eliminated or what can be kept; may initiate terrible retributions; the final destruction of established patterns.

♀   Seeing that there are two extremes: good and evil; choosing one and dedicating your life toward eliminating other; a realistic look at life direction; elimination of ineffective practices; extreme times of change.

Significant Examples of People and Events Using Saturn/Pluto

General: **STRONG:** Winston Churchill; Joseph Joffre; Johann Von Goethe; George Patton; Komar; Jean Cocteau; Arthur Ford; Albert Camus; Steve Wozniak; Grant Lewi; Nikola Tesla; Johnny Carson; Manly Palmer Hall; Ida Rolf; John Dillinger
WEAK: Dustin Hoffman; Sir Laurence Olivier; Carl Sandburg; Jean Paul Sartre; Alex. Graham Bell; Edgar Degas; Dr. Sam Sheppard; Sydney Omarr
EVENTS: Chernobyl Nuclear Accident; John F. Kennedy Shot; Kent State Shootings; Pres. Nixon's Resignation; (Franklin Roosevelt Wins First Election).

☉   Helen Reddy; Arturo Toscanini; Johnny Carson; H. Kissinger; G. Marconi

☽   Stephen King; Jean Houston; O. J. Simpson; Albert Einstein; Hugh Downs

☿   Jacques Cousteau; Earl Warren; Edmund Halley; Carroll Righter; Gregory Peck; John Lennon; Jack Paar; Al Unser

♀   Steve Allen; Dr. Tom Dooley; Jean Cocteau; Hermann Goering; J. Nicklaus

♂   First Medicare Patient Accepted; Sydney Omarr; Erich Maria Remarque; Charles Steinmetz; Auguste Rodin; Olivia Newton-John

♃   Franklin Roosevelt; Charles Addams; Sean Connery; Thomas H. Huxley; F. Scott Fitzgerald; Charles Kettering

♄, ♀   Cheiro; Billy Rose; Johnny Carson; Arnold Schwarzenegger; Gen. Joseph Joffre; Charles Kettering; Audrey Hepburn

♅   Hermann Goering; Erwin Rommel; P. Yogananda; Nixon's Resignation

♆   Emperor Hirohito; Pearl Harbor Attack; Steven Spielberg; Francisco Franco; Komar; Ritchie Valens

☋   Jean Cocteau; Bob Hope; Johnny Carson; Ellen Burstyn; Paul Cezanne

A   Stonewall Jackson; George Patton; Robert DeNiro; Winston Churchill

M   Albert Camus; John Paul I; Arthur Ford; O. J. Simpson; Steven Spielberg

SATURN/NODE   ♄/☊

Basic Ideas:
These themes represent finding a purpose for life by using your contacts with other people, groups, or organizations. Through these motifs there may be many disappointing directions which your life will follow as you try to find the best conditions for whatever it takes to find happiness. You should try to incorporate both simplicity and credibility in your life. These planets do not suggest motives, but show that you search out other people, groups, connections, and ties to determine which of these, if any, it will take to provide you with the assistance you seek. You may learn much about the concept of loyalty, support, and mutual assistance through this mixture. The concept of enduring with and through others, breaking through the disappointments and restrictions imposed by others, and creating a path for yourself is shown. Also indicated are suggestions for meeting prior obligations through others.

In Your Personal Life:
Thesis   Finding support for your ideas, goals, ambitions and plans through the support of other people, groups, or ties; permanent alliances and connections to others; new habits which help make you a better person.

Anti   Moving from person to group to new friends because you are not able to find the inner peace you desire within yourself; using friendships as an easy excuse to not look inwardly at self for the growth you require.

In Your Relationships:
Thesis   Focusing on consistency and loyalty as a mutual goal with your partner; disciplining yourself to accept disillusionment or frustrations from your partner without falling apart psychologically.

Anti   Blaming others for failures or mistakes; an inability to create a meaningful or lasting set of friendships, or to maintain a support group to help you get through difficult personal times.

With Body or Mind:
The constriction of tubes or passageways in the body; blocked or constricted bowels; blocked throat or air passages; weak connecting muscles.

In Politics or Business:
Thesis   The creation or building of authority or pride; new ties to allies; help from others in times of internal difficulties; foreign enterprises which offer assistance; long-standing ties and relationships to old friends.

Anti   A country in inner turmoil which does not request help from others; a country which does not know how to use organizations for assistance or aid; trying to do things internally without outside help or aid.

SATURN/NODE with Planets and Points

☉ Your inner determination to end a line of potentially self-destructive forces which drive you to not value the use of friendships and the good will of others; purposefully seeking and using needed assistance.

☽ Appreciation for the compassion others bring when you are in need of assistance; sensitivity to the manner in which others offer help to you; using public assistance to find value in life; ties to female run societies.

☿ Thoughts of using assistance from others to further your goals in life; questions about the help others offer; restlessness about your direction and purpose in life; talking to others about help; quickly seeing others.

♀ Using people with connections to bankers, artists, musicians, etc. to help you meet goals; appreciating responses received when you request help; joint beautification projects; functional currency exchanges.

♂ Inner anger associated with being unable to find stability in life's patterns; established athletic contests or sporting events; irritation for what others are not able to contribute ; hastily rejecting assistance.

♃ Generous assistance when you require it; fortunate support and meetings with friends who are able to provide you with the assistance you need (if you can recognize and accept same); sincere help in finding yourself.

♅ Strange twists of fate when seeking help from others; innovative forms of assistance from groups; disruption in your ability to find and attract the kind of help you require; encourages unpredictable events at business meetings.

♆ Inspiration from others as a form of assistance toward finding your path in life; deceit with friendship given; having to pay a price for help which is more than you expected; friends who deceive or confuse you.

♇ Incidents which push you beyond self-help and into plights which require you to rely on others; obsession with helping yourself when others are available to help you; help with conditions attached.

A Important situations or events which may alter your life; discussions on the wisdom of continuing or supporting an effort; events which may cause you suffering, loss, or pain; a scarcity of help through depressing times.

M Growing and maturing through the help of others; using the assistance that others provide to mature and find your destiny in life; able assistance from groups or through meetings with others; your work carried on by others.

SATURN/NODE CONCEPTS

Endures through Delays	Isolated Criticism	Brief Barriers
Unhappy with Sexual Ties	Inner Feelings for Destiny	Careful Interviews
Noiseless Publicity	Lasting Layoffs	Simple Cooperation
Perpetuates Familiarity	Restrained Occasions	Continual Kinship
Disappointing Alliances	Monotonous Ridding	A Simple Life's Aim
Practical Co-workers	Pessimism at a Conference	Definite Breaks
Naive in Relationships	Hinders Partnerships	Realistic Alliances
Lasting Ties to Others	Respectable Connections	Relentless Supporters
Modest Acquaintances	Insufficient Attachments	Lessens Mergers
Postpones Separations	Honorable Ties to Others	Silent Alliances
Eliminates Organization	Becomes More Cautious	An Obvious Fate
Disappointing Sexual Ties	An Inferior Conference	Secure Coalitions

Prolongs Finding Others	Postpones Sexual Ties
Responsible for Separations	Avoids Acquaintances
Silent when Meeting Others	Final Acquisitions
Utilitarian Ordering	Disappointing Associations
Cautious when Meeting Others	Travels the Paths of Life Alone
Meets Few with Similar Ideas	Almost No Bureaucracy
Unsure of Personal Adaptability	Sees Life as Restrictive
Monotonous Meetings	Delays Pushing Forward
Realizes How to use Friendships	Simple and Direct Presentations
Uses Proper Introductions	Silently Leaves Others Behind
Delays in Seeing Others	Lacks Social Graces at Meetings
Painstaking Gatherings	Life's Destiny as a Lonely Affair
Endures through Boring Proposals	Avoids Assessing Life's Progress
Restricted by Meeting Others	Friends who Rely on You
Disappointed with Life's Lot	Maneuvers the Bureaucracy
Able to Locate the Right Person	Uneasy with Joint Ventures
Narrow Passageways	Promises of Delays from Friends
Unwilling to Find New Friends	Cautious Acquaintances
Depressed over Friendships	A Distressing Bureaucracy
Unsure about Relationships	Responsible for Presentations
Restricts Acquaintances	Established Regulations
Constrained by Losses	Few Sexual Ties
Hinders Ability to Meet Others	Cautious about Life's Prospects
Uneasy about Delays	Feels Uneasy about Separations
Constant Spiritual Growth	Uneasy Presentations
Gloomy Episodes	Legitimate Criticism
Prohibits Attachment	Restricts Ties to Others
Restricted by Obligations	Depends on Assistance
Realistic about Offers	Delays in Finding Support
Learns to Discipline Self	Limited Opportunities
Prolongs Exchanges	Silent Acquaintances

SATURN/NODE With Itself

♄ Short meetings with others; completing a prior obligation; groups using methodical or traditional procedures; increased chances for rebuffs from colleagues about ideas or work; breaks in relations or procedures.

☊ Added needs to locate people who have similar ideas; opportunities to work with people or groups; meeting older and wiser people who offer assistance; the likelihood of having to confront karmic challenges.

Significant Examples of People and Events Using Saturn/Node

General: STRONG: F. Scott Fitzgerald; Henry Mancini; Hank Williams; Percy Bysshe Shelley; Alexander Graham Bell; Willie Mays; Charles E. O. Carter; Enrico Caruso; Edna Ferber; Paul Joseph Goebbels; Edouard Manet
WEAK: Ernest Pyle; Stephen Sondheim; Audrey Hepburn; A. Schwarzenegger; Sally Ride; Merv Griffin; Bertrand Russell; Vincent Van Gogh
EVENTS: Apollo 11 Moon Landing; Wright Brothers First Flight; Pres. Nixon's Resignation; John F. Kennedy Shot; (First Atomic Bomb Explosion).

☉ Henri Matisse; Olivia Newton-John; Alan Leo; Elton John; W. Churchill

☽ Rollo May; Olivia Newton-John; Alb. Speer; Ulysses S. Grant; H. G. Wells

☿ Charles E. O. Carter; Winston Churchill; Norman Mailer; Francisco Franco

♀ Stephen Crane; Gustav Dore; John Fremont; Sir Alexander Fleming; Georges Seurat; Jonathan Winters

♂ Jackie Robinson; Gus Grissom; Scott Carpenter; Jeddu Krishnamurti; Merv Griffin; Albert Camus

♃ Paul Joseph Goebbels; Ramstein Airshow Crash; Bobby Fischer; David O. Selznik; Charles Steinmetz

♄, ☊ Jim Thorpe; Jean Paul Satre; Paul Newman; Jack Nicklaus; A. Modigliani

♅ Johnny Carson; Jerry Reed; Challenger Explosion; Friedrich Nietzsche

♆ Richard Alpert; Joseph Joffre; Carroll Righter; Bob Dylan; H. Kissinger

♇ David Frost; Sir Alex. Fleming; Bob Fosse; Evel Knievel; Richard Alpert

A Rex Harrison; Jack Nicklaus; Tom Jones; Edouard Manet; Watergate Burglary occurs; Carroll Righter

M Burt Reynolds; Wright Bros. First Flight; Jerry Rubin; Percy B. Shelley

SATURN/ASCENDANT   ♄/A

Basic Ideas:

This combination represents an inward focus and a preference to shut the world away from view. Finding an inner enjoyment in the silence of your own space, you do not show much interest in the impressions or reactions of others and you prefer to keep your concerns and observations about life to yourself. You find it easy to close yourself off in your inner world, and to exclude the reactions of people around you from your personal space, even when you are in a crowd. You derive satisfaction in this self-imposed mental isolation. You experience the world through abbreviated views of outer reality, you find your surroundings uninteresting (for the most part), and you restrain your attitudes and interactions so that you can remain in your own mental space. You discipline yourself to avoid receiving impressions from others, and are selective in your personal responses.

In Your Personal Life:

Thesis   You find peace in solitude, and are happy to live in your inner mental space; you do not rely on others for personal stimulation, and prefer to entertain yourself; you need only short amounts of time with others.

Anti   You restrict sensory input from others, and are precise and formal with your approach to people; you feel frustrated and alone when around others, and prefer the serenity of your own inner space to people.

In Your Relationships:

Thesis   A need for one who will give you room and time to be yourself as silence and introspection form a large part of your way of relating to others; this pair inhibits all other reactions from outside influences.

Anti   When required you find it difficult to communicate openly about your feelings to another; you prefer space and time to sort out your reactions regarding the relationship; you are easily disappointed by others.

With Body or Mind:

Hemorrhoids; arthritis; swollen or painful joints; cataracts; vision problems; torn cartilage; knee troubles; bones or teeth that are fragile, brittle, or break.

In Politics or Business:

Thesis   Difficulty for others to understand internal leadership or direction; policy or authority dictated or restricted by external demands; inflexibility or an inability to adapt to necessary change.

Anti   A replacement or a lowering in status of advisors or leaders; curtailment of programs for the disadvantaged; a disregard for checks and balances within an enterprise; repression as a function of policy.

SATURN/ASCENDANT with Planets and Points

☉   Increased need for approval; developing your personality so that you appear friendly, but reserved; a need to dominate others; a need for identification with the real you; effective business practices.

☽   One of your parents preferred to remain in the background and taught you a lesson in self-sufficiency; your care for others is heightened, although you are reluctant to act spontaneously and steal attention from others near you.

☿   Developing a shrewd mind and becoming a better analyst; increased ability to correlate facts and data; dealing with numbers easily; mentally computing well; ability to be articulate with facts or numbers.

♀   Enhanced enjoyment received from being in your own mental space; pleasure derived from listening to music or enjoying art by yourself; building appreciation within yourself about your abilities and skills.

♂   You vacillate between wanting to restrain your impulses and being physically active; you have great patience with certain things, and no patience with other activities; you have much energy, but prefer to be by yourself.

♃   You inflate perceptions of yourself easily, but are still reticent about sharing your views; a silent ego; enhanced comprehension of large amounts of facts and data, especially about people or places.

♅   You often surprise people with your astute perceptions because you seem to be quiet and introspective; you prefer to study others silently, and may use computers, applying astrological or statistical methods of analysis to people.

♆   Developing an understanding about that side of life which is not easily explained by the physical sciences; spending much time dreaming about what the world should be like, as opposed to what it is like.

♇   A need to accumulate and control data and facts about perceptions of others; you easily dismiss information about how life works which does not fit the views of the world which you have formulated.

☊   You meet others who share the same type of serious need for introspection and analysis; you join groups of people who have interests similar to yours; you find friends who understand your silence and study.

M   The acclaim you receive due to the isolated analysis you performed; a slow start in life that included many restrictions; career goals that are achieved very slowly, but steadily; personal guarantees that you keep and fulfill.

SATURN/ASCENDANT CONCEPTS

Limited Surroundings
Cautious Attention Seeking
Retards Perceptions
Reticent around Others
Inadequate Sense of Reality
Endures through Concern
Sparse Conditions
Careful Introspection
Depends on Perceptions
Limited Personal Style
Perpetuates Pretenses
Simple Demeanor
Slow in Relating to Others
Restrains Impressions

Tedious Introspection
Little Awareness
A Monotonous Presence
Delayed Reactions
Unbending Mannerisms
Narrows Mental Focus
Diminished Personal Style
Subdues Inhibitions
Detects Rebuffs Easily
Guarded Perceptions
Simple Mannerisms
Shortens Presence
Silent Portrayals
Missing Perceptions

Rigid Attitudes
Reliable Responses
Silent Concern
Inhibited Settings
Delays Conditions
Suspends Impressions
Simple Attitudes
Few Observations
Unyielding Notions
Quiet Personal Style
Practical Traits
Uninteresting Views
Simple Responses
Restrained Reactions

Uneasy with Impressions Received
Postpones Attention Seeking
Disciplined Mental Concentration
Realistic Understanding of Others
Silences Repressive Mechanisms
A Realistic Way of Seeing People
Restricts Personal Beliefs
Monotonous Attention Seeking
Restricts Understanding of Others
Disappointed with Appearance
Disciplined Observations
Postpones Reactions to Others
Lessens Impressions Received
Monotonous Personal Style
Shy in Front of Others
Endures through all Experiences
Continues to Develop Personality
Deficient Responses
Restrained by Knowing Others
Inflexible Mannerisms
Disciplined Postures
Frustrated when Reading Others
Isolated Hunches Received
Inhibits Ideas on Sorrow
Deliberate Idea Suppression
Pessimistic on Interpersonal Roles
Obvious Personal Responses
Pessimistic Viewpoints
Continuous Impressions Received

Disappointing Personal Style
Limited Perceptions of Others
Hides Few Pretenses
Continuing Introspection
Muted Attention Seeking
Boring Daily Routine
Dependable Sense of Reality
Cautious Personal Style
Endures through Personal Beliefs
Undisguised Reactions
Rigid when Relating to Others
Silently Understands Others
Unbending Interpersonal Roles
Relies on Sense of Reality
Disappointing Reactions
Hinders Interpersonal Roles
More Reliable with Practice
Spartan Personal Style
Frustrating Mental Focus
Lasting Attention Seeking
Inconvenient Circumstances
Depends on Studying Others
Practical Surroundings
Prolongs Sensations
Bored by Understanding Others
Dissatisfied with Attitudes
Realistic Experiences
Sincere about Relationships
Realistic Reactions

SATURN/ASCENDANT With Itself

♄
Added needs for discipline or consistency in any efforts; seeking silence and solitude when faced with situations in life which are difficult to manage; persistence when faced with adversity or delay.

A
Increased awareness of situations or conditions which exist in life; your need to have experiences which are thrilling or out of the ordinary is diminished as your preference for ordinary routine is increased.

Significant Examples of People and Events Using Saturn/Ascendant

General: **STRONG:** John F. Kennedy; Dr. Francis Regardie; Alexis Carrel; Sir Alexander Fleming; Arthur Ford; Manly Palmer Hall; Jacques Cousteau; Bob Dylan; Percy Bysshe Shelley; Sydney Omarr; Edward R. Murrow
WEAK: Gianni Agnelli; Henri Matisse; Auguste Rodin; Al Unser; Rossano Brazzi; Ferdinand Foch; Melvin Belli; Yehudi Menuhin
EVENTS: Lee's Surrender at Appomattox; Chernobyl Nuclear Explosion; Ramstein Airshow Disaster; Franklin Roosevelt Wins First Election; (Apollo 11 Moon Landing).

☉   Ellen Burstyn; Carroll Righter; Willie Mays; Ira Progoff; South Carolina Secession; Mary Martin; Olga Worrall

☽   William K. Douglas; Lee's Surrender; J. Krishnamurti; Alexis Carrel

☿   Edmund Halley; Johnny Carson; Dave Garroway; Paul Cezanne

♀   Jackie Robinson; Giacomo Puccini; Fidel Castro; Alexis Carrel; Muh. Ali

♂   Bolsheviks Take Power; Norman Mailer; Elvis Presley; Sydney Omarr

♃   Jonathan Winters; George Patton; Willie Mays; Albert Speer; Robin Williams; Albert Schweitzer; Tom Jones

♄, A   Alan Leo; First A-Bomb Explosion; Percy Bys. Shelley; Sean Connery

♅   Harry Shoaf; Jackie Robinson; Ida Rolf; Rollo May; Dr. Tom Dooley

♆   Jacques Cousteau; Neil Diamond; Dr. Tom Dooley; Sally Ride; Fidel Castro; Liberace; Charles Kettering

♇   Teilhard de Chardin; Charles E. O. Carter; Sally Ride; Bob Newhart

☊   Israel Regardie; Grant Lewi; Vittorio DeSica; Paul Newman; Cheiro

M   Charles Kettering; J. Von Ribbentrop; Richard Byrd; Ivar Kreugar

SATURN/MIDHEAVEN   ♄/M

Basic Ideas:

A difficult and spartan early life sets the tone for your developing into a person who becomes determined to stand alone in life. You grow to find that much of your life is spent in taking a realistic look at self and capabilities, and developing and using these so people will notice your accomplishments and contributions. You like to start at levels which place you subordinate to others, but you are willing to work harder than most to surpass all. You find vindication and success only through much hard work, persistent application of your schooling or learning, and full dedication to self, work, and/or personal interests. The legacy you leave behind you endures, and you spend much time in early middle life trying to find the person you are and what your life's goals can be. Discipline becomes a close companion from an early age, and you find that you prefer solitude to friendships.

In Your Personal Life:

Thesis Becoming a better person through hard work and persistent dedication to learning about self and life; your role as a self-starter; added personal reserve and restraint about your achievements; you work for status.

Anti Worrying about what you have not done well; examining tasks to see if all have been completed perfectly; self-imposed restrictions which denote greater self-control; insecurity about receiving recognition for efforts.

In Your Relationships:

Thesis Appearing as a strong and steady person, but with a dependency need on another; a willingness to let your ambitions be subordinate to those of your partners; growing together in a meaningful relationship.

Anti Subordinating yourself even further into the needs of your partner; placing yourself in a dependent position where your desires are secondary; added personal rigidity and formality; sorrow or loss over a love.

With Body or Mind:

Seeking psychological counseling to find the person you are or should be; adopting personality restrictions or inhibitions in severe or damaging ways.

In Politics or Business:

Thesis Simplifies the purposes of an enterprise, and establishes goals that may be hard to meet; restrictions on the development of resources or businesses; formal rules or roles imposed on the executive branch.

Anti Restrictions on development within the enterprise; may end the struggle for independent activity after repression or colonialism; formal and strict rules for conducting transactions.

SATURN/MIDHEAVEN with Planets and Points

☉   Becoming the master of your own fate despite an early life which limited or restricted your growth or development; recognition for the work you do or are able to accomplish; driven to perform for praise.

☽   A restrictive but nurturing parent; stifled in your childhood; a family which dominates your early life; subordinating yourself to the needs of the family; traditional values with ordinary or plain starts; strict family values or ethics.

☿   Apply your intelligence toward making your position or mark in the world; an articulate, thinking, intelligent person who relies on logic and persistence to analyze situations; rigid formal schooling rules.

♀   Softening self-generated critical evaluations of self or others; feeling more worthwhile about your abilities and efforts; a love of music and the arts in special ways; personal pleasure as you age; a love of traditional music or art.

♂   Personal effort and energy put into growing and developing self; added struggles and intensity of the battles you face; courage and stamina for coping with life's various tests; a drive to succeed at work.

♃   Others to give you counsel and advice about your self-imposed limitations; advice on how to grow as a person; an avid reader and student; happiness about life's progress; growing social acumen.

♅   Emotional detachment when assessing interpersonal qualities and status; a scientific or sterile outlook for assessing events; friendships with serious astrologers or researchers; unusual ways to mark progress.

♆   Unnecessary fears about your alleged problems; added delusions that you can not easily cope with problems; increased needs to escape through drugs; inspiration achieved through maturity and discipline.

♇   A need to be in control at all times; great changes in life's conditions; a strong repression of your work or abilities by others; added will power to accomplish whatever it is you set your mind to do.

☊   Increased struggles to succeed in life; the importance of working with the people who can offer help or assistance; a need to work along with others and to share accomplishments and goals through them; dependency on people.

A   Focusing on achieving recognition for work done; a serious demeanor in your appearance; others see that you have had a formal and proper early training or education; you may relate well to only a few people.

SATURN/MIDHEAVEN CONCEPTS

A Strong Family Morality	A Respected Position	Defines Principles
Plans for Objectives	Early Frustrations	Disciplined Resolution
Comes Far in Life	Struggles with Life	Narrows Intentions
Cautious Attainment	Delays a Start in Life	Firm Principles
Becoming Secure in Life	Competent and Reliable	Limiting Plans
Prolonged Self-Restraint	Disciplined Methods	Narrows Expertise
A Few Ground Rules	Cautious Behavior	Plain Conclusions
Quiet Purposes	Realistic Expertise	Limits Distinction
Copes with Problems	Insufficient Justification	Few Self-Concepts
Training to be Vigilant	Utilitarian Coping	Economical Results
Restrained Recognition	Unhappy with Failure	Final Mastery
Cautious Self-Restraint	Perfects Behavior	Barely Copes with Life
Realistic Adjustments	Delays Learning Skills	Drab (Poor) Origins
Restricts Accomplishments	Restricts Outcomes	Limits Rewards

Selective Self-Restraint	Abbreviates Accomplishments
Endures and Continues Maturing	Poor Self-Management
Disciplined and Restrained	A Family Needing Discipline
Retards Personal Development	A Lack of Confirmation
Studies to Gain Expertise	A Strong Personal Identity
Orderly Reconciliations	Formal Learning and Growing
Disappointing Personal Growth	Conservative Behavior
Inhibits Maturation Processes	Principles of Self-Discipline
Sent to an Isolated Position	Legitimate Recognition
An Inferior Stature (Standing)	Slow, Steady Self-Integration
Endures with Self-Guidance	Adopts a Conservative Outlook
Gloomy about Plans for Life	Stifles Self-Restraint
Struggles to Become Mature	Responsible for Self-Growth
Slow, Steady Personal Growth	A Difficult Start in Life
Worries about Protecting Family	Prolongs Public Projection
Frustrated Learning and Growing	Respected Professional Growth
A Functional Career	Conscientious Workmanship
Slow Personal Development	Final Conclusions
Disappointing Results	Tedious Training
Obligated to Safeguarding	Limited Personal Assurances
Restrictive Self-Concepts	Uninteresting Experiences
Monotonous Rules of Conduct	Frustrating Outcomes
Perseveres despite Inadequacy	Becomes Older and Wiser
Worries over Finding Security	Pessimistic Results
Frustrating Fulfillment	Painstaking Proficiency
Becomes Bored with Life	Born into Simple Origins
Restrained by Family Standing	A Recognized Reputation
Formal Training	Realistic Starts
A Stable Family Origin	Simple Expertise

SATURN/MIDHEAVEN With Itself

♄ A need for additional preparation for planning your life and how to achieve your goals; lessened desire to seek deserved recognition for efforts or accomplishments; steady progress toward using the accepted traditional ways.

M Recognition for prior work accomplished; credits for work completed earlier; strong respect shown for important efforts; finding confirmation from experiences in life for your convictions and goals.

Significant Examples of People and Events Using Saturn/Midheaven

General: **STRONG:** Burl Ives; Louis Pasteur; Marc Edmund Jones; Ivar Kreugar; Steve Wozniak; Joachim Von Ribbentrop; Ada Lovelace Byron; William K. Douglas; Arthur Rimbaud; Manly Palmer Hall; Komar; Robert DeNiro
WEAK: Hank Williams; Friedrich Nietzsche; Scott Carpenter; Jim Thorpe; Percy B. Shelley; Earl Warren; David O. Selznik; Bob Newhart
EVENTS: George Washington's First Inauguration; S. Carolina Secession; Lewis & Clark Expedition starts; Mt. St. Helens Explosion; (Challenger Explosion).

☉ J. Von Ribbentrop; Albert Einstein; Ira Progoff; Lewis & Clark Exped. Starts

☽ Louis Pasteur; Carl Sandburg; Gus Grissom; Arthur Rimbaud; Henry Mancini; Jack Schwartz; Kareem Abdul-Jabbar

☿ Kareem Abdul-Jabbar; Stephen King; Neil Diamond; John McEnroe

♀ Benito Mussolini; Ritchie Valens; Lewis & Clark Exped.; Dick Gregory

♂ Neil Diamond; Ritchie Valens; Stephen Foster; John Glenn; H. Mancini

♃ First A-Bomb Explodes; Paul Gauguin; Walt Whitman; Albert Speer

♄, M Marc Edmund Jones; Henry Winkler; Jackie Robinson; Carl Sandburg

♅ Watergate Burglary; Paul Gauguin; Charles Kettering; Dick Gregory

♆ Manly Palmer Hall; Evel Knievel; Shirley Jones; Komar; Jimi Hendrix

♇ Arturo Toscanini; Marlon Brando; Sam Sheppard; Wm. Butler Yeats

☊ Steve Allen; Paramhansa Yogananda; John McEnroe; Thomas H. Huxley; John Glenn; Stephen Sondheim; Yehudi Menuhin

A John Fremont; Paul Joseph Goebbels; Alan Alda; Jacques Cousteau; Cheiro; Lindburgh Lands in Paris; Benito Mussolini

URANUS/NEPTUNE ♅/♆

Basic Ideas:
These themes symbolize indifference and rebelliousness combining with illusions and dreaminess, or your need for the new or novel blending with the mystical and imaginative. You may find it easy to walk away from or abandon people or activities which you no longer need, or to turn away from disagreements or places where confusion exists and to start upon new paths. You may also find that these motifs reflect circumstances where confusion arises in peculiar and unpredictable ways, that you have an urge to replace that which is worn out or weakened, or that ideas which are vague or subtle upset you and cause you to reconsider your involvement with them. These themes also show an impersonal view of your devotion to religious ideas, your initiative or participation in reforms which have lofty ideals, and your unusual ideas on the role of holiness or sanctity.

In Your Personal Life:
Thesis   You are insightful and inventive in ways which others are not; you have insight into mystical ideas and concepts; you act friendly toward those with whom you share worship.

Anti   You are not able to accept dissent or confusion and easily leave the people or places which create this; you can be deceptive with your disruption of people or events; an unfriendly attitude toward religions.

In Your Relationships:
Thesis   You need a partner who gives you great freedom and latitude of action; sharing revelations and insights on mysticism, astrology, and the occult is important to you; you need another person, yet need freedom also.

Anti   You allow your ideals of what the relationship can be to cloud your mind and ignore its reality; you give unusual devotion to others, but also demand periods of solitude and time to be within yourself and ideas.

With Body or Mind:
Unpredictable, abrupt reactions to drugs; shock or remission due to causes difficult to define; sudden insect bites or stings; tiredness; fungus infections.

In Politics or Business:
Thesis   Changes in social and political structures due to new ideals and dreams of the future; revolution or strikes which are focused on new ways of thinking; groups which form to exploit oil or chemical resources.

Anti   Sudden upsurges in the availability of illegal drugs; subversion using a new method of acquiring information; movements which diminish the power or authority of the nation's leadership or police systems.

URANUS/NEPTUNE with Planets and Points

☉   The motivation you get from insight and inspiration in dreams or meditations; the commitment you have to developing the "non-thinking" side of yourself; experience with directing confused people.

☽   Heightened sensitivity for the need to go within yourself for insight and inspiration; hesitation thru confusion with new processes; inconsistent results when you can not work where disagreement reigns.

☿   Increased need for meditation; sudden inspiration for plans you wish to develop; application of insight into new information or engineering techniques; artificial intelligence processes, ideas, and thoughts.

♀   Increased need for peaceful, pleasant surroundings and people; a need for music or art around you; the pleasure you derive from meditation, the occult, or astrology; your enjoyment from new age religions.

♂   Increased tolerance for unusual activities which become your source of inspiration and ideas; exiting quickly when disagreements upset you; unusual forms of mental stimulation, exercise, or activity.

♃   Need to be within yourself for inspiration and ideas; opinion formed on esoteric subjects; increased interest in the philosophy of the occult, astrology, or computing methods; inspiring metaphysical studies.

♄   Increased need for solitude and silence to gain inspiration; restricted ability to withdraw from unpleasant tasks or surroundings; restraint on how you can effect reforms using ideals which are too visionary.

♀   Inspirations for ideas which can change your world; the extreme destruction caused by disagreements or rebelliousness of those around you; your participation and support of these or similar methods.

☊   Enhanced ability to meet those people who are able to effect your ideas and dreams; the close ties you develop to leaders who introduce change through revolt or turmoil; your closeness with important religious leaders.

A   Enhanced ability to focus on the people or tasks you concentrate on; the conditions around you and how they affect your concentration and ability to generate ideas; your views of others gained through insight and inspiration.

M   The reputation you develop from your insight into ideas, gadgets, or people; your proficiency at being able to use the right side of your brain, and how you work to develop this talent; the restraint you place on half-baked ideas.

URANUS/NEPTUNE CONCEPTS

Unpredictable Weakness	Disruptive Omission	Sudden Neglect
Deviant Mysteries	Stirs up Fantasies	Unusual Imagination
Accidental Disregard	Unusual Shortcomings	Unplanned Laxity
Casual Confusion	Indifferent to Avoidance	Unique Disguises
Inspires a Rebellion	A Troubled Imagination	Sudden Omission
Indifferent to Carelessness	Abnormal Make-Believe	Resists Myths
Progressive Costumes	Stirs up Confusion	Disturbed by Weakness
Confused Astrologers	Disrupts Compliance	Sudden Disguises
Progressive Delusion	Extraordinary Deception	Resists Vagueness
Innovative Fraud	Unexplained Weakness	Casual Amends
Remarkable Shoddiness	Irregular Concealment	Upsetting Mysteries
Out of Place Daydreams	Changes Disguises	Irregular Faith

Innovative Acquiescence	Disinterested in the Weak
Indiscriminate Shoddiness	Lackadaisical Carelessness
Unique Inefficiency	Unpredictable Mysteries
Rebels against Laxity	Infrequent Musings
Mixes Astrology and the Occult	Progressive Impracticality
Nebulous Challenges	Modifies Imperfections
Undependable Inspiration	Rebels against Fantasies
Scientific Deceit	Exclusive Counterfeits
Accidental Indiscretion	Avoids Disruptions
Casual Compliance	An Uncustomary Blunder
Indifferent to Omissions	Unfriendly Confusion
Subtle Discrimination	Peculiar Disregard
Innovative Imagination	Distinctive Dreams
Irregular Incoherence	Unusual Submission
Random Shortcomings	Out of the Ordinary Myths
Disrupting Confinement	Noteworthy Compliance
Unprecedented Dilapidation	Revives a Perplexity
Remarkable Subtlety	Peculiar Fallacy
Special Shortcomings	Individual Indiscretions
Particular Visions	Unique Inspiration
Uncommon Enigmas	Weakens the Rebels
Odd Miracles	A Sudden Fantasy
Impersonal Atonement	Misleading Insight
Modern Nuances	Modifies Camouflage
Accidental Inspiration	Distinctive Neglect
Unshared Losses	Particular Tolerance
An Unpredicted Escape	Neglects Science
A Substitute for Faith	Subtle Transformations
Nebulous Friendliness	Confuses the Scientists
Inspires Astrologers or Mystics	Progressive Guilt
Modern Solicitation	Unusual Inspiration

URANUS/NEPTUNE With Itself

⛢ Additional needs for freedom and independence; breaking of routines which no longer suit; inability to recognize the difficulties which lie behind a task; resistance to change thru avoidance of confrontation.

♆ Using evasion and deception to remove yourself troubling situations; seeing an imaginative world as if it were real; the power to dream plans into fruition; a release from prior obligations to give assistance.

Significant Examples of People and Events Using Uranus/Neptune

General: **STRONG:** Jack Paar; Benito Mussolini; John Glenn; Shirley Jones; John Denver; Robert McNamara; Sam Peckinpah; Anne Murray; Arthur Ford; Stephen Sondheim; Friedrich Nietzsche; Jerry Reed; Hank Williams
WEAK: Nikola Tesla; Richard Byrd; Lawrence Welk; Evel Knievel; Edmund Halley; Robert DeNiro; Dr. Sam Sheppard; Richard Strauss
EVENTS: Woman's Suffrage Amendment Passed; USS Maine Explosion; Pearl Harbor Attack; George Washington's Inauguration; (RMS Titanic Hits Iceberg).

☉ Vincent Van Gogh; J. Meredith Enrolled; Abraham Lincoln; Dr. T. Dooley

☽ William Butler Yeats; Yehudi Menuhin; Sean Connery; Vittorio DeSica

☿ Enrico Caruso; Drew Pearson; Stephen Sondheim; S. Carpenter; Jn. Glenn

♀ Jack Paar; Winston Churchill; Art Linkletter; Bob Newhart; Louis Pasteur; Jean Paul Satre; Thomas H. Huxley

♂ Bobby Fischer; Erich M. Remarque; Richard Strauss; Jim Thorpe; Ivar Kreugar; Komar; Auguste Rodin; Henry Mancini

♃ Carl Sagan; Olga Worrall; Olivia Newton-John; Robin Williams; Steve Rosenbloom; Bob Fosse; Henry Kissinger; Ellen Burstyn

♄ Stephen King; Maurice Ravel; Jerry Rubin; Hugh Downs; USS Maine Expl.

⛢, ♆ Benito Mussolini; Bobby Fischer; John Lennon; Maurice Ravel; Enrico Caruso; USS Maine Explosion; Ernest Pyle

♇ Anne Murray; Henry Winkler; First A-Bomb Expl.; Cl. Debussy; A. Camus

☊ Harry Shoaf; Jack Paar; Arturo Toscanini; Paul Gauguin; USS Maine Explosion; Shirley Jones; Jacques Cousteau

A Mark Spitz; Marlon Brando; Benito Mussolini; Moshe Dayan; Bobby Fischer; Marc Edmund Jones; Cheiro; Glen Campbell

M Hugh Downs; Tommy Smothers; S. Peckinpah; Sigmund Freud; S. Foster

URANUS/PLUTO   ♅/♇

Basic Ideas:

Impulses to remain aloof, detached, and eccentric find intensity, concentration, corruption, and tyranny within this theme. You experience internal urges to create a unique and personal lifestyle away from all pressures to conform to the needs, demands, or wishes which others establish. You desire to concentrate on your own interests, and seek to be left alone with your ideas. You find it easy to resist anyone else's call, and may become obsessed with the ruin of anything that is not of your creation or design. You may become fanatic with secret desires for personal freedom, gain insight and create new but peculiar inventions, or nurture secret desires to reform lifestyles which do not conform to your ways. You may become obsessed with the misuse of anything, enjoy sexual invention and experimentation, and ignore the destruction of protected settings.

In Your Personal Life:

Thesis   You have a great need to be left alone; you develop ideas on how to improve on old habits; you desire to be in control of any activity which alters or changes the old and brings in the new.

Anti   You take pleasure at seeing the overthrow of any activity which marks the old order; you may become obsessed with manipulating people and processes; you have secret needs to change the lifestyles of other people.

In Your Relationships:

Thesis   You have a need for a freethinking partner who shares your views of how to avoid life's responsibilities; you enjoy inventing new forms of sexual pleasure; you like people who appreciate your need for freedom.

Anti   You find it difficult to relate to another because you have such strong desires to be your own person; you need great freedom, but also are not willing to relinquish your control over your partner's lifestyles.

With Body or Mind:

Stress reactions which cause colon spasms or problems; hemorrhoids; piles; abnormal cell regeneration; sudden toxic symptoms; drug dependencies.

In Politics or Business:

Thesis   Helps modernize and improve secretive agencies; new devices to allow the collection or analysis of secret information; revolutions in industrial management or practices to improve production, trade, or goods.

Anti   Violent upheavals or rioting which bring changes in government; intruders who cause disruptions of processes; strikes and labor movements which are intent on forcing changes; sudden new criminal acts.

URANUS/PLUTO with Planets and Points

⊙   Determination to pursue unusual subjects, in such fields as astrology, computers, artificial intelligence, etc.; extreme dedication to your own ideas to the exclusion of the rest of the world's interests and needs.

☽   Sensitivity to and awareness of the needs of others, despite desires to work alone; insight into tradition allows you to introduce new and unique ways for representing old methods in new explanations.

☿   Manual dexterity and adept thinking which helps you create in reality the ideas which form in your head; you discuss rationally your ideas about need for changes to the various activities you see in life.

♀   Added softness to the rough and unusual character you can show; you bring reform and newer, more effective ways of presenting art ideas; you can be cordial and courteous but still seek great changes in others.

♂   You can exhibit many forms of anger at others, and enjoy devising loud or disruptive activities to purposely make others feel uncomfortable; you can be impulsive, headstrong, or demanding when forcing your ways and ideas.

♃   Added insight into legal and political processes which you use for expressing ideas about reform and change; an excess of strong feelings about imposing major changes into the many various paths of life.

♄   Needs to appear rebellious are diminished but not dispelled; enhanced ability to persist despite obstacles on your path toward reform; you have many desires to be alone, and ask others to respect your solitude.

♆   You spend much time with your own dreams of what reality is and how the nonphysical and physical worlds operate; you enjoy astrology and the occult; you desire to use computers and new-age sciences

☊   You are drawn to others who have ideas similar to yours about how to change the world through new approaches; your association with others who share ideas similar to yours for new paths is enhanced with this contact.

A   An enhanced ability to focus on the kind of world which must grow out of today into tomorrow; you read others and their restlessness with the status quo; an increased need to appear unique as an individual.

M   The influence your family supplied in early life causes you to rebel at their lifestyles; you have a reputation about having unique ideas on how to live and you present various lifestyles which others do not yet envision.

URANUS/PLUTO CONCEPTS

Insight into Corruption
An Abnormal Friendliness
Arbitrary Intensity
Dismisses Challenges
Obsessed with Rebelling
Emotionless Corruption
Casual Destruction
Novel Admonishment
Resourceful Changes
A Disgraceful Rebel
Upsetting Curses
Remorse for Disruptions

Inventive Destruction
Rebels with Intensity
Uncommon Punishment
Impartial to Using Force
Refines Astrology
Irregular Retaliation
Sporadic Morbidity
Innovative Dishonesty
Unsolicited Remorse
Suspicious of Innovation
Fixed on Antagonism
Emotionless Intensity

Defies Corruption
Disruptive Chaos
Unshared Obsession
Decaying Novelties
Unique Intensity
Upsetting Suspicions
Bizarre Deaths
Unusual Intensity
Reckless Pursuit
Novel Corruption
Sudden Destruction
Unusual Infections

Accidental Accusations
Disinterested in Intensity
Indifferent to Compulsions
Distinctive Suspicion
Impersonal Purification
Infrequent Retaliation
Uncustomary Prosecution
Modern Morbidity
Indiscriminate Condemnation
Regulates Impurity
Astrological Intensity
A Distinctive Monopoly
Impersonal Suspicion
Unpredicted Reversals
Immune from Preoccupation
Detaches from Corruption
Unpredictable Crimes
Ignores Elimination
Individual Intensity
Indifferent to Death
Impartial to Retribution
Eccentric Restitution
Indiscriminate Wasting
New Forms of Innovation
Unpredictable Erasure
Impersonal Reproofs
Rebels against Corruption
Uncontrolled Crime
Defames the Disobedient
Indifferent when Using Force
Resourceful Destruction

Innovative Funerals
Unforeseen Elimination
Insight into Contamination
Condemns Astrology
Indifference to Using Poison
Defies Punishment
Uninhibited Admonishment
Disruptive Destruction
Uncommon Violence
Unique Destruction
Sudden Contamination
Revives Wilfullness
Uncontrolled Restitution
Insight into Obtaining Purity
A Voluntary Conversion
Weakens Regulations
Innovative Corruption
Changes Hiding Places
Unexplained Depression
Retaliates against Irregularities
Unsolicited Stealth
Immune from Catastrophe
Scientific Rebirth
A Disruptive Death
An Unusual Fixation
Novel Condemnation
Peculiar Adulterations
Resists Rediscovery
Sudden Intensity
Condemns a Revision
A Distinctive Funeral

URANUS/PLUTO With Itself

♅ You need to spend time with your ideas; you see the effects of personal and inner changes bought on by your attitudes and feelings about life; you need to separate yourself from the ordinary ideas of others.

♀ Experiencing inner changes which you build on to improve your outlook on life; you change or alter your lifestyle to bring in new ideas or activities; you change fundamental ways you operate or think.

Significant Examples of People and Events Using Uranus/Pluto

General: **STRONG:** Albert Einstein; Art Linkletter; Jean Francoise Millet; Charles E. O. Carter; Burl Ives; David O. Selznik; Arthur Ford; Dave Garroway; Lance Reventlow; Ulysses S. Grant; Grant Lewi; William K. Douglas
WEAK: Ellen Burstyn; Alan Alda; Edmund Halley; Walt Whitman; Stephen Sondheim; Steve Allen; Stonewall Jackson; Edgar Degas
EVENTS: RMS Titanic Hits Iceberg; First Medicare Patient Applies; Challenger Explosion; Kent State Shootings; (Woman's Suffrage Amendment Passed).

☉ Hermann Melville; Norman Mailer; Benjamin Disraeli; Evel Knievel

☽ Tom Jones; Edna Ferber; Charles E. O. Carter; Louis Pasteur; Ernest Hemingway; Liberace; Emperor Hirohito; Al Unser

☿ Charles E. O. Carter; Chernobyl Nuclear Explosion; Arnold Schwarzenegger; Jeddu Krishnamurti

♀ Chernobyl Nuclear Expl.; Henry Winkler; Drew Pearson; Manly P. Hall

♂ Jack Paar; Stephen Crane; Gustav Dore; Rollo May; Richard Alpert

♃ David Frost; Jean Francoise Millet; O. J. Simpson; Gus Grissom; RMS Titanic Hits Iceberg; Rex Harrison; Henry Winkler

♄ Transcontinental Railroad Completed; Erich Maria Remarque; Jack Nicklaus; Sigmund Freud; Guglielmo Marconi

♅, ♀ First Medicare Patient Accepted; Gianni Agnelli; John Glenn; Ira Progoff

♆ Willie Mays; Mario Andretti; Neil Diamond; Thomas H. Huxley; Jerry Reed; Guglielmo Marconi; Amadeo Modigliani

☊ J. F. Kennedy Shot; Bob Dylan; S. Carolina Secedes; Art Linkletter; Gr. Lewi

A Dave Garroway; Arnold Schwarzenegger; Ulysses S. Grant; Bob Newhart; Elton John; Olivia Newton-John

M Enrico Caruso; Albert Einstein; Arthur Ford; Elvis Presley; David Frost

URANUS/NODE ⛢/☊

Basic Ideas:

These themes combine your needs for expressing unexpected thoughts as well as meeting new people by offering opportunities to effect unusual or unforeseen alliances . You may gain some insight into how and why others form relationships, or how the cosmic process of attraction between people works. When you need certain people to appear in your life , you create the right external circumstances for this to happen. People who share unconventional views like yours, or others you meet who have similar insights into new ways of doing things are described here. Meetings with scientific or computer groups, and an urge to share insight into or study astrology with friends, are also shown here, as is any fuss you experience or initiate at meetings. You become more aware of sexual, intuitive, or former life bonding to others through the effects of these motifs.

In Your Personal Life:

Thesis   People you meet suddenly or unexpectedly who share a similar destiny; the peculiar or unique abilities you have for attracting friends; how others contact you about changing life's various situations around you.

Anti   The disruptions you cause to others because you are not happy with the present status within groups; your indifference to the help others are able to give you toward effecting your destiny.

In Your Relationships:

Thesis   Attracting people who have an astrological or scientific bent; unpredictable outcomes to chance meetings with others; enhanced ability for sexual contact with people who share similar interests.

Anti   Your inability to use the information and assistance which you receive from others who offer you their advice; indifference to sexual advances offered to you; any unpredictable behavior during friendly encounters.

With Body or Mind:

Sudden onset of complications due to stress in life; deafness as you close out any assistance from others; unusual social diseases or behavior; nerve blockage.

In Politics or Business:

Thesis   The changes which accompany new efforts to alter the direction of events; alliances which follow revolution or unexpected changes in leadership; help from others who assist with modernization activities.

Anti   Treaties for modernizing facilities which benefit another more; revolution for the effecting of popular changes; a society which does not appreciate modernizing; business changes which evolve with society.

URANUS/NODE with Planets and Points

☉ Acceptance of your plans for modernization; the dedication you put into being different from others during meetings and presentations; the impressions you leave after you have effected reforms.

☽ Heightened sensitivity and consideration when introducing changes; prompts some inconsistency in following plans for reform or change; the people's acceptance of your scientific or astrological ideas.

☿ Concentration on education and study before effecting change; grasping new or complicated scientific concepts and explaining them in ways that others can understand; scientific or astrological intelligence.

♀ A soft way of introducing your version of change into the world; novel ideas in music or the arts that you introduce; glamor which accompanies changes you initiate; satisfying sexual ties after encounters.

♂ Energy and impetus to push ahead with needed changes; strength to push ahead against any opposition to your ideas or insights; sexual attraction and love become intertwined themes in relationships.

♃ Fortunate connections which help others accept your ideas or insights; introducing new scientific or astrological theories; the publication of ideas or theories in respected journals; the mixing of sex and politics.

♄ Lengthy struggle to gain acceptance, but persistence in your efforts to have your theories discussed and used by others; developing astrological or scientific theories in isolation before presenting them.

♆ Mental or spiritual inspiration for developing important and new scientific or astrological ideas; presenting theories or ideas to your friends; some confusion about your ideas or work and its meaning; intuitive guidance.

♇ Revolutionary new scientific or astrological ideas which you present at the meetings you attend; creating extremely novel solutions or ways for streamlining old thinking; friends who put down your ideas or your work.

A A strong mental focus on the need for changing the world so that your ideas on how life operates become more popular; discussions you have with others about your theories and ideas; your need for feedback from others.

M The popularity and acclaim you achieve due to the acceptance of your ideas and theories; personal assurances you receive from those who share your destiny about the help and assistance you will receive from them.

URANUS/NODE CONCEPTS

Revising Old Habits
Sudden Ties to Others
Rebels against Alliances
Eccentric Criticism
Insight into Karma
Astrologers as Friends
Rebels at Consolidation
Resourceful Relatives
Chance Meetings with Others
Rethinks Familiarity
Exceptional Acquaintances
Meetings with Reformers

A Unique Life's Aim
Arbitrary Sequencing
Upsetting Separations
Unusual Groupings
Unique Acquaintances
Distinctive Sexual Ties
A Scientific Federation
An Unusual Life's Path
Connections to Innovators
Disruptive Circumstances
Challenging Opportunities
Modifies Cooperation

Unusual Karma
Revises Life's Aim
An Infrequent Backer
Insight into Criticism
Stirs up Sexual Ties
Resists Alliances
Unique Episodes
Noteworthy Occasions
Rids Self of Substitutes
Sudden Friendship
Set against Mergers
Regulates a Partition

Individual Attraction
Insight into your Destiny
Indifferent to Meetings
Impersonal Sexual Advances
Disruptive Exchanges
Contrived Presentations
Unique Forms of Attraction
Discloses Meetings with Others
Astrological Conventions
Rebels during Interchanges
Indifferent at Interviews
Breaks up Ties to Others
Peculiar Familiarity
Unsolicited Gatherings
Compromises Appointments
Insight during Presentations
Resourceful Preoccupation
Arranges to Find Others
Surprised by Supporters
Preoccupied with Innovation
Distinctive Diversions
Unconventional Obligations
A Personal History of Defiance
Unusual Acquaintances
Infrequent Meetings
Substitute Supporters
Unshared Discourses
Revises Annulments
Unpredicted Friendships
Scientific Conventions
Detaches from Backers

Attracted to New Friends
Compromises your Life's Aim
Unexpected Publicity
Unusual Group Connections
Rebels against Bureaucracy
Restless Acquaintances
Indifferent to Alliances
Scientific Interchanges
A Distinctive Life's Aim
Impersonal Familiarity
Starts to Learn Astrology
Innovative Performances
Infringes on Group Connections
Accidental Connections
Sources of Discontent
A Singular Sense of Destiny
Unpredictable Preoccupation
An Impersonal Separation
Exclusive Exchanges
Irregular Results
Awakens Gatherings
Peculiar Attachments
Resourceful Arrangements
Unplanned turns of Events
Aloof to Relationships
Irregular Supporters
Challenges Delaying Tactics
Upsets a Conference
Unexpected Separations
Individual Criticism
Unbiased Sources

URANUS/NODE With Itself

♅   You become more introspective about the role that others play in your life; you bring an air of creativity to the way you want to present yourself to others; irregular desires to be either alone or with people.

☊   Realizing the importance the opinions of others can play in helping you formulate and devise different ideas about your work, or how you should appear or work; you seek new friends who can be supportive.

Significant Examples of People and Events Using Uranus/Node

General: **STRONG:** Rupert Murdoch; John Lennon; Steve Wozniak; John F. Kennedy; Edouard Manet; Edgar Degas; Vida Blue; Hank Williams; Franklin Roosevelt; Winston Churchill; Jim Thorpe; Richard Alpert; Friedrich Nietzsche
WEAK: Adolf Hitler; Nikola Tesla; William K. Douglas; Robert Redford; Helen Reddy; Bob Dylan; Robert DeNiro; David O. Selznik
EVENTS: East Coast Power Blackout; Watergate Burglary Discovered; Alaskan Earthquake occurs; Mt. St. Helens Explosion; John F. Kennedy Shot; (First A-Bomb Explosion).

☉   Jim Thorpe; Steve Wozniak; Olivia Newton-John; Georg. Seurat; C. Sagan
☽   Richard Strauss; Albert Camus; John F. Kennedy Shot; Paul Newman; John Lennon; East Coast Power Blackout; Willie Brandt
☿   Arthur Rimbaud; Giacomo Puccini; Bobby Fischer; Chernobyl Nuclear Ex.
♀   Cheiro; Sir Alx. Fleming; Vittorio DeSica; Elvis Presley; First Medicare Pat.
♂   Gregory Peck; Lord Byron; Challenger Explosion; Joseph Joffre; Edward R. Murrow; Mick Jagger; Olga Worrall; Wayne Gretzky
♃   Vida Blue; Fidel Castro; Willie Mays; R. D. Laing; Charles E. O. Carter
♄   Steve Wozniak; Jean Paul Satre; Jean Francoise Millet; Stephen Foster; Audrey Hepburn; Amadeo Modigliani; John Glenn
♅, ☊   Edmund Halley; Ernest Pyle; Emp. Hirohito; Henry Kissinger; Gustav Dore; Rupert Murdoch; Richard Alpert; Glen Campbell
♆   Ivar Kreugar; Elvis Presley; John F. Kennedy; Edw. R. Murrow; Jn. Winters
♀   Carroll Righter; Arturo Toscanini; Shirley Jones; Kareem Abdul-Jabbar; Richard Chamberlain; Sean Connery
A   Sigmund Freud; Shirley Jones; Erich M. Remarque; Cheiro; Kareem Abdul-Jabbar; Burt Reynolds; Francisco Franco
M   Ulysses S. Grant; Guglielmo Marconi; John Denver; Jerry Rubin; Alan Alda; Bertrand Russell; John McEnroe

URANUS/ASCENDANT   ⛢/A

Basic Ideas:

These themes symbolize an ability to disrupt others in clever ways and for this you may be accused of having hints of mischief in your eyes. You are not one who can easily concentrate on only one subject at a time, and you have an interest in the study and application of many subjects, especially those with scientific, psychological, or astrological themes. You may be quiet one minute and then suddenly burst forth into the consciousness of others like a tornado. You have a strong need to appear as an individual and often do so with mannerisms or preferences that are completely unconscious. You enjoy being unconventional in subtle but prominent ways, and you have singular ways of imposing yourself on the inner ideas of others. You have a quick grasp of electromechanical devices and ideas. Playing with the newest electronic gadgetry consumes much of your attention and time.

In Your Personal Life:

Thesis   An ability to see life differently from others; you nurture a progressive outlook and are generally ahead of your time; your unconventional style prevents you from doing things as others come to expect of you.

Anti   A lonely eccentric, you find it hard to relate your sense of who you are to others; your unpredictable nature makes it hard for others to want to know you; disruptive improper attempts to bring notice to yourself.

In Your Relationships:

Thesis   You have a unique way of relating to or satisfying your partner's needs; you enjoy presenting new ways of showing affection; attracting others to your life who have unconventional or socially rebellious lifestyles.

Anti   An unpredictable manner of sharing close intimacy; needs for friendship instead of intimacy in relationships; peculiar reactions from others who are not able to understand your attitudes.

With Body or Mind:

Emphasizes finding mental balance and stability; added stress from having to conform to another's ideas and rules; rapid changes in body chemistry.

In Politics or Business:

Thesis   A unique sense of internal identity; modernization projects which are intended to seek notice from others; allying the enterprise with others in bonds of mutual support; election results which surprise everyone.

Anti   Causing disruptions in the affairs of others; use of verbal intimidation to garner support from others; a legislature which has difficulty relating to the reform or modernization ideas of its constituents.

URANUS/ASCENDANT with Planets and Points

☉   Your ability to be a unique person; notoriety for achievements or inventions in electromechanical fields; friendship with leaders and important persons; attempts to suppress unpredictable urges.

☽   An emotional need to be noticed and appreciated by others for the individual you are or for your achievements; sudden fluctuations in your emotional temperament; friendship with ordinary people.

☿   Clever ways of making your mark of uniqueness on life; questioning your need for being disruptive toward others; a hint of genius in your thinking and reasoning; rapid debates stirred up among friends.

♀   Softening the impact of a harsher side of self which can be very disruptive to others; appreciating the individuality in others; study and observation of what makes a good social relationship.

♂   Adding forcefulness to how you interrupt others; setting demands for your needs and requirements; your impulses to be different and disruptive; noisy ways of disruption; spirited agitation for your needs.

♃   A fortunate set of circumstances where others appreciate your innovation and uniqueness; new approaches to solving social or legal problems; new opinions which are contrary to accepted social norms.

♄   Disapproval about your sense of individuality; restraint on your improper antisocial urges; stifled desires to express your true inner self to others; becoming more cautious, thorough, and studious in a scientific way.

♆   Confusion about socially acceptable forms of behavior; the illusion that your uniqueness is appreciated; self-deception about the importance of pursuing your dreams; magic shows; turning to your idea of god for guidance.

♇   Others lower their opinion of you because you appear too unconventional; extremes and varieties of behavior peculiarities; eliminating habits others find distasteful; changes with morbid outcomes.

☊   An attraction to people who need to bring attention to themselves; presentations to others which have a unique flair or an unusual innovation in their manner of display; sudden and unexpected encounters with friends.

M   Using technology for understanding self or others; fulfillment of your aims even though unexpected changes occurred; agitation for an increase in safety and protection; experience prevails over disruption.

URANUS/ASCENDANT CONCEPTS

An Abnormal Experience
An Indifferent Demeanor
A Casual Disposition
Innovative Portrayals
Surprising Personal Beliefs
An Unshared Reality
Progressive Surroundings
Noteworthy Settings
A Remarkable Presence
Indifferent to Environs
Distinctive Surroundings
Defies Impressions

Modifies Mental Focus
Abnormal Pretenses
Extraordinary Responses
Imaginative Introspection
Pretends to be Special
Unique Surroundings
Insight into Others
Progressive Portrayal
Disruptive Mannerisms
An Uncustomary Context
Innovative Reactions
Unusual Points of View

Atypical Attitudes
Unique Leanings
Alters Awareness
Original Techniques
Unusual Opinions
Sudden Reactions
Irregular Views
Unstable Leanings
Upsetting Events
Alters Reality
Opposes Conditions
Revises Perceptions

Indifferent to Reality
Innovative Mannerisms
Unusual Impressions
Studies People using Astrology
Experiences by Accident
Unique Ways of Relating
Innovative Perceptions
Separates Personal Motives
Revises Responses to Others
Detached Recognition
A Disruptive Personal Style
Unusual Sense of Reality
Remarkable Circumstances
Unconventional Experiences
Perceives Chaotic Notions
Eccentric Attention Seeking
Disgruntled by Convention
Represses Upsetting Conditions
A Casual Sense of Reality
Shows Indifference to Settings
Insightful Reactions
Uncritical of People Roles
Individual Characteristics
Infrequent Observances
A Remarkable Consciousness
An Unpredictable Disposition
Indifferent to Rejoinders
Chaotic Scenarios
Disruptive Attention Seeking
Unplanned Insights
Emotionless Inhibitions

Rebels through Mannerisms
Focuses on Astrology
Resourceful Assessments
Unrestricted Portrayals
Sudden Consciousness
Modern Portrayals
Distinctive Reactions
Sudden Pretenses
Unrestricted Inhibitions
Unhampered by Opinions
Quirky Attention Seeking
Sees the Novel in People
Observes Personal Styles
Unconventional Traits
Astrological Perceptions
Scientific Inclinations
A Progressive Personal Style
Unsettling Impressions
Against Standard Responses
A Distinctive Personal Reality
Unpredictable Point of View
Surprising Sentiment
Noteworthy Peculiarities
Relates well to Astrologers
Remarkable Convictions
Insightful Perceptions
Independent Reactions
Unusual Personal Motivation
A Distinctive Personal Style
Sudden Insight into Others
A Unique Set of Beliefs

URANUS/ASCENDANT With Itself

♅ Increased personal restlessness; finding new ways to express individuality; adopting unusual methods of working; detachment from present environment; emphasis on the impersonal part of relating.

A Focusing on your need for uniquely relating to others; examining the differences between self and others; an impact on your ability to find personal privacy; concentration on measurement and production.

Significant Examples of People and Events Using Uranus/Ascendant

General: **STRONG:** Dr. Francis Regardie; Steve Wozniak; Edgar Degas; Jack Paar; Arthur Ford; Neil Diamond; Sam Peckinpah; Joseph Joffre; R. D. Laing; Franklin Roosevelt; Gustav Dore; Steve Rosenbloom; Billy Rose
WEAK: Dr. Tom Dooley; Dr. Sam Sheppard; Stephen Foster; Norman Mailer; Ralph Nader; Benjamin Disraeli; Glen Campbell; Emperor Hirohito
EVENTS: RMS Titanic Hits Iceberg; Franklin Roosevelt Wins First Election; John F. Kennedy Shot; First A-Bomb Explosion; (Alaskan Earthquake occurs).

☉ Steve Wozniak; Billy Rose; Gustav Dore; John F. Kennedy Shot; Neil Diamond; Bob Newhart; Shirley Jones

☽ Claude Debussy; Johnny Carson; Liberace; Merv Griffin; Drew Pearson

☿ Edgar Degas; Ellen Burstyn; Charles Addams; Paul Joseph Goebbels; Paul Newman; Pierre Renoir; O. J. Simpson

♀ Israel Regardie; Jackie Robinson; Woman's Suffrage Passed; Komar

♂ Charles Kettering; Johann Von Goethe; Art Linkletter; Evel Knievel

♃ Merv Griffin; Willie Brandt; Woman's Suffrage OK'd; R. Chamberlain

♄ Giacomo Puccini; Paul Gauguin; Gustav Dore; J. Krishnamurti; Shir. Jones

♅, A Chernobyl Explosion; Bjorn Borg; Ada Lovelace Byron; J. Krishnamurti

♆ Henry Kissinger; Sam Peckinpah; Bobby Fischer; John Paul I; David O. Selznik; Muhammad Ali; Benito Mussolini

♀ Earl Warren; Arthur Rimbaud; John Denver; Cheiro; Steve Wozniak

☊ Joachim Von Ribbentrop; Percy Bysshe Shelley; Ralph Waldo Emerson

M Anne Murray; Sam Peckinpah; Apollo 11 Moon Landing; R. D. Laing

URANUS/MIDHEAVEN ⛢/M

Basic Ideas:

This combination suggests that not all of life is laid out in well-defined patterns and goals. Through these themes you learn to adjust to the rapidly changing panorama of life and adapt yourself to ever changing situations. This pattern also shows how and where you are able to excel in areas like engineering, mechanics, electricity, computers, information theory and its application, or the use of astrology as a tool for helping yourself understand stages of life. You may find that you have an increased awareness of or need for scientific or engineering gadgetry. You may feel you need added personal freedom or need to retreat from others. Your tendency to be independent, or rebel at situations which force you to conform, is heightened. These points may bring you sudden recognition, or indicate unusual work talents or expertise within your occupation. You may achieve sudden or unwanted notoriety.

In Your Personal Life:

Thesis   Urge to consider unusual or uncommon pursuits and practices; a need to investigate different ideas; gaining renown or expertise in unusual fields;opening yourself to new ideas, habits, or occupations.

Anti   You are marked as a rebellious and uncontrollable person who wishes to be left alone when busy; many peculiar concepts about who you are and what you should do in life; agitating for increased freedom.

In Your Relationships:

Thesis   Realizing the importance of having a relationship; pursuing friendship rather than intimacy with your partner; added needs for people who have unusual work habits or occupations to share your life and time.

Anti   You appear indifferent to affection and it is difficult to tie yourself to one person in a relationship; you need and demand freedom and find it hard to make commitments to other people.

With Body or Mind:

Stress in your work environment; a stubbornness or resistance to change; varicose veins; injuries to the lower legs; muscle crampings.

In Politics or Business:

Thesis   Reform as a national goal; a new legislative platform calling for correction of old policies and people; social changes force leadership to new ways of looking at old policies or practices.

Anti   Radical movements which prompt changes in the method of enforcing policy; modernization movements which begin with labor unrest; strife which forces new internal policy or methods; unruly scientists.

URANUS/MIDHEAVEN with Planets and Points

☉ Determination to proceed despite opposition to your ideas or plans; added personal power and resolve to continue with your independent ways; successful forces pushing for added freedom or reform.

☽ Care and concern about the impact your ideas may have; added inner uncertainty about paths to success; vacillating on how to proceed with plans; demands for more isolation and personal freedom from people.

☿ A greater mental cleverness and variety of expression; being creative and inventive when expressing yourself; great creativity and insight into learning methods; gaining scholarly notoriety for past endeavors.

♀ Increased creativity and imagination in areas like music or the arts; experimenting with synthetic forms of art or music; using machines to assist you in expressing your ideas or thoughts in music, art, or love.

♂ Increased energy for pursuing your ideas despite opposition or resistance; mechanical skills and ability to make objects or inventions; rebellious and pushy, you take out your aggressions on others.

♃ Ability to use electronic means to publish ideas; success in pursuing innovative work or ideas; others notice your contributions and assign appropriate credit to you; success for social modernization efforts.

♄ An added need to do tasks alone and without interference or relief from others; lessened rewards for tasks done, but increased reputation as a solid and reliable worker; new pitfalls while working.

♆ Native creativity and desire to produce results which are new or different; indifference about how these effects are introduced or presented; enlightened creativity by using modern forms of expression.

♇ You could achieve worldwide fame and recognition for your efforts, or be dropped alone and unnoticed to the depths of despair; added personal intensity put into work efforts; possible disgrace at work.

☊ Finding friends and allies who are invaluable to you; going to much effort to apply your political talents wisely; becoming accustomed to using the bureaucracy for your own ends; becoming a good opportunist.

A Concentrating on your projects and becoming a good judge of the people you meet; an increasing reputation for being a personally independent and freedom loving person who needs much recognition and personal space.

URANUS/MIDHEAVEN CONCEPTS

Emotionless Coping	Set against Credentials	Innovative Starts
Modified Intentions	Detaches from Objectives	A Limited Beginning
Unregulated Workmanship	Distinctive Assurances	Revises Principles
Infrequent Protection	Atypical Expertise	Ignores Mastery
A Remarkable Reputation	Modifies Regrets	Upset by Reactions
Indifferent to Principles	Uncontrolled Behavior	Disrupts Standards
Peculiar Self-Restraint	Regulates Career	Upsetting Experiences
Extraordinary Mastery	Impartial to Integration	Unique Intentions
Peculiar Authorization	Sudden Recognition	A Distinctive Infancy
Weird Respectability	Innovative Fulfillment	Unplanned Outcomes
Insight into Principles	Remarkable Origins	Irregular Integrity
Defies the Experts	Casual Protection	Peculiar Rewards

Remarkable Personal Growth	Voluntary Self-Restraint
Unfriendly and Matures Slowly	Revises Guiding Philosophy
Impartial to Credentials	Sudden Self-Discipline
Revises Earlier ways of Living	Out of the Ordinary Principles
Insight into How to Mature	Unexpected Rules of Conduct
Indifference to Conscience	Novel ways of Training
Unusual Workmanship	Progresses using Computers
Reputed to act Impersonally	Unhampered Attainments
Atypical ways of Coping	Opposes Personal Development
Unpredictable Results	Unshared Recognition
Modernizes Attitudes	Exposure to Astrologers
Uncustomary Stature (Standing)	Indifferent to Qualifications
Rebels against Standards	Surprising Personal Reserve
Unpredictable Self-Restraint	Unique Expertise
Indifferent to Credentials	Irregular Rules of Conduct
Recognition as an Astrologer	Respect as a Scientist
Uncommon Personal Growth	Challenges the Experts
Irregular Proficiency	Original Training
Novel Learning and Growing	Unusual Expertise
Distinctive Needs for Security	Unique Credentials
Uncontrolled Conduct	Novel Self-Restraint
Weird Self-Concepts	Progressive Rewards
Abrupt Accomplishments	Eccentric Conduct
Exclusive Experiences	Distinctive Guiding Principles
Changes Life through Experiences	Unpredictable Advancement
Upsets Reputation	Irregular Recognition
Unusual Learning and Growing	A Surprising Turn of Events
Impartial to Rules of Conduct	Resists Self-Restraint
Remarkable Persevering	Discourteous Respectability
Unusual Experiences	A Change in Basic Attitudes
Agitates over Assurances	Disinterested in Experience

URANUS/MIDHEAVEN With Itself

⛢ Realizing that there are parts to your personality which need adjusting; desiring to change your present lifestyle; seeing new ways of living and becoming more like the person you want to be remembered.

M Highlighted need to achieve recognition and confirmation for ideas and contributions; working thru consequences of activities to ensure that past, outstanding issues are resolved; rewards for scientific work.

Significant Examples of People and Events Using Uranus/Midheaven

General: **STRONG:** Paul Newman; Tom Jones; Claude Debussy; Stephen Crane; Thomas H. Huxley; Liberace; Muhammad Ali; Jack Schwartz; Lawrence Welk; Manly Palmer Hall; Emperor Hirohito; Herman Melville; Maurice Ravel
WEAK: Henry Winkler; Lance Reventlow; Drew Pearson; Jack Paar; Sally Ride; Jimi Hendrix; Yehudi Menuhin; Bob Hope
EVENTS: Nixon's Resignation; Lindburgh Lands in Paris; USS Maine Explosion; East Coast Power Blackout; Chernobyl Nuclear Explosion; (First Atomic Bomb Explosion).

☉ Woman's Suffrage OK'd; Audrey Hepburn; Abraham Lincoln; S. Wozniak

☽ Chernobyl Nuclear Explosion; John Dillinger; Tom Jones; Emperor Hirohito; Robin Williams; Rollo May

☿ Ulysses S. Grant; Liberace; Paul Newman; Thomas H. Huxley; Evel Knievel; Arthur Ford; Stephen Spielberg

♀ Nixon's Resignation; Paul Joseph Goebbels; Nikola Tesla; R. Chamberlain

♂ O. J. Simpson; Pres. Nixon's Resignation; Lindburgh Lands in Paris; Gregory Peck; Maurice Ravel; Giacomo Puccini

♃ Marlon Brando; Albert Camus; Sydney Omarr; Francisco Franco; A-Bomb

♄ Paul Newman; Mt. St. Helens; Chas. E. O. Carter; Helen Reddy; M. E. Jones

⛢, M Earl Warren; Stephen Crane; Charles Addams; Maurice Ravel; S. Koufax

♆ Nikola Tesla; Enrico Fermi; Johann Von Goethe; Sydn. Omarr; H. Matisse

♇ Charles E. O. Carter; Edward R. Murrow; Ada Lovelace Byron; Nikola Tesla; Gregory Peck; David Frost

☊ Transcont. RR done; Alex. Graham Bell; Jackie Robinson; Mario Andretti

A Stephen Sondheim; Muhammad Ali; Adolf Hitler; Steve Allen; Bjorn Borg; Sean Connery; Cheiro

NEPTUNE/PLUTO   Ψ/♇

Basic Ideas:

Looseness and relaxation meet seething and intensity, and these themes may indicate that you ignore or neglect the preoccupation you have had with matters which previously absorbed your interests. You may study mysticism or the occult arts for their ability to help you maintain control of self or others. You may find that your need for sexual fulfillment diminishes. You may seek out new themes for your idealism, use drugs which provide artificial stimulation, or revisit your feelings about the nature of reality or your life's purposes. Your decisions to start projects or matters anew, neglect of your basic passions or desires, or any dramatic change in your intensity to pursue goals can also start here. Feelings of ambiguity about your aims or goals, or inner attitudes toward the necessity for certain forms of reality (like a job, a career, a home, marriage, etc.) may also be confronted.

In Your Personal Life:

Thesis   Transforming your life by abandoning pursuits which are innately disruptive to your aims; using artificial means (drugs) to speed up your self-growth processes; study of occult ideas for achieving self-mastery.

Anti   Abandoning anything because you feel that there is little or no hope for this in yo͟   ͟fe; allowing ambiguity or helpless feelings to cloud y͟   ͟s for progress toward goals; equating decay with pro͟   ͟n life.

In Your Relationships:

Thesis   Using ideas from others to help you to understand the role of relationships in your life; taking the best of what others can bring you for creating new mutual plans and/or goals for future progress together in life.

Anti   Giving in to needs for an escape from reality when this course of action destroys what is left of your self-esteem within a relationship; confusion over the roles that you or your partner should practice.

With Body or Mind:

Extreme reactions to drugs; weakness in the endocrine gland system; extreme cell formation or regeneration; body changes due to a lack of caring.

In Politics or Business:

Thesis   Creating new ideals for the power bases within any enterprise; calls for new measures for protection from natural disasters; new ideas in waste processing, pollution control, mass medical care, or psychiatry.

Anti   Controls over centers of political power; organized crime; activities involving plans for mutual destruction; subversion within security agencies; breakdowns in health, medical, or social care.

NEPTUNE/PLUTO with Planets and Points

☉ Transforming your life to shortcut, alter, or otherwise change normal or existing patterns of personal growth; your sense of determination to progress on your own with or without artificial supports or activities.

☽ You bring increasing care to transforming the lives of self or others for emotional betterment; added need to purchase devices, drugs, or other means to transform present reality ideas; need for short escapes.

☿ Needs to educate or enlighten yourself about processes which cause change; learning how to create ways to gain control or power; gathering thoughts and information about transforming your lifestyle.

♀ Demands to escape the pressures of living by using drugs or other reality bending tools; the use of music or art to describe feelings of helplessness about being able to change society or regain lost love.

♂ Potential use of drugs or artificial devices to speed up or alter your life; added compulsion to use violence to achieve your dreams; hostility emphasized by any imminent destructive or punishing activity.

♃ Increased need to find a better way to spend your life; desire to use drugs; improving your mental state but only by the neglect of others; expanded desires to enjoy a better future; social or political pressures.

♄ Bringing a sense of reality and discipline to efforts you undertake to alter old habit patterns and begin anew; frustrations encountered in moving yourself away from dependencies on those things which alter your reality.

♅ Emphasizes unusual means to escape from or change reality; rebellion against artificial supports or pursuits; adds to impersonal attitudes about any destructive or antisocial activities; tendencies to go to extremes with drugs.

☊ Meeting others who are able to show you how to implement your ideas for better living; vague or unrealistic associations with criminal elements; friends who are able to relate to your needs for changes in life.

A A focus on your need to experience and work thru the various kinds of changes you experience; a deep, penetrating study of what reality can be and how it can be altered to fit whatever context you desire.

M Adjusting your personal aims or ambitions about changing yourself; pushing ahead to make life better for yourself or those you cared for; added demands to be noticed by others for your self-growth; worldly revolutions.

NEPTUNE/PLUTO CONCEPTS

Abnormal Dreams
Draining Impoverishment
Hidden Inspirations
Abnormal Punishment
Inefficient Purification
A Terminal Weakness
Insignificant Destruction
Inspires Destruction
Confused Fanatics
Secretive Illusions
Imaginary Concealment
Concedes Suspicion

Avoids Conclusions
Imaginary Punishment
Compulsions to Abandon
Concealed Mysteries
Wasting Depletion
A Release from Morbidity
Secret Deceptions
Rediscovers Deception
Mixed up Violence
Artificial Destruction
Inspires Decadence
Avoids Corruption

Imaginary Power
Hides Neglect
Intense Nebulousness
Artificial Decadence
Imaginary Intensity
Prompts Suspicion
Wasteful Decadence
Merciful Duress
A False Mystic
Weak and Exhausted
Removes Guilt
Stops Adulterating

Enmeshed in Perversion
The End of Compassion
Insignificant Intensity
Confusion with Constraints
Frivolous Dismissal
Imaginary Destruction
An Unreasonable Monopoly
Confused by Punishment
Disjointed Destruction
An End to Insignificance
Disguised at Funerals
A Contrived Rediscovery
Loosens Oppression
A Lack of Prosecution
Confused by Reversals
Dreams of Transformation
Incomplete Prosecution
Inappropriate Corruption
Confusion over a Censure
Fanatical about Artificial Means
Assumes Completion
Frivolous Condemnation
Unreasonable Overhauls
Pretended Intensity
Mystical Frenzy
Compassionate Punishment
Improbable Evolution
Lessens Contamination
Avoids Prosecution
A Speculative Use of Force
Covers Up Control

Mystical Purification
Inspires Remorse
Temporary Waste Products
Retaliation is Impossible
Punished for Abandoning
An Obsession to Avoid
Dishonest Mystics
Fictitious Elimination
Condemns Waste
Temptations to Renovate
Dubious Defamation
Impractical Adulteration
A Flimsy Accusation
Suspicious of Ambiguities
Purifies Wastes
Wasted Punishment
Suspicious and Confused
Tolerates Retaliation
Impractical Cleansing
Concealed Hatred
Illusive Suspicions
Punishment for Garbles
Corrects a Weakness
Inspires a Compulsion
An Improbable Conclusion
Unimaginable Transition
Destruction of a Romance
Neglects the Ending
Avoids all Extremes
Temporary Destruction
Meaningless Subversion

NEPTUNE/PLUTO With Itself

Ψ Weakened intensity and drive to use others, their work, or their skills; being mislead about the purposes or intentions of others; dreams for power or passion; a letting go of power previously held or wielded.

♀ Being pushed to extremes when events have gone too far; disfavor from others for avoiding punishment due; impurity in systems which are designed to remove contaminants; subdues violent discharges.

Significant Examples of People and Events Using Neptune/Pluto

General: **STRONG:** Alexander Graham Bell; Erwin Rommel; Jeddu Krishnamurti; Nikola Tesla; John F. Kennedy; Jackie Robinson; Rupert Murdoch; John Paul I; Dane Rudhyar; Sam Peckinpah; Paul Cezanne; Mark Spitz
WEAK: Francis Regardie; Manly Palmer Hall; Benito Mussolini; Sir Alex. Fleming; Edna Ferber; Richard Chamberlain; Charles Kettering
EVENTS: Lindburgh Lands in Paris; Transcontinental Railroad Completed; Mt. St. Helens Explosion; Pres. Nixon's Resignation; (Challenger Explosion).

☉ Jean Paul Satre; John Glenn; Franklin D. Roosevelt Wins Election; Gregory Peck; John Fremont; Peter Max

☽ Henry Winkler; Paul Cezanne; Rupert Murdoch; Wayne Gretzky

☿ Rosanno Brazzi; Olivia Newton-John; Merv Griffin; Challenger Explosion; Abraham Lincoln

♀ Burl Ives; Ritchie Valens; Erwin Rommel; John Glenn; Richard Strauss

♂ Paul Gauguin; Percy Bysshe Shelley; Ritchie Valens; Dane Rudhyar

♃ Erwin Rommel; Percy Bysshe Shelley; Transcon. RR Done; W. Churchill

♄ Sam Sheppard; Stephen Crane; Albert Speer; Mario Andretti; Henry Mancini; Winston Churchill

♅ Bob Newhart; Richard Byrd; Wayne Gretzky; Thomas H. Huxley

Ψ, ♀ Erwin Rommel; Hermann Goering; P. Yogananda; Francisco Franco

☊ Tommy Smothers; Percy Bysshe Shelley; Steven Spielberg; William Butler Yeats; Arthur Ford

A Bertrand Russell; Claude Debussy; Grant Lewi; Franklin Roosevelt Wins His First Election; Edward R. Murrow

M Ervin Nyiregyhazi; Dane Rudhyar; Lawrence Welk; Marlon Brando

NEPTUNE/NODE   Ψ/☊

Basic Ideas:

These themes indicate your retreat from the friendship, advice, and counsel of others to a more private world where you hold the exclusive membership. When you need the time and the space to be with yourself away from the influence of others, when you need an opportunity to be by yourself, or when you need to be free from the ties and obligations that others create, then you can draw upon the power of these patterns. They denote confusion about the intentions of others, the way you shy away from and intentionally avoid meetings with associates, and your opportunities to gather friends together for inspiring meetings or ventures. When you exhibit shortcomings due to meeting others, when confusion abounds within groups or clubs, or when deceit and misleading arguments are used during or about such exchanges, then these issues may be active and working.

In Your Personal Life:

Thesis   Examining yourself and taking the time to isolate your feelings from other influences; influencing your friends and exciting them about the dreams and visions you are experiencing.

Anti   Retreat from others when you really need their counsel and advice; the urges to avoid those you should not meet; allows fantasizing about what people can be rather than seeing what they are.

In Your Relationships:

Thesis   Enhanced feelings of tenderness and romance for another, but hinderance in your ability to express these; an element of mystical contact and a sense of 'soul companionship' with or from your partner.

Anti   Added need to retreat from or use excuses for avoiding contact during times of difficulties; excuses for using drugs as your means for not having to relate to others; avoiding confrontations with partner.

With Body or Mind:

Use of drugs to isolate self from society; subjugating yourself to the influence of another; weakens the body's joints, ligaments, or connecting tissues.

In Politics or Business:

Thesis   A leadership which is unwilling or unable to consider the demands of its people; ideals or national glamor as an excuse for neglecting the growth and progress demands of the population or important groups.

Anti   Spies or terrorists which enter for villainous purposes; drug policies which avoid important concerns; an ill-adapted and inadequate hospital or medical care system; scandals caused by foreign concerns.

NEPTUNE/NODE with Planets and Points

☉   Encouragement to be your own person in deciding what influences you will or will not accept from other people; determination to be basic and original in your own interpretation of which paths to travel in life.

☽   Increased needs to isolate yourself from others; fluctuating attitudes toward staying with or avoiding others; increased needs for romance and escapism; enhanced intuition; attracting psychic women.

☿   Seeking more impersonal means of communicating, such as by telephone or letter as opposed to face-to-face; needs for explanations about your reclusiveness and isolation; avoiding communicating.

♀   Added contentment and satisfaction when you find time to be alone with yourself; increased needs to pamper and indulge your personal retreats with comfortable, tasteful surroundings, and music, art, etc.

♂   An insistant demand to remain isolated from others; angry reactions from within to others who place too much demand on your time or space; active defense to be left alone in your private, personal world.

♃   Aspirations and yearnings to expand your thoughts and beliefs about what life is and what your goals in life should be; much thinking and inner exploration about the meaning of life, religion, soul, god, reincarnation, etc.

♄   Added stability in your planning for what you want from life, but also an added need for isolation; increased ideas that you need only a very few close friends; enjoyment of isolation and solitude become more tolerable for you.

♅   A tendency to be disruptive and agitated by the actions of other people; sudden displacement and then isolation from associates; inspiration and progress for scientific, occult, engineering, etc. work attempted.

♇   Increased needs to isolate yourself from the influences of society; willingness to use strong destructive forces to protect your privacy and isolation if necessary; suffering depressions alone and silently.

A   Increased ideas that you do best when you are alone; ignoring the reactions and attitudes of people you meet; mentally repressing outside influences and concentrating more fully on your own needs.

M   Doing your best self-evaluation and coping with your problems and worries when alone and away from people's influences and distractions; increased enjoyment in gaining inspiration from the works of others as you mature.

NEPTUNE/NODE CONCEPTS

A Confusing Bureaucracy
Misleading Presentations
Unintelligible Exhibitions
A Flawed Sense of Destiny
Illusory Ties to Others
Neglects Acquaintances
Inspiring Exhibits
Awkward Separations
Unsure of Life's Aim
Confusing Discourses
Frivolous Companions
Neglects Publicity

Confused by Life's Aim
Dreams of Relationships
Abandons New Habits
Inspires Separations
Illogical Interviews
Unreasonable Barriers
Garbled Interviews
Hidden Opportunities
Fading Attachments
Inspiring Approaches
Devoted to Companions
Evasive Supporters

Artificial Barriers
Frivolous Mergers
Weakens Results
Illusive Life's Aim
Weak Presentations
Inspires New Habits
Evades Criticism
Abandons Friends
Mystical Ridding
Dubious Processes
Unclear Karma
Ignores Friends

Envisions Connections to Others
Inefficient Ways of Meeting
Defrauded by Supporters
Groups which use Pretenses
An Illusion of Familiarity
Mystical Methods of Attraction
Duped by Presentations
Unreal Meetings with Others
Neglects Obligations
Deceived by Close Friends
Confusion at Meetings
Unsure during Interviews
Visionary about Life's Destiny
Inspires Joint Ventures
Conceals Sexual Ties
Neglects Meetings with Others
Mysterious Delaying Tactics
Misuse of an Annulment
Confused about Sexual Ties
Mislead through Obligations
Unexpected Meetings
Illusive during Interviews
Inspired by Childhood
Confused by Acquaintances
Envisions Alliances
Inconclusive Criticism
Unrecognized Assemblies
Has Sexual Visions
Difficult to Find Others
Deceit during Meetings
Muddled Exchanges

Inspired with Life's Aim
Abandons Others and Separates
Contrived Demonstrations
Awkward Sexual Ties
Artificial Alliances
The Mysteries of Karma
Unintelligible Treaties
Evades Life's Aim
Miraculous Connections
Uncertainty from Bureaucracy
Unconvincing Interchanges
Mysterious New Habits
Weakens Ties to Others
Lax at Meetings with Others
Deceives by Dividing
Vague about Obligations
An Unexplained Opportunity
Coalitions which Disappear
Dishonesty in Segregation
Inappropriate Ties to Others
Eludes Familiar People
Mystical Associates
Makes up Ties to Others
Dreams about Delays
Pious Familiarity
Inefficient Passageways
Separates Out the Weak
Allied through Joint Visions
Dreams of Separation
Dreams about Life's Aim
Evasive Presentations

NEPTUNE/NODE With Itself

Ψ   Indecision about life's direction; incorporating evasion of others as a part of reality; avoiding or neglecting those who offer help; a lack of knowledge about where to turn for help; avoiding help offered.

☊   Meeting inspiring and knowledgeable people who offer fresh perspectives or insight; increased attraction to groups who have a mystical, religious, or occult orientation; increased desires to meet religious or spiritual persons.

Significant Examples of People and Events Using Neptune/Node

General: **STRONG:** Dr. Francis Regardie; Sir William Crookes; Ralph Nader; Yehudi Menuhin; Henri Matisse; Bjorn Borg; Bob Hope; Percy Bysshe Shelley; Rex Harrison; Nikola Tesla; Steven Spielberg; Charles Steinmetz; Lance Reventlow
     WEAK: Elton John; Norman Mailer; John McEnroe; Hugh Downs; Burl Ives; Edmund Halley; Albert Einstein; Tom Jones
     EVENTS: President Nixon's Resignation; Bolsheviks Seize Power; Alaskan Earthquake; Titanic Hits Iceberg; (Lewis & Clark Expedition starts).

☉   Olga Worrall; Charles Steinmetz; Hermann Goering; Ralph W. Emerson

☽   Lawrence Welk; Sam Peckinpah; Dave Garroway; Georges Seurat

☿   Bob Fosse; Sean Connery; Gus Grissom; David O. Selznik; Albert Speer

♀   Sam Peckinpah; South Carolina Secedes; Liberace; Arthur Ford; Sean Connery; Thomas H. Huxley; Audrey Hepburn

♂   Sir Laurence Olivier; Sir Alex. Fleming; John Denver; Dick Gregory

♃   Manly Palmer Hall; Dick Gregory; Mick Jagger; Gregory Peck; U. S. Grant

♄   Jeddu Krishnamurti; Ramstein Airshow Crash; Nikola Tesla; Dick Gregory; Muhammed Ali; Ervin Nyiregyhazi

♅   Tommy Smothers; John Denver; Bolshevik's Seize Power; Arthur Godfrey; Stonewall Jackson; Robert DeNiro

Ψ, ☊   Rex Harrison; Jimmy Carter; Nixon's Resignation; Israel Regardie; Edna Ferber; Drew Pearson; Carl Sandburg

♀   John F. Kennedy Shot; Alaskan Earthquake; Earl Warren; Edgar Degas; Liberace; Watergate Burglary Discovered

A   Liberace; Paul Cezanne; Wright Brothers First Flight; Jack Nicklaus; Ralph Nader; Gregory Peck; Jimmy Carter

M   Charles Steinmetz; Anne Murray; Richard Chamberlain; Jerry Reed

NEPTUNE/ASCENDANT   Ψ/A

Basic Ideas:

These themes indicated that you overlook the reality of what is happening before you and rely instead on what you believe the situation should be. You easily overlook what is obvious to others about their human feelings, intentions, needs, or processes. These motifs show the use of intuition to tune in to the intentions and motivations of others. You learn to trust your instincts, body language or attitudes, or nuances of speech more than you trust the sensory facts which others present. You encourage yourself to build a false sense of reality about others. You learn you can inspire or charm others easily and present your views of reality in ways that uplift and inspire others. You also appear more elusive and hard to pin down, and you may change or shift moods rapidly. You find it easy to dismiss or walk away from people or situations which you no longer want or need.

In Your Personal Life:

Thesis Creating a believable reality with only your ideas; an enhanced ability to receive and process intuitive rather than sensory clues about the disposition of others, or possibilities for future events.

Anti Enhances the reality of the fiction you like to build inside your mind; helps you to deceive or lie to others in a convincing way; helps you rely more on your intuition of others than the reality of what they present.

In Your Relationships:

Thesis Reading the motives behind your partner's activities; being less than honest about interpreting feelings within a relationship; enhanced feelings of a mystical oneness with your partner or friends.

Anti Looking away from the reality of your relationship and distorting ideas about your compatibility; beginning to believe the fiction of your romantic ideas; added ability to deceive your partners.

With Body or Mind:

Enhanced needs for drugs to alter reality; an affinity or craving for different stimulants or depressants (nicotine, caffeine, alcohol, marijuana, etc.).

In Politics or Business:

Thesis Responding to the ideals of the people; deluding others about the current state of the economy or affairs; scandals which are in the news; the need for additional glamor or glory; distortions of the facts.

Anti Subversion by those who are trusted and close to operational aspects; internal decay or neglect of hospital or health care systems; misleading news concerning the intentions; overlooking decay or neglect.

NEPTUNE/ASCENDANT with Planets and Points

☉   Effectively using your perceptive powers to read and understand the motives of those around you; determination to stay free from drugs; enhanced idealism about your chances or abilities for success.

☽   Added compassion for the feelings and circumstances of others; an increased tendency to be easily swayed by the needs of others; a sensitivity about the attitudes of others; tuning in to the needs of consumers or the public.

☿   Reading others in sales or business situations; communicating important ideas to others; raising questions about another's motives or attitudes; discussions about the impact of your visions on life.

♀   Increased ability to feel deep affection for your close friends; added intuition; gaining an inner appreciation for music or the arts; added needs to be comforted with fine things; desires for luxury or comfort.

♂   Increased physical energy to help push through your ideas or dreams; spirited discussions of your dreams or ideas; added need to bully or motivate others to accept your ideas; pushing ideas for success.

♃   An increased religious philosophy or outlook; added need for legal actions or responses; a need to be generous to those for whom you feel compassionate; relating your ideas persuasively; ideas for publicity or public relations.

♄   Delays and setbacks when trying to implement your visions and dreams; added ability to sense disappointment from others even though they may tell you otherwise; caution when describing feelings.

♅   Sudden impressions about the feelings or motives of others; unpredictable inspirations when relating your dreams and visions; perception of future upheavals or changes; a need to use the occult; interested in seeing trends.

♇   Creating plans for evolving and selling schemes of power; using pressure when selling others on your ideas; not caring whether facts presented are false as long as they properly serve your needs; underhanded transactions.

☊   Ability to attract others to your schemes or dreams of the future; aims and goals involve persuading groups of people to your points of view; ties to others who are visionaries; meeting people who need to sell.

M   Becoming a better person by analyzing and interpreting your dreams for a better world; gaining recognition for your visions, insight, or prophecies; recognizing improbable schemes or plans.

NEPTUNE/ASCENDANT CONCEPTS

Refuses to See Neglect
Contrived Leanings
Improbable Attitudes
Lacks a Sense of Reality
Recognizes Disguises
Disregards Techniques
Illusive Sense of Style
Confused by Perceptions
Doubts Personal Ability
Impractical Points of View
A Deceitful Disposition
Confusing Viewpoints

Unsure of what Reality is
Inspiring Personal Style
Neglects Surroundings
Attention on Fantasy
Inspired by Settings
Withdraws Sentiment
Surrounded by Deceit
A Frivolous Disposition
Ignores Reality
Subtle Sensations
Inspires Reactions
Pious Personal Beliefs

Inspires Recognition
Weak Convictions
Confusing Attitudes
Perceives Illusions
Casts off Mannerisms
Unclear Settings
Awkward Opinions
Weak Hunches
Nebulous Positions
Temporary Inclinations
Evasive Responses
Hidden Portrayals

Rambles on before Others
A Careless Mental Focus
Vague Ideas on Relating
Ignores Inclinations
Receives Visions
Speculative Assessments
Unsure when Relating
Neglects Responding
Inspired by First Impressions
Repressed Unwanted Thoughts
Improbable First Impressions
Sees Self as a Visionary
Dubious about Observations
Neglects Impressions Received
Imagines Experiences
Ignores the Unreal
Evades those Seeking Them
Unsound Forms of Judgment
Perceptive Visions
Focuses Internally
Loosens Personal Style
Neglects Consciousness
Focuses Strongly on Visions
Peculiar Explanations
Unexplained Convictions
Makes up Impressions
Neglects Interpersonal Roles
Understands Kindness
Confusion about Personal Style
Appears Ambiguous
Visionary with a Sense of Style

Surrounded by the Unreal
Inefficient Concentration
Enhances Ability to Read Others
Mysterious Satisfactions
Unsure of Attention Seeking
Evades Recognition
Inspires Introspection
Compassionate Attitudes
Mystical Sense of Style
Recognition which Eludes
Inspiring Mannerisms
Inconclusive Personal Responses
Deceit when Relating to Others
Uncertain Impressions
Inappropriate Identification
Unsure of Gaining Attention
Mixed up Mental Focus
Subtle Mannerisms
Strives to Make Dreams Real
Confuses Recognition
Inspired by Meeting Others
Confused by Reactions
Sees Ambiguity and Deceit
Deceived by Perceptions
Confused by Circumstances
Inconclusive Masquerades
Disposed to Daydreams
Mysterious Reactions
Unsure of Personal Beliefs
Devoted to Sensations
Leaves Reality Behind

NEPTUNE/ASCENDANT With Itself

Ψ   Abandoning situations or people when your attitudes toward them change; ignoring the reality of what is occurring around you; the ability to read future trends or people's motives; added inspiration.

A   Added language barriers which prevent you from understanding fully all of the attitudes and concerns of others; elaborate masquerades relying on deceptive practices which mask reality; receiving subtle impressions.

Significant Examples of People and Events Using Neptune/Ascendant

General: **STRONG:** Benito Mussolini; Pierre Auguste Renoir; Benjamin Disraeli; Steve Allen; Rossano Brazzi; Cheiro; Georges Seurat; James Earl Carter; Sigmund Freud; Johnny Carson; Jack Schwartz; O. J. Simpson; Jack Nicklaus
WEAK: Bertrand Russell; F. Scott Fitzgerald; Charles Addams; Alexander Graham Bell; Jean Houston; Lance Reventlow; Sir William Crookes
EVENTS: Apollo 11 Moon Landing; Mount St. Helens Explosion; First Medicare Patient Accepted; Pres. Nixon's Resignation; (Challenger Explosion).

☉   Olivia Newton-John; Maurice Ravel; Robert DeNiro; O. J. Simpson

☽   Gianni Agnelli; Lindburgh Lands in Paris; Jean Cocteau; Olivia Newton-John; Winston Churchill; Anne Murray

☿   Steve Rosenbloom; Willie Mays; Elvis Presley; S. Carolina Secedes

♀   Georges Seurat; Wayne Gretzky; First Medicare Patient Accepted; Thomas H. Huxley; Dane Rudhyar; John Dillinger

♂   Vida Blue; Olga Worrall; First A-Bomb Explosion; Edna Ferber

♃   Walt Whitman; Yehudi Menuhin; Pearl Harbor Attack; John Paul I

♄   Robert McNamara; Jack Nicklaus; Lord Byron; Adolf Hitler; Edgar Degas

♅   Kent State Shootings; Lee's Surrender; Arthur Godfrey; Bobby Fischer

Ψ, A   Pierre Renoir; Audrey Hepburn; Benito Mussolini; Benjamin Disraeli

♇   Gregory Peck; Mick Jagger; Bob Fosse; Apollo 11 Moon Landing; A. Carrel

☊   Drew Pearson; Billy Rose; John F. Kennedy; Albert Schweitzer; J. Denver

M   Steve Allen; Georges Seurat; Albert Speer; Sam Peckinpah; Lawrence Welk; Elton John; Charles Gordon

NEPTUNE/MIDHEAVEN   Ψ/M

Basic Ideas:
Indecision about life's direction, added inner doubts about any personal progress being made, and dreams of being a leader in the "New Age" begin here. Abandoning your carefully built up self-restraint and slipping into habits which make it more difficult for you to plan effectively are also indicated. You may find yourself growing apart from your roots or family as you struggle to define your personal uniqueness and where you wish to go with life. There is a possibility of failure to specify career directions or educational interests, of ambiguity about how to define life's goals, and of slowness in mastering lessons from life's experiences. However, these points show enhanced capacity to dream or plan future directions for personal growth and increased ability to see yourself maturing through a better appreciation of the role of faith, religion, hope, god and/or soul in life.

In Your Personal Life:
Thesis — An enhanced ability to visualize future directions and goals in life; gaining inspiration from your dreams and ideas about the future; finding mystical or foreign concepts or principles to enrich your life.

Anti — Deluding yourself about your ability to compete in life; added confusion about who you are or what you should be or do with your life; feeling inadequate when coping against others in life.

In Your Relationships:
Thesis — Enhances mystical feelings of oneness with those persons with whom you like to be physically close; enhanced feelings and intuition about the current status of your relationships; reading partner's feelings.

Anti — Makes it easier for you to deceive yourself about another's motives and intentions; clouds your ability to clearly see what you are able to contribute to others, or what it is that others want from you in a relationship.

With Body or Mind:
Possible genetic weakness or body reaction to certain allergens, drugs, alcohol, etc; examine family heredity patterns for tendencies to certain genetic traits.

In Politics or Business:
Thesis — Leaders reevaluate or rexamine the ideals of their enterprises and plan toward those goals; hints about planning for the future originate within dreams and visions of the leadership.

Anti — Increased likelihood that leaders will allow others to deceive them about their intentions and motives; spies which undermine the national security; official scandals of very large scope or proportions.

NEPTUNE/MIDHEAVEN with Planets and Points

☉   Personal power and self-determination for lifting yourself out of self-pity and delusion about what you are as a person or where your life is going; ablility to visualize and effectively set your life's direction.

☽   Increased receptivity about your plans and direction in life; a sensitivity to how others can or will deceive you about the help they give in fulfilling your dreams and visions; hesitations about your goals.

☿   You think and visualize your future plans well, but it is easy for you to proceed with wrong ideas about the support you will receive from others; you are aided in your schemes and plans about how to live.

♀   You visualize progress or new ideas in love, arts, or music; an increased need to show off your glamor or wealth as you progress in life; using your charm to progress from lowly origins to loftier heights.

♂   Increased anger and frustration when you fail to put consistent efforts forth toward goals; giving in to rash impulses without restraint; a need to activate plans derived from mystical images, meditation, or metaphysical sources.

♃   Proceeding despite poorly defined goals; an increased awareness and perception of how other people think or what their needs are; falling into self-delusion or deception; expanding vistas of life.

♄   Bringing reality to what might otherwise be fruitless planning or a frivolous use of resources; planning more thoroughly for your goals, but success comes slowly; lessened ability to idly dream about future possibilities.

♅   Sudden, unexpected insights about possible goals or plans for future use of your time and resources; the resistance you receive for unpopular ideas with little basis in reality; rewards from studying astrology.

♇   Added intensity and depth in the reality you feel is coming in the future; little abnormalities which create big problems in reaching your goals; concealing your plans from others while you scheme and plan about future directions.

☊   Finding others who share your dreams and visions for the future and who will work with you; acquiring help from support groups; people who listen to your dreams of the future; friends who create reality from your visions.

A   Enhanced need to discuss your dreams and visions of life with others; a strong mental focus on plans about your future direction which need to be developed; settings which let you dream of the future.

NEPTUNE/MIDHEAVEN CONCEPTS

Neglects Self-Restraint	Dreams of Outcomes	Illogical Objectives
Confusion about Behavior	Weakens Self-Restraint	Inspires Results
Speculative Qualifications	Inconclusive Planning	Mystical Expertise
Inefficient ways of Maturing	Unable to Cope with Life	Wasted Childhood
Confused by Experts	Unsound Credentials	Intangible Results
Protects the Deceitful	Ambiguous Purposes	Loses a Reward
Abandons Perseverance	Doubtful Consequences	A Lack of Purpose
Neglects Schooling	An Unlikely Start	Inspires Goals
Masters Evasion	Flawed Results	Unsound Training
Lacks Self-Integration	Mysterious Proficiency	Confused Purposes
Bluffs about Aptitudes	Envisions Fulfillment	Miraculous Stature
Metaphysical Principles	Meaningless Maturing	Unthinkable Effects
Dreams about Outcomes	Evades Self-Concepts	Forsakes Expertise

Unexplained Credentials	Unsure of Stature (Standing)
Imagines Learning and Growing	Confused about Aging Gracefully
Neglects Workmanship	Nebulous Personal Growth
Meaningless Recognition	A Visionary with Expertise
Deludes Self about Position	Doubtful Self-Restraint
Learns to Develop Compassion	Nebulous Security Seeking
Neglects Learning and Growing	Dreams about Position
Imagines a Need for Security	Inappropriate Qualifications
Confused about Beginnings	Unsuitable Schooling
Tolerates Inappropriate Conduct	Nebulous Outcomes
Illusive Learning and Growing	Imaginary Principles
A Conscience which Deceives	Seeks Answers through Mysticism
Inspires Personal Development	Speculative Reconciliation
Visions of Prospering	Subtle Sense of Fairness
Unconvincing Efforts	Abandons Education
Enlightens Self on Goals	Pretends to have a Purpose
Confusion over Development	Inspires Self-Concepts
Inspired to Learn and Grow	Uncertain Integrity
Intangible Proficiency	Inspires Others to Mature
Confusion about Intentions	Unable to bring it Together
Deceived by Credentials	Weak Image of Self
Empathic Personal Development	A Lack of Qualifications
Mysterious Results	Unsure of how to Mature
Uses Metaphysics to Grow	Guilt over Family Protection
Fantasizes over Outcomes	Withdraws Guarantees
False Attainment	Intangible Self-Discipline
Illogical Habits when Working	Temporary Results
Conceals Details of Early Life	Withdraws from Public
Neglects Personal Development	Deceives Self on Abilities
Matures Despite Inner Confusion	An Expert in a Trivial Subject

NEPTUNE/MIDHEAVEN With Itself

Ψ   Added neglect of or inability to see the need for thoroughly planning work; heightened pretenses of self-importance; decreased recognition; stirred up feelings about a lack of direction in career or in life.

M   Recognizing the importance of proper credentials and attention from others; coping with situations where you have wasted much effort and resources for little gain; a better outcome after consistently poor starts.

Significant Examples of People and Events Using Neptune/Midheaven

General: **STRONG:** Jean Francoise Millet; Abraham Lincoln; Herman Melville; Kareem Abdul-Jabbar; Elvis Presley; Arthur Godfrey; David Frost; Al Unser; John F. Kennedy; Vittorio DeSica; Charles Kettering; Melvin Belli; Franklin Roosevelt
     WEAK: Mick Jagger; Drew Pearson; Adolf Hitler; Jack Nicklaus; Dr. Sam Sheppard; Enrico Fermi; Willie Mays; Albert Camus
     EVENTS: James Meredith Enrolls at U. Miss.; RMS Titanic Strikes Iceberg; Lindburgh Lands in Paris; First Atomic Explosion; (Pearl Harbor Attack).

☉   Alexander Graham Bell; Friedrich Nietzsche; Arthur Godfrey; Chernobyl Nuclear Explosion; Herman Melville; Melvin Belli

☽   R. D. Laing; Winston Churchill; Tom Jones; Dave Garroway; Bob Dylan

☿   Mount St. Helens Explosion; Wayne Gretzky; Guglielmo Marconi; Lindburgh Lands in Paris; Percy Bysshe Shelley

♀   Audrey Hepburn; Enrico Caruso; Lord Byron; Abraham Lincoln; Henry Mancini; Ida Rolf; John Dillinger

♂   Steven Spielberg; Bob Newhart; Guglielmo Marconi; Robin Williams

♃   Jean Houston; Henry Mancini; Arthur Rimbaud; Audie Murphy

♄   Enrico Fermi; Mark Spitz; Jack Schwartz; Helen Reddy; Herman Melville

♅   Henry Mancini; Paul Cezanne; Manly Palmer Hall; Charles Kettering

Ψ, M   Abraham Lincoln; Paul Cezanne; Vittorio DeSica; Richard Byrd; B. Disraeli

♇   Pres. Nixon's Resignation; Steve Rosenbloom; Jean Houston; William K. Douglas; Louis Pasteur; Maurice Ravel

☊   Arthur Godfrey; Arturo Toscanini; Lord Byron; Herman Melville

A   Stephen Foster; Jack Paar; Marc Edmund Jones; Vittorio DeSica; Claude Debussy; Auguste Rodin

PLUTO/NODE ♀/☊

Basic Ideas:

These themes show increase in your social influence and encouragement from those people or groups who can provide important connections. Your compulsion to seek others out, the obsessions you have with meeting the right people, or the needs you have to start new friendships with influential people are encouraged here. These issues help you discover the consequences of past actions through your experiences with life, and to realize the rewards or gains you may accumulate from these. Your need to find others for fulfillment, your tendency to abuse friendships, the role of friends who disappear or die, or the drains on your personal and material resources which others create may originate here. These motifs also mirror your need to seek vengeance, your use or abuse of poisonous substances, and the sexual or carnal opportunities you seek from others.

In Your Personal Life:

Thesis   Seeking and finding important or influential people to help you; compulsions or insatiable desires for attracting others to you; opportunities to make great gains in life through others who offer help to you.

Anti   Increased obsession for using others for your own purposes; meetings where you are assessed or where you evaluate the abilities of others; planning retaliation for past activities; hidden slurs returned.

In Your Relationships:

Thesis   Use of professional or community groups to meet new partners; personal contacts acquired thru connections; establishing new or breaking old ties; noticing new attraction or sexuality.

Anti   Using others solely as sexual objects; added inability to understand the human side of relationships; using partner or friends while expecting to return little to them; taking sexual advantage in the wrong way.

With Body or Mind:

Blockages which affect your pituitary or endocrine glands; sexual preferences or capacities; accumulation of toxins due to blockage of tubes or passages.

In Politics or Business:

Thesis   Agreements about reciprocal rights for information obtained through clandestine methods; violent or criminal persons who enter the country secretly at any given opportunity; sewage or waste compacts.

Anti   Treaties involving the exchange of secretive or clandestine data; people who may not have the country's or business's best interests in mind; breakdowns in security or treaties due to the actions of other persons.

PLUTO/NODE with Planets and Points

⊙ Evaluating and making use of the people you encounter thru your activities; the importance you attach to such meetings or encounters; the approval you feel from others during meetings; respect you gain.

☽ The depth of emotions, good and bad, which arise from meetings with others who arouse sensitive passions; the ups and downs of encounters taken to extremes; uncertainties after meeting powerful people.

☿ Reading others and judging their needs; feeling shifts of power or direction from others, and taking advantage of these; conversing easily and fluently with influential people; getting the right education.

♀ Influential artists or bankers met thru contacts or groups; accumulating friendships for wealth or power potentials; intimacy from people you meet; intimate questions about the role of love in attraction or sex.

♂ Influential business people met through contacts or groups; force or invective in your emphasis at meetings; an urgency in your needs to find or meet others; sexual competitiveness; impulses for kinship.

♃ An enhanced ability to read the political motives of the people you meet and assess their needs for power; potential success thru your ability to use people to their highest potential as a manger of their affairs or activities.

♄ Lessened desires to use and discard others; realizing that personal trust must be built up in people over time and that relationships with others are not to be rushed or used to extremes; ability to read people.

♅ Impersonal decisions to eliminate others from your association; unusual meetings on morbid subjects; meetings with powerful people in the sciences or engineering (including astrologers); discussing differences at meetings.

♆ Increased potential for you to be deceived by others, or for you to deceive them with your intentions; seeing that people are not always what they seem to be; added doubts about the effectiveness of friends.

A Reading the potential and intentions of the people you meet; added ability to focus on how groups can help you; emphasizing your intentions and ideas at meetings; reading the intentions of others from their appearance.

M Growing and learning from what more accomplished people in your profession can teach you; learning from the contacts and assistance you receive from important groups or associations from which you seek advice.

PLUTO/ASCENDANT ♀/A

Basic Ideas:

This combination denotes strength in your mental intensity and increased concentration and attention on matters important to you, as well as ability to ignore any irrelevant disturbances. Your powers of insight and observation about the nature or character of other are enhanced, and your demeanor has a look of penetration and intensity. You have the urge to always act as you see fit, and you may spend much time wringing pain from your inner self for errors you made or for inappropriate activities. Your obsession with the roles and needs of others is heightened, and you may bring a sexual and passionate mannerism to the way you show attention to others. With these themes you excel at observing other people and situations, and you are prompted to bring logical order to situations. You have an increased need for controlling the feelings and reactions of others.

In Your Personal Life:

Thesis   Reading and judging people's reactions; a need for concentrating and observing all; noticing another's mannerisms; understanding what others seek from socializing; researching psychological qualities.

Anti   Remaining in the background and observing the reactions of others; already strong passions and feelings increase; conducting research and study as an emotional outlet; intense focus as a release from pressures.

In Your Relationships:

Thesis   Understanding the needs of your partner and responding in a sexual and passionate manner; heightened excitement and pleasure at being able to satisfy another's needs or passions.

Anti   Seeing that much of life is based upon sexual ability and inclining to judge others in this way; hiding your feelings and covering them with sexual identity; repressing your inner feelings about your relationship.

With Body or Mind:

Endocrine and pituitary gland functions; toxic reactions; waste matter in environment; exposure to virus or bacteria; waste or vermin nearby.

In Politics or Business:

Thesis   The identification and reversal of potentially destructive ideas or attitudes; focusing consciousness on elements intending to do harm to others; inspection of waste disposal procedures; space colonization.

Anti   Introducing immoral or profiteering ways into practice; natural disasters which strike without warning; serious psychotic or self-destructive reactions; global trends for the environment, pollution, or poisons.

PLUTO/ASCENDANT with Planets and Points

☉   Determined and effective efforts to read and study people to know what they want or how to motivate them; a determination to end forms of injustice and replace harmful practices; authority which is aware.

☽   An instinct for avoiding powers or people which can be destructive to self or the environment; a sensitivity about reading and understanding the motives of others; difficulties with abusive females; intense mood swings.

☿   Intellectually studying the motives and reactions of others; a mental outlook which you may use to destroy or eliminate others who oppose you; rationalizing thoughts or ideas to work outside of the law.

♀   Added softness in an intense demeanor helps others relate better to the inner you; an increased need for affection, and to give and receive both love and sexual pleasure; added grace and charm in your disposition.

♂   Magnified intensity of feelings and of your insistence on having your way over others; quick anger; loud and persistent arguing during situations which call for calmer and smoother approaches to others.

♃   An enhanced love of politics and the law, and the use of knowledge of people and their motives to push ahead in life; excessive urgency to control the feelings and lives of others; an increased aura of sincerity.

♄   You appear more stern and unforgiving than you are; you give an impression that you are older and wiser; you condense and organize your thoughts and ideas; you remain aloof, detached, or uninvolved.

♅   An increased need to be disruptive toward practices of which you do not approve; a need to study the psychological ways of other people; an interest in using astrology to understand others and life.

♆   An appearance of being a dreamer and visionary; a need to use drugs to heighten experiences and reactions to the world; a consideration of fraud and deception as a personal policy and deliberate activity.

☊   An enhanced ability to work effectively through groups or associations; meeting people with whom you have a deep and intense affiliation or bonding; ridding yourself of unneeded friends; psychological interests.

M   An increase in the respect and admiration others have for you as you age and become better accepted; increased confidence in motivating people; becoming a person who keeps his or her word; internal struggles with integrity.

PLUTO/ASCENDANT CONCEPTS

An Intense Mental Focus	Eliminates Introspection	Reverses Leanings
Diminished Inhibitions	Sexual Disposition	Deters Responses
Reacts to Punishment	A Stubborn Mannerism	Refines Attitudes
Sees Another Reality	Destroys Conceptions	A Radical Focus
Conceals Pretenses	Withholds Perceptions	Sexual Reactions
Observes Shadowy Activities	Hidden Inhibitions	Alters Mannerisms
Overwhelms Surroundings	Thins Out Habitat	A Morbid Context
Destructive Personal Style	Pursues Convictions	Drastic Notions
Compulsive Mannerisms	Destructive Experiences	Hidden Attitudes
Depletes Surroundings	Carnal Relating to Others	Reverses Demeanor
An Intense Disposition	Uses Observations	Pursues Sensations
Retaliates within Context	Punishes Self Internally	Troubled Sentiments

Intensifies Experiences	Hides Impressions
Retaliates over Attitudes	Eliminates Unwanted Attitudes
Too Intense when Relating	Compresses Consciousness
Fanatical Concentration	Overwhelmed by Perceptions
Widens Focus of Attention	Reexamines Repressions
Alters ways of Relating	Obsessed with Surroundings
Receives Sexual Impressions	Troubles with Sense of Reality
Powerful Portrayals	Secretive with Personal Views
Revises Impressions Received	Seeks a Basis for Attitudes
Censures Attitudes of Others	Eliminates Unnecessary Traits
Troubles with Recognition	Extreme Circumstances
Refuses to Look at Reality	Strong Interpersonal Roles
An Overwhelming Personality	Belittling Mannerisms
Diminished Impressions	Fanatical Sentiments
Provokes Inner Understanding	Destroys Relationships
Disposed to Punishment	Violates the Environment
Lessens Detection	Provocative Treatment
Wasted Personal Attention	Single-Minded Mental Focus
Too much Attention Seeking	Pursues Relations to Others
Carnal Sensations	Reciprocates with Rejoinders
Sees Defects in Reality	A Destructive Mental Focus
Provocative Sense of Style	Evolves Interpersonal Roles
Excludes Awareness of Others	Intense Focus on Tasks
Exhaustive Responses	Hides Interpersonal Roles
Destroys Personal Privacy	Prevents Relating to Others
Turns Reality Around	Excessive Personal Motives
Refines Reactions to Others	Abnormal Characteristics
Shortens Visits to Others	An Exasperating Personal Style
Able to Overturn Reality	Tunes out Surroundings
Ends Personal Responses	Provocative Mannerisms
Reverses the Context	Pursues Impressions Received

PLUTO/ASCENDANT With Itself

♀ Focusing within and concentrating on reevaluating old matters; seeing more clearly what others want or are; possible fallout with others who are using you for your talents or position; needs to destroy property.

A Becoming more aware of people and how they react in the world; added interest in others and what makes them unique; an interest in keeping surroundings and personal spaces apart from others; withdrawal within.

Significant Examples of People and Events Using Pluto/Ascendant

General: **STRONG:** Paul Joseph Goebbels; Jack Paar; Norman Mailer; Muhammad Ali; Vida Blue; Nikola Tesla; F. Scott Fitzgerald; Gus Grissom; Steven Spielberg; Bjorn Borg; Liberace; Bob Newhart; Maurice Ravel
WEAK: Sandy Koufax; Melvin Belli; Arthur Godfrey; Ulysses S. Grant; Richard Strauss; Thomas H. Huxley; Edgar Degas; Burl Ives
EVENTS: Transcontinental RR Completed; Bolsheviks Take Power; Ramstein Airshow Crash; (Washington's Inauguration).

☉ Henry Winkler; John Denver; Arthur Rimbaud; H. G. Wells; Vida Blue

☽ Muhammad Ali; Mary Martin; Sir Laurence Olivier; First Medicare Patient Accepted; Lord Byron; Sigmund Freud

☿ Woman's Suffrage OK'd; J. Von Ribbentrop; Johnny Carson; Steve Allen

♀ Willie Mays; Edouard Manet; Ralph Waldo Emerson; Transcon. RR Done

♂ Ellen Burstyn; Billy Rose; Paul Joseph Goebbels; Dane Rudhyar; Willie Mays; Robert DeNiro; John F. Kennedy

♃ Mt. St. Helens Explosion; Norman Mailer; Rupert Murdoch; Arthur Ford

♄ Bolsheviks Seize Power; John Glenn; Jonathan Winters; Abraham Lincoln; John McEnroe; Richard Byrd

♅ Gustav Dore; Manly Palmer Hall; Charles Steinmetz; Kareem Abdul-Jabbar; Mario Andretti; Norman Mailer

♆ Watergate Burglary Found; Ellen Burstyn; Norman Mailer; Bob Newhart; Richard Alpert; Thomas H. Huxley

♀, A Richard Alpert; Liberace; Challenger Explosion; Shirley Jones; Gen. Joseph Joffre; Jimmy Carter; Gus Grissom

☊ Gustav Dore; Winston Churchill; Stephen Crane; F. Scott Fitzgerald

M Maurice Ravel; Arthur Rimbaud; Muhammad Ali; Ramstein Air Crash

PLUTO/MIDHEAVEN   ♀/M

Basic Ideas:
These themes show growth with and through life's experiences, lessons, and trials and becoming a better, if different, person. You realize that you cannot be all things to all people. You are introduced to ideas very different from those which your family and early life taught you, and guided you to develop self-control in all areas of life, perhaps excessively. You may be obsessed with the need for correcting your personal or family distresses, for clarifying your personal goals and needs, and with confronting your reputation. Your problems in coping with feeling secure about who you are, in eliminating self-restraints imposed in your past, or in denying principles for which you inwardly stand, are also emphasized by these points. The efforts you go through to clear your name, a family member's name, or an ancestor's reputation may also originate here.

In Your Personal Life:
Thesis   Pursuing activities designed to make you a stronger person inwardly and let you feel better about you, the person; a turn-around in your feelings about your family members, their reputations, or their traditions.

Anti   Situations where others force you to stand and fight for your beliefs and ideals; obsession with improving your standing before others; imposing self-punishment for the sins of living.

In Your Relationships:
Thesis   Recognizing that two people working together can accomplish more than one individual; devoting much effort to helping yourself and your partner grow thru and in your relationship.

Anti   Finding partners who are psychologically dependent upon you for growth; destroying a part of your partner's identity so that you can enhance yourself; imposing on those who offer help.

With Body or Mind:
Toxins accumulate due to the stress of living or work; colon or elimination problems due to inadequate attention to your body's basic needs.

In Politics or Business:
Thesis   The pursuit of large and expensive research or social projects; studies involving the concept of the earth, the solar system, etc., as a living organism; practices concerning the disposal of toxins or waste products.

Anti   Inadequate preparation, supplies for emergencies, or similar large disasters; overloaded waste disposal systems; destructive self-centered terrorist actions; focusing on weapons systems for great destruction.

PLUTO/MIDHEAVEN with Planets and Points

☉   Increased determination to become a better person thru accumulating power, wealth, or fame; seeking leadership and notoriety for power; tremendous pride in your accomplishments; a rise from obscurity.

☽   An emotional drive to overcome indecisiveness and forge ahead with your pursuits; a need for maternal-like comforting when coping with your inadequacies; uncertainty over how your family feels about you.

☿   Added need for educational credentials to help you become better appreciated; overcompensating for an obscure origin by concentrating upon developing yourself academically and/or thru public speaking.

♀   Powerful urges to become rich and famous so that others can notice you; demands for high professional fees due to your popularity or political stature; a fated attraction or love for one who has social stature or standing.

♂   Increased willingness to battle for your objectives; added energy to develop yourself as a person who has much to prove to others; the need to push ahead and keep driving toward your goals at all costs.

♃   Fortunate events propel you into positions where you can add to your prestige or power; increased need for political power and recognition; thoughts of using your personal powers in selfish ways to advance .

♄   Early frustrations help you work hard to achieve your desires; increased desire to work hard to add to your recognition in life; questioning the dedication of others helping you achieve your ends.

♅   Sudden or drastic reversals which change your stature or reputation; progressive ideas for helping others; friends who encourage you to achieve your goals; coping with the unusual; an interest in applying astrology.

♆   Inwardly seeing the need for change on a larger scale; temporary setbacks due to illusions about how to effect some progress; thinking of using dubious practices to increase your reputation or power.

☊   Others notice your abilities and ambitions; membership in associations or clubs which can help you achieve your purposes; ridding yourself of undesirable habits which retard progress; the importance of connections.

A   Concentrating more on your goals; increased ability to seek out practical ways of meeting success; added ability to persuade others to your ideas; an extreme intensity and power when addressing others; personal power.

PLUTO/MIDHEAVEN CONCEPTS

Destroys Security Seeking	Achievements Erased	Discards Principles
Hidden Ways of Maturing	Pursues Integration	Drastic Protection
A Master Contaminator	Reduces Consequences	Prevents Fulfillment
Deficient in Credentials	Looks for Experts	The Original Purifier
Pursues Self-Restraint	The End of Childhood	Deficient Principles
Attains Purification	Depletes Wisdom	Depletes Outcomes
Removes Protection	Dismisses Origins	Changes Morals
Excessive Self-Restraint	Terminates Protection	Drastic Outcomes
Matures Using Sexuality	The Final Purification	Abolishes Protection
A Compulsive Expert	Initiates Schooling	Reverses Behavior
Worldwide Public Projection	Exhausts Designs	Carnal Proficiency
Hidden Self-Concepts	A Destructive Expert	Pursues Intentions

Undertakes Personal Development	Drastic Self-Restraint
Compulsive Needs for Security	Violates Self-Concepts
Destroys Self-Restraint	Obsessed with Competence
Drastic Personal Development	Pursues Anything to Origin
Dismisses Guarantees	Rejects Outcomes
Provokes Security Seeking	Willful Needs for Security
Carnal Self-Restraint	Pursues Security Seeking
Obsessed with Mastery	Reduces Standing in Society
Reduces Self-Restraint	Diminished Sense of Fairness
Hidden Persevering	An Obsession with Principles
Depressing Personal Growth	Tarnished Self-Concepts
Intense Pursuit of Conclusions	Destructive Intentions
Compulsive Schooling	Excessive Self-Discipline
Corrupting Principles	Deters Integration
Opposes Personal Guarantees	Copes with Contamination
Drastic Learning and Growing	Genital Behavior
Worries about Recognition	Provokes Self-Restraint
Wasted Reactions	Carnal Consequences
Punishes the Immature	Shortens Proficiency
Reverses Learning and Growing	Punishes Security Seekers
An End to Safekeeping	Troubled by Rules of Conduct
Compulsive Personal Growth	Completes Maturation
Reverses Immunity	Concentrated Provocations
Obsessed with Self-Concepts	Defective Protection
Destroys Stature (Standing)	Intense Career Demands
Deficient Mastery	Concentrates on Maturing
Evolves a Reputation	Clarifies Goals in Life
A Perverted Sense of Fairness	Reconstructs Standards
Penalizes Self-Restraint	Experience from Living
Evolves Conclusions	Repulsive Conduct
The Pursuit of Morality	Intends to Provoke

PLUTO/MIDHEAVEN With Itself

♇   Increased needs to be recognized by others for who you are or what you can do; stooping to less than honest means for achieving recognition and help with your ambitions; added ruthlessness to your ideas.

M   Overcoming the worst of the obstacles in your way; added persistence to try and finish whatever it is you start; realizing that the end objective is not always as important as preserving personal moral integrity and position.

Significant Examples of People and Events Using Pluto/Midheaven

General: **STRONG:** Jean Francoise Millet; Willie Mays; Vincent Van Gogh; Johnny Carson; Gus Grissom; Steve Wozniak; Dustin Hoffman; John McEnroe; Henry Mancini; Jack Nicklaus; Albert Einstein; Erich Maria Remarque
WEAK: Norman Mailer; Stephen King; Helen Reddy; Melvin Belli; Ervin Nyiregyhazi; Rossano Brazzi; H. Toulouse-Lautrec; Gregory Peck
EVENTS: Ramstein Airshow Disaster; South Carolina Secedes from Union; Lindburgh Lands in Paris; J. Meredith Enrolled at U. Miss.; (Challenger Explosion).

☉   Dick Gregory; Sally Ride; Jack Paar; Alexis Carrel; Gus Grissom; Jean Houston; Paul Cezanne; Charles E. O. Carter

☽   Dustin Hoffman; Paul Cezanne; East Coast Blackout; Sir Wm. Crookes

☿   Stephen Sondheim; Van Cliburn; Sam Peckinpah; Erich Maria Remarque; Mario Andretti; Abraham Lincoln

♀   Johnny Carson; John Fremont; Giacomo Puccini; Gus Grissom; Israel Regardie; Rosanno Brazzi; Steve Wozniak

♂   Alan Alda; Abraham Lincoln; Thomas H. Huxley; Charles Kettering

♃   Elvis Presley; Benito Mussolini; Francisco Franco; Albert Camus; Jack Paar

♄   Drew Pearson; F. D. Roosevelt Wins Election; R. W. Emerson; Sigmund Freud

♅   John McEnroe; James Meredith Enrolled at U Miss; Lance Reventlow

♆   Carl Sandburg; Bolsheviks Seize Power; Cheiro; Jim Thorpe; Dick Gregory; Lawrence Welk; Johnnie Carson

♇, M   Komar; Jimmy Carter; Alan Alda; Emperor Hirohito; Tom Jones

☊   Henry Mancini; Sydney Omarr; Rupert Murdoch; Rollo May; Liberace

A   Hermann Goering; Richard Strauss; Willie Mays; Gen. Ferdinand Foch

NODE/ASCENDANT   ☊/A

Basic Ideas:
With these motifs you focus attention on finding and meeting people who share mutual obligations, impressions, interests, or influences, and you satisfy your needs for associating with such persons, groups, or societies. Your ability to retain a personal identity in your society, and the familiarity you develop with friends you meet through groups having mutual interests is also represented. These themes show opportunities for concentrating on meeting the kinds of people you seek to fulfill obligations during the various phases of your life. Your desires to meet in comfortable, familiar surroundings, personal friendships which evolve from groups which attract you, and benefits you achieve from associating with people who share a similar life's purpose with you begin here. Also noted are eactions to imposed separations, and the mutual assistance derived from others.

In Your Personal Life:

Thesis — Increased awareness and consciousness about the people with whom you meet or socialize; benefits derived from exchanging ideas with friends; people who help you identify with spiritual causes or ideas.

Anti — Tensions created because of involvement between people who share similar destinies; reading the intentions and thrust of mutual efforts; misuse of social or interpersonal contacts; dismissing help from others.

In Your Relationships:

Thesis — Working together with a partner to solve various problems; the strength of the ties you feel with others who share similar destinies; attitudes of shared intimacy; a close relationship.

Anti — Using others without involving yourself in their mutual closeness; determining and satisfying another's needs; an inability to focus beyond personal needs to improve your lifestyle.

With Body or Mind:

The overall soundness of psychological health; support from others; handling the mental pressure of living; group therapy; role modeling.

In Politics or Business:

Thesis — Mediating or resolving disputes involving others; opinions of the leadership about problems which exist beyond their control; originating solutions to benefit others as well as self; social pressures or drifts.

Anti — Strong reactions from others about internal policies which affect them; alliances which drain the leadership's time or resources; refusals to cooperate or fulfill prior promises; isolation imposed for self-fulfillment.

NODE/ASCENDANT with Planets and Points

☉   Showing personal authority and sincerity when working with others; the reliability of your word or promises; the influence your friends have on you, or you over them; focusing on developing personal goals.

☽   Doubts which arise about the sincerity of effort you give or receive from groups or friends; the sincerity of your work efforts; your influence or effect on family members; your affect upon the members at large of your societies.

☿   Influence wielded by an effective communicator; expressing your ideas to others; developing skills to gather advice or support; educating others to your methods; ability to get ideas across to groups.

♀   Admiration and satisfaction from associates; focusing on values received from mutual participation; how others perceive your personal charm and manners in social situations; groups interested in the arts.

♂   Activating and leading groups to mutual causes of fulfillment; impulsive behavior at meetings through speaking out abruptly or aside comments; the irritation you inwardly feel about those not grasping the overall picture.

♃   Expanding your participation and acceptance within groups or among friends with whom you share efforts; promises made to support and work with others; the politics behind guiding or shaping opinions.

♄   Demonstrations of organizational or administrative skills; simplifying group structures; explaining problems; slowly, patiently teaching others about your ideas or methods; barriers to socializing efforts.

♅   Focusing upon sudden outbursts at meetings; interruptions at gatherings; meetings focus upon astrological or computing methods; remaining impartial from ideas and emotional issues under discussion.

♆   Receiving inspiration from others who share similar goals and interests; encountering people unable to follow through with work promised at prior meetings; dissolving your ties or friendships to others.

♀   Changes in the fabric of society due to your support of groups and friends with whom you share common bonds; the revenge, recrimination, or retaliation you notice from associates or co-workers; powerful friends and allies.

M   Maturing and growing as a person due to the effect your friends have on your life; the personal guarantees and assurances you carry forward for the greater benefit of groups or friends; recognition received for social efforts.

NODE/ASCENDANT CONCEPTS

Ceases to Concentrate	Develops a Personality	Familiar Attitudes
United by Personal Style	Realizes about Pretenses	Sexual Overtures
Those Who Act the Same	Accepted Sense of Style	Similar Concepts
Uniform Attention Seeking	Discloses Convictions	Struggles for Poise
Occupies Attention	A Similar Mental Focus	Seeks the Context
Detects Current Morale	Allied through Pretenses	Uniform Objectives
Seeks Interpersonal Roles	Looks at Other's Habits	Strives for Reactions
Relations with Others	Sexual Attention Seeking	Explores Possibilities
Attracted by Mannerisms	Allied through Conditions	Personal Attitudes
Establishes Personal Space	Rids Self of a Situation	Joint Perceptions
Precludes Reactions	Similar Sense of Reality	Similar Outcomes
Connects through Attitudes	Sensual Mannerisms	Observes Sexuality

Allies through a Sense of Reality	Similar Interpersonal Roles
Rids Self of Impressions	Evolves from Impressions
Attracts Others thru Style	Friends with Similar Concerns
Similar Impressions Received	New Ways of Identifying
Separates Self from Incidents	Meets Others with Style
Allies by Relating to Others	Acquainted with Mannerisms
Seeks Others for Recognition	Familiar with Attitudes
Customary Approaches	Observant during Encounters
Rids Self of Inhibitions	Sexual Consciousness
Strives for Sensory Repression	Recognizes what to Notice
Shows an Interest in Reality	Destined to Seek Attention
Aware of Mental Focus	Inborn Postures
Peculiar Separations	Recognizes Everyday Reality
Meets and Evaluates Others	Attracts Others through Attitudes
Combines Interpersonal Roles	Different Personal Styles
Touches on Personal Beliefs	Eliminates Another's Views
Separates from Portrayals	Meetings about Relationships
Allied in Repressing Reactions	Connects through Sense of Style
Rids Self of Convictions	Visits Others who Understand
Detects a Presence	Eliminates Certain Actions
Receives Familiar Impressions	Masters a Personal Style
Looks for Public Projection	Habitual Inhibitions
Aware of what is Observed	Strives for a Sense of Style
Discovers Relating to Others	Sexual Perceptions
Meets Attention Seekers	Rids Self of Circumstances
Disconnects from Introspection	Kindred Surroundings
Connects through Personal Views	Presented with a Backdrop
Accustomed to Assurances	Shows an Interest in Reactions
Strives for Interpersonal Roles	Demonstrates Introspection
Feels an Attraction to Others	Acceptable Personal Attitudes
Attracts Others by Mannerisms	Seeks to Understand Others

NODE/ASCENDANT With Itself

♋ Questions about your purpose and role in life; finding groups or others who can help provide needed answers; the roles of others in bringing fresh impetus and direction; a fated meeting which proves important.

A Immediate needs to find and socialize with others; needs to find others who can communicate with you; contacting others to release the social or internal pressures generated by your lifestyle or living habits.

Significant Examples of People and Events Using Node/Ascendant

General: **STRONG:** Steve Wozniak; Bob Fosse; Mark Spitz; Winston Churchill; James Earl Carter; Albert Camus; Percy Bysshe Shelley; Vincent Van Gogh; Jean Cocteau; Vittorio DeSica; Audrey Hepburn; Bob Dylan
WEAK: Hugh Downs; Willie Brandt; Walt Whitman; Stephen Foster; Giacomo Puccini; Ferdinand Foch; William Butler Yeats; Jerry Rubin
EVENTS: Watergate Burglary Occurs; Lee's Surrender at Appomattox; John F. Kennedy Shot; Lewis & Clark Expedition Starts; (First A-Bomb Explosion).

☉ Ida Rolf; Paul Joseph Goebbels; Gustav Dore; Mario Andretti; Al Unser

☽ Bjorn Borg; Charles E. O. Carter; Benjamin Disraeli; Arthur Rimbaud

☿ Edgar Degas; Vida Blue; Earl Warren; Charles E.O. Carter; Chas. Steinmetz

♀ Bob Fosse; William K. Douglas; Earl Warren; Carl Sandburg; Gug. Marconi

♂ Marlon Brando; First Medicare Patient Received; Arthur Rimbaud; David Frost; Burl Ives; Al Unser

♃ Franklin Roosevelt Wins His First Election; Mark Spitz; Watergate Burglary Discovered; Francisco Franco

♄ Henry Mancini; Pierre Renoir; Gustav Dore; John Dillinger; Richard Alpert; Bjorn Borg; Mary Martin

♅ Lindburgh Lands in Paris; Arnold Schwarzenegger; Jean Cocteau; Rex Harrison; Joachim Von Ribbentrop

♆ Henry Kissinger; John Glenn; Van Cliburn; Bertr. Russell; Marlon Brando

♇ Ira Progoff; F. Scott Fitzgerald; Kent State Shootings; Paul Gauguin

♋, A Arthur Godfrey; Steve Wozniak; Ida Rolf; Van Cliburn; Sydney Omarr

M Steve Wozniak; Albert Camus; Percy Bysshe Shelley; Chernobyl Nuclear Explosion; Gregory Peck; Jack Paar

NODE/MIDHEAVEN   ☊/M

Basic Ideas:

A basic theme here is working with people who share a similar social, political, or business standing with yourself. Locating people who have similar goals or aspirations, friends who cause situations which help you develop as a person, and uncovering people who have needs similar to yours are also described here. The process of attracting people who can help or assist you in becoming a better or more well-rounded person, those who are familiar to you yet not necessarily acquainted or friends, and ties to others who are able to help you develop and mature as a person are also shown within these motifs. Separation from your early or family ideas, habits acquired or adopted as you become a better or different person, changes within you which make you a better person, and integration of your destiny with your daily activities also begin with these combined themes.

In Your Personal Life:

Thesis   Seeking and finding others who have similar ideas about how to develop or learn and grow from your present sense of self into a better and more mature you; sexual ties with persons of the same social class.

Anti   Becoming acquainted with or attracted to people who have good intentions but who lead you astray with ideas that are not directly suited for your personal situation; release of self from obligations made earlier.

In Your Relationships:

Thesis   Opening yourself to another who can help or assist you in becoming a more well-rounded person; finding another with whom you feel compatible and familiar; sexual liaisons with friends you meet.

Anti   Newfound friends who create drains on your time or resources; people who lead you astray with their patterns of good intentions; familiarity which leads to deeper troubles between partners or friends.

With Body or Mind:

Psychological coping or adaptation with roots or origins; encounters with those qualified to answer questions on psychological conditions or diagnoses.

In Politics or Business:

Thesis   Support for new ideals and goals from associates; assistance in the form of aid and personnel help; food aid; legal actions intended to promote or spur activity and growth for all.

Anti   Aid or forms of assistance which cause more difficulties than expected; assistance from well-intentioned sources even when it is not requested or required; leaders who convince others of their sincerity and trust.

NODE/MIDHEAVEN with Planets and Points

☉   Determination to find others who think like you when meeting life's challenges; meetings with responsible, mature people who help you identify your goals; channeling ambition through the efforts of others.

☽   Compassion from others about your life's situation; meeting people who are sensitive to your personal growth and who care about your intentions and principles; obscure persons who help you gain stature.

☿   Insight into situations and circumstances when you meet others who are able to support your goals; learning situations with people who want to develop aspirations, goals, or plans similar to yours.

♀   Intimacy formed from friendships with those you met through groups which perform for the arts, music, or sculpture; garden or beautification clubs with those who have interests similar to your own.

♂   Immediate or rapid meetings with people who have principles similar to yours; aggressive people or groups who try to force their attitudes upon you; noisy encounters or meetings with others who have similar ideas to yours.

♃   Meeting with people who share familiar ideas about philosophy, religion, or law; large numbers of people who have similar origins or expertise; acquaintances who share similar beliefs and ideas.

♄   Admiration for those who have upheld principles similar to yours; frustration in not being able to make proper contacts; losing contact with friends who share your ideas and goals; sharing expertise at basic levels with others.

♅   Impersonal reactions from new acquaintances who share similar goals or principles; political associates who distance themselves from your principles, but support you anyhow; goal revisions at meetings.

♆   Deceit from well-meaning people who offer to help you meet your goals or increase your stature; illusive goals set at meetings; encountering others whose ambitions are vague but which sound familiar.

♇   Suspicions about the intentions of others who offer to help you find your destiny or purpose in life; achieving positions of power through the use of groups of people with aims and goals similar to yours; hidden allies appear.

A   Encounters with people who have a familiarity with the principles you need for advancing self in life; finding others who are willing and able to help you meet your goals; groups which come to you when you need them.

NODE/MIDHEAVEN CONCEPTS

An Accomplished Socializer
A Sexual Reputation
Acquainted Way back when
Recognizes the Results
Habitual Schooling
Pursues Soul Growth
Routine Personal Betterment
Knows Personal Intentions
Routine Personal Reserve
Familiar with Behaving
A Traditional Resolution
Finalizes Self-Learning

Allied through Experiences
Familiar Conduct
Seeks Personal Guarantees
Mutual Security Seeking
Carnal Experiences
Returns to Family Sources
Encounters Immunity
Acquires Self-Growth
Strives for Standards
Finds Personal Growth
Overcomes Beginnings
Establishes Guarantees

Shows Expertise
Presents Results
Meets Experts
Pursues Principles
Familiar Outcomes
Routine Experience
Strives to Cope
Personal Defenses
Innate Capacity
Finds a Refuge
Friends from Birth
Drawn to Distinction

Acquainted with Status
Gains and Loses Proficiency
Matures with Experience
Loses Preconceived Notions
Attracts Others through Principles
Consolidates Intentions
Destined for Self-Growth
The Rewards of Friendship
Familiar with Personal Growth
Introduced to Experience
Works for Personal Recognition
Presented with Self-Concepts
Works to Become Self-Reliant
Understands Personal Morality
Accumulates Experiences
Attracts Others with Ideas
Trustworthy Cooperation
Works to Establish Reputation
A Master Demonstrates
Attracts Others for Self Growth
Acquires Authorization
The Old-Boy Network
Consolidates and Integrates
Discovers Self-Restraint
Attracted by Innate Capability
Sexual Learning and Growing
Acquires Personal Training
Allied through Profession
Friendships made in School
Strives for Self-Restraint
Evolves and Learns Restraint

An Interest in Respectability
Encounters Ambitious People
Destined for Public Projection
Breaks a Pact with Self
Separates from Self-Concepts
Built in Personal Guarantees
Looks for Inner Peace
Withdraws from Recognition
Similar Personal Development
Removed from Repercussions
Seeks Learning and Growing
Finds Friends at School
Habitual Security Seeking
Presented with Protection
Adds to Reputation
Separation from Expertise
Drawn to Competence
Destined for Fulfillment
Strives for Objectives
Connections with Experts
Rids Self of Birth Image
Seeks Qualified Assistants
Separates from Outcomes
Encounters Security Seeking
Attracts Others through Maturity
Realizes the Outcome
Acquainted with Self-Restraint
Has Chances to Learn
Events which help you Grow
Strives for Recognition
Seeks Personal Development

NODE/MIDHEAVEN With Itself

☊ Friendships cultivated and acquired during your early life which persist and help you over the years; the familiarity you gain with how to make friends and work with people; an innate ability to show competence among peers.

M Rewards and personal satisfactions from friendships; recognition because you pursued opportunities opened by friends; personal interests or talents which allow you to develop innate abilities in life.

Significant Examples of People and Events Using Node/Midheaven

General: **STRONG:** Emperor Hirohito; Carl Sagan; Steve Wozniak; Dr. Tom Dooley; Albert Speer; Jack Schwartz; Erwin Rommel; Manly Palmer Hall; Hank Williams; Alexis Carrel; Henri Toulouse-Lautrec; Louis Pasteur
WEAK: Elvis Presley; Georges Seurat; Jonathan Winters; Neil Diamond; Henry Winkler; Benjamin Disraeli; Paul Cezanne; Jacques Cousteau
EVENTS: George Washington's Inauguration; Nixon's Resignation; Transcontinental Railroad Completed; Wright Brothers First Flight; (Apollo 11 Moon Landing).

☉ Alexis Carrel; Louis Pasteur; Lawrence Welk; John Fremont; B. Mussolini

☽ Emperor Hirohito; Johann Von Goethe; John Denver; Pearl Harbor Attack

☿ Claude Debussy; Steve Wozniak; RMS Titanic Hits Iceberg; First A-Bomb Explosion; Carl Sagan; Carroll Righter

♀ Charles Steinmetz; H. Toulouse-Lautrec; Ivar Kreugar; Moshe Dayan

♂ Jackie Robinson; Mick Jagger; Transcon. RR done; Wright Bros. First Flight

♃ Ervin Nyiregyhazi; Elton John; Jack Schwartz; Dave Garroway; Abraham Lincoln; R. D. Laing; Paul Cezanne

♄ Tom Jones; John McEnroe; Charles Addams; Guglielmo Marconi

♅ Robert McNamara; Percy Bysshe Shelley; Lord Byron; Pearl Harbor Attack; Alan Alda; Alexander Graham Bell

♆ Louis Pasteur; Hugh Downs; Henri Toulouse-Lautrec; Rollo May; Yehudi Menuhin; Henry Kissinger

♇ Nixon's Resignation; Ernest Hemingway; Shirley Jones; R. W. Emerson

☊, M Jerry Reed; G. Washington's Inauguration; Carl Sagan; Steve Wozniak

A Transcontinental Railroad Completed; Pearl Harbor Attack; Abraham Lincoln; Gianni Agnelli; Steve Wozniak

ASCENDANT/MIDHEAVEN   A/M

Basic Ideas:

The understanding you bring to interpersonal situations through the expertise or knowledge you have accumulated, and your perceptions and comprehension about what you must do to become a better person or better your lot in life, are represented here. These themes show your efforts (education, work, friendships formed, travel, etc.) to enrich your life's experiences, the attention you receive for the work you do, and recognition for your endeavors. Your sense of belonging within a community or family environment, the growth of your intellectual capabilities by absorbing the lessons of life, your effort to enrich yourself or expand your lifestyle, and your reflection about situations in life all start here. How you can or cannot relate and grow thru life's experiences, and the feedback you receive from friends about personal status and development also start here.

In Your Personal Life:

Thesis   Learning and maturing as you develop in life; the effects of the lessons of life and how you absorb these; your self-concept and how this changes as you encounter difficulties; your attitudes toward principles.

Anti   Perceptions that you are going nowhere in life and are not able to alter your destiny; ignoring the object lessons that life continues to repeat for you; your inability to learn through using self-growth or restraint.

In Your Relationships:

Thesis   Devoting more attention to growing with others; learning and growing due to the mental perspective that a new relationship brings to you; seeing others as unique individuals, each with different needs.

Anti   An inability to appreciate the differences between others and self; your refusal to learn from associating with other people; an inability to get the type of help you need in life from friends, partners, or backers.

With Body or Mind:

Psychological growth experiences; the maturing you do through your reactions to circumstances or situations in life; a measure of your maturity.

In Politics or Business:

Thesis   Feedback and judgment on the quality and appreciation of an enterprise's services and reputation; the leadership's ability to guide enterprises through periodic cycles of expansion and contraction.

Anti   Lack of progress in improving of the quality of life; an inability to find common or shared goals with neighbors or with those who contributed to your origins; exclusion of racial groups.

ASCENDANT/MIDHEAVEN with Planets and Points

☉   Acclaim and recognition for efforts at improving the quality of your personality and awareness; your contributions to life and the world as gained from personal experiences and interaction with others.

☽   A strong sense of attachment to the rhythms of life; sensitivity about people you encounter, and about how you use these impressions to recognize yourself for what you are and what you can contribute to your own progress in life.

☿   Your thinking or analysis about the effects of your daily contacts with the people in your life who are meaningful to you; the versatility you show when adapting to the examples of those who influence you.

♀   Incorporating your admiration for the qualities of others into respect for self and contentment with your goals; appreciation of the role of entertainment and how it can enhance life; the role of love in your life.

♂   Learning to fight for the appreciation you want and demand; arousing your need for self protection against those you feel threaten your lifestyle; your need to use competitive sports to gain fame.

♃   An awareness of the political needs and nature of others; expanded need to develop your instincts about how to read and use the reactions of others; the ways you idealize the motives of others you meet.

♄   Difficulty in recognizing the motives and intentions of the people you encounter daily; sensing disappointment from others about the way you have conducted your life; simple plans for self-growth.

♅   Abrupt changes to your lifestyle or occupational circumstances which force you to reassess what you want out of life and how to attain it; extraordinary and unusual demands upon self from others; infrequent looks at progress.

♆   You are intuitive about others, and yet at the same time your assessment of their intentions is clouded; an inability to plan or foresee the consequences of your daily activities on the personal growth opportunities you encounter.

♇   Intense drive to work for the recognition that you feel is due to you; depression over your lack of recognition from others; your firm intention to gain influence at any price.

☊   Encountering others who are able to help you with the personal assessment you make about your life and your progress as a person; associating with the right kind of people to help you formulate and succeed with your plans.

Appendix A
A Cross Reference of Planetary Combinations

Use this cross reference to find all combinations equivalent to the individual descriptions given in this book. Appendix B contains the same information as Appendix A, but is sorted in alphabetical order. The listings under each reference heading (e.g., ☉/☽) are astrological equivalents. That is, a description of 'Sun in the 4th House' in a horoscope can be found under the explanation of the ☉/☽ midpoint. Please see Chapter 2 for a more complete description of the origin of the material contained here. Read down the left hand column and then down the right hand column to use these pages.

☉/☽

Sun in the 4th House
Moon in the 5th House
Sun in Cancer
Moon in Leo
Sun opposition (anything)
Moon conjunct (anything)

☉/☿

Sun in the 3rd House
Sun in the 6th House
Mercury in the 5th House
Sun in Gemini
Sun in Virgo
Mercury in Leo
Sun decile (anything)
Sun quintile (anything)
Mercury conjunct (anything)

☉/♀

Sun in the 2nd House
Sun in the 7th House
Venus in the 5th House
Sun in Taurus
Sun in Libra
Venus in Leo
Sun sextile (anything)
Venus conjunct (anything)

☉/♂

Sun in the 1st House
Sun in the 8th House
Mars in the 5th House
Sun in Aries
Sun in Scorpio
Mars in Leo
Sun semi-square (anything)
Mars conjunct (anything)

☉/♃

Sun in the 9th House
Sun in the 12th House
Jupiter in the 5th House
Sun in Sagittarius
Sun in Pisces
Jupiter in Leo
Sun trine (anything)
Jupiter conjunct (anything)

☉/♄

Sun in the 10th House
Saturn in the 5th House
Sun in Capricorn
Saturn in Leo
Sun square (anything)
Saturn conjunct (anything)

☉/♅

Sun in the 11th House
Uranus in the 5th House
Sun in Aquarius
Uranus in Leo
Sun undecile (anything)
Uranus conjunct (anything)

☉/♆

Sun in the 9th House
Sun in the 12th House
Neptune in the 5th House
Sun in Sagittarius
Sun in Pisces
Neptune in Leo
Sun novile (anything)
Neptune conjunct (anything)

☉/♇

Sun in the 1st House
Sun in the 8th House
Pluto in the 5th House
Sun in Aries
Sun in Scorpio
Pluto in Leo
Sun semi-sextile (anything)
Pluto conjunct (anything)

☉/☊

Node in the 5th House
Node in Leo
Node conjunct (anything)

☉/A

Sun in the 1st House
Leo on the Ascendant
Ascendant conjunct (anything)

☉/M

Sun in the 10th House
Leo on the Midheaven
Midheaven conjunct (anything)

☽/☿

Moon in the 3rd House
Moon in the 6th House
Mercury in the 4th House
Moon in Gemini
Moon in Virgo
Mercury in Cancer
Moon decile (anything)
Moon quintile (anything)
Mercury opposition (anything)

☽/♀

Moon in the 2nd House
Moon in the 7th House
Venus in the 4th House
Moon in Taurus
Moon in Libra
Venus in Cancer
Moon sextile (anything)
Venus opposition (anything)

☽/♂

Moon in the 1st House
Moon in the 8th House
Mars in the 4th House
Moon in Aries
Moon in Scorpio
Mars in Cancer
Moon semi-square (anything)
Mars opposition (anything)

☽/♃

Moon in the 9th House
Moon in the 12th House
Jupiter in the 4th House
Moon in Sagittarius
Moon in Pisces
Jupiter in Cancer
Moon trine (anything)
Jupiter opposition (anything)

☽/♄

Moon in the 10th House
Saturn in the 4th House
Moon in Capricorn
Saturn in Cancer
Moon square (anything)
Saturn opposition (anything)

☽/♅

Moon in the 11th House
Uranus in the 4th House
Moon in Aquarius
Uranus in Cancer
Moon undecile (anything)
Uranus opposition (anything)

☽/♆

Moon in the 9th House
Moon in the 12th House
Neptune in the 4th House
Moon in Sagittarius
Moon in Pisces
Neptune in Cancer
Moon novile (anything)
Neptune opposition (anything)

☽/♇

Moon in the 1st House
Moon in the 8th House
Pluto in the 4th House
Moon in Aries
Moon in Scorpio
Pluto in Cancer
Moon semi-sextile (anything)
Pluto opposition (anything)

☽/☊

Node in the 4th House
Node in Cancer
Node opposition (anything)

☽/A

Moon in the 1st House
Cancer on the Ascendant
Ascendant opposition (anything)

☽/M

Moon in the 10th House
Cancer on the Midheaven
Midheaven opposition (anything)

☿/♀

Mercury in the 2nd House
Mercury in the 7th House
Venus in the 3rd House
Venus in the 6th House
Mercury in Taurus
Mercury in Libra
Venus in Gemini
Venus in Virgo
Mercury sextile (anything)
Venus quintile (anything)
Venus decile (anything)

☿/♂

Mercury in the 1st House
Mercury in the 8th House
Mars in the 3rd House
Mars in the 6th House
Mercury in Aries
Mercury in Scorpio
Mars in Gemini
Mars in Virgo
Mercury semi-square (anything)
Mars quintile (anything)
Mars decile (anything)

☿/♃

Mercury in the 9th House
Mercury in the 12th House
Jupiter in the 3rd House
Jupiter in the 6th House
Mercury in Sagittarius
Mercury in Pisces
Jupiter in Gemini
Jupiter in Virgo
Mercury trine (anything)
Jupiter quintile (anything)
Jupiter decile (anything)

☿/♄

Mercury in the 10th House
Saturn in the 3rd House
Saturn in the 6th House
Mercury in Capricorn
Saturn in Gemini
Saturn in Virgo
Mercury square (anything)
Saturn quintile (anything)
Saturn decile (anything)

☿/♅

Mercury in the 11th House
Uranus in the 3rd House
Uranus in the 6th House
Mercury in Aquarius
Uranus in Gemini
Uranus in Virgo
Mercury undecile (anything)
Uranus quintile (anything)
Uranus decile (anything)

☿/♆

Mercury in the 9th House
Mercury in the 12th House
Neptune in the 3rd House
Neptune in the 6th House
Mercury in Sagittarius
Mercury in Pisces
Neptune in Gemini
Neptune in Virgo
Mercury novile (anything)
Neptune quintile (anything)
Neptune decile (anything)

☿/♇

Mercury in the 1st House
Mercury in the 8th House
Pluto in the 3rd House
Pluto in the 6th House
Mercury in Aries
Mercury in Scorpio
Pluto in Gemini
Pluto in Virgo
Mercury semi-sextile (anything)
Pluto quintile (anything)
Pluto decile (anything)

☿/☊

Node in the 3rd House
Node in the 6th House
Node in Gemini
Node in Virgo
Node quintile (anything)
Node decile (anything)

☿/A

Mercury in the 1st House
Gemini on the Ascendant
Virgo on the Ascendant
Ascendant quintile (anything)
Ascendant decile (anything)

☿/M

Mercury in the 10th House
Gemini on the Midheaven
Virgo on the Midheaven
Midheaven quintile (anything)
Midheaven decile (anything)

♀/♂

Venus in the 1st House
Venus in the 8th House
Mars in the 2nd House
Mars in the 7th House
Venus in Aries
Venus in Scorpio
Mars in Taurus
Mars in Libra
Venus semi-square (anything)
Mars sextile (anything)

♀/♃

Venus in the 9th House
Venus in the 12th House
Jupiter in the 2nd House
Jupiter in the 7th House
Venus in Sagittarius
Venus in Pisces
Jupiter in Taurus
Jupiter in Libra
Venus trine (anything)
Jupiter sextile (anything)

♀/♄

Venus in the 10th House
Saturn in the 2nd House
Saturn in the 7th House
Venus in Capricorn
Saturn in Taurus
Saturn in Libra
Venus square (anything)
Saturn sextile (anything)

♀/♅

Venus in the 11th House
Uranus in the 2nd House
Uranus in the 7th House
Venus in Aquarius
Uranus in Taurus
Uranus in Libra
Venus undecile (anything)
Uranus sextile (anything)

♀/♆

Venus in the 9th House
Venus in the 12th House
Neptune in the 2nd House
Neptune in the 7th House
Venus in Sagittarius
Venus in Pisces
Neptune in Taurus
Neptune in Libra
Venus novile (anything)
Neptune sextile (anything)

♀/♇

Venus in the 1st House
Venus in the 8th House
Pluto in the 2nd House
Pluto in the 7th House
Venus in Aries
Venus in Scorpio
Pluto in Taurus
Pluto in Libra
Venus semi-sextile (anything)
Pluto sextile (anything)

♀/☊

Node in the 2nd House
Node in the 7th House
Node in Taurus
Node in Libra
Node sextile (anything)

♀/A

Venus in the 1st House
Taurus on the Ascendant
Libra on the Ascendant
Ascendant sextile (anything)

♀/M

Venus in the 10th House
Taurus on the Midheaven
Libra on the Midheaven
Midheaven sextile (anything)

♂/♃

Mars in the 9th House
Mars in the 12th House
Jupiter in the 1st House
Jupiter in the 8th House
Mars in Sagittarius
Mars in Pisces
Jupiter in Aries
Jupiter in Scorpio
Mars trine (anything)
Jupiter semi-square (anything)

♂/♄

Mars in the 10th House
Saturn in the 1st House
Saturn in the 8th House
Mars in Capricorn
Saturn in Aries
Saturn in Scorpio
Mars square (anything)
Saturn semi-square (anything)

♂/♅

Mars in the 11th House
Uranus in the 1st House
Uranus in the 8th House
Mars in Aquarius
Uranus in Aries
Uranus in Scorpio
Mars undecile (anything)
Uranus semi-square (anything)

♂/♆

Mars in the   9th House
Mars in the 12th House
Neptune in the 1st House
Neptune in the 8th House
Mars in Sagittarius
Mars in Pisces
Neptune in Aries
Neptune in Scorpio
Mars novile (anything)
Neptune semi-square (anything)

♂/♀

Mars in the 1st House
Mars in the 8th House
Pluto in the 1st House
Pluto in the 8th House
Mars in Aries
Mars in Scorpio
Pluto in Aries
Pluto in Scorpio
Mars semi-sextile (anything)
Pluto semi-square (anything)

♂/☊

Node in the 1st House
Node in the 8th House
Node in Aries
Node in Scorpio
Node semi-square (anything)

♂/A

Mars in the 1st House
Aries on the Ascendant
Scorpio on the Ascendant
Ascendant semi-square (anything)

♂/M

Mars in the 10th House
Aries on the Midheaven
Scorpio on the Midheaven
Midheaven semi-square (anything)

♃/♄

Jupiter in the 10th House
Saturn in the 9th House
Saturn in the 12th House
Jupiter in Capricorn
Saturn in Sagittarius
Saturn in Pisces
Jupiter square (anything)
Saturn trine (anything)

♃/♅

Jupiter in the 11th House
Uranus in the 9th House
Uranus in the 12th House
Jupiter in Aquarius
Uranus in Sagittarius
Uranus in Pisces
Jupiter undecile (anything)
Uranus trine (anything)

♃/♆

Jupiter in the 9th House
Jupiter in the 12th House
Neptune in the 9th House
Neptune in the 12th House
Jupiter in Sagittarius
Jupiter in Pisces
Neptune in Sagittarius
Neptune in Pisces
Jupiter novile (anything)
Neptune trine (anything)

♃/♀

Jupiter in the 1st House
Jupiter in the 8th House
Pluto in the 9th House
Pluto in the 12th House
Jupiter in Aries
Jupiter in Scorpio
Pluto in Sagittarius
Pluto in Pisces
Jupiter semi-sextile (anything)
Pluto trine (anything)

♃/☊

Node in the 9th House
Node in the 12th House
Node in Sagittarius
Node in Pisces
Node trine (anything)

♃/A

Jupiter in the 1st House
Sagittarius on the Ascendant
Pisces on the Ascendant
Ascendant trine (anything)

♃/M

Jupiter in the 10th House
Sagittarius on the Midheaven
Pisces on the Midheaven
Midheaven trine (anything)

♄/♅

Saturn in the 11th House
Uranus in the 10th House
Saturn in Aquarius
Uranus in Capricorn
Saturn undecile (anything)
Uranus square (anything)

♄/♆

Saturn in the 9th House
Saturn in the 12th House
Neptune in the 10th House
Saturn in Pisces
Neptune in Capricorn
Saturn novile (anything)
Neptune square (anything)

♄/♀

Saturn in the 1st House
Saturn in the 8th House
Pluto in the 10th House
Saturn in Aries
Saturn in Scorpio
Pluto in Capricorn
Saturn semi-sextile (anything)
Pluto square (anything)

♄/☊

Node in the 10th House
Node in Capricorn
Node square (anything)

♄/A

Saturn in the 1st House
Capricorn on the Ascendant
Aquarius on the Ascendant
Ascendant square (anything)

♄/M

Saturn in the 10th House
Saturn in Capricorn
Capricorn on the Midheaven
Aquarius on the Midheaven
Midheaven square (anything)

♅/♆

Uranus in the 9th House
Uranus in the 12th House
Neptune in the 11th House
Uranus in Sagittarius
Uranus in Pisces
Neptune in Aquarius
Uranus novile (anything)
Neptune undecile (anything)

♅/♀

Uranus in the 1st House
Uranus in the 8th House
Pluto in the 11th House
Uranus in Aries
Uranus in Scorpio
Pluto in Aquarius
Uranus semi-sextile (anything)
Pluto undecile (anything)

♅/☊

Node in the 11th House
Node in Aquarius
Node undecile (anything)

♅/A

Uranus in the 1st House
Aquarius on the Ascendant
Ascendant undecile (anything)

♅/M

Uranus in the 10th House
Uranus in Capricorn
Aquarius on the Midheaven
Midheaven undecile (anything)

♆/♀

Neptune in the 1st House
Neptune in the 8th House
Pluto in the 9th House
Pluto in the 12th House
Neptune in Aries
Neptune in Scorpio
Pluto in Sagittarius
Pluto in Pisces
Neptune semi-sextile (anything)
Pluto novile (anything)

Ψ/☊

Node in the 9th House
Node in the 12th House
Node in Sagittarius
Node in Pisces
Node novile (anything)

Ψ/A

Neptune in the 1st House
Neptune in the 12th House
Sagittarius on the Ascendant
Pisces on the Ascendant
Ascendant novile (anything)

Ψ/M

Neptune in the 10th House
Sagittarius on the Midheaven
Pisces on the Midheaven
Midheaven novile (anything)

♀/☊

Node in the 1st House
Node in the 8th House
Node in Aries
Node in Scorpio
Node semi-sextile (anything)

♀/A

Pluto in the 1st House
Aries on the Ascendant
Scorpio on the Ascendant
Ascendant semi-sextile (anything)

♀/M

Pluto in the 10th House
Aries on the Midheaven
Scorpio on the Midheaven
Midheaven semi-sextile (anything)

☊/A

Node in the 1st House

☊/M

Node in the 10th House

Appendix B
A Sorted Reference of Astrological Equivalents

There are two parts to each column, a word explanation and an astrological equivalent paired with it which you can reference in the main part of this book. For example, Aquarius on the Ascendant in a chart will have correspondences to the midpoint writeup given with ♅/A; Jupiter in Aries in a chart can be referenced in the writeup on ♂/♃; and so forth. Read down the left column pairing and then down the right column pairing on each page for the alphabetical listing of all such astrological equivalences.

Aquarius:
- on the Ascendant .... ♄ / A
- on the Ascendant .... ♅ / A
- on the Midheaven .... ♄ / M
- on the Midheaven .... ♅ / M

Aries:
- on the Ascendant .... ♂ / A
- on the Ascendant .... ♇ / A
- on the Midheaven .... ♂ / M
- on the Midheaven .... ♇ / M

Ascendant:
- in Aries .... ♂ / A
- in Aries .... ♇ / A
- in Taurus .... ♀ / A
- in Gemini .... ☿ / A
- in Cancer .... ☽ / A
- in Leo .... ☉ / A
- in Virgo .... ☿ / A
- in Libra .... ♀ / A
- in Scorpio .... ♂ / A
- in Scorpio .... ♇ / A
- in Sagittarius .... ♃ / A
- in Sagittarius .... ♆ / A
- in Capricorn .... ♄ / A
- in Aquarius .... ♄ / A
- in Aquarius .... ♅ / A
- in Pisces .... ♃ / A
- in Pisces .... ♆ / A
- conjunct (anything) .... ☉ / A
- decile (anything) .... ☿ / A

Ascendant (continued):
- novile (anything) .... ♆ / A
- opposition (anything) .... ☽ / A
- quintile (anything) .... ☿ / A
- semi-sextile (anything) .... ♇ / A
- semi-square (anything) .... ♂ / A
- sextile (anything) .... ♀ / A
- square (anything) .... ♄ / A
- trine (anything) .... ♃ / A
- undecile (anything) .... ♅ / A

Cancer:
- on the Ascendant .... ☽ / A
- on the Midheaven .... ☽ / M

Capricorn:
- on the Ascendant .... ♄ / A
- on the Midheaven .... ♄ / M

Gemini:
- on the Ascendant .... ☿ / A
- on the Midheaven .... ☿ / M

Jupiter:
- in Aries .... ♂ / ♃
- in Aries .... ♃ / ♇
- in Taurus .... ♀ / ♃
- in Gemini .... ☿ / ♃
- in Cancer .... ☽ / ♃
- in Leo .... ☉ / ♃
- in Virgo .... ☿ / ♃
- in Libra .... ♀ / ♃

Jupiter (continued):
- in Scorpio .... ♂ / ♃
- in Scorpio .... ♃ / ♇
- in Sagittarius .... ♃ / ♆
- in Capricorn .... ♃ / ♄
- in Aquarius .... ♃ / ♄
- in Aquarius .... ♃ / ♅
- in Pisces .... ♃ / ♆
- in the 1st House .... ♂ / ♃
- in the 1st House .... ♃ / A
- in the 2nd House .... ♀ / ♃
- in the 3rd House .... ☿ / ♃
- in the 4th House .... ☽ / ♃
- in the 5th House .... ☉ / ♃
- in the 6th House .... ☿ / ♃
- in the 7th House .... ♀ / ♃
- in the 8th House .... ♂ / ♃
- in the 8th House .... ♃ / ♇
- in the 9th House .... ♃ / ♆
- in the 10th House .... ♃ / ♄
- in the 10th House .... ♃ / M
- in the 11th House .... ♃ / ♄
- in the 11th House .... ♃ / ♅
- in the 12th House .... ♃ / ♆
- conjunct (anything) .... ☉ / ♃
- decile (anything) .... ☿ / ♃
- novile (anything) .... ♃ / ♆
- opposition (anything) ..... ☽ / ♃
- quintile (anything) .... ☿ / ♃
- semi-sextile (anything) ... ♃ / ♇
- semi-square (anything) .. ♂ / ♃
- sextile (anything) .... ♀ / ♃
- square (anything) .... ♃ / ♄
- undecile (anything) .... ♃ / ♅

Leo:
- on the Ascendant .... ☉ / A
- on the Midheaven .... ☉ / M

Libra:
- on the Ascendant .... ♀ / A
- on the Midheaven .... ♀ / M

Mars:
- in Aries .... ♂ / ♇
- in Taurus .... ♀ / ♂
- in Gemini .... ☿ / ♂
- in Cancer .... ☽ / ♂
- in Leo .... ☉ / ♂
- in Virgo .... ☿ / ♂
- in Libra .... ♀ / ♂
- in Scorpio .... ♂ / ♇
- in Sagittarius .... ♂ / ♃
- in Sagittarius .... ♂ / ♆
- in Capricorn .... ♂ / ♄
- in Aquarius .... ♂ / ♄
- in Aquarius .... ♂ / ♅
- in Pisces .... ♂ / ♃
- in Pisces .... ♂ / ♆
- in the 1st House .... ♂ / ♇
- in the 1st House .... ♂ / A
- in the 2nd House .... ♀ / ♂
- in the 3rd House .... ☿ / ♂
- in the 4th House .... ☽ / ♂
- in the 5th House .... ☉ / ♂
- in the 6th House .... ☿ / ♂
- in the 7th House .... ♀ / ♂
- in the 8th House .... ♂ / ♇
- in the 9th House .... ♂ / ♃
- in the 9th House .... ♂ / ♆
- in the 10th House .... ♂ / ♄
- in the 10th House .... ♂ / M
- in the 11th House .... ♂ / ♅
- in the 12th House .... ♂ / ♃
- in the 12th House .... ♂ / ♆
- conjunct (anything) .... ☉ / ♂
- decile (anything) .... ☿ / ♂
- novile (anything) .... ♂ / ♆
- opposition (anything) ..... ☽ / ♂
- quintile (anything) .... ☿ / ♂
- semi-sextile (anything) .. ♂ / ♇
- sextile (anything) .... ♀ / ♂
- square (anything) .... ♂ / ♄
- trine (anything) .... ♂ / ♃
- undecile (anything) .... ♂ / ♅

Mercury:

- in Aries ☿ / ♂
- in Aries ☿ / ♇
- in Taurus ☿ / ♀
- in Gemini ☿
- in Cancer ☽ / ☿
- in Leo ☉ / ☿
- in Virgo ☿
- in Libra ☿ / ♀
- in Scorpio ☿ / ♂
- in Scorpio ☿ / ♇
- in Sagittarius ☿ / ♃
- in Sagittarius ☿ / ♆
- in Capricorn ☿ / ♅
- in Aquarius ☿ / ♄
- in Aquarius ☿ / ♅
- in Pisces ☿ / ♃
- in Pisces ☿ / ♆
- in the 1st House ☿ / ♂
- in the 1st House ☿ / A
- in the 2nd House ☿ / ♀
- in the 3rd House ☿
- in the 4th House ☽ / ☿
- in the 5th House ☉ / ☿
- in the 6th House ☿
- in the 7th House ☿ / ♀
- in the 8th House ☿ / ♂
- in the 8th House ☿ / ♇
- in the 9th House ☿ / ♃
- in the 9th House ☿ / ♆
- in the 10th House ☿ / ♄
- in the 10th House ☿ / M
- in the 11th House ☿ / ♄
- in the 11th House ☿ / ♅
- in the 12th House ☿ / ♃
- in the 12th House ☿ / ♆
- conjunct (anything) ☉ / ☿
- novile (anything) ☿ / ♆
- opposition (anything) ☽ / ☿
- quintile (anything) ☿
- semi-sextile (anything) ☿ / ♇
- semi-square (anything) ☿ / ♂
- sextile (anything) ☿ / ♀
- square (anything) ☿ / ♄

Mercury (continued):

- trine (anything) ☿ / ♃
- undecile (anything) ☿ / ♅

Midheaven:

- in Aries ♂ / M
- in Aries ♇ / M
- in Taurus ♀ / M
- in Gemini ☿ / M
- in Cancer ☽ / M
- in Leo ☉ / M
- in Virgo ☿ / M
- in Libra ♀ / M
- in Scorpio ♂ / M
- in Scorpio ♇ / M
- in Sagittarius ♃ / M
- in Sagittarius ♆ / M
- in Capricorn ♄ / M
- in Aquarius ♄ / M
- in Aquarius ♅ / M
- in Pisces ♃ / M
- in Pisces ♆ / M
- conjunct (anything) ☉ / M
- decile (anything) ☿ / M
- novile (anything) ♆ / M
- opposition (anything) ☽ / M
- quintile (anything) ☿ / M
- semi-sextile (anything) ♇ / M
- semi-square (anything) ♂ / M
- sextile (anything) ♀ / M
- square (anything) ♄ / M
- trine (anything) ♃ / M
- undecile (anything) ♅ / M

Moon:

- in Aries ☽ / ♂
- in Aries ☽ / ♇
- in Taurus ☽ / ♀
- in Gemini ☽ / ☿
- in Cancer ☽
- in Leo ☉ / ☽
- in Virgo ☽ / ☿
- in Libra ☽ / ♀
- in Scorpio ☽ / ♂

Moon (continued):

- in Scorpio .... ☽ / ♇
- in Sagittarius .... ☽ / ♃
- in Sagittarius .... ☽ / ♆
- in Capricorn .... ☽ / ♄
- in Aquarius .... ☽ / ♄
- in Aquarius .... ☽ / ♅
- in Pisces .... ☽ / ♃
- in Pisces .... ☽ / ♆
- in the 1st House .... ☽ / ♂
- in the 1st House .... ☽ / ♇
- in the 1st House .... ☽ / A
- in the 2nd House .... ☽ / ♀
- in the 3rd House .... ☽ / ☿
- in the 4th House .... ☽
- in the 5th House .... ☉ / ☽
- in the 6th House .... ☽ / ☿
- in the 7th House .... ☽ / ♀
- in the 8th House .... ☽ / ♂
- in the 8th House .... ☽ / ♇
- in the 9th House .... ☽ / ♃
- in the 9th House .... ☽ / ♆
- in the 10th House .... ☽ / ♄
- in the 10th House .... ☽ / M
- in the 11th House .... ☽ / ♄
- in the 11th House .... ☽ / ♅
- in the 12th House .... ☽ / ♃
- in the 12th House .... ☽ / ♆
- conjunct (anything) .... ☉ / ☽
- decile (anything) .... ☽ / ☿
- novile (anything) .... ☽ / ♆
- quintile (anything) .... ☽ / ☿
- semi-sextile (anything) ... ☽ / ♇
- semi-square (anything) .. ☽ / ♂
- sextile (anything) .... ☽ / ♀
- square (anything) .... ☽ / ♄
- trine (anything) .... ☽ / ♃
- undecile (anything) .... ☽ / ♅

Neptune

- in Aries .... ♂ / ♆
- in Aries .... ♆ / ♇

Neptune (continued):

- in Taurus .... ♀ / ♆
- in Gemini .... ☿ / ♆
- in Cancer .... ☽ / ♆
- in Leo .... ☉ / ♆
- in Virgo .... ☿ / ♆
- in Libra .... ♀ / ♆
- in Scorpio .... ♂ / ♆
- in Scorpio .... ♆ / ♇
- in Sagittarius .... ♃ / ♆
- in Capricorn .... ♄ / ♆
- in Aquarius .... ♄ / ♆
- in Aquarius .... ♅ / ♆
- in Pisces .... ♃ / ♆
- in the 1st House .... ♂ / ♆
- in the 1st House .... ♆ / A
- in the 2nd House .... ♀ / ♆
- in the 3rd House .... ☿ / ♆
- in the 4th House .... ☽ / ♆
- in the 5th House .... ☉ / ♆
- in the 6th House .... ☿ / ♆
- in the 7th House .... ♀ / ♆
- in the 8th House .... ♂ / ♆
- in the 8th House .... ♆ / ♇
- in the 9th House .... ♃ / ♆
- in the 10th House .... ♄ / ♆
- in the 10th House .... ♆ / M
- in the 11th House .... ♄ / ♆
- in the 11th House .... ♅ / ♆
- in the 12th House .... ♃ / ♆
- conjunct (anything) .... ☉ / ♆
- decile (anything) .... ☿ / ♆
- opposition (anything) ..... ☽ / ♆
- quintile (anything) .... ☿ / ♆
- semi-sextile (anything) ... ♆ / ♇
- semi-square (anything) .. ♂ / ♆
- sextile (anything) .... ♀ / ♆
- square (anything) .... ♄ / ♆
- trine (anything) .... ♃ / ♆
- undecile (anything) .... ♅ / ♆

Node:

- in Aries ....♂ / ☊
- in Aries ....♇ / ☊
- in Taurus ....♀ / ☊
- in Gemini ....☿ / ☊
- in Cancer ....☽ / ☊
- in Leo ....☉ / ☊
- in Virgo ....☿ / ☊
- in Libra ....♀ / ☊
- in Scorpio ....♂ / ☊
- in Scorpio ....♇ / ☊
- in Sagittarius ....♃ / ☊
- in Sagittarius ....♆ / ☊
- in Capricorn ....♄ / ☊
- in Aquarius ....♄ / ☊
- in Aquarius ....♅ / ☊
- in Pisces ....♃ / ☊
- in Pisces ....♆ / ☊
- in the 1st House ....♂ / ☊
- in the 1st House ....♇ / ☊
- in the 1st House ....☊ / A
- in the 2nd House ....♀ / ☊
- in the 3rd House ....☿ / ☊
- in the 4th House ....☽ / ☊
- in the 5th House ....☉ / ☊
- in the 6th House ....☿ / ☊
- in the 7th House ....♀ / ☊
- in the 8th House ....♂ / ☊
- in the 8th House ....♇ / ☊
- in the 9th House ....♃ / ☊
- in the 9th House ....♆ / ☊
- in the 10th House ....♄ / ☊
- in the 10th House ....☊ / M
- in the 11th House ....♄ / ☊
- in the 11th House ....♅ / ☊
- in the 12th House ....♃ / ☊
- conjunct (anything) ....☉ / ☊
- decile (anything) ....☿ / ☊
- novile (anything) ....♆ / ☊
- opposition (anything) .....☽ / ☊
- quintile (anything) ....☿ / ☊
- semi-sextile (anything) ...♇ / ☊
- semi-square (anything) ..♂ / ☊
- sextile (anything) ....♀ / ☊
- square (anything) ....♄ / ☊

Node (continued):

- trine (anything) ....♃ / ☊
- undecile (anything) ....♅ / ☊

Pisces:

- on the Ascendant ....♃ / A
- on the Ascendant ....♆ / A
- on the Midheaven ....♃ / M
- on the Midheaven ....♆ / M

Pluto:

- in Aries ....♂ / ♇
- in Taurus ....♀ / ♇
- in Gemini ....☿ / ♇
- in Cancer ....☽ / ♇
- in Leo ....☉ / ♇
- in Virgo ....☿ / ♇
- in Libra ....♀ / ♇
- in Scorpio ....♂ / ♇
- in Sagittarius ....♃ / ♇
- in Sagittarius ....♆ / ♇
- in Capricorn ....♄ / ♇
- in Capricorn ....♄ / M
- in Aquarius ....♄ / ♇
- in Aquarius ....♅ / ♇
- in Pisces ....♃ / ♇
- in Pisces ....♆ / ♇
- in the 1st House ....♂ / ♇
- in the 1st House ....♇ / A
- in the 2nd House ....♀ / ♇
- in the 3rd House ....☿ / ♇
- in the 4th House ....☽ / ♇
- in the 5th House ....☉ / ♇
- in the 6th House ....☿ / ♇
- in the 7th House ....♀ / ♇
- in the 8th House ....♂ / ♇
- in the 9th House ....♃ / ♇
- in the 9th House ....♆ / ♇
- in the 10th House ....♄ / ♇
- in the 10th House ....♇ / M
- in the 11th House ....♄ / ♇
- in the 11th House ....♅ / ♇
- in the 12th House ....♃ / ♇
- in the 12th House ....♆ / ♇

Pluto (continued):
- conjunct (anything) ....☉ / ♇
- decile (anything)..............☿ / ♇
- novile (anything).............♆ / ♇
- opposition (anything).....☽ / ♇
- quintile (anything) ....☿ / ♇
- semi-square (anything)..♂ / ♇
- sextile (anything) ....♀ / ♇
- square (anything) ....♄ / ♇
- trine (anything) ....♃ / ♇
- undecile (anything) ....♅ / ♇

Sagittarius:
- on the Ascendant ....♃ / A
- on the Ascendant ....♆ / A
- on the Midheaven...........♃ / M
- on the Midheaven ....♆ / M

Saturn:
- in Aries.............................♂ / ♄
- in Aries.............................♄ / ♇
- in Taurus ....♀ / ♄
- in Gemini ....☿ / ♄
- in Cancer...........................☽ / ♄
- in Leo ....☉ / ♄
- in Virgo ....☿ / ♄
- in Libra ....♀ / ♄
- in Scorpio ....♂ / ♄
- in Scorpio..........................♄ / ♇
- in Sagittarius....................♃ / ♄
- in Sagittarius ....♄ / ♆
- in Capricorn .... ♄
- in Capricorn ....♄ / M
- in Aquarius ....♄ / ♅
- in Pisces ....♃ / ♄
- in Pisces ....♄ / ♆
- in the 1st House ....♂ / ♄
- in the 1st House ....♄ / A
- in the 2nd House ....♀ / ♄
- in the 3rd House ....☿ / ♄
- in the 4th House ....☽ / ♄
- in the 5th House.............☉ / ♄
- in the 6th House ....☿ / ♄
- in the 7th House ....♀ / ♄

Saturn(continued):
- in the 8th House..............♂ / ♄
- in the 8th House ....♄ / ♇
- in the 9th House..............♃ / ♄
- in the 9th House ....♄ / ♆
- in the 10th House ....♄ / M
- in the 11th House ....♄ / ♅
- in the 12th House............♃ / ♄
- in the 12th House ....♄ / ♆
- conjunct (anything) ....☉ / ♄
- decile (anything)..............☿ / ♄
- novile (anything) ....♄ / ♆
- opposition (anything).....☽ / ♄
- quintile (anything) ....☿ / ♄
- semi-sextile (anything) ...♄ / ♇
- semi-square (anything)..♂ / ♄
- sextile (anything) ....♀ / ♄
- trine (anything) ....♃ / ♄
- undecile (anything).........♄ / ♅

Scorpio:
- on the Ascendant ....♂ / A
- on the Ascendant ....♇ / A
- on the Midheaven...........♂ / M
- on the Midheaven ....♇ / M

Sun:
- in Aries ....☉ / ♂
- in Aries ....☉ / ♇
- in Taurus ....☉ / ♀
- in Gemini ....☉ / ☿
- in Cancer ....☉ / ☽
- in Leo .... ☉
- in Virgo ....☉ / ☿
- in Libra ....☉ / ♀
- in Scorpio ....☉ / ♂
- in Scorpio ....☉ / ♇
- in Sagittarius ....☉ / ♃
- in Sagittarius ....☉ / ♆
- in Capricorn ....☉ / ♄
- in Aquarius.......................☉ / ♄
- in Aquarius.......................☉ / ♅
- in Pisces............................☉ / ♃

Sun (continued):
in Pisces .... ☉ / ♆
in the 1st House .... ☉ / ♂
in the 1st House .... ☉ / ♇
in the 1st House .... ☉ / A
in the 2nd House .... ☉ / ♀
in the 3rd House .... ☉ / ☿
in the 4th House .... ☉ / ☽
in the 5th House .... ☉
in the 6th House .... ☉ / ☿
in the 7th House .... ☉ / ♀
in the 8th House .... ☉ / ♂
in the 8th House .... ☉ / ♇
in the 9th House .... ☉ / ♃
in the 9th House .... ☉ / ♆
in the 10th House .... ☉ / ♄
in the 10th House .... ☉ / M
in the 11th House .... ☉ / ♄
in the 11th House .... ☉ / ♅
in the 12th House .... ☉ / ♃
in the 12th House .... ☉ / ♆
conjunct (anything) .... ☉
decile (anything) .... ☉ / ☿
novile (anything) .... ☉ / ♆
opposition (anything) .... ☉ / ☽
quintile (anything) .... ☉ / ☿
semi-sextile (anything) .... ☉ / ♇
semi-square (anything) .... ☉ / ♂
sextile (anything) .... ☉ / ♀
square (anything) .... ☉ / ♄
trine (anything) .... ☉ / ♃
undecile (anything) .... ☉ / ♅

Taurus:
on the Ascendant .... ♀ / A
on the Midheaven .... ♀ / M

Uranus:
in Aries .... ♂ / ♅
in Aries .... ♂ / ♇
in Taurus .... ♀ / ♅
in Gemini .... ☿ / ♅
in Cancer .... ☽ / ♅
in Leo .... ☉ / ♅

Uranus (continued):
in Virgo .... ☿ / ♅
in Libra .... ♀ / ♅
in Scorpio .... ♂ / ♅
in Scorpio .... ♅ / ♇
in Sagittarius .... ♃ / ♅
in Sagittarius .... ♅ / ♆
in Capricorn .... ♄ / ♅
in Capricorn .... ♅ / M
in Aquarius .... ♅
in Aquarius .... ♄ / ♅
in Pisces .... ♃ / ♅
in Pisces .... ♅ / ♆
in the 1st House .... ♂ / ♅
in the 1st House .... ♅ / A
in the 2nd House .... ♀ / ♅
in the 3rd House .... ☿ / ♅
in the 4th House .... ☽ / ♅
in the 5th House .... ☉ / ♅
in the 6th House .... ☿ / ♅
in the 7th House .... ♀ / ♅
in the 8th House .... ♂ / ♅
in the 8th House .... ♅ / ♇
in the 9th House .... ♃ / ♅
in the 9th House .... ♅ / ♆
in the 10th House .... ♄ / ♅
in the 10th House .... ♅ / M
in the 11th House .... ♅
in the 11th House .... ♄ / ♅
in the 12th House .... ♃ / ♅
in the 12th House .... ♅ / ♆
conjunct (anything) .... ☉ / ♅
decile (anything) .... ☿ / ♅
novile (anything) .... ♅ / ♆
opposition (anything) .... ☽ / ♅
quintile (anything) .... ☿ / ♅
semi-sextile (anything) .... ♅ / ♇
semi-square (anything) .... ♂ / ♅
sextile (anything) .... ♀ / ♅
square (anything) .... ♄ / ♅
trine (anything) .... ♃ / ♅

Venus:
in Aries .... ♀ / ♂

in Aries ....♀ / ⚷
in Taurus................................ ♀
in Gemini ....☿ / ♀
in Cancer.............................☽ / ♀
in Leo ....☉ / ♀
in Virgo ....☿ / ♀
in Libra .... ♀
in Scorpio ....♀ / ♂
in Scorpio ....♀ / ⚷
in Sagittarius ....♀ / ♃
in Sagittarius ....♀ / ♆
in Capricorn ....♀ / ♄
in Aquarius ....♀ / ♄
in Aquarius ....♀ / ♅
in Pisces ....♀ / ♃
in Pisces ....♀ / ♆
in the 1st House................♀ / ♂
in the 1st House................♀ / A
in the 2nd House .... ♀
in the 3rd House ....☿ / ♀
in the 4th House ....☽ / ♀
in the 5th House..............☉ / ♀
in the 6th House ....☿ / ♀
in the 7th House .... ♀
in the 8th House ....♀ / ♂
in the 8th House ....♀ / ⚷

Venus (continued):
in the 9th House ....♀ / ♃
in the 9th House ....♀ / ♆
in the 10th House ....♀ / ♄
in the 10th House ....♀ / M
in the 11th House ....♀ / ♅
in the 12th House ....♀ / ♆
in the 12th House ....♀ / ♃
conjunct (anything) ....☉ / ♀
decile (anything)..............☿ / ♀
novile (anything)..............♀ / ♆
opposition (anything) .....☽ / ♀
quintile (anything) ....☿ / ♀
semi-sextile (anything) ...♀ / ⚷
semi-square (anything) ..♀ / ♂
square (anything) ....♀ / ♄
trine (anything) ....♀ / ♃

Venus:
undecile (anything).........♀ / ♅

Virgo:
on the Ascendant..............☿ / A
on the Midheaven ....☿ / M

Appendix C
Resources

Resources on the subject of midpoints, computer printouts of midpoints, midpoint tools, etc. follow. While I have tried to include as many references as possible I apologize in advance if I have omitted any author, work, or tool which may help others in working with or using midpoints. Please write the firms or people listed in bold type for information. (Not all books, devices, or services may be available when you request them.)

BOOKS, General Midpoint Information:

Ebertin, Reinhold, *Astrological Healing,*
 Samuel Weiser, PO Box 612, York Beach, ME 03910, 1989.

Ebertin, Reinhold, *The Combination of Stellar Influences,*
 1940, Ebertin - Verlag, West Germany

Ebertin, Reinhold, *The Cosmic Marriage*

Ebertin, Reinhold, *Applied Cosmobiology*

Ebertin, Reinhold, *The Contact Cosmogram*

Ebertin, Reinhold, *Fixed Stars and Their Interpretation*

Ebertin, Reinhold, *Rapid and Reliable Analysis*

Ebertin, Reinhold, *Transits*

 Ebertin - Verlag, West Germany; in the U.S., Ebertin-Verlag publications can be obtained from: **The American Federation of Astrologers,** PO Box 22040, Tempe, AZ 85285.

Harding, Michael, and Charles Harvey, *Working with Astrology,*
 Viking Penguin, Inc.; 40 W 23rd St., New York City,
 NY 10010, 1990.

Munkasey, Michael, *The Concept Dictionary,*
 Neological Systems, Inc., Falls Church, VA, 1991.
 Distributed by **ACS Publications,** Box 34487, San Diego, CA 92163.

Simms, Maria Kay, *The Dial Detective,*
 ACS Publications, Box 34487, San Diego, CA 92163, 1989.

Tyl, Noel, *Times to Come, Vol 12 of The Principles and Practice of Astrology*
 Llewellyn Pub., PO Box 64383-895, St. Paul, MN, 55164, 1974.

BOOKS , Chart Data:

Rodden, Lois, *Astro-Data II.*
Rodden, Lois, *Astro-Data III.*
Rodden, Lois, *Astro-Data IV.*
Rodden, Lois, *Profiles of Women.*
 American Fed. of Astrologers, PO Box 22040, Tempe, AZ 85285.

BOOKS, Chart Data (continued):

Erlewine, Michael, *The Circle Book of Charts*
  Matrix Software, 315 Marion Ave., Big Rapids, MI 49307.

CHART and/or SPECIALIZED MIDPOINT SERVICES:

Astro Communications Services, Inc.
  Box 34487, San Diego, CA 92163, 619 -297-9203
  (A wide variety of charts, list calculations and tools are available,
  such as *Midpoint Structures, Graphic Midpoint Sorts, Dial Charts*, etc.
  Free catalog available on request.)

Munkasey, Michael, *Midpoint Weighting Analysis,*
  (The *Midpoint Weighting Analysis,* which is used and referenced in this
  book, is available from Neological Systems as a computer service for
  individuals. Due to an impending long-distance move at the time this
  book went to press, those requesting the service should write to **Michael
  Munkasey, c/o ACS**, Box 34487, San Diego, CA 92103.)

DEVICES:

Robinett, Patricia , *Astro-Template* & *Astro-Ruler*
  Smart Art, Box 940, Marcola, OR 97454.

Custom Laminated Dials, Computer Plotted Dial Charts
  Astro Communications Services, Inc., PO Box 34487,
  San Diego, CA 92163, 619-297-9203. Free catalog on request.

Kramer, Arlene A., *Star Dial* (a unique and accurate 90° dial)
  Arlene A. Kramer, 24410-1 Victory Blvd.; Woodland Hills, CA 91367.

Mechanical Midpoint/Halfsum Locator
  Astrological Investigations, Windsor, CA.

PERSONAL COMPUTER PROGRAMS FOR ASTROLOGERS:

Erlewine, Michael, *Blue Star*
  Matrix, 315 Marion Ave., Big Rapids, MI 49307, 616-796-2483.

Pottenger, Mark, *CCRS Horoscope Program*
  Astrolabe, P. O. Box 28, Orleans, MA 02653, 508-896-5081.

Haskell, Dennis, *Graphic Astrology*
  Time Cycles Research, 27 Dimmock Rd.; Waterford, CT 06385
  203-444-6641.

Cochrane, David, *Kepler*
  Cosmic Patterns, P. O. Box 14605, Gainesville, FL 32604,
  904-373-1504.

Hand, Robert, *Nova*
  Astrolabe, P. O. Box 28, Orleans, MA 02653, 508-896-5081.

Appendix D
Examples Used

Examples of persons and events used here came from three sources: the *Astro Data II* and *Astro Data III* books by Lois Rodden, and examples taken from real life events as researched by the author. The people whose names follow have their chart data and a short biography listed in the *Astro-Data* books. Please refer to those books for this information. These people were carefully chosen so that no one one career category overshadowed another. In general about fifteen career categories, with no more than fifteen people in each, were selected. The people chosen are listed alphabetically. A short description of their field of endeavor or popularity follows their name and is included for your assistance. Refer to the *Astro-Data* books for more information. All examples are from the *Astro-Data II* book except those marked with a (III) which are from the *Astro-Data III* book.

Most of the selections come from the section of the *Astro-Data* books containing verified birth times (i.e., "A" or "AA" data.) Two exceptions are Charles Kettering, the lead engineer at General Motors who invented most of the common household appliances and the automobile ignition system used for years, and Henry Kissinger, the Secretary of State during the Nixon and Ford presidencies. In the case of Charles Kettering an article on his life in *Smithsonian* magazine provided additional information about him (his birth data is listed as "C" in *Astro-Data II*), and an article in the *Urania* (Uranian SIG newsletter of NCGR) provided a more accurate time of birth for Dr. Kissinger. Both people were in occupations and had enough public exposure to warrant inclusion in this work.

ABDUL-JABBAR, Kareem	Sports, basketball
ADDAMS, Charles	Cartoonist, U.S. (III)
AGNELLI, Gianni	Industrialist, Italian (III)
ALDA, Alan	Actor, movies
ALI, Muhammad	Sports, boxer
ALLEN, Steve	Entertainer, TV show host, comedian
ALPERT, Richard (Ram Dass)	New Age guru
ANDRETTI, Mario	Sports, U.S., auto racer (III)
BELAFONTE, Harry	Entertainer, singer
BELL, Alexander Graham	Scientist, inventor of telephone
BELLI, Melvin	Lawyer, U.S. (III)
BING, Rudolph	Executive, New York City Opera
BLUE, Vida	Sports, U. S. baseball

BORG, Bjorn	Sports, Swedish tennis player (III)
BRANDO, Marlon	Actor, U. S. movies
BRANDT, Willie	Politician, Germany
BRAZZI, Rosanno	Actor, Italian and U.S. movies
BURSTYN, Ellen	Actress, movies, TV
BYRD, Richard	Scientist, explorer, went to North Pole
BYRON, Ada Lovelace	Scientist, mathematician
BYRON, Lord	Poet, British
CAMPBELL, Glen	Entertainer, U.S. country music singer
CAMUS, Albert	Writer, French essayist and novelist
CARPENTER, Scott	Astronaut, U.S.
CARREL, Alexis	Scientist, French biologist and surgeon
CARSON, Johnny	Entertainer, U.S. TV show host
CARTER, Charles E. O.	Astrologer, British (III)
CARTER, James Earl	Politician, U.S. President (III)
CARUSO, Enrico	Singer, Italian operatic tenor (III)
CASTRO, Fidel	Politician, Cuban dictator (III)
CEZANNE, Paul	Artist, French
CHAMBERLAIN, Richard	Actor, U.S. television dramas
CHEIRO	Palmist, numerologist
CHURCHILL, Sir Winston	Politician, British statesman and PM
CLIBURN, Van	Entertainer, U.S. pianist
COCTEAU, Jean	Artist, French poet, novelist
CONNERY, Sean	Actor, movies
COUSTEAU, Jacques	Scientist, oceanographer, inventor
CRANE, Stephen	Writer, American novelist
CROOKES, Sir William	Scientist, British chemist, physician
DAYAN, Moshe	Politician, Israeli general (III)
De NIRO, Robert	Actor, U.S. movies
De SICA, Vittorio	Director, movies and stage
DEBUSSY, Claude	Composer, musical genius, pianist
DEGAS, Edgar	Artist, French sculptor
DENVER, John	Singer, U.S. popular country music
DIAMOND, Neil	Singer, U.S. songwriter (III)
DILLINGER, John	Gangster, U. S. bank robber
DISRAELI, Benjamin	Statesman, British Prime Minister
DOOLEY, Dr. Tom	Humanitarian, medical doctor
DORE, Gustav	Artist, French painter and sculptor
DOUGLAS, William K.	Scientist, physician to astronauts (III)
DOWNS, Hugh	Entertainer, U.S. TV talk show host
DYLAN, Bob	Singer, U.S. folk musician, songwriter

EINSTEIN, Albert	Scientist, mathematician, physicist
EMERSON, Ralph Waldo	Writer, U.S. poet, essayist, thinker (III)
FERBER, Edna	Writer, U.S. novelist and playwright
FERMI, Enrico	Scientist, Italian atomic physicist
FISCHER, Bobby	Chess champion
FITZGERALD, F. Scott	Writer, U.S. novelist
FLEMING, Sir Alexander	Scientist, British bacteriologist
FOCH, Ferdinand	Soldier, French WW1 general
FORD, Arthur	Medium, U.S., clairvoyant (III)
FOSSE, Robert	Dancer, choreographer, director (III)
FOSTER, Stephen	Composer, U.S. songwriter
FRANCO, Francisco	Politician, Spanish dictator
FREMONT, John	Explorer, U.S. general
FREUD, Sigmond	Psychologist, Austrian physician
FROST, David	Entertainer, U.S. TV talk show host
GARROWAY, Dave	Talk show host, entertainer (III)
GAUGUIN, Paul	Artist, French painter, woodcarver
GLENN, John	Astronaut, U.S. Senator
GODFREY, Arthur	Entertainer, television and movies
GOEBBELS, Paul Joseph	Politician, Nazi propagandist
GOERING, Hermann	Military, German general in WWII
GOETHE, Johann Von	Writer, German literary genius
GORDON, Charles	Military, British general
GRANT, Ulysses S.	Politician, U.S. Civil War general (III)
GREGORY, Dick	Comedian, activist (III)
GRETZKY, Wayne	Hockey player (III)
GRIFFIN, Merv	Entertainer, U.S. TV talk show host
GRISSOM, Virgil	Astronaut, U.S.
HALL, Manly Palmer	Philosopher, Canadian, lecturer (III)
HALLEY, Edmund	Scientist, British explorer (III)
HARRISON, Rex	Actor, movies; director
HEMINGWAY, Ernest	Writer, novelist, adventurer
HENDRIX, Jimi	Musician, U.S. singer, rock superstar
HEPBURN, Audrey	Actress, Belgian, ballet dancer (III)
HIROHITO	Japanese Emperor, marine biologist
HITLER, Adolf	Dictator, politician, Nazi (III)
HOFFMAN, Dustin	Actor, U.S. movies
HOPE, Bob	Entertainer, actor, comedian
HOUSTON, Jean	Psychologist, U. S., writer
HUXLEY, Thomas H.	Scientist, British zoologist, lecturer
IVES, Burl	Folk and ballad singer, actor, U.S.

JACKSON, Thomas (Stonewall)	Military, U.S. Civil war general (III)
JAGGER, Mick	Musician, British rock superstar
JOFFRE, Joseph	Military, French Marshall in WW1
JOHN PAUL I	Catholic Pope, reformer
JOHN, Elton	Musician, British singer
JONES, Marc Edmund	Astrologer, U.S., writer
JONES, Shirley	Actress, singer, U.S. (III)
JONES, Tom	Singer, Welsh, actor (III)
KENNEDY, John F.	Politician, U.S. President (III)
KETTERING, Charles	Scientist, U.S. inventor and engineer
KING, Stephen	Writer, U.S. novelist (III)
KISSINGER, Henry	Politician, U.S. statesman
KNIEVEL, Evel	Daredevil, U.S., stuntman
KOMAR	Phenomena, fakir, performer (III)
KOUFAX, Sandy	Sports, baseball pitcher
KREUGAR, Ivar	Business promoter, made fortunes
KRISHNAMURTI, Jeddu	Religious leader, philosopher (III)
LAING, R. D.	Psychiatrist, U.S., analyst, writer
LENNON, John	Musician, British songwriter
LEO, Alan	Astrologer, British
LEWI, Grant	Astrologer, U.S. (III)
LIBERACE	Musician, pianist
LINCOLN, Abraham	Politician, U.S. President
LINKLETTER, Art	Entertainer, TV personlaity
MAILER, Norman	Writer, U.S. novelist, playwright, actor
MANCINI, Henry	Musician, U.S. songwriter, conductor
MANET, Edouard	Artist, French modernist, artistic rebel
MARCONI, Guglielmo	Scientist, Italian inventor
MARTIN, Mary	Actress, singer, U.S., writer (III)
MATISSE, Henri	Artist, French decorative pointer
MAX, Peter	Artist, U.S., pop culture hero (III)
MAY, Rollo	Psychologist, U.S., writer, lecturer
MAYS, Willie	Sports, U.S. baseball player
McENROE, John	Sports, U.S. tennis player (III)
McNAMARA, Robert	Manager, U.S., financial analyst
MELVILLE, Herman	Writer, U.S. novelist
MENUHIN, Yehudi	Musician, U.S. violinist, child prodigy
MILLET, Jean Francois	Artist, French, temperamental
MODIGLIANI, Amadeo	Artist, Italian portrait artist
MURDOCH, Rupert	Business entrepreneur, Australian (III)
MURPHY, Audie	Military hero, U.S., actor (III)

MURRAY, Anne	Singer, Canadian, pop music (III)
MURROW, Edward R.	Broadcaster, news commentator (III)
MUSSOLINI, Benito	Italian dictator during WW2
NADER, Ralph	Attorney, U.S., consumer activist (III)
NEWHART, Bob	Actor, U.S., comedian, writer (III)
NEWMAN, Paul	Actor, U.S. movies, director
NEWTON-JOHN, Olivia	Singer, Australian, pop (III)
NICKLAUS, Jack	Sports, U.S. golfer
NIETZSCHE, Friedrich	Philosopher, German, writer
NYIREGYHAZI, Ervin	Violinist, virtuoso, iconoclast (III)
OLIVIER, Sir Laurence	Actor, British, producer, director
OMARR, Sydney	Astrologer, U.S. (III)
PAAR, Jack	Entertainer, U.S. TV talk show host
PASTEUR, Louis	Scientist, French biochemist
PATTON, George	Military, U.S. general in WW2
PEARSON, Drew	Journalist, news commentator (III)
PECK, Gregory	Actor, U.S.
PECKINPAH, Sam	Movie director, U.S., screenwriter
PRESLEY, Elvis	Entertainer, U.S. rock and roll singer
PROGOFF, Ira	Psychologist, U.S., writer
PUCCINI, Giacomo	Musician, Italian opera composer
PYLE, Ernest	Journalist, U.S. writer
RAVEL, Maurice	Musician, French composer
REDDY, Helen	Popular music singer, Australian
REDFORD, Robert	Actor, U.S.
REED, Jerry	Singer, U.S., acts, writes country music
REGARDIE, Israel (Dr. Francis)	Occultist, British, writer
REMARQUE, Erich Maria	Writer, German novelist
RENOIR, Pierre Auguste	Artist, French impressionist
REVENTLOW, Lance	Heir, U.S. financier, auto racer
REYNOLDS, Burt	Actor, U.S., stuntman
RIBBONTROP, Joachim Von	Politician, Nazi general and diplomat
RIDE, Sally	Astronaut, U.S. (III)
RIGHTER, Carroll	Astrologer, U.S. (III)
RIMBAUD, Arthur	Poet, French
ROBINSON, Jackie	Sports, U.S. baseball player
RODIN, Auguste	Sculptor, French
ROLF, Ida	Psychologist, U.S. (III)
ROMMEL, Erwin	Military, German WW2 general
ROOSEVELT, Franklin	Politician, U.S. President (III)

ROSE, Billy	Entertainer, U.S., businessman
ROSENBLOOM, Steve	Manages and owns football team (III)
RUBIN, Jerry	Political activist, U.S.
RUDHYAR, Dane	Astrologer, U.S., writer, musician (III)
RUSSELL, Bertrand	Writer, mathematician, philosopher
SAGAN, Carl	Scientist, astronomer, lecturer (III)
SANDBURG, Carl	Poet, U.S. writer
SARTRE, Jean Paul	Writer, French philosopher
SCHWARTZ, Jack	Psychic healer, Dutch, actor (III)
SCHWARZENEGGER, Arnold	Physical body builder, Austrian, actor
SCHWEITZER, Albert	Humanitarian, French, physician
SELZNIK, David O.	Film producer, U.S.
SEURAT, Georges	Artist, French
SHELLEY, Percy Bysshe	Poet, British
SHEPPARD, Sam	Physician, exonerated murderer
SHOAF, Harry	Scientist, U.S., engineer, executive (III)
SIMPSON, O.J.	Sports, U.S. Football player, actor
SMOTHERS, Tom	Comedian, U.S.
SONDHEIM, Stephen	Composer, U.S., writer (III)
SPEER, Albert	Scientist, Nazi architect, engineer
SPIELBERG, Steven	Film producer, U.S. (III)
SPITZ, Mark	Sports, swimmer, Olympic medalist
STEINMETZ, Charles	Scientist, inventor, electrician
STRAUSS, Richard	Musician, German, songwriter
TEILHARD De CHARDIN, Pierre	Jesuit priest, geologist, writer
TESLA, Nikola	Scientist, inventor, genius
THORPE, Jim	Sports, U.S., football, olympics (III)
TOSCANINI, Arturo	Musician, conductor, cellist
TOULOUSE-LAUTREC, Henri	Artist, French, painter, lithographer
UNSER, Al	Sports, U.S., race car driver, owner (III)
VALENS, Ritchie	Singer, rock star
VAN GOGH, Vincent	Artist, French, had mental problems
WARREN, Earl	Lawyer, U.S. Chief Justice, politician
WELK, Lawrence	Musician, U.S. bandleader
WELLS, H.G.	Writer, British, science fiction
WHITMAN, Walt	Writer, U.S. Poet
WILLIAMS, Hank	Singer, country music songwriter (III)
WILLIAMS, Robin	Comedian, U.S., actor (III)
WINKLER, Henry	Actor, U.S. television

WINTERS, Jonathan	Comedian, U.S. mimic, entertainer
WORRALL, Olga	Psychic healer, U.S., minister (III)
WOZNIAK, Steve	Businessman, entrepreneur (III)

YEATS, William Butler	Poet, British
YOGANANDA, Paramhansa	Mystic, yogi, writer

A total of 220 persons were selected for this MWA study.

EVENTS

Alaskan EARTHQUAKE	Mar 27, 1964	Kodiak Island, AS
APOLLO 11 Moon Landing	July 20, 1969	Houston, TX
ATOM BOMB Explosion, First	July 16, 1945	Alamagordo, NM
BOLSHEVIKS Take Power	Nov. 8, 1917	Petrograd, Russia
CHALLENGER Explosion	Jan 28, 1986	Cape Canaveral, FL

CHERNOBYL Nuclear Explosion	Apr. 25, 1986	Piratyn, Russia
East Coast POWER BLACKOUT	Nov. 9, 1965	New York City, NY
F. D. ROOSEVELT's Election	Nov 8, 1932	Palo Alto, CA
GEO. WASHINGTON Sworn in	Apr 30, 1789	New York City, NY
J. F. KENNEDY Assassination	Nov 22, 1963	Dallas, TX

JAMES MEREDITH Enrolled at U. Miss.	Sep 30, 1962	Oxford, MS
KENT STATE Shooting	May 4, 1970	Kent, OH
LEE'S SURRENDER	April 9, 1865	Appomattox, VA
LEWIS & CLARK Expedition	May 14, 1804	St. Louis, MO
LINDBURGH Arrives in Paris	May 21, 1927	Paris, France

First MEDICARE Patient Accepted	July 1, 1966	New York City

MOUNT ST HELENS Explosion	May 18, 1980	Mt. St. Helens, WA
Richard NIXON's RESIGNATION	Aug 9, 1974	Washington, DC
PEARL HARBOR Attack begins	Dec 7, 1941	Honolulu, HI
RAMSTEIN Airshow Collision	Aug 28, 1988	Ramstein, Germany

South Carolina SECEDES from Union - effectively starts U.S. Civil War
Dec 20, 1860   Charleston, SC

RMS TITANIC Strikes Iceberg   April 14, 1912 North Atlantic Ocean

TRANSCONTINENTAL Railroad Completed and East meets West
May 10, 1869 Promontory Pt. UT

USS MAINE Explosion   Apr 15, 1898 Havana Harbor, Cuba

WATERGATE Burglary Occurs   July 17, 1972 Washington, DC

WOMAN's SUFFRAGE Constitutional Amendment Adopted
                                Aug 26, 1920 Washington, DC

Wright Brothers FIRST Sustained POWERED FLIGHT
                                Dec 17, 1903   Kitty Hawk, NC

The 27 events selected for the MWA study represent a cross section of different types of events. They were primarily chosen because their dates and times are verifiable from accurate sources. Please consult your local library sources for additional information on these events.

A synopsis of the statistical results of the MWA study used to produce this midpoint book, as well as a one page MWA printout on each person and event described in this book, is available for sale as a separate book. This book, called *The MWA Data Book,* is about 450 pages in length, standard paper size.

The original computer output containing the ranking of the MWA's for the 220 people and the 27 events used in this book is available to serious astrological researchers who may wish same. This material is hundreds of pages in length. It is in columnar and tabular form, not narrative form. The material consists of either computer files or printed listings from its FoxBase (Macintosh version) output format by person; by midpoint; by hit; etc. There is a Macintosh readable version of this material, but no IBM PC readable version presently available. The material is not intended for general public release, and it is expensive. A reason for requesting the material is necessary.

Because of an impending move at the time of this printing, a direct address for Neological Systems, publisher of the above materials, is not availabe. For further information and costs for either *The MWA Data Book* or for the computer files or listings described above, write to Michael Munkasey, c/o ACS Publications, PO Box 34487, San Diego, CA 92163.

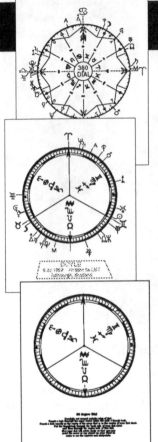